THE TRUE STORY OF
THE GREAT ESCAPE

THE TRUE STORY OF
THE GREAT ESCAPE

STALAG LUFT III, MARCH 1944

Jonathan F. Vance

Greenhill Books

The True Story of the Great Escape: Stalag Luft III, March 1944

Greenhill Books

Greenhill Books, c/o Pen & Sword Books Ltd,
47 Church Street, Barnsley, S. Yorkshire, S70 2AS, England
For more information on our books, please visit
www.greenhillbooks.com, email contact@greenhillbooks.com
or write to us at the above address.

CIP data records for this title are available from the British Library

ISBN 978-1-78438-438-8

Typeset and designed by JCS Publishing Services Ltd
Typeset in 10pt Minion Pro
Printed and bound by CPI Group (UK) Ltd, Croydon, CR0 4YY

CONTENTS

This book is dedicated to the memory of
The Fifty

GLOSSARY AND GUIDE TO ABBREVIATIONS

Abort	Lavatory
Anschluss	Nazi takeover of Austria
Appell	Roll call
Ausweis	Identity card
Autobahn	Highway
BATDU	Blind Approach Training Development Unit
BEF	British Expeditionary Force
Big S	Code name for George Harsh, head of security for the escape organization
Big X	Code name for Roger Bushell, leader of the escape organization
Circuit	A path around the perimeter wire of the camp
CO	Commanding officer
Cooler	Punishment block
Dean and Dawson	Escape organization's forging operation
DFC	Distinguished Flying Cross
Dispersal	Means of hiding earth removed from a tunnel
DSC	Distinguished Service Cross
DSO	Distinguished Service Order
Dulag Luft	*Durchgangslager Luftwaffe*, or Luftwaffe transit camp
Duty pilot	Prisoner responsible for monitoring movement of guards through main gate
EFTS	Elementary Flying Training School
Ersatz	Substitute
FAA	Fleet Air Arm
Ferrets	Nickname for German guards specially trained to foil escape attempts
FL	Flight Lieutenant

FO	Flying Officer
FTS	Flying Training School
Gestapo	*Geheimestaatspolizei*, or state security police
Ghost	Prisoner who fakes an escape and then hides, so that when he makes his genuine escape later, his absence will not be noticed
Goon	Nickname for German guards
Goonbox	Guard tower
Goonskin	False German uniform
Hardarser	Escaper planning to travel on foot
HCU	Heavy Conversion Unit
HMS	His Majesty's Ship
Hundführer	Camp official responsible for guard dogs
Kit	Prisoner's possessions, including clothing and toiletries
Kiwi	New Zealander
Klim	Canned powdered milk sent in Red Cross food parcels
Kommandantur	Administrative building of a prison camp
Kriegie	*Kriegsgefangene*, or prisoner of war
Kriegsmarine	Germany navy
Kripo	*Kriminalpolizei*, or criminal police
Little S	Deputy security officer for each hut
Little X	Escape officer designated for each hut
Luftwaffe	German air force
Muck cart	Wagon used to remove sewage from camp lavatory hut
NCO	Non-commissioned officer
Oflag	*Offizierlager*, or officers' POW camp
OKW	*Oberkommando der Wehrmacht*, or Armed Forces High Command
Orderly	Enlisted man responsible for maintenance duties in POW compound
Orpo	*Ordnungspolizei*, or regular uniformed police
OTU	Operational Training Unit
Penguin	Person engaged in the dispersal of tunnel soil
Permanent Staff	POWs responsible for administrative matters in Dulag Luft

PO	Pilot Officer
POW	Prisoner of war
PRU	Photo-Reconnaissance Unit
Purge	Group of POWs moved into or out of a camp
RAAF	Royal Australian Air Force
RAF	Royal Air Force
RAFVR	Royal Air Force Volunteer Reserve
RCAF	Royal Canadian Air Force
Reichsmarschall	Special rank created for Hermann Göring as head of the Luftwaffe
RFC	Royal Flying Corps
RNZAF	Royal New Zealand Air Force
RSHA	*Reichsicherheitshauptamt*, or Reich Main Security Office
SAAF	South African Air Force
SBO	Senior British officer
SFTS	Service Flying Training School
Shoring	Wood used to brace a tunnel to prevent collapse
Short service commission	Limited-term commission in RAF
SL	Squadron Leader
Stalag	*Stammlager*, or other ranks' POW camp
Stalag Luft	Air force prison camp
Stooge	Lookout
Trapführer	POW responsible for controlling a tunnel entrance
USAAF	United States Army Air Forces
Vorlager	Small separate compound housing service facilities
WAAF	Women's Auxiliary Air Force
Warning wire	Low wire inside the main prison camp fence that marks the beginning of the danger zone
WO	Warrant Officer
X Organization	Code name for Stalag Luft III's escape organization

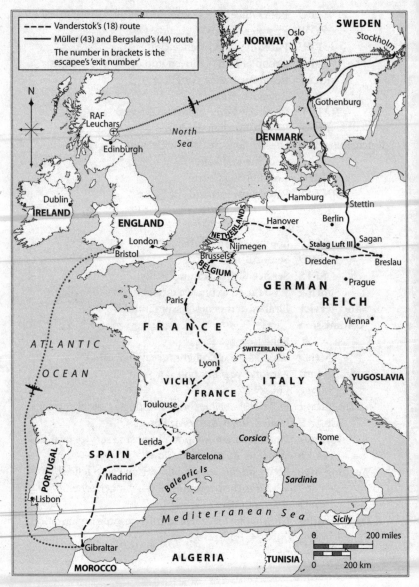

The Escapees' Routes from Stalag Luft III

Location of Stalag Luft III

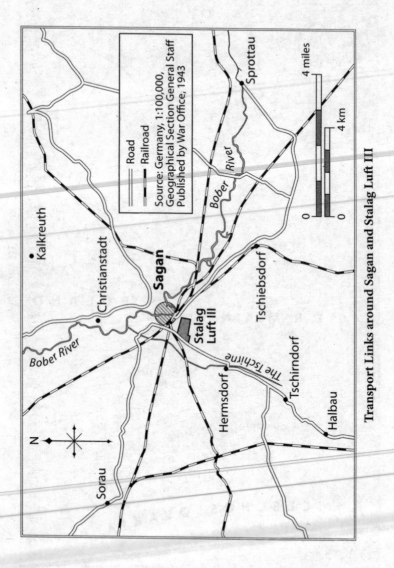

Transport Links around Sagan and Stalag Luft III

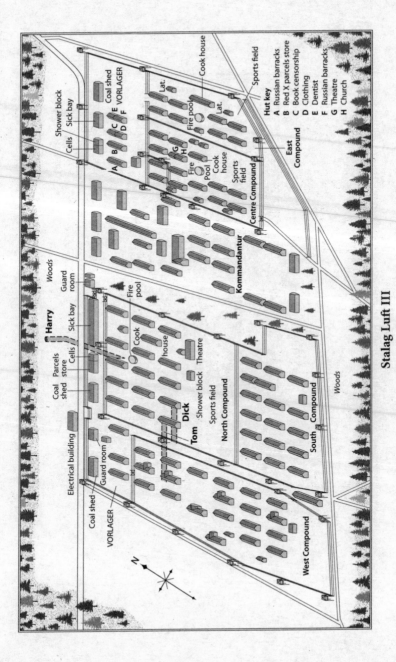

Stalag Luft III

Shower block
Sick bay
Cells
Coal shed
VORLAGER
A B C D E F

Lat.
Cook house
Fire pool
Lat.
Sports field

Hut key
A Russian barracks
B Red X parcels store
C Book censorship
D Clothing
E Dentist
F Russian barracks
G Theatre
H Church

G H
Fire Pool
Cook house
Sports field

East Compound

Centre Compound

Kommandantur

Woods
Guard room

Harry
Sick bay
Cells
Parcels store
Coal shed

Electrical building
Coal shed
Guard room
VORLAGER

Fire pool
Cook house
Dick
Theatre
Shower block
Sports field
Tom

North Compound

South Compound

West Compound

Woods

N

FOREWORD

LIKE MOST PEOPLE, I was first exposed to the March 1944 escape from Stalag Luft III through the film. It was Victoria Day in my hometown of Waterdown, Ontario, and I was probably eight or nine years old. Victoria Day in Canada means fireworks, and my family was planning to walk to the local park to watch the display. But I was glued to the television. My mother had switched on *The Great Escape*, and I was transfixed, so much so that I refused to leave the house until the film was over. Maybe it was the stirring score by Elmer Bernstein, or Daniel Fapp's gorgeous cinematography. The fine ensemble cast certainly held my attention, and, years later, ex-POWs I talked to would roll their eyes when I told them that Steve McQueen's motorcycle ride had made a huge impression on me. Even though I missed the fireworks that night, I gained a passion that remains with me to this day.

In some ways, I may have always known that I would write this book, for I began 'researching' it when I was still a teenager. By 'researching,' I mean writing to ex-POWs and asking them questions that occurred to me – or even just requesting an autograph. They were remarkably kind, often inviting me to visit them when we were on family vacations or allowing me to attend their reunions. One of my first contacts was the legendary escaper H.M.A. 'Wings' Day, who invited my family to his retirement home in Rustington and introduced us to his friends there, former airmen all. I recall one particularly well – an American from the deep south (Alabama, I think) who had joined the Royal Flying Corps during the First World War and liked England so much that he never left. Wings had a charming little cat, who spent much of the afternoon sitting on his shoulders.

I was fortunate to begin working on the Great Escape when so many of the main characters were still alive – they gave me some remarkable information on the escape and its participants, but also were wonderful hosts, kind and generous to a fault. Per Bergsland fed me and my wife grilled salmon that had come into the docks in Oslo just hours earlier. The raffish and utterly charming Sydney Dowse treated us to a fabulously expensive dinner in Menton, in the south of France. He had a villa there, and I asked him if he had learned to speak French. 'If you have money, you don't need to learn the language,' was his reply. Bob Stanford-Tuck drove me around the south coast of England, reminiscing as he drove, at some considerable speed – I wondered at the time if he should be paying a little more attention to the road. Ivo Tonder was never without a smile as he related the experience of spending so much time as a young adult escaping from one enemy or another. I was even able to become something of a regular at the RAF Club on Piccadilly, once for a memorable reunion dinner of escapers, including characters like Bill 'Tex' Ash and Oliver Philpot, of Wooden Horse fame.

When I started to contact the relatives of the fifty escapers who were executed, they were just as friendly, and thrilled that someone was interested in their long-gone but still beloved relative. At the beginning, I had hopes of tracking families of a dozen of the fifty – in the end, I was able to get in touch with descendants of almost all of them. Mimi Martin-Picard hosted us for days in her tidy house in Belgium. She was an adventurous cook, and tried out many new dishes on us – 'les cobailles,' she called us, guinea pigs. David and Mary Hayter threw open their beautiful home Kinghams to us on more than one occasion, and introduced us to the extended Hayter family. Sylvia Swain taught me that steak and kidney pie could actually be tasty. Sir Kenneth Cross literally opened his brother Ian's life to me – because everything the family had saved was kept in a battered suitcase.

These unforgettable experiences allowed me to do more than just research. They allowed me to come as close as possible to the men of Stalag Luft III. I really felt that I got to know some of them – one can't spend hours listening to family stories, poring over photo albums, and reading letters and diaries without developing a connection to the subjects. The men of the Great Escape became very real to me, and I became extraordinarily protective of them. The first version of this book was privately published, mostly just for the many people who had helped me, because I couldn't bear to turn it over to an editor, who might ask me to consider suggested deletions. The second edition was done by Pacifica Military History in California, the imprint of a wonderful historian named Eric Hammel. Eric has forgotten more about the US Marine Corps than most people will ever know, but he liked the story of these intrepid airmen and gave me every encouragement to improve the narrative. He also arranged for the third edition, published by Simon & Schuster in one of its reprint series.

The men of the Great Escape remain very real to me, and I'm delighted that the 75th anniversary of the escape is the occasion for a re-issue of this book. Since it was first published under the title *A Gallant Company* (the phrase was taken from an In Memoriam notice in *The Times*), other writers have tackled the subject with general histories of the escape or biographies of individual airmen. I am grateful for the opportunity to correct errors or add important new details, but I am even more grateful to be able to introduce these men to readers again, and to revisit the remarkable events that even Hollywood couldn't better. To read of the resourcefulness, determination, and courage of this group of men is, frankly, humbling.

PROLOGUE

Escape literature has long been a staple of the reading matter preferred by schoolboys. Many British men who grew up in the interwar years were keenly aware of the escapers of the First World War and will admit to having consumed a steady diet of classics such as A. J. Evans's *The Escaping Club* or Duncan Grinnell-Milne's *An Escaper's Log*. Wartime escapers were even popular guest speakers at British schools in the 1920s and 1930s, thrilling the lads with tales of flights to freedom. This tradition formed the intellectual underpinnings to escape during the Second World War, but a host of other factors acted as more immediate motivators to the prisoner of war. Escape offered the hope of a speedy return to loved ones, or an antidote to the stultifying boredom of prison camp life. For men who believed they were not pulling their weight in the war effort, escaping provided the opportunity to get back into action, albeit on a more limited scale, and perhaps make some further contribution to the war. Others probably turned to it simply because it so angered their captors, or because they were moved by the notion that it was a prisoner's duty to attempt escape.

These motives were common to men of all services, but there were a number of reasons why airmen were overrepresented among escapers, and more likely to succeed at escape. Men who enlisted in the air force in peacetime found that the rigorous selection process demanded a high level of education, and during wartime even the lowliest air gunner would have had to show intellectual ability to earn his qualification. At the same time, airmen compensated for being part of the most junior of the services by becoming generally more aggressive, an aggression that made itself felt in prison camp. Airmen, too, were accustomed to relatively exciting service lives and likely chafed at the inactivity of the prison camp more than other POWs. They were also used to operating alone or in small groups, experience that provided excellent training in the kind of self-reliance and cooperation that escaping demanded. Furthermore, in all of the Allied air forces, the rank structure encouraged escape activity. Operational aircrews were almost always officers or NCOs, or men whose initiative and zeal had already earned them promotion; that same zeal would fuel their escape attempts. Airmen who had not shown sufficient initiative to be promoted, and therefore were unlikely candidates for escape, generally did not fall into enemy hands because they were rarely posted to operational duties.

The airman, then, was almost the ideal escaper. Well educated, aggressive, used to working in solitude, and actuated by all the normal impulses that make a human seek freedom, he brought an impressive arsenal of escape skills to the prison camp in which he was incarcerated. It was a combination that many airmen would put to good effect.

The POW branch of the Luftwaffe, the German air force, was fully aware of this fact. British aviators had given them no end of trouble during the Great War (Evans and Grinnell-Milne were, after all, airmen), and it is entirely likely that, in September 1939, the Luftwaffe had some inkling of what was to come. When the number of Allied airmen being shot down remained small, until the fall of 1941, their imprisonment caused little difficulty. They could all be centralized in a single camp, Stalag Luft I at Barth on the Baltic coast. The aviators were immediately up to their old tricks, though, and it occurred to the Luftwaffe that it might not have been such a good idea to keep them all together. So there was a change in policy: newly captured airmen were split up between a handful of camps, on the rationale that, if dispersed, they might be less troublesome. This hope proved in vain – instead of one problem camp, it created half a dozen problem camps – and by the spring of 1942 the Luftwaffe had returned to its policy of centralization. Allied air force prisoners would all be transferred to a new camp, Stalag Luft III at Sagan in Silesia, which was purpose-built to frustrate potential escapers. When Luft III opened in March 1942, it marked the beginning of a two-year battle of wits that pitted hundreds of well-educated, well-trained, and highly motivated POWs against an equally determined and wily staff of guards and security officers. That battle culminated in the episode that has gone down in history as the Great Escape.

*

It was not the largest escape in the annals of military history, nor was it the most successful. There were more audacious breakouts, and ones that presented more significant engineering challenges. But no plan was more ambitious, and none was carried through in the face of such overwhelming odds. No other escape had such an impact on the Second World War, and few took such a toll in lives.

They were only fifty men. The number seems small and almost insignificant when compared to the total fatal casualties sustained by the Royal Air Forces during the Second World War. Fifty men out of more than 90,000 – fewer than eight Lancaster crews. Had the RAF lost only eight crews on any of the major raids of the strategic bombing offensive, the operation would have been deemed a great success. But the deaths of *these* fifty men were anything but insignificant. When they and twenty-six other airmen escaped from Stalag Luft III on the night of March 24–25, 1944, there began a chain of events that was to have greater ramifications than anyone could have expected. And when the fifty were murdered by Hitler's Gestapo in the weeks after the escape, with their very deaths they continued the battle they had begun upon enlistment.

They were not supermen, though. They were average, normal individuals, like the thousands of other airmen who died before and after them. They were bank clerks and farmers, students and professional soldiers, journalists and engineers. They came from all over the world: from remote and dusty Australian towns, from the heat of the South African veld and the cold of a Canadian winter, from the bustle of London and the quaintness of Warsaw. Under the leadership of a remarkable lawyer-turned-fighter-pilot, they came together in Luft III, pooling their skills and talents in a common enterprise. This is their story.

Chapter 1

THE FIRST TO FALL

IT WAS COOL AND breezy on the evening of September 8, 1939, and for the second time in the war, Pilot Officer Alfred Burke Thompson warmed up his Armstrong Whitworth Whitley twin-engine bomber on the tarmac of 102 Squadron's base at Driffield in Yorkshire, England. The controller's reassuring voice crackled in the headphones and, with a wave to the other Whitley ticking over behind him, 'Tommy' Thompson was off. Piled in the fuselage of the aircraft were bundles of pamphlets that reminded the enemy, in no uncertain terms, that the struggle was a futile one and that the forces of right would triumph in due course. The leaflets sat in large, menacing stacks, waiting to be pushed down the funnel in the bomb bay. Some bombing mission, thought Tommy.

As they crossed the English coast and headed out over the North Sea, Squadron Leader Philip Murray called out a heading from the navigator's position and Tommy turned the Whitley toward the Continent. He was about to call 'Wank' Murray for another course heading when a hand thrust a scrap of paper up into the cockpit. It was a page from Murray's scratch pad, and scribbled on it were the words 'Intercom dead – use notes instead,' followed by a course heading. Tommy was dubious, but the system worked fairly well, and the aircraft reached the German frontier without incident. The leaflets were pushed out the chute, and Tommy banked the Whitley around toward home. No sooner had the bomber come to an even keel than the engines began to sputter and the temperature gauges climbed alarmingly. No amount of fiddling could get the motors to run more smoothly, and the altimeter started to wind down as one engine stopped altogether. It was soon apparent that they wouldn't make it to friendly airspace, let along England, so Tommy reluctantly motioned to Wank to bail out.

Once Murray had escaped, Tommy clambered out the escape hatch and watched as the Whitley dove past him. Fascinated by the bomber's plunge, he didn't notice the ground coming up beneath him until it knocked the wind out of his lungs. Dawn was breaking, and German soldiers were quick to round up the downed airmen. They were taken to cells at a small airfield, stripped of everything with which they could possibly harm themselves, and left to pass an uneasy morning. For Tommy Thompson it was the beginning of an odyssey that would last nearly six years and include more jail cells than he cared to recall.

*

It began in Penetanguishene, Ontario, where Tommy was born on August 8, 1915, the son of the local member of Parliament. He started high school in 1929 but left after four years for a job with an insurance company in Toronto. Even though his father had pulled strings to secure the position, Tommy didn't take to the work and preferred to spend his time taking flying lessons. Once, when he felt particularly strongly about not going to work, he decided to call in sick. Then he donned a pair of skis and, for the next two days, skied back home for a vacation. Unfortunately the company took it upon themselves to send a nurse to check on their ailing employee, and when she found no one at home, Tommy was out of a job.

He wasn't overly concerned at being unemployed and in late 1936 went to England to join the RAF under a special enlistment scheme. Soon after arriving at the flying school at Hamble in Hampshire, Tommy was sure he had made the right decision. He loved the comradeship of like-minded men but at times had a tendency to be a bit too boisterous during training. Thompson was once put up on charges for flying under a bridge and wrote home that he would go to Spain to fight in the civil war if the RAF discharged him over the incident. Luckily, Tommy received nothing more than a reprimand and on November 15, 1937, was assigned to 102 Squadron. He was to remain with that unit until shot down.

Thompson had plenty of time to reflect on his past as he and Murray sat in the cells at the airfield, but Thompson's musings were interrupted when an interpreter appeared with some ominous remarks about last wishes and a long journey. After a moment of panic, Tommy and Wank learned they were to leave for Berlin that afternoon and might wish for some refreshment before setting out. They accepted with thanks and arrived at a small hospital on the outskirts of Berlin after a seven-hour trip. The two were interrogated off and on through the night and were feeling drained when two guards appeared the next morning to take them to meet 'someone of great importance.' Mystified, they followed their escorts through a forest, across a railroad siding, and through a railroad passenger car to a large grassy clearing. Under a great tree at the edge of the clearing sat a large platform. On it was a massive desk and, behind the desk, the huge, bemedaled figure of Hermann Göring.

It was impossible not to be impressed by the bulky *Reichsmarschall*, and Tommy and Wank were taken aback for a moment until Wank recovered himself and strode up the steps to give a salute. Murray and Göring chatted amicably for a few minutes before Tommy was invited onto the platform to join the interview. The *Reichsmarschall* jokingly upbraided the two for disturbing his sleep and forcing him to take cover in a bomb shelter but sympathized with them for losing the freedom of the skies, as he put it. He seemed a little puzzled by Tommy's presence, especially as Canada had not yet entered the war, but quickly left the subject to discuss the finer points of Canadian ice hockey. The interview lasted nearly thirty minutes and ended with Göring promising that RAF prisoners would be treated decently. He waved a flabby hand, and Tommy and Wank were led from the platform.

In late September, the two newest kriegies (the word is a corruption of the German *Kriegsgefangenen*, meaning prisoners of war) were transferred to a permanent camp, at Itzehoe near Hamburg. A couple of French airmen and six hundred Poles were their only companions until a New Zealander downed on September 6 joined them. Each had a private room, and conditions were quite comfortable, but recreational activities were at a premium. Luckily, one of the Frenchmen had a deck of cards, so the five spent hours playing endless rubbers of bridge. Two weeks after their arrival, Tommy, Wank, and the New Zealander were on the move again when the Germans decided to segregate the air force officers from the Poles. The fliers and their guards were packed into a truck and set off for the long drive to their new camp.

They finally arrived at their destination after thirty-six hours on the road, and Tommy peered out of the truck to see a squat medieval castle perched on a hilltop. He could only see the brown stone walls and steep slate roofs, but soon a decrepit clock tower came into view and, below the castle, Tommy picked out the walls of a moat. 'It doesn't look too inviting,' he said to Wank. Spangenberg Castle, or Oflag IXA/H, as it was designated, certainly did not look very welcoming as the Luftwaffe truck wound its way up the tree-lined road to the massive stone gates.

Clambering out of the truck and clutching their meager possessions, Tommy, Wank, and the Kiwi were heartened to see a small knot of airmen standing in the cobbled courtyard. Among them were Gerry Booth and Larry Slattery, the first RAF prisoners of the war and survivors of low-level attacks on German warships at Wilhelmshaven on September 4. It was small comfort for Thompson and Murray that these two had been in the bag even longer than they had. Over the next couple of weeks, various other unfortunates dribbled into the camp, including two Fleet Air Arm pilots, Captain Guy Griffiths and Lieutenant Dick Thurston, downed over the North Sea on September 14. A few others turned up in early October, and soon the nucleus of the Allied air forces in German captivity was formed.

Conditions in Spangenberg were much less comfortable than they had been in Itzehoe, where the prisoners had been able to buy fruit, soft drinks, and other extras. In the new camp they lived on the lowest scale of German military rations, which included such unappetizing fare as a heavy, black bread baked from potatoes, a nearly inedible cheese made from fish by-products, small pieces of stringy and heavily salted bacon fat, honey or jam extracted from coal and sweetened with saccharine, and a thick stew containing an occasional piece of some unidentifiable meat. It was washed down with coffee made from scorched grain or chestnuts, a combination that was enough to spoil the appetite of the most ravenous eater.

The accommodations were also a far cry from the private rooms of Itzehoe. At Oflag IXA/H, the prisoners lived in a long dormitory on the ground floor of the castle and slept on straw-filled mattresses, or palliasses, in iron beds lining the whitewashed walls of the room. The only other furnishings were two long tables with benches in the center of the room. The kriegies spent much of their day lounging around the dormitory, for it was becoming too cold to spend much time in the tiny, cobbled courtyard. The tables were the center of activity and were used for doling out the rations, playing cards, or exchanging stories. Conversation usually continued until well after lights out, and the sound of low voices in the warm and stuffy dormitory was strangely comforting to new prisoners. There was little thought of escape, and most of the kriegies were content to accustom themselves to the loss of freedom. On the whole, they managed to cope quite well in those difficult early weeks and, without knowing how long their captivity would last, started to settle into a routine.

*

One day in mid-October, a bus pulled up to the castle and disgorged a load of immaculate and heavily laden French Air Force officers and a tall, middle-aged fellow with a gaunt face and balding head. In contrast to the French, this officer carried no luggage and looked quite disheveled thanks to a sprouting beard and a swath of dirty bandages. Above the beard sat two very dark, very alert eyes that quickly scanned the prisoners in the castle courtyard. His back straight and his head erect, Wing Commander Harry Melville Arbuthnot Day had finally arrived in a Luftwaffe permanent camp.

Born in Sarawak on August 3, 1898, Day was schooled in England, an experience that proved strange for a lad who had grown up in Borneo, far from cricket and rugby. When the First World War broke out, Harry Day enlisted in the Royal Marine Light Infantry as a cadet and in 1916 was commissioned. His first assignment was to the marine detachment aboard the cruiser HMS *Britannia*. Two days before the Armistice, the *Britannia* was torpedoed by a German submarine off Gibraltar and, in the ensuing explosions, several crew members were trapped belowdecks. Lieutenant Day made his way into the wardroom through a tiny hatch and discovered two wounded crew members inside. Rather than try to drag them back through the hatch on his own, Harry returned topside and found a couple of stewards to help him carry the wounded to safety. Before leaving the cabin, he battened all the scuttles and hatches to prevent the spread of fire. It was a rescue achieved at great personal risk, and in January 1919 Harry Day was awarded the Albert Medal. He later claimed that he was only trying to rescue the key to the wardroom liquor cabinet.

After this feat of gallantry, Day rose quickly in the marines, commanding detachments on various ships. By 1924, he had seen the world with the marines, from Malaya to Memel and Singapore to Smyrna, and was craving a new challenge. It wasn't long before he discovered flying. Day wangled a transfer and did his first solo at the flying school at Netheravon, in southern England. By 1929 he was a flight lieutenant with 23 Squadron and two years later he was chosen to lead the synchronized aerobatic team at the Hendon Air Show. Harry Day continued to rise in the RAF, receiving a promotion to squadron leader while in Egypt and, as war drew near, learned that he was to take up a staff job when hostilities began. This did not suit Day, and a few hurried calls and visits secured a promotion to wing commander with a squadron of Bristol Blenheim medium bombers. In September 1939 Day, who had acquired the nickname 'Wings' when he was promoted, took 57 Squadron to France.

The unit's first operation was a reconnaissance sweep of the Bochum–Essen area. The last minutes of Friday, October 13, 1939, were ticking away as Harry Day taxied his Blenheim down the runway at Metz. At 22,000 feet he looked down to see a thick carpet of cloud shielding the way to Germany. Just after crossing the German frontier, the comforting white blanket disappeared, leaving the lone aircraft in full view of any German who might be watching. Things were suddenly very dangerous. Soon the muffled voice of the air gunner came over the intercom to warn of flak. Then, guided by flak bursts, three Messerschmitt Bf 109 fighters moved in for the kill. Wings had just begun a tight turn when the first bullets slammed into the aircraft, and before long the cockpit was filled with smoke as the gasoline tanks began to burn. Checking that the gunner and the navigator had already bailed out, Wings threw the Blenheim into a vertical turn and ripped open the escape hatch. With a single kick, he was free.

The first person to reach him when he landed was a smiling old forest guard, who said only *'Engländer'* and shook Wings's hand with a kindly squeeze. He was marched a short distance to the village of Langweiler, where his scorched forehead was tended by an elderly Luftwaffe doctor. Curious about his crewmates, Day was shown their blackened bodies in the back of a truck; both had bailed out with their parachutes on fire. The lean wing commander snapped to attention to salute his comrades and paused for a moment before being led away.

The first days of Wings's captivity were spent in the villa of a German Army major, his wife, and their young daughter. His next stop was the local army hospital, and even there, the only sign of captivity came at night, when a single sentry guarded the door of Wings's ward. After two days in the hospital he was taken to a compound on the grounds of an agricultural academy near Mainz. The only other inmates were a dozen French officers, and Day felt very much alone as he went through the usual questioning. The next morning a bus pulled up outside the small compound to take the prisoners to another camp. Wings still had not resigned himself to the fact that he was a prisoner of war and was feeling at a low ebb as the bus clattered up the steep hill to Spangenberg Castle. His mood changed quickly when he spotted a smiling and familiar face in the crowd. The grinning chap was Mike Casey, an old friend from 57 Squadron, and Wings was never more glad to hear his warm Irish brogue. Mike strode forward with an open hand, greeted Wings heartily, and then introduced Thompson, Murray, and the rest of the tiny RAF contingent.

'It's fine to see you,' said Casey to the new arrival, 'but for your sake, I'm sorry you're here!' With a clap on the back, Wings was led off to the British dormitory by his squadronmate.

*

Wings had quite a bit in common with the soft-spoken yet powerful Irishman. Like Day, Flight Lieutenant Michael James O'Brien Casey was a product of the British Empire, born in Allahabad on February 19, 1918, the son of the inspector-general of the Indian Police. Casey was educated in England and was popular at school, both for his athletic prowess in boxing, rugby, and cricket, and for his moral strength, manifest in his attention to religious duties. Mike finished school in July 1936 and applied for a short service commission in the RAF. Shortly before the war, Casey's sister married the son of an influential and respected Tyneside businessman, a young man whom Mike had known at school. Through this union Mike met the young man's sister Margery, whom he eventually married at Bicester on September 19, 1939. Sadly, the couple had an all-too-short time together, for Mike's squadron was posted to France before the month was out.

On October 16, 1939, Mike and his crew were ordered to fly a reconnaissance of the main road between Wesel and Bocholt. They failed to return to their base at Amy, but it wasn't until October 21, through a story in *The Times*, that the squadron learned what had happened to the Blenheim. The article, titled 'An Aerial Steeplechase', quoted a German newspaper account of a duel between a German fighter and a Blenheim. According to the German pilot, the Blenheim led him in and out of cloudbanks before taking him on a mad pursuit across the countryside around Emden. Casey, described as a 'good, adroit and skillful airman,' used every dip in the ground, every hedge, and every tree as cover; he skimmed over rooftops and scattered branches in his wake to disrupt his adversary's aim. They flew on, sometimes barely six feet off the ground, but finally the German's gunfire found the vitals of the Blenheim. With no time to lower the undercarriage, Mike dumped the aircraft into an open field. Moments before the Blenheim burst into flames, the crew piled out and gave a hearty wave to the German pilot circling overhead.

After Mike related the story of his final flight to Wings, the latter grinned and shook his head. 'At least you ruffled a few feathers,' he said. 'My sole contribution to our war effort has been to force a trio of Messerschmitts to expend some ammunition on me!' Mike laughed and pushed Wings up the dormitory stairs for a brew of tea.

*

After Day's arrival, the little RAF group settled back into its routine, with the wing commander acting as senior British officer (SBO). There was little to liven things up in the last months of 1939, and so it was with some enthusiasm that an order was received in December for the transfer of twelve British and French airmen to another camp. To join the draft, the Germans selected Wings, Mike Casey, and the two Fleet Air Arm pilots, Guy Griffiths and Dick Thurston, with Mike's air gunner as orderly.

The camp to which they were taken was Dulag Luft, or Luftwaffe transit camp, near the town of Oberursel, ten miles from Frankfurt-am-Main. At first the prisoners occupied a large, attractive building that had once formed part of an experimental farm. They lived in small rooms off a central corridor and were locked in at dusk but were free to roam around the building during the daylight hours. Just after New Year's, a small compound was provided for the kriegies. In April 1940 the men were moved to a newly constructed camp nearby. This compound contained three barracks: East Block, with a recreation room and wash facilities as well as twelve double and two single rooms; Center Block, with rooms for about sixty-five prisoners; and West Block, which held the messes, kitchen, and food store.

Shortly after they arrived in Dulag Luft it became apparent to the prisoners that this wasn't a normal camp. It had been opened purely as a transit center, in which new prisoners could be interrogated and helped to acclimatize to captivity. To assist in this process the Germans appointed a committee of prisoners called the Permanent Staff, which eventually grew to comprise about twenty-five officers. These officers would remain in the camp and be responsible for liaison with the camp staff, distribution of food and clothing, discipline within the camp, and providing aid and guidance to new prisoners. Those chosen for the Permanent Staff were older and, theoretically, more responsible officers, many with some distinction in their family backgrounds. In fact, Commandant Theo Rumpel hoped they would epitomize what he saw as the essence of the British ruling class.

Wings Day became the senior British officer and selected as his adjutant Lieutenant Commander Jimmy Buckley, trained at the Royal Naval College at Dartmouth and one of the earliest Fleet Air Arm pilots. Jimmy had served as a flight commander on the aircraft carrier HMS *Glorious* before the war and was shot down while strafing German gun emplacements at Calais on May 29, 1940. He made the march to captivity with tens of thousands of soldiers and had escaped briefly along the way. An old friend of Jimmy's, Lieutenant Commander John Casson, was also on the Permanent Staff. The two had served together in Malta and on *Glorious,* and John was shot down over Trondheim fjord on April 13, 1940. Before arrangements were made to send church parties into the local village, John held Sunday morning services in the camp. However, he thought it tactful to omit the traditional blessing to the armed forces from the service, leading to an oft-heard jest around the camp, 'We want our blessing – but John won't let us have it!'

When new POWs arrived in the camp, they went first to the interrogation center for questioning by skilled intelligence officers. When the interrogation was completed, the prisoner was released to the care of the Permanent Staff. He was given a toilet kit and a Red Cross parcel and was told to come to the clothing store once he knew what sort of supplies he needed. Then, with the formalities taken care of, he was given a good meal. It was, all in all, a pleasant introduction to life in captivity. Indeed, POWs in Dulag Luft lived quite well for the short time they were there. They lived in rooms of two to four men and had plenty of food parcels. In addition, a good feast was scheduled every few weeks to ensure that everyone had a chance to satisfy their appetite before going to a permanent camp. There were occasional parole walks in the woods around the camp, and parties were sometimes allowed into town to attend church services.

For the Permanent Staff, conditions also were good. The commandant was a very congenial host who held occasional dinner parties for members of the Permanent Staff. Both sides had motives for this high living. The Germans hoped that their hospitality would cause prisoners to drop their guard and reveal some point of information that could be useful; they also hoped that the 'killing with kindness' tactic would subdue the aggressive urges of the prisoners, something that was not altogether unsuccessful in some cases. For their part, the Permanent Staff wanted the Germans to believe that the prisoners were becoming soft and compliant; while trying to foster this notion, they made plans for escape.

*

Wings Day put Buckley in charge of an escape organization, and Jimmy chose as his deputy and intelligence head an officer new to the Permanent Staff. He was just under six feet tall and fairly well built, but the most remarkable thing about him was his eyes. They were a steely blue and seemed to pierce right through you from the dark, heavy rings that surrounded them; to make the impression even stronger, the left eye had a sinister droop in the outer corner, the result of a skiing accident. All things considered, Squadron Leader Roger Joyce Bushell was a formidable-looking character.

His prewar life was, in many ways, not unlike that of an Evelyn Waugh character. Born on August 30, 1910, in Springs, Transvaal, South Africa, Roger was the son of an English-born mining engineer who had immigrated to South Africa. The younger Bushell was educated first in Johannesburg and then in England. In November 1926 he applied to study honors engineering at Pembroke College, Cambridge; when he was enrolled in October 1929, Roger had elected to pursue a legal career instead.

At Cambridge Bushell became what Waugh called one of the 'bright young things.' He competed with the university ski team in Switzerland and was a member of the well-known Kandahar Club at Mürren. His daring on the ski runs was legendary, for his tactics were simple: point the skis downhill and go as fast as possible. Where others would have flinched or held back, Roger merely quickened his pace; he was widely considered to be the fastest British skier of the prewar years, and he held the speed record for the flying kilometer at St. Moritz.

In 1932 Bushell became a member of the renowned 601 Squadron, Royal Auxiliary Air Force, nicknamed the Millionaires' Squadron. The members of the unit were already well known in England, though their reputation was not entirely good. As Max Aitken wrote, 'They were the sort of young men who had not quite been expelled from their schools, whom mothers warned their daughters against – in vain – who stayed up far too late at parties and then, when everyone else was half dead with fatigue, went on to other parties.'

To go along with his reputation as a skier and pilot, Roger Bushell had been making a name for himself as a lawyer. He was called to the bar in November 1934 and was involved in several sensational cases. On one occasion he successfully defended a noted London underworld leader accused of murder. When the verdict was passed down, the defendant went to shake Bushell's hand. 'No, thank you,' replied Roger. 'I don't shake hands with murderers. I only do what I'm paid to do.' Unperturbed, his client smiled and said 'Fine – but if you ever run into trouble in this city, just mention my name and you'll be okay.' It was a favor that Roger was glad he never had to use. Bushell also became known as a successful advocate in courts-martial of RAF personnel, often on charges of dangerous flying. In fact, he was so successful that the RAF command suggested he be discouraged from taking further cases because his success rate was having an adverse effect on public relations.

Roger was a flight lieutenant in 601 when war broke out, and on October 12, 1939, he was assigned to form and command 92 Squadron, a Blenheim night-fighter unit at Tangmere. He was the first auxiliary air force officer assigned to form a new squadron. When he arrived at the station three days later, though, he discovered that he had no equipment, no other officers, and only a skeleton ground crew. Nevertheless, the welcome extended by the officers of the other squadron based at Tangmere was so warm that, as 92 Squadron's diary put it, Roger 'retired to his bed at a late hour, feeling that Tangmere was the best station to be found in the best country in the best of all possible wars.'

By the spring of 1940, 92 had converted to Spitfires, and on May 23, 1940, Bushell twice led his squadron to the beaches of France to cover the evacuation of the British Expeditionary Force. On the second trip,

Bushell got into a duel with Messerschmitt Me 110 twin-engine fighters. He knocked down one and was chasing a second at very low altitude when he was bounced by a third; the enemy's first burst scored many hits, and Roger's Spit caught fire. He was able to extinguish the blaze by shutting everything off, and he turned toward Boulogne to make a forced landing. He came down just east of the city and, assuming he was in friendly territory, waited by the wrecked aircraft and had a cigarette. Eventually a motorcyclist appeared; Bushell assumed he was French but he turned out to be a heavily armed German. Escape was out of the question, and Roger gave up gracefully, vowing to continue the fight in other ways. His appointment to the escape committee in Dulag Luft gave him that opportunity.

*

Buckley and Bushell immediately realized that there would be problems in planning escapes from Dulag Luft. Because they were so well known to the camp authorities, the Permanent Staff would not be able to attempt walking out of the gate in disguise, and the small size of the compound made a climb over the fence too dangerous. Nor could any of the prisoners in transit be recruited for these schemes, because their stay at Dulag Luft was always indefinite. There was little point in planning an escape for someone who might well be moved the next day. The most obvious answer seemed to be a tunnel. The various members of the Permanent Staff could work on it in turn, at different times so their absence would not be noticed, and interested newcomers could dig a few shifts before their transfer to another camp. Anyone who was really interested in escaping would be glad of the experience.

For their first effort, Buckley and Bushell decided to dig a tunnel toward a small footbridge across a ditch just outside the wire fence. They thought that, with careful surveying, they could break the tunnel underneath the bridge and quite a few prisoners could get out before an alarm was raised. Roger and Mike Casey began work on this tunnel with a few other prisoners. If it broke, they would make for Schaffhausen on the Swiss frontier, an area Roger knew well from his skiing days. Unfortunately, the diggers soon found that the ditch they had targeted was filled with water, much of which drained into their tunnel. After six weeks of digging in mud, they gave up. Two other tunnels were started shortly after, but neither came to anything.

*

Meanwhile, a tall and bulky army major had joined the Permanent Staff. He was an older fellow, balding and with a small mustache, and he spoke with a refined American accent. At first no one seemed to know what he was doing in a Luftwaffe camp, but eventually the whole story came out. And in captivity, where odd stories were more the rule than the exception, John Bigelow Dodge set a new standard for strange tales.

Born in New York on May 15, 1894, John Dodge was raised in the upper echelons of international society. The grandson of Abraham Lincoln's minister to France and related by marriage to Winston Churchill, he was educated at St. Mark's School in the United States and in Montreal. When war came in 1914, his influential relative pulled some strings in the Admiralty and the young Dodge was given a commission in the Hood Battalion of the Royal Naval Division. He served gallantly during the war, first at Antwerp in 1914, then at Gallipoli in 1915, where he was awarded the Distinguished Service Cross. In 1916 Johnny transferred to the army and went to France, where he was wounded twice. By 1918, he was commanding the 16th Battalion, Royal Sussex Regiment, and had a Distinguished Service Order and two mentions in dispatches to go along with his DSC.

A naturalized British subject since 1915, Dodge set out in 1919 on what he called an investigation of the problems of trade congestion created by the war. After visiting Australia, New Zealand, and Japan, he trekked through China and Mongolia and rode on horseback seventeen hundred miles beyond the railroad in Siberia. Unable to get to Moscow, Johnny returned east, mapped a new route from Bangkok to Mandalay, and then visited Afghanistan and Mesopotamia before exploring Persia and Georgia in the spring of 1921. However, he fell afoul of the Soviet secret police in Batum and was arrested when sketches of agricultural implements found in his pack aroused suspicion. Released after a few weeks, he immediately tried to establish a trading station near where he had been arrested. Throughout his travels Johnny Dodge remained a confirmed capitalist, something he never tired of reminding his fellow prisoners.

Having soothed his travel itch, Johnny settled down to the kind of life for which he had been bred. He served on the London County Council as the member for Mile End from 1925 to 1931, though he failed twice in his bid to represent the constituency in Parliament, and became a member of the London Stock Exchange. He married, had two sons, and took on the directorship of a New York bank. He was fast becoming one of the people who mattered in London society.

Again, Dodge's plans were interrupted by war. This time, he wangled his way into the Middlesex Regiment and was attached to the South Kensingtons. He went with the regiment to France, only to find himself caught in the debacle at St. Valéry. On June 13, 1940, he was roaming the beach, contemplating the disintegration of his division, when he spotted a small steamer several miles offshore. Quickly kicking off his boots, he started to swim out to it and was halfway there when German artillery gunners on the shore spotted it, too. In a hail of shells, the ship hastily sped off, leaving Johnny to swim back to shore. A few hours later he and several other officers were captured while walking along the shore toward Dunkirk.

Though his feet had been badly cut from walking barefoot on the stony beach, Johnny had escape on his mind and saw his chance on June 28, when he and a few hundred other prisoners were heading up the Scheldt estuary on a steamer. Early in the morning he leaped off the stern of the ship and was soon lost in the maze of small vessels around him. Escape was not as easy as he had hoped, though, and half an hour later he was pulled from the water and put back in custody. The bewildered policeman who arrested Dodge had no idea what to do with him and turned him over to the first officer who appeared. That fellow happened to be from the Luftwaffe, and Johnny found himself in air force hands. When Rumpel met Dodge, he decided that the big major was just the sort of respected and responsible person he needed for the Permanent Staff. With a few changes to Dodge's POW registration card, he was transferred to the RAF. Though Rumpel didn't know it at the time, Johnny Dodge would be responsible for little more than trouble during his stay with the Luftwaffe.

Chapter 2

LEARNING THE ESCAPING GAME

WITH THE FALL OF France, the Germans suddenly found themselves with thousands of new prisoners to house and feed, and their fledgling POW organization was quickly swamped. A central POW office within the Armed Forces High Command, or OKW, took an active hand in the running of the camps, but the camps themselves were administered by each of the three services. Not surprisingly, this arrangement led to much confusion and mismanagement. If that wasn't complicated enough, the security services also had a role to play in POW affairs, for they were responsible for recapturing escaped prisoners. The operations of the various branches of the security service were run from the Reich Main Security Office, or RSHA, in Berlin. Within the RSHA was the *Kriminalpolizei*, or Kripo, and the *Geheimestaatspolizei*, or Gestapo; the former was officially responsible for the search for and recapture of escaped POWs, while the latter was responsible for, among other things, the apprehension of 'enemies of the state.' Once the police recaptured escapers, they were to hold them until they could be returned to the military; any punishment of escapers was administered by the military authorities, in accordance with the Geneva Convention.

*

Of course, these details were the least of the Permanent Staff's worries. Through the fall and winter of 1940, there was a steady stream of new kriegies to receive, outfit, and send on their way. With the exception of the Battle of Britain, the past few months had not been kind to the RAF. Bomber Command had been badly mauled during the Battle of France and took more heavy casualties in the succeeding months as they tried to solve the problems of the bombing campaign. The RAF lost many experienced crews during those months, and the prisoners who drifted into Dulag Luft were representative of the mainstay of the RAF's strength during the first years of the war.

There was Flight Lieutenant Paul Gordon Royle, an Australian who had joined the RAF on a short service commission in March 1939.

He flew with 53 Squadron before force-landing his Blenheim south of Cambrai on May 19, 1940. Another typical airman was Flight Lieutenant Richard Sidney Albion Churchill, a twenty-year-old pilot who enlisted in August 1938. On the night of September 2–3, 1940, Dick took his 144 Squadron Hampden to raid an oil plant at Ludwigshafen but was attacked by a night fighter before reaching the target. With the aircraft alight, the crew bailed out, but only Dick and his navigator survived. There was also Pilot Officer Bertram Arthur 'Jimmy' James, the twenty-five-year-old second pilot of a 9 Squadron Wellington twin-engine bomber. James joined the RAF in 1939 and was shot down south of Rotterdam on June 5, 1940. He sprained an ankle on landing and was captured when he went to a farmhouse for some food.

Dozens of other chaps like Royle, Churchill, and James fell into German hands during the last half of 1940. They came from all corners of the empire and had been the backbone of the prewar air force. Now they were to form the backbone of the RAF escape club. For these new prisoners, though, there was a change. Instead of shipping them to Spangenberg, the Luftwaffe had decided to centralize its prisoners in a new camp, Stalag Luft I, a drab and depressing facility near the town of Barth on the Baltic coast.

The camp was of a design that would become increasingly familiar to POWs: low wooden huts in a barren compound; thick barbed wire around the perimeter; guard towers at each corner; and a deep ditch and single strand of wire just inside the perimeter that marked the outer boundary for strolling prisoners. A small adjacent compound, called the *Vorlager,* held the solitary-confinement cells (known as the cooler), the sick bay, and the guardhouse, all in a single building; an adjoining compound contained six huts for NCOs. One gate led out of the officers' compound, which measured about one hundred by seventy yards.

It was the location of Luft I that really made it dismal. Situated on a sandy isthmus near the Baltic, the camp was windswept and desolate, protected only by a stand of glum pine trees on one side. The wind blew constantly, and it was difficult to keep sand out of the huts. It was a gloomy and unpleasant camp, and only the morale of the airmen made it bearable. As usual, they turned their energies to finding a way out.

*

One night in early August 1940, the first organized escape conference at Barth was held under a naval aviator named Lieutenant Peter Evelyn Fanshawe, usually known as 'Hornblower'. Fanshawe had entered the Royal Naval College at Dartmouth in 1925 at age thirteen, and by 1940 was with 803 Squadron on the aircraft carrier *Ark Royal*. He was John Casson's navigator when they were downed while attacking the *Scharnhorst* in Norway.

Fanshawe and the other prisoners decided that a tunnel was the best way to proceed. A trap had already been cut in the floorboards of a room in the north end of the Center Block, and a brief reconnaissance had revealed plenty of space under the floor for dispersal of soil, with the advantage that the sides of the hut were boarded up to shield from prying eyes. With this encouraging intelligence they elected to dig straight down for about four feet and then head toward the wood. It was estimated that the tunnel would have to be at least 150 feet long.

Because the guards were as new to preventing escapes as the prisoners were to attempting them, security posed no problem; all it took was one man standing at the door of the hut. He could see the main gate and beyond and could warn of the approach of hostile parties in plenty of time to close the trap. The tunnel progressed well despite the fact that, in the words of one worker, it was 'amateurish and bloody dangerous' and had reached the wire by the time it was discovered in November.

It was a learning experience for both sides and, during the three weeks that the officers were banished to the *Vorlager* after the tunnel was blown, considerable changes were made in camp security. The skirting boards were removed from the sides of the huts, and new Luftwaffe guards dressed in blue-gray overalls appeared in the compound. They carried thin metal rods for poking into the ground to search out tunnels and eventually were christened ferrets.

On the other side of the fence, the kriegies were more anxious than ever to try their hand at escaping. A small six-man tunnel had started (and failed) in October, and during the brief sojourn in the *Vorlager*, the workers began another tunnel, dispersing the dirt in the roof. It had progressed only a few feet when the Germans moved the lot of them back to the main compound. A week later, two others smuggled themselves into a work party of NCOs but didn't get very far. In September three kriegies cut their way through the wire. One was free for three days, but the others were caught trying to disentangle themselves. Another fellow fashioned himself a pair of Luftwaffe work overalls and gained very temporary freedom, and two more walked out of the gate as German workmen a couple of weeks later. None of these attempts was successful, but all were part of the learning experience.

*

Back at Dulag Luft, new kriegies continued to arrive as the RAF stepped up its attacks on targets in occupied Europe. One newcomer was a slim chap of medium height with rather large ears and a thin face. He greeted the kriegies draped around the room with a wide smile and a cheerful hello and then sauntered past the table and tossed his kit on an empty bunk in the corner. He thrust an open hand toward the nearest kriegie.

'Name's Brian Evans,' he said in a quiet voice. 'From Cardiff.' The other prisoners came forward to greet him with a firm handshake or a clap on the back, and it wasn't long before they got around to hearing a bit more about him.

Born in Shaldon in Devon on February 14, 1920, Brian Herbert Evans was the elder son of Captain Herbert Evans, a master mariner with the Clan Line Steamers, and his Australian-born wife, Dorothy. After the birth of Noel, the Evanses' second son, the family moved to Upton near Birkenhead, the last loading port for Clan Line vessels before leaving the British Isles. Life near the port city was a delight for the boys. Every three or four months, when Mr. Evans's ship came in, the family would troop down to the docks to welcome him home. As they got older, the boys were sometimes allowed to climb the rope ladder to the deck. Then, a week later, the four would make the same trip down to the docks to see Mr. Evans off, though that was a considerably less happy occasion.

In 1933 Alan Cobham's air circus came to a little paddock near the Evans home, and Brian was seized with a new passion: flying. From that day on, he spent as much time as possible at local flying clubs, and later managed to see the finish of the King's Cup Air Race. At about this time Brian met Joan Cook at Sunday school. She was three years younger, but the two quickly became fast friends and often got together with a group of friends for a game of tennis or a swim.

During the summer of 1935, the Evans family moved to Cardiff. Brian's father had been made a ship's master two years earlier, and had earned the privilege of having his wife accompany him during coasting for unloading and loading. Cardiff offered an ideal central location with respect to the usual ports. The family moved into a large house, and the boys quickly settled into their new environment.

Brian still had a burning desire to pursue a career in civil aviation but realized that the costs involved were prohibitive, so for the time being he had to be content with day trips to the local flying club to watch the action. It soon became apparent that the only way to realize the dream was to join the RAF as a stepping-stone to commercial aviation.

He was hindered, however, by his difficulty with the required mathematics examination. A more aggressive person might have worked himself into enough of a temper to overcome his fear of exams, but Brian was too good-natured and gentle for that. He was downhearted for a short while; then his quiet sense of humor took over and he looked for a way to make the best of a bad situation. Finishing high school in 1938, he went to Liverpool to become a trainee in a grocery wholesale enterprise and moved to Upton. He renewed his friendship with Joan Cook and, in the short time that he was in Liverpool, became very close to Joan and her family. It was soon apparent that future prospects in the grocery trade were limited, so Brian returned to Cardiff, where he was fortunate enough to be apprenticed to a firm of auctioneers, surveyors, and real-estate agents. At the same time, he continued his struggle with math through correspondence courses.

Though his efforts to enlist in the RAF had been thwarted, Brian's love of flying remained undiminished, and he joined the Cardiff Aero Club to earn his pilot's license. He continued his part-time schooling and eventually passed the real-estate agent's examination in mathematics, which the RAF deemed equivalent to the exam required for enlistment. The last hurdle overcome, Brian could now join the service. He was granted a short service commission with effect from August 8, 1939, when he was posted to the Civil Flying School at Gatwick.

His goal finally realized, Brian threw himself into his training. By April 1940 he was with 14 Operational Training Unit (OTU) at Cottesmore. His first trips were what he called 'kipper patrols,' antishipping reconnaissance flights in twin-engine Avro Ansons. Brian reveled in these training operations, and it was clear that flying was all he had hoped it would be. 'I spent quite the most pleasant days of my sweet life toying about with those Ansons,' he wrote. He also did some operational flying as second pilot on Hampdens ('glorious position . . . doing nothing but navigating on operational flights') and quickly gained respect for the ungainly bomber. 'Hampdens are wizard machines once in the air,' he wrote; 'the takeoff is just like a rocket.' By September 1940 Brian had done a few hours as captain on practice flights but still needed to reach the forty-hour mark as second pilot on night operations before he could be posted to an operational squadron as first pilot. This assignment was uppermost in Brian's mind ('So roll on forty hours, or else stay here, which I don't want to do!'), and on September 30 he was sent to an operational unit, 49 Squadron, at Scampton.

Throughout his time on operations, Brian managed to get home for occasional weekend leaves, and he regaled his family with tales of the Hampden bomber. He talked of the discomfort of long flights, after which some crew members had to be lifted out of the aircraft, and mentioned his dislike of parachute jumping; he would much rather risk a crash-landing than hit the silk, he told Noel. Brian soon found the opportunity to experiment with his preference. On October 16, 1940, his Hampden took some heavy flak over Bordeaux Harbor, jamming the bomb-bay doors. The crew tried to free the mechanism but, running low on fuel, Brian elected to turn for home. He found the southern coast of England covered with fog and, unable to locate an airfield to land the damaged Hampden, eventually had to force-land. They came down heavily, the rear gunner being thrown clear and the navigator breaking both legs, and as Brian clambered from the cockpit, fire broke out in the fuselage, trapping the radio operator. Half-blinded and badly concussed, Evans stumbled back to the aircraft to free the sergeant but was driven away by the flames. Slumping down in the field, he watched through bleeding eyes as his crewmate burned to death.

His own wounds were considerable, and Brian was kept off operations until late in November. His first mission after the crash ended with another forced landing, this time at Christchurch. On December 6, 1940, his luck went from bad to worse. While flying as second pilot with an experienced crew for a raid on German airfields in France, Brian's aircraft ran into a snowstorm over Paris. The deicing gear failed, both engines seized, and the pilot had to crash-land the Hampden in a field near Courville. Only the radio operator was uninjured, and he went to the nearest farm to seek assistance. The farmer agreed to shelter the crew but sent a stable boy to get the police; they arrived just as the four airmen were settling down to sleep in the barn.

*

After Brian told the story of his last flight, a few of the kriegies rolled back into their bunks, and a couple of others ambled outside to brave the cold for a few circuits around the compound. Brian returned to his bunk and sorted out his kit before heading down the corridor to search for familiar faces. By the time he had canvassed the camp, word came through that he was to join the next group leaving for Barth.

On February 16, 1941, the party trooped down to the station to begin their journey. They were happy to be heading to a permanent camp, and the mood was boisterous as the train chugged out of the Frankfurt station. In one corner of the railroad car, a few of the prisoners were engaged in a game of cards. One of the guards watched them for a time but found the game so utterly incomprehensible that he wandered off to the other end of the car shaking his head. From behind dark glasses worn to shade his still-sensitive eyes, Brian Evans watched the guard's movements and, after a few minutes, gave a slight nod to the fellow opposite, a naval airman named Filmer. He in turn nudged the officer beside him, Flight Lieutenant Henry Cuthbert Marshall, commonly known as Johnny, a 3 Photo-Reconnaissance Unit (PRU) pilot who had bailed out of his Spitfire over Laval on January 12, 1941. Johnny Marshall was older than most of the other kriegies and had just entered his seventeenth year of service in the RAF. He was dark and good-looking, with slightly thinning hair and perfect white teeth.

From the guard's vantage point, the kriegies were still playing a harmless game of cards but, in fact, Johnny Marshall was slowly prying the nails out of the window with a flattened bit of metal that had been smuggled out of Dulag Luft by the fourth member of the group, Ben Everton-Jones. It was slow work, but as darkness fell, Marshall finished the last of the nails. The card game slowly wound up, and the prisoners began to doze off in the dimness. The car was quiet, and Brian noticed that the guard had decided to take advantage of the calm to make a trip to the lavatory.

At that moment, as the train approached the crest of a slight hill, the escapers made their move. The first three clambered through the window without incident, but then the train began to accelerate again. As the speed increased, the fourth man, Brian Evans, finally forced himself out of the window, but his leg struck a signal post with a glancing blow as he landed. It was the same leg he had injured in his crash, and it was with some effort that he hobbled painfully toward the bush behind which the others had concealed themselves. Luckily, no alarm was raised, and the four were able to collect their thoughts for a few minutes before setting out along the railroad line toward Berlin.

After a few hours of walking, it was evident that Brian's leg was slowing down the group, so the four elected to split up. Filmer and Evans, realizing that Brian's limp would attract attention, decided to leave the rail line and find a less conspicuous route. Their choice turned out to be the wrong one, and the pair were picked up within an hour. Marshall and Everton-Jones, however, had better luck and were able to hitch rides on passing freight trains. In a couple of days they had reached the northern outskirts of Berlin and began to walk westward. Two days later, hungry and exhausted, they were stopped by a police patrol and arrested. When they finally reached Barth, they found that Evans and Filmer had preceded them.

They also found that two other kriegies had escaped from the same train, at almost the same time. H.D. 'Tim' Newman, a short service commission officer from New Zealand, and an Australian officer had squeezed out of a window at the opposite end of the train. On the second day of their trek they reached Pasewalk, but they were recaptured while trying to go around the town.

When they reached Barth, this batch of recaptured escapers found a number of schemes in progress. Jimmy James and a Scotsman named Ian 'Muckle' Muir were working on a tunnel from the East Block that survived for a few weeks, and when that was found, energies shifted to a hole originating in the newly built West Block. In June 1941 the trap was sunk to a depth of about five feet through the floor in the corner of one of the barracks rooms. The soil was firm enough to make shoring unnecessary, and there was a rough ventilation system with air lines crafted out of wallpaper that had been stiffened with a mixture of water and clay dust scraped from bricks. As the tunnel pushed toward its planned one-hundred-foot length, other escapes were being undertaken. In one attempt in May, a kriegie named Harry Burton unfastened the bars on his cell window and burrowed under the gate to freedom. On the last day of the month he reached Sweden, the first successful RAF escaper of the war.

On August 20, 1941, the West Block tunnel was finally ready to break and about thirty workers, including Jimmy James, Muckle Muir, and Tim Newman, prepared to make their exit. The first five crawled into the tunnel and found that progress was much more difficult with full escape kit. Furthermore, they made so much noise trying to squeeze out of the exit that a guard was alerted and several shots were fired. In the ensuing confusion, only Tim Newman and two others got away. Another fellow got wedged in the tunnel and was dragged out by the guards. The rest were able to regain the comparative safety of the West Block. Newman was caught after three days, but the other two had better luck. Both managed to get onto the docks at Rostock, where the first fellow was picked up trying to board a Swedish ship. The second was able to get aboard and hide in a coal bin, planning to stay there until the ship reached Sweden. Sadly, he was so exhausted by his exertions that he fell asleep and his snores alerted the crew. Reluctantly, they explained to the exhausted escaper the consequences if they were discovered trying to smuggle a fugitive out of Germany and said they would have to turn him over to the Germans.

With the comparative failure of this scheme, another plan was soon in the works. John 'Death' Shore and Jimmy James had set their sights on a small brick incinerator near the perimeter wire. They figured that if a trap could be sunk under the incinerator, there would only be about twenty-five feet to dig to the sports field outside the wire. The two soon set to work with a gang of diversionists, including Dick Churchill, Paul Royle, and Lawrence Reavell-Carter, a former British Olympian and an air gunner on a Hampden that had been shot down on a minelaying mission in June 1940. Another who joined the scheme was John Shore's second pilot, James Leslie Robert Long, a stout and jolly fellow who earned the nickname 'Cookie' because of his skill in brewing kriegie hooch. Long, a big, bearded chap who lived in Jimmy James's room, was strong and reliable, and very anxious to get into escape work.

Born on February 21, 1915, in Bournemouth, on the southern coast of England, Long was a likable, thick-set boy with a full face, dark complexion, and straight black hair. He was educated in Somerset; the family moved to Taunton when his father, Cecil, bought a large grocery store there. Les did well in school, and at age eleven won a scholarship to a private school. He was always in the top half dozen academically and also made a name for himself on the sports field.

By this time Cecil Long had bought a block of stores in Taunton, and the family had moved into a very large apartment above the prosperous Long's Grocers. Cecil Long was equally well known in local society as the secretary of the Octagon Chapel, a closely knit congregation of the Plymouth Brethren where Charles Wesley had once preached. Les Long, too, was an active member of the chapel community, and it was through the church that he met a young woman named Dorothy Broom. Courtship was difficult in those days, especially with the strictness of the Plymouth Brethren, and Les and Dorothy even had to travel to the next town to go to the movies, something that was frowned on by the church elders. Still, the couple managed somehow. By December 1939 they were engaged.

While at school, Les passed the Oxford entrance exam with honors, but a university education was too expensive at that time, and he became apprenticed to the General Accident Insurance Company to train as an inspector. Les received a small stipend and was expected to take correspondence courses. By 1939 he had passed two of the three exams required in his apprenticeship. Les had always been interested in things mechanical, often going to air shows or to local motor races to see the German Auto-Unions compete, but it wasn't until a few years before the war that his interest really jelled. For a vacation, he flew to Ireland and, when he returned from his 'trip of a lifetime,' as he called it, he had made up his mind to become a pilot. He even talked about working as a bush pilot in Canada someday. His first step was to join the Civil Air Guard, a civilian organization that trained pilots, and got his flying license in 1938. One day a week and on weekends he traveled to Locking near Weston-super-Mare to learn in single-seaters. By September 1939 he had completed much of his instruction but had yet to solo.

When word of the German invasion of Poland came, Les and his younger brother Norman were on a camping trip in Wales and were all set for a climb of Mount Snowdon. They talked about the coming war but decided to make their climb regardless. After all, this would likely be the last day of normalcy for quite some time. When they returned home to Taunton, Les's call-up papers were waiting. Because he had not yet soloed, his mobilization was deferred, and it wasn't until April 19, 1940, that he was taken into the Royal Air Force Volunteer Reserve

(RAFVR). In June he began training and by December had been awarded his wings. He did officer training at Torquay, where Dorothy was able to visit him for a week, with his elder sister Kathleen acting as chaperone. Just before Christmas, Les was commissioned and assigned to 19 Operational Training Unit.

On March 3, 1941, Pilot Officer Long was transferred to 9 Squadron and flew his first operation less than two weeks later. Though he had only been in operations a short time, it was clear that his experiences in the RAF had changed him. He told Dorothy that he had no desire to go back to the narrow life in which they had been raised and intended to give up insurance and study economics instead. He hoped that Dorothy would be a part of his new life.

On March 27, 1941, five Wellingtons from 9 Squadron were detailed to join a raid on Cologne and, just before 8:00 P.M., Long, John Shore, and the rest of the crew took off from their base at Honington. From the beginning it was evident that the engines weren't right, but John elected to press on regardless. They made it to the target, albeit almost an hour behind schedule, and dropped their bombs. Shore wheeled the Wellington around and set course for home. Just after 10:30 P.M., though, the starboard engine stopped abruptly and then immediately started up again. Seconds later, both engines gave out and, despite Shore's efforts, nothing could get them going again. At eight thousand feet he ordered the crew to bail out, and at fifteen hundred feet he hit the silk himself. Most of the crew came down east of Eindhoven, in Holland. Some were captured immediately, but Les, having aggravated an old rugby injury to his knee, spent the night sheltering in a church porch before being picked up the next morning. The crew met up at the police station in Heusden and were driven to the Luftwaffe barracks in Amsterdam before being transferred to Dulag Luft.

*

Every morning at about ten-thirty, Cookie Long joined the cluster of men standing on and around Barth's incinerator to get a better view of the day's soccer match. Using the crowd as cover, John Shore and Jimmy James climbed into the incinerator and built a trap in the sand floor, which was propped open for ventilation. They scraped away the sand in the tunnel with a table knife and ferried it in bowls back to the incinerator, where it was mixed with the ash and rubbish. Then, at about 5:00 P.M., another match was organized, and the diggers climbed out of the incinerator and melted into the crowd. It was all very neat. The tunnel was completed in only four working days, but because of a series of searches, those days had to be spaced over a period of three weeks, so it was October before the tunnel was actually ready. Shore and James were to go first, crawling through traps cut in their room floors and across the compound to the incinerator. Four hours later, Muckle Muir, Tim Newman, and two others were to follow them. The escapers had decided to go during an air raid, so for several days they had to be ready at a few minutes' notice.

Finally, on the night of October 19, 1941, the sirens wailed in the distance, and the six knew that the time had come. Shore went first and snaked across the compound to the incinerator. After a suitable delay, Jimmy James was helped through his trap by Cookie Long and followed Shore's path to the tunnel. Unfortunately, James's exit coincided with an unusual amount of activity in the camp, and he found himself lying in the middle of the compound while guards wandered in various directions. Eventually there was a lull and Jimmy continued his crawl, only to see the figure of the camp security officer loom in front of him. A flashlight shone and, discretion being the better part of valor, Jimmy scuttled back to his block. However, he could not find the trap that led up into his room and was eventually dragged ignominiously from under the hut. There was a bright spot in the evening's proceedings, though. John Shore made it all the way to Sassnitz and there boarded a ferry for Sweden. He became the second successful escaper from Barth.

*

The escapers had had the last of the mild weather to work in, and by November the chilling east winds had started to blow across the compound. The mornings dawned dull and frosty, and the ornithologists in the camp reported large flocks of birds flying south. Snow came shortly after, and the prisoners were able to build a small ice rink in the garden. They had to make do with pieces of iron bedstead for skates and charcoal briquets for hockey pucks, but it was enough to provide some entertainment and exercise. Despite the cold, work on various tunnels continued below the compound. In December a new hole was started by a mixed team of diggers, including William Jack Grisman and Leslie George Bull, crewmates who had only recently arrived in Barth.

Jack Grisman, the eldest son of a postman, was born in the family home in Hereford, England, on August 30, 1914. A quiet and shy child, Jack matured quickly when he took up swimming and rugby at school. Outgoing and extroverted as he had become, Jack did not find his métier until leaving high school. Then, to the surprise and delight of his family, he announced his intention to join the RAF. The air force seemed to offer all he wanted: fine training in engineering; ample opportunity to indulge his love of sports; and the chance to see the world. On January 13, 1931, Jack arrived at Halton as a member of the 23rd Entry of Aircraft Apprentices. He was not yet seventeen years old.

Another member of the class, Wally Gardiner, remembers Jack as a determined and intelligent fellow who quickly gained popularity at Halton. The two roomed together there for a year, played rugby, and became firm friends. When they graduated from Halton in December 1933, both were posted to Boscombe Down, Jack to the new Handley-Page Heyford bombers of 10 Squadron and Wally to 9 Squadron, still equipped with older Vickers Virginia bombers. Life at Boscombe Down was good. Jack and Wally continued on the rugby squad, and Jack swam for the station, as he had done at Halton. By January 1936 both were leading aircraftmen about to begin their tour of duty overseas.

It was a rough journey to Basra in Iraq, the first stop on their Middle East assignment. The Bay of Biscay was in the throes of a raging storm, and the airmen spent days on end bundled up in their greatcoats. They arrived none the worse for wear and soon found themselves assigned to the aircraft depot at Hinaidi. Though classified as an engine fitter, Jack was temporarily assigned to the motor-transport section. Like many of his fellow airmen, he loved the time in Iraq. There were constant sports matches to watch or play, swimming pools (Jack could still beat most challengers in the water), and the movies, so social life at the station was good; for the more adventurous among them, Baghdad was close at hand. Some, Jack and Wally included, began attending classes for their high-school equivalency but found their interest waned quickly. They were young and too inquisitive to spend time with books, and it was far too hot to study.

In November 1936, Jack was given a temporary appointment to the British embassy in Baghdad to start a seven-month stint as driver to the ambassador. Wally Gardiner saw less and less of Jack and eventually returned to England, while Jack moved on to the aircraft depot at

Dhibban. Then, having completed two years in Iraq, Jack received the usual assignment to the North-West Frontier Province (or 'the Grim,' as it was known in RAF slang), in what is now Pakistan, in April 1938. He was assigned to temporary flying duties as an air gunner, a 'rigger and fitter,' on the biplanes of 28 Squadron.

Though the years in Iraq and India were a delight for Jack, it was with some relief that he returned to England in December 1938 after volunteering for aircrew duties. Following the completion of an observer's course he was posted to 99 Squadron, which was stationed at Mildenhall, on July 27, 1939. During this period Jack Grisman renewed his friendship with Marie Marchant, his high-school sweetheart. Many years had passed since their school days, when the two used to meet at the local swimming pools and go for long walks in the countryside, but neither seemed to have changed much. Jack was to move around quite a bit over the next two years, but his relationship with Marie gradually intensified.

At the outbreak of war, 99 Squadron was assigned to take part in pamphlet raids on Germany. After a navigation course and a promotion to sergeant, Jack returned to duty and showed sufficient promise on operations to be posted for officer training in June 1940. Even with the rigors of the course, Jack still managed to find time to visit Marie, and the two spent many happy, if rushed, afternoons together. On August 2, 1940, they were married. The wedding took place on the last day of a short leave, and the honeymoon lasted only until Jack had to return to base later that same evening. He was soon back on operations, earning a mention in dispatches on October 6, and on December 20 he received his commission.

Having completed one tour of operations as a sergeant, Grisman found himself back at Boscombe Down in December, with 109 Squadron, which was involved in the development of new radar aids and radio countermeasures. Because of the nature of that work he was reluctant to talk about his operations but enjoyed working with the most modern technological developments. More important, his time at Boscombe Down brought him together with another man who worked on the Barth tunnel: Les Bull.

Leslie George Bull was born in Highbury, London, on November 7, 1916, and upon finishing school entered the London County Council School of Building at Brixton with the intention of becoming an architect. Les did well at the school but after three years of full-time study decided that the building trade wasn't for him. He liked the sound of the RAF and in July 1936 joined the service. He spent his first years in the air force flying Handley-Page Harrow bombers with 75 Squadron and hoped one day to be a test pilot. In 1938, while stationed at Driffield, Les married Kathleen Organ, whose parents kept a bed-and-breakfast near the airfield. Les and Kathleen had a son, David, born in 1940.

On February 24, 1940, Bull was posted to 9 Squadron at Honington and flew Wellingtons on five operations with the unit, primarily against communications targets. He was commissioned in June and was then transferred to the Blind Approach Training Development Unit (BATDU) at Boscombe Down. The BATDU later became the Wireless Intelligence Development Unit and, from December 1, 1940, 109 Squadron. Les and Kathleen moved to Salisbury, and with a new son and the numerous flights made by the unit, Les Bull was quite busy. Now crewed up together, Les and Jack Grisman flew frequently, often to monitor the German radar chain or test a new piece of equipment. Occasionally they made two or three trips in a day. In June Les Bull was promoted to flying officer, and in July he was awarded the Distinguished Flying Cross for completing his first tour of operations.

On the night of November 5, 1941, Bull, Grisman, and the rest of the crew took off in their Wellington to investigate the German radar chain on the western coast of France. The trip was proceeding without incident when, just before midnight, the starboard engine began to fail over Lorient. Les played with the controls but soon the engine died completely, and Bull peered out of his side window to see that the starboard propeller had come off in midflight, a not unusual occurrence with the Bristol Pegasus radial engine. Bull wrestled the Wellington to an even keel to allow the crew to bail out, and all seven escaped safely, coming down at various places around the town of Pontivy. Les was picked up immediately, and four crewmen were captured within hours, but Jack was more fortunate. He walked south for the rest of the night, took shelter in a barn at dawn, and then started his trek again at dusk. Walking for most of the night, Jack was driven by hunger and thirst to approach a farm for help. There his luck ran out. The farmer alerted the authorities while Jack ate, and Grisman found himself in the bag.

*

With just a month of captivity under their belts, Grisman, Bull, and the others worked tirelessly in the tunnel but found the going very difficult. Aside from the fact that the earth was rock-hard, the diggers could work only short shifts before being forced to return to the hut to thaw out their numbed bodies. There were more pleasant ways to spend the holiday season, but at least they were better off than Jimmy James. He was spending yet another spell in the cooler after being found in a tunnel under his block.

Things would warm up considerably over Christmas, though, for the kriegies were making their first forays into home brewing. An early attempt to make alcohol from potato skins was declared an abject failure, but a later effort, using dried fruit from Red Cross parcels and yeast obtained from a guard, proved to be more successful. Under the careful supervision of a former distillery employee, the fermented mixture was distilled in a contraption made from a large milk can, part of an old football, and pieces of a trombone. What came off was pure alcohol, though some prisoners tried to pass their own brews off as rum, whiskey, or gin. One kriegie even bottled his under rather nice labels that proclaimed it to be 'Le Grand Vin du Bordel.'

Well lubricated with homemade hooch, a few of the kriegies put on a Christmas pantomime in the NCOs' recreation room. Even the commandant and his staff were invited, and Wings Day sat them in the front row, looking forward to a tasteful performance in the best tradition of the English theater. His hopes were dashed by the title of the performance, 'Alice and Her Candle,' and what followed was a particularly lewd exercise in kriegie humor. Expecting the commandant to have a fit at any minute, Wings was surprised that he sat through the entire performance and was even more shocked when he politely complimented the kriegies on their effort at the conclusion. Apparently the commandant's knowledge of English profanities was somewhat lacking.

The Christmas celebration was an excellent way for the kriegies to blow off steam and, though making alcohol was technically forbidden, the Germans usually turned a blind eye to it. As long as things didn't get out of hand, they were quite willing to let the prisoners have their fun. And a bit of fun they needed, for the war news was not encouraging. The Germans were quick to report their successes on the Russian Front, and the sinking of the *Prince of Wales* and *Repulse* off Malaya overshadowed the cheering news that the United States had entered the war. Some kriegies refused to believe any news that originated from enemy sources, but new purges (transferees from other camps) that reached Barth at Christmastime confirmed most of the German claims.

*

The latest group included Flight Lieutenant Roy Brouard Langlois, a dark, twenty-four-year-old Channel Islander. Roy joined the RAF in May 1936 and was flying with 12 Squadron on August 5, 1941, when his Wellington force-landed near Antwerp after a raid on Aachen. He managed to get away from the wreck and link up with the Resistance but was eventually arrested in Brussels on October 2.

The new arrivals were directed to various huts by the adjutant, and Langlois wandered off to locate his room. As he entered, his attention was immediately drawn to the farthest corner, where strains of Cuban folk music rose softly from a battered gramophone. Above, on a bunk painted with exotic and colorful flowers, reclined a slender, extremely handsome man with thick black hair and a dark mustache. He wore a brightly striped caftan and yellow silk bedroom slippers and was engrossed in a copy of *The Sexual Life of Savages*. He seemed so oblivious to Roy's presence that the latter started when he spoke.

'Soothing, isn't it?' said the figure. 'I always find it helps me regain my equilibrium after a busy morning. You're new, aren't you?' he inquired, looking up for the first time. Langlois nodded and introduced himself.

'A fellow foreigner of sorts!' smiled the figure. 'Pleased to make your acquaintance. I'm Tom Kirby-Green, late of Tangier.'

*

Squadron Leader Thomas Gresham Kirby-Green had to rank as one of the more unusual officers in Barth, for his life could have been taken straight from the pages of a boy's adventure book. Born February 27, 1918, in Dowa, in Nyasaland (now Malawi), he was the son of Sir William Kirby-Green, the district governor of Nyasaland, and his brilliant if eccentric wife, Ada. Even the circumstances of Tom's birth were out of the ordinary. During the period that Ada was expecting, Sir William was upcountry, where his party came upon a baby boy who had been abandoned in the woods. This was a very unusual occurrence, and Sir William took the baby home, where he learned that Tom had been born on the very night that the abandoned baby had been found. The native child was christened Putti, and the two boys were raised as brothers.

After growing up in Nyasaland, Kirby-Green was sent to the very foreign environment of Dover College to continue his education. Unused to the ways of the English private school, Tom had some difficulties adjusting. One of his first acts upon arrival was to do a little duck hunting with his shotgun on the school's pond, an episode that brought down the wrath of the headmaster. However, Tom got used to the atmosphere at Dover and eventually became a house prefect and a respected, even feared, member of the rugby team. Tom finished school in 1935 and went to live with his parents in Tangier, but was back in England in August 1936 to join the RAF on a short service commission. Having already earned his private pilot's license, he sped through training and was posted to 216 Squadron on May 27, 1937. The following January, Pilot Officer Kirby-Green was transferred to 99 Squadron at Mildenhall, where he remained until 1939. After a gunnery course he was posted to 9 Squadron in January 1940 to begin operations.

Throughout the first half of 1940 the squadron was constantly in action. By the end of July Tom had completed twenty-seven raids, mostly against road and rail targets in France and the Low Countries. He was a well-known figure around the squadron's base at Honington. Now a fairly senior flying officer, he had a dignified and businesslike mien and could often be found in the mess, assiduously reading *The Times*. In September, for a well-earned rest, Kirby-Green was posted to the newly formed 311 (Czech) Squadron to act as flight instructor. He was popular with the bright and fiery Czechs and was well respected for his disdain of the enemy. At a time when rumors were rife about the fate of Continental airmen captured by the Germans, Tom always insisted on wearing Czech shoulder insignia to inspire his students. When he was posted back to an operational unit in September 1941, Tom left 311 with many new friends among the Czechs.

Tom was sent to 40 Squadron, whose Wellingtons were engaged in almost nightly raids on the Continent. Newly promoted to squadron leader, he soon found that the operations were a little different from those flown by 9 Squadron. On September 10 the unit was assigned to make the long trip to Turin in northern Italy. It was a filthy night, and

Tom was the only squadron pilot to reach and bomb the target, a feat of endurance that earned him a mention in dispatches. A month later, he and his crew circled Nuremberg for ninety minutes while attempting to pinpoint the target. They eventually gave up trying to locate the aiming point and dumped their load on the first likely looking spot.

On October 17, 1941, Tom and his crew were assigned to a raid on Duisburg. It was Kirby-Green's thirty-seventh operation. However, nothing was heard from the Wellington after it left base, and it was assumed that the popular squadron leader had been lost. Tom's good friend and commanding officer, Wing Commander Pickard, immediately flew down to Selsey, where Tom's wife, Maria, was living, and told her the news, saying he was certain that Tom was a prisoner. Sure enough, on November 16, Lord Haw-Haw, the British traitor who made radio broadcasts for the Nazis, gloated over the capture of the eminent Squadron Leader Kirby-Green; by this time he had already passed through Dulag Luft and arrived at Barth.

At Stalag Luft I, Tom quickly made a name for himself as a character, and not simply for his exotic dress. He was very enthusiastic about Latin music and often accompanied his records on a homemade set of bongo drums. His personal parcels included strange and wonderful foods, such as figs, garbanzos, atun, and bacalao. They weren't for all tastes but they certainly did provide a respite from the same old menu. Kirby-Green was also a popular speaker on the camp's lecture list. Shortly after his arrival in Barth he gave a detailed and entertaining account of the war situation that was appreciated by many of the older kriegies. 'You see I read *The Times* regularly,' he said with a smile at the close of his talk.

*

As more POWs arrived at Barth, the pace of escape attempts increased. On January 5, 1942, Nick Tindal tried to get out under the muck cart, used for pumping out the camp latrines, but was found at the gate. On the fourteenth two prisoners marched toward the gate in goonskins, the nickname given to false German uniforms made by the prisoners, but were revealed as fakes in the glare of the searchlights. One kriegie buried himself in the snow on the sports field but was spotted by a sentry, who noticed steam rising from his body. A few days later the same fellow tried again, disguised as the ferret Charlie Pfelz. Tom Kirby-Green carved a fake flashlight for an airman who got away from the parcels store in the *Vorlager* dressed in a German uniform; he made it as far as Sassnitz, where he was retaken and purged to Colditz, the infamous castle prison where the Germans incarcerated inveterate escapers. Pat Leeson made a good attempt as a chimney sweep and then later tried again with two others as a Luftwaffe corporal and two prisoners. Later, Jimmy James made a straightforward attempt. He waited until some disturbance caused the lights to go out and then donned a goonskin and ran toward the main gate shouting 'Los! Los!' ('Go! Go!'), hoping that the guard would let him through in the confusion. Halfway to his destination, though, the lights came on again and Jimmy dashed back to his hut and hid the uniform.

There was also a tragedy that winter. In the NCOs' compound, Sergeant Johnny Shaw, Brian Evans's pilot, and another kriegie made an assault on the wire in a heavy snowstorm. They had just started to cut their way through when a guard spotted them and yelled a warning. Johnny Shaw stood up and raised his arms, but the guard ignored his surrender and fired a single shot, killing him. Johnny was the first fatal casualty of the escape campaign.

Chapter 3

THE DULAG LUFT TUNNEL

Stalag Luft I provided the main irritant to the Luftwaffe, but the RAF's campaign against their captors was not merely a single-front affair. During Barth's first year of existence the number of Allied airmen falling into German hands had necessitated the formation of air force contingents at other camps. Luft I turned out to be too small to handle all the captured airmen, so groups of fliers were farmed out to various camps, each of which became a center for RAF escape work. And each became a thorn in Germany's side.

*

After the first winter of settling in at Dulag Luft, the Permanent Staff had turned its energies seriously to escape and got back to tunneling. In the summer of 1940 a tunnel had been started from a washroom in the East Block but had been closed in October because of flooding. In March 1941 it was decided to reopen the hole to see if it could be used. The first workers who went down found the tunnel partly flooded with freezing water, but they were able to draw the worst of it off by sinking drainage holes beside a large boulder that had impeded progress the previous year. By April the tunnel was again ready for full-scale work.

Following the plan drawn up before, most of the digging was done by members of the Permanent Staff, with the aid of any prisoners in transit who wanted to lend a hand. Digging progressed well through the firm earth, and the planners were content to take their time, anticipating that the tunnel would be used in the fall, when the escapers could forage for food in fields. However, things went so well that the tunnel was completed in May, and it was decided to break it at the next moonless period, the first weekend in June. Eighteen of the workers geared up for the escape.

Roger Bushell had proposed a different scheme for himself. Because he needed to catch a connecting train from Frankfurt to the Swiss frontier, he planned to hide in a goat shed near the recreation field and slip away in the early evening. To discourage a close search of the shed by guards, one bright light suggested that Bushell hide in a pile of goat dung.

'But what about the smell?' Roger protested.

'Oh, I don't imagine the goats will mind,' came the reply.

Bushell's exit went like clockwork, and he reached the village of Stuhlingen on the Swiss frontier in the late afternoon of the following day. At that point he was faced with a dilemma: He must either wait until nightfall and try the difficult border crossing in darkness or make the attempt in daylight. Confidence won out over prudence, and Roger chose the latter course. He was on his way through the village when the inevitable happened: A man emerged from a house and stopped him. Picking a role he knew well, Roger pretended to be a drunken ski instructor on his way home from a nearby village. The man was almost convinced but said that Roger had to be checked by police, whereupon Bushell smiled disarmingly and bolted. He darted around the corner and into a cul-de-sac; his escape attempt ended there.

Covered by a raucous party, the other escapers made their way to the tunnel entrance on that warm June night and began their crawl to freedom. Few of them got far from the camp. Wings Day was picked up by a forest ranger on the second day, while Jimmy Buckley got to Minden before a train guard cottoned on to him. Guy Griffiths and his running mate spotted a motorcycle that they wanted to steal until they noticed the vicious-looking dog chained to it. They beat a hasty retreat and were later picked up in a marshaling yard near Darmstadt. Johnny Dodge and his partner boldly walked south along the autobahn, despite the fact that pedestrians were forbidden. In broad daylight they passed a flak battery, where a bored-looking guard merely stared at them, not even cracking a smile when Johnny tripped and went sprawling on the tarmac. Shocked into greater care, they went to ground for the rest of the day. After dark the pair set off again, having munched on their food packets but with nothing to slake their thirst. Not wishing to risk being spotted on the autobahn, they looked for the first available bridge to cross and get into less well traveled country. Unfortunately, the bridge was guarded, and their trek ended there.

The last pair out was Mike Casey and his running mate. Emerging from the tunnel, they headed south, crossed the Main River by bridge, and walked for a full twenty-four hours before sheltering in a wood the night after the escape. Starting early the following morning, they had reached a small village a few miles north of Darmstadt when they were stopped by a local policeman. He immediately asked to see their papers and, when they could produce nothing, arrested the two. After a few hours in the local jail, they were taken by bus to the civilian prison in Frankfurt, and from there, directly to Barth.

Commandant Rumpel was removed from his post after the escape, but he took it very well. When the recaptured escapers boarded the train taking them to Luft I, they found in their carriage a case of champagne, with Rumpel's compliments.

*

In addition to Dulag Luft and Barth, other camps also had RAF contingents. In July 1941 about fifty unlucky souls were purged from Barth to Stalag XC at Lübeck, a camp that held mostly British officers captured in Crete. It was dirty and primitive, and there seemed to be a chronic shortage of food. To make matters worse, the RAF was none too popular because a Wellington had recently dropped a bomb on the German officers' mess. Bushell and Filmer started a tunnel there but were delighted when in October the entire camp, including a group of recent arrivals from Dulag, was moved to Oflag VIB at Warburg.

Never one to miss an opportunity, Bushell mobilized the airmen and assembled a team to cut their way out of the boxcars in which they were traveling. There were about thirty men in each car, with three guards near the door, so Bushell arranged for a bunch of kriegies to huddle over a game of cards. In the middle, he and Filmer hacked away at the floorboards with a notched table knife. Hours later, their fingers ragged and bleeding, they finally had a hole big enough to squeeze through.

Filmer went first and waited for the train to slow on an incline before lowering himself gingerly onto the tracks. Then it was merely a matter of rolling off the tracks between the wheels. Bushell and a Czech officer, Jack Zafouk, went next, followed by another pair. They all made a clean getaway, albeit somewhat panicked by a rifle shot that they later discovered was fired at two men escaping from another part of the train. Filmer didn't get far, but one pair of escapers made it all the way to Stettin before being nabbed while skulking around the docks. It would be months before the rest of the kriegies learned the fate of Bushell and Zafouk.

While all this was happening, another group of airmen was on its way to Warburg from Spangenberg. They arrived on October 10, 1941, and found the camp occupied by twenty-five hundred British Army officers who had just taken up residence. It was a large, oddly shaped compound about a mile in length, and it sat on the side of a desolate slope astride a country road. Its wooden huts were in a terrible state. They were damp and flea-infested, many were unlit, and the cooking and sanitary arrangements were hopelessly inadequate. All in all, it was not a very encouraging situation.

Nevertheless, morale was high, and when the now-depleted Lübeck group arrived a few days later, the RAF contingent began to organize itself and settle in. It was soon obvious that there was much to be learned from their new campmates. The army officers had been in captivity for nearly a year and a half and had put that time to good use in improving their escape techniques. They had much to share with the airmen about tunneling, surveying, mapping, and forgery. For their part, the RAF provided a much-needed fillip of morale. They were always in high spirits and made a great game of singling out members of the German staff for ridicule. The second-in-command, a corpulent and pompous character dubbed 'Bulk Issue,' was a favorite target. Whenever he waddled through the camp, one of the fliers invariably took it upon himself to act as a traffic policeman, directing the progress of Bulk Issue with such warnings as 'Make way there – give the man some space,' while other airmen flattened themselves against the walls of the huts, as one does when a truck comes down a narrow lane.

When not baiting the camp staff, the airmen spent their time learning the tricks of the escaping trade from the army officers, and in November the RAF contingent made its first attempt. Wearing roughly tailored German uniforms, Peter Stevens assembled a group of eleven officers and, armed with a forged gate pass, prepared to march them out of the compound. The sentry told Stevens that the pass lacked the signature, so Peter marched the party back toward the barracks and went straight to the forgers to get the necessary signature. A few minutes later he was at the gate again, only to be told that two guards and an NCO were needed to escort a group of that size. Stevens began with an explanation but the sentry was unconvinced and started shouting. Immediately the group broke up and scattered back to the barracks, closely followed by Stevens. Still a little confused, the sentry called a couple of guards to round up the fleeing prisoners. They caught only two of the twelve but had broken up a very plucky escape attempt.

Meanwhile, a mixed bag of Canadian, British, Polish, and Czech airmen had started a tunnel from one of the orderlies' huts. With the help of some army surveyors, they had picked an exit point just outside the glare of the searchlights and predicted that a two-hundred-foot-long tunnel would bring them up in darkness. There was no need to shore the tunnel, for the earth was a sticky clay, but it was necessary to floor it with boards taken from one of the dining rooms. For dispersal, the diggers stashed the soil in the attic of the hut. On April 19, 1942, the tunnel was finally ready for use, and a Czech officer went down to dig the last six feet, a task that took him nearly four hours. When he did get it open, he discovered that the surveying had been inaccurate and that the tunnel came up in the middle of a floodlit area. Some of the officers decided that the risk was too great and gave up their places in the exit order, but five intrepid souls decided to have a try. They crawled across the lighted space and disappeared into the night. One of the Czechs, Josef Bryks, remained at large until May 5, when he was picked up near Erbach, but the other Czech, a Polish officer, and a Montreal-born flight lieutenant named Eddie Asselin were caught within a few days.

The fifth escaper, Stanisław Zygmunt (Danny) Król, was also recaptured, not far from the camp. Dark-haired with a square face and a cleft chin, Król was born on March 22, 1916, in Zagorzyce, Poland, and enlisted in the Polish Air Force on September 21, 1937. He trained at the officer cadet center at Deblin, specialized in fighter techniques, and was commissioned on September 1, 1939. The next day, though, Deblin's aircraft were bombed, and Danny and his comrades were reduced to spectators for the rest of the campaign; after a week, the cadets began a trek to Romania, which they reached on September 17. The following month they got to France, where General Sikorski had re-formed the Polish government. In February 1940, Sikorski established a Polish Air Force center at Lyon–Bron, and most of the Poles settled in there with hopes of continuing the fight with French equipment. The Deblin cadets formed part of the Finnish Group, so named because it was destined for Finland under the terms of an agreement for assistance to that country. However, the French government decided to keep the Finnish Group, and it remained at Lyon–Bron with its Morane fighters.

The German invasion of France brought more heavy fighting for the Poles. On May 10, 1940, Lyon-Bron was bombed and, over the next month, the Deblin group moved around France to fill gaps in the defense. Eventually most of the Poles were evacuated to England and taken into the RAF for assignment to various training stations, with Danny going to 57 OTU. Then he began his third separate campaign of the war, though this one was also short. On July 2, 1941, while flying a 74 Squadron Spitfire from Gravesend, Król was downed on his eleventh sweep over the Continent.

Danny Król was a familiar figure at Warburg. In the summer months he was known for practicing his championship fencing moves on the sports field, while in the winter he could often be seen standing naked outside his hut, washing himself with snow. He always maintained that it improved his resistance and stamina. There was obviously some truth in it, too, for Danny was a tough and strong little man, just over five feet tall but with immense power packed into his small frame.

Król was one of the first of a wave of Polish airmen who would fall into German hands while serving with the RAF. However, it would be months before the Poles arrived in the camps in significant numbers. In the autumn of 1941, the majority of airmen falling into captivity were still from Britain and the empire. In fact, they created such pressure on space as to necessitate the re-creation of the RAF community at Spangenberg, and, from January 1942, most of the officers passing through Dulag were transferred to this fortress near Kassel. One who arrived in February was a Canadian flight lieutenant, George McGill. For hard-luck stories, the tale of George's last flight had to rank pretty high.

*

George Edward McGill was born on April 14, 1918, the second of five children, in Toronto, Ontario. Upon graduation from high school in 1936, George did a year of applied science and engineering at the University of Toronto but eventually left to work in the family coal business. His greatest achievement during those years was in athletics; he was a strong and able athlete and won the Ontario championships in the quarter-mile run. Much of his time, though, was spent on Toronto Island, a cottage area in Lake Ontario where he lived with his grandparents. The island was a perfect spot for running, and George was also fond of canoeing. It was there that McGill met Betty Goodman, who was to become his wife in September 1940. They would have a son, Peter, born two months before George went overseas.

Despite the fact that many of his friends had joined the army, George opted for the RCAF and started his navigation training on December 9, 1940, at Malton, Ontario. The quiet and determined McGill really took to the work and had no difficulty with it. By the time he got his commission in May 1941, George had received high ratings in all aspects of the observer's trade. On July 16, 1941, McGill left Gander, Newfoundland, for the long flight to Britain. The following month he went to 21 OTU to begin operational training. On October 17 he was posted to 103 Squadron, based at Elsham Wolds.

On January 10, 1942, George and his crew were headed to Wilhelmshaven in their Wellington for their fifth operation. Everything went well until the bomb run, when the pilot reported that he thought one of the bombs had hung up on the first pass. He was going to wheel the Wellington around and try again. On the second run, by a wild stroke of bad luck, a flare entered the bomb bay, starting a terrific blaze in the fuselage. Crewmen tried to put it out, only to be driven back by the burning flare. As the inferno in the fuselage grew, the pilot ordered a bailout. George McGill and three other crewmen jumped; then the co-pilot decided to have a try at the flare. He attacked it with a fire extinguisher, and eventually the force of the spray caused it to fall out through a hole in the aircraft's skin. He then set to work putting out the burning fabric with his gloved hands, and returned to the cockpit. The Wellington staggered back to make a landing in England, and the pilots were awarded immediate DFCs (DFCs for a single action). However, George and the other crewmen were left languishing in enemy hands.

*

When he arrived at Spangenberg in February 1942, McGill soon learned that escape attempts were constantly being planned. One ambitious scheme was the brainchild of three other recently arrived prisoners, all from 3 PRU: Tony Barber, downed in early January 1942; Tommy Calnan, captured on December 30, 1941; and Flight Lieutenant Charles Piers Hall (born C. P. Egerton-Hall), brought down on December 28 on only his third flight with the unit. Birmingham-born but resident in Halstead near Sevenoaks in Kent, 'Chaz' Hall was a quiet and reserved young man, an ex-Halton photographer who had once served on *Ark Royal*. He badly wanted to escape but was not sure that it was possible. Still, he was practical and methodical and could fabricate almost anything with his hands.

The trio soon came up with an escape plan that called for split-second timing and no mean feat of athletic skill. The moat of the castle was used as an exercise yard, while on the other side of the moat was a gymnasium, also used by the prisoners. Covered by suitable diversions, someone in the gymnasium party would lower a rope to the three pilots, allowing them to climb up to the gym. There they would hide until dark, when they would make their way away from the castle. On paper it looked fairly simple, but the problems of equipment and diversion were not to be taken lightly. Finding the necessary equipment proved simple. A grappling hook was found in a hollow table leg, probably left by some previous escaper, while Calnan and Hall broke into a storeroom and stole a fifty-yard coil of rope. With the material procured, it was left to plan the bid for freedom down to the last second. The greatest problem was getting out of the moat without being shot and, after days of drawing diagrams, timing sentries, and calculating blind spots, it was decided that two guards would have to be diverted for at least a couple of minutes. Because neither Hall nor Calnan had done any rope-climbing before, the longer the diversion, the better.

A group of army officers gladly agreed to arrange something on the gymnasium side of the moat to draw the guards' attention there, and another airman offered to run a rugby match to keep the sentries occupied. Alas, all the planning came to nothing, for just as the scheme was ready to be put into operation in late April, the RAF group was transferred from Spangenberg. On the way there, the three vented their frustrations by trying to cut their way out of the train, but Barber and Hall were forced to give up after breaking numerous saws in the hard, thick wood of the railroad car. There would be even greater challenges ahead, however, for the Luftwaffe was in the process of centralizing its POWs. They were all destined for a new camp, and a new phase of the escaping war.

Chapter 4

THEY CAME TO SAGAN

D URING THE TWO AND a half years they had spent behind barbed wire, the airmen had registered few actual successes. Only two of their number had succeeded in reaching neutral territory (or making a home run, as it was known in POW slang), while hundreds more had been recaptured in various stages of escape bids. Nevertheless, the first stage of the escaping war had kept their morale high. Buoyed by the successes of Harry Burton and John Shore, few had slipped into the inactivity and melancholy that so often signaled the onset of deeper psychological difficulties of captivity. Furthermore, the airmen had created problems for their captors that were disproportionate to their numbers and were clearly making a contribution to the war effort by forcing the Germans to divert an inordinate amount of resources to guarding and searching for them. And the number of airmen in captivity was rising. Captures had increased as the strategic bombing offensive gathered steam and fighter sweeps over the Continent grew in intensity, and 1942 also brought the first members of the American air forces into captivity. The Germans had no choice but to build new and larger prison camps to cope with the influx of air force POWs who seemed so bent on escape.

*

For the biggest of the new camps, the Luftwaffe went to Silesia in eastern Germany and began construction near the city of Sagan, about halfway between Berlin and Breslau. A mile south of the city, in the apex of an inverted vee formed by the Bober River and a muddy stream called the Tschirne, they carved a small, open space from the thick pine forest and laid out two new compounds, one for officers and one for NCOs.

The Germans had drawn some lessons from more than two years of supervising unwilling guests, and they put all they had learned into the new camp. The huts, six in each compound, were built on stilts so the earth underneath could be examined, and trapdoors in the floors and ceilings allowed easy access for inspection. In case anyone got a tunnel started, the huts were situated well back from the perimeter to make it that much farther to dig. Next came the two barbed-wire fences, ten feet high and six feet apart. The gap was filled with concertina wire, and an overhang sloped toward the compound to discourage climbers. Finally, a single strand of wire ran around the perimeter of the compound about ten yards inside the main fence. Eighteen inches high, it was known as the warning wire, and anyone who crossed it could expect to draw a spray of bullets. Fifteen feet above the ground, at intervals of one hundred yards, stood wooden guard towers manned by sentries with automatic weapons and searchlights. From their vantage point, it looked as if they could watch every inch of the sandy camp.

*

The compounds of the new Stalag Luft III were completed in early spring, and the first officers arrived from Barth on March 21, 1942, to take up residence. However, they were certainly not the fresh-faced and recently captured airmen who were arriving with such frequency as to stretch the resources of the Germans. These were some of the most persistent troublemakers in the Luftwaffe's keep, and they came from camps across Germany. From Spangenberg came Chaz Hall and Canadians Tommy Thompson and George McGill. Another bunch, including Danny Król and the legendary legless fighter pilot Douglas Bader, was weeded out of Oflag VIB at Warburg. But by far the largest number came from Barth, and the group that piled onto the train in the Baltic coast camp was a veritable rogues' gallery of air force escapers. There were the two naval types, Jimmy Buckley and Peter Fanshawe, and two of the original kriegies, Wings Day and Mike Casey. Most of the diggers from the West Block tunnel were there, including Tim Newman, Jimmy James, and Muckle Muir. Cookie Long (who tried unsuccessfully to escape in transit), Johnny Dodge – the list went on and on. The commandant of Barth knew he was shipping a dangerous group and concluded his farewell speech by saying, 'You vill all arrive at ze new camp – dead or alive!' followed by a toothy smile.

Mike Wood and 'Scruffy' Weir were unimpressed by this threat and took turns prying the nails out of the window screens while the two guards in the railroad car were occupied. Using a rough map, they deduced that the train would pass through or near Stettin and planned to jump off at the closest possible point. By reading the place names on station boards, they checked their progress against the map until the train arrived at a small station some twenty miles south of Stettin. Mike and Scruffy quickly arranged for a diversion and, at a prearranged signal, jerked down the window and clambered out. Scruffy went first, and after a quick look at the guards, Mike followed. Rolling down a grassy embankment, they lay still for a few moments and breathed a sigh of relief as the train puffed away into the darkness. It was a daring and dangerous escape that was carried off brilliantly, but it was all for naught. Five days later, the two were picked up in Stettin while trying to steal food, and they spent ten days in the police lockup before being shipped to Sagan. By the time they arrived, Jimmy Buckley had already set up an escape committee and started to plan for the future.

This time the committee was divided into three sections to control the different types of escape: over (wire escapes), under (tunnels), and through (gate escapes). Special sections were set up to produce and duplicate maps and to make tools and escape gear, from air pumps for the tunnels to German insignia for walk-out escapes. There was a tailoring department; a food section under naval aviator and nutritional expert David Lubbock; and a fully outfitted forgery branch, known as the Dean and Dawson Travel Bureau, supervised by Flight Lieutenant Gilbert William Walenn.

'Tim' Walenn was a delightful man, carefree and consistently cheerful with an even temper and an always courteous manner. Inwardly he was a man of steely resolution, strong self-discipline, and intense determination. Throughout his years as a POW, he remained a nonsmoker and tried to train his body to live on a reduced fluid intake, in preparation for the escape he knew he would one day make.

Born in London on February 24, 1916, Tim inherited two character traits from his father, a commercial artist who had served in the Royal Flying Corps during the First World War: considerable artistic ability and a desire to fly. As a child, he loved going to the Hendon Air Display and would spend hours drawing the aircraft he had seen; indeed, Tim hoped for a career in aircraft design. However, flying was an expensive and uncertain occupation at the time, and Walenn accepted an apprenticeship at his uncle's Silver Design Studio in London, where he worked on the design of wallpaper and fabric. Later, after realizing that design was not the career for him, Tim took a clerk's position in Midland Bank in the hope of saving enough money to pursue his first love, flying.

Early in 1936 he approached the management of the bank with a proposal to form a gliding club, and the response from the staff was so great that it was decided to start a flying club instead, with the bank's directors making a grant toward the club's expenses. The Midland Bank Flying Club was accordingly founded in 1937 with Tim, as the originator of the idea, as the club's honorary secretary. At first there were well over a hundred applicants, though only thirty-two could be accepted into the first draft. Tim Walenn was granted six months' leave by the bank to train as a flying instructor and thereafter spent his weekends training other air-minded employees.

Tim joined the RAFVR in December 1937 and continued training bank employees in the years before the war; by March 1939 he had been transferred to 97 Squadron. When hostilities began, Tim took a couple of refresher courses in preparation for assignment to 10 Elementary Flying Training School (EFTS) as a flying instructor. He was a popular teacher, thanks to his very forgiving nature and great patience, and was equally well known for his wonderful sense of humor. On one occasion he broke a leg in a training accident and had to propel himself around on a pair of crutches. Going to the movies with his sister Joy one day, Tim spotted the bus they had to take, and Joy realized that they would never reach the stop in time. 'Never mind,' said Tim nonchalantly, and he promptly walked into the middle of the road and stood directly in the bus's path, waving his crutches. The bus screeched to a halt and the conductor hustled out to help the wounded hero onboard; he even refused to let the Walenns pay their fares. 'You see?' said Tim with a smile later. 'That was much easier than running, wasn't it?'

After more than a year instructing, Tim was itching to get into action and applied for assignment to an operational unit. Finally, after numerous applications and delays, he was posted to 25 OTU in August 1941. His training flights progressed normally, but on the night of September 9–10, 1941, Tim took a new crew on a practice bombing run from their base in the north of England. They dropped two bombs and then got a return heading from the control tower. No further messages were received from Tim's crew. At first it was assumed that the aircraft had somehow drifted off course and crashed into the sea. So it was with some surprise that the squadron learned that Tim's aircraft had gone hundreds of miles astray, finally crash-landing near Rotterdam. Tim Walenn was a prisoner of war.

With his wings temporarily clipped, Tim turned to his other love: art. Now sporting a huge, bushy mustache that gave him a striking resemblance to Pilot Officer Prune, the stereotypical British aviator made famous in cartoons, he set to work arranging the operations of the forgery department.

*

The largest section of the escape organization was the tunneling department, under the short and stocky Robert 'Crump' Ker-Ramsay, a prisoner since September 1940, and Wally Floody, a tall Canadian fighter pilot who had been a mining engineer in northern Ontario before the war. It wasn't long before the diggers discovered the first problem. The gray sandy soil on which the Germans had built the camp concealed a loose yellow sand that started six or eight inches under the surface. It was difficult to disperse and, more important, dangerous to work in, for it was very unstable and apt to collapse with little warning.

The first tunnels were much like those constructed at Barth – fairly shallow, unshored, and ventilated by small holes pushed through the roof with a thin wooden rod. Within a week a number of shafts had been sunk, and work was pushing ahead. Mike Casey led one effort, Peter Fanshawe another, and Muckle Muir a third. Though the latter two were deeper – about fifteen feet – they still experienced bad cave-ins, some of which almost reached ground level. One by one these tunnels were discovered by various means. Some collapsed when the goons flooded the compound with a fire pumper, and others caved in when heavy trucks or wagons were driven around the camp. Some simply fell in of their own accord, leaving a suspicious-looking furrow pointing toward the wire.

In fact, by the time summer came to Sagan there were only two of these original tunnels left: Fanshawe's, and Floody's new effort from Hut 67, both made secure by a unique system of dummy traps. The first shaft was sunk to a depth of eight feet, and the tunnel went out horizontally for about forty feet. Then, in the floor of that tunnel, another shaft was sunk to a depth of twenty feet, and the main tunnel progressed from there. In this way, if the first shaft was found, it was merely a matter of sinking another shaft to link up with the main tunnel. Fanshawe's, the shallower of the two, was discovered after three months, but the other one pushed on under the care of Floody, Johnny Marshall, and Crump Ker-Ramsay. It was certainly an ambitious effort. Hut 67 was a good four hundred feet from cover but had been chosen because the Germans would think it a less likely starting point for a tunnel. In spite of this, the dummy shaft was found, forcing the diggers to sink a linking shaft. Then the dispersal area under the floor of the hut reached capacity, forcing them to dig a tunnel to the next hut, where the rest of the sand was dispersed.

While all this burrowing was going on, other means of escape were tried as well. Wearing tailored German uniforms and carrying money, maps, and forged papers, Wings Day, Nick Tindal, and a Czech airman tried to walk out of the gate disguised as a party of accountants. The guard barely glanced at their passes, and they were halfway down the road when one of the tower sentries recognized Wings and let out a yell. Other prisoners got out by faking the count of the wash parties that left the compound for the shower block in the *Vorlager*. One managed to smuggle himself onboard a Swedish ship before being turned over to the Germans. Using a similar ruse, Jimmy James and another prisoner faked the count of a party leaving the camp for typhus vaccinations and hid in the coal shed in the *Vorlager*. They had hoped to cut the wire from there, but the organization had no wire cutters available, and the two were forced to tunnel out. They sank a short shaft and had dug twenty feet toward the wire when a guard came into the shed to shelter from a thunderstorm and happened to see them behind a pile of coal.

*

The late spring of 1942 saw much of import occurring in various theaters of the war, rumors of which eventually reached the kriegies in Luft III. In early May the American garrison at Corregidor surrendered to the Japanese, and a week later the Soviets opened an offensive in the Kharkov area that would lead to another major Soviet defeat in weeks. On May 30 the RAF mounted its long-awaited Operation Millennium, the thousand-plane raid on Cologne. Though the immediate damage inflicted by Millennium was not decisive by a long shot, the raid did demonstrate the growing strength of Bomber Command. Aircrew morale was buoyed by Millennium, and the feeling that they had at last crested the hill was obvious in successive raids.

As usual, Happy Valley (as the crews called the Ruhr) was hopping on the night of June 8–9, 1942, as Halifax four-engine bomber H-Harry of 405 Squadron RCAF droned toward the Krupps works in Essen with two hundred other heavy bombers. It was a clear night and, having hit the city just over a week ago, the crew was confident that this mission, too, would be routine. In the fuselage of the bomber, navigator Jim Wernham shared a few jokes with radio operator Bill Kerr as the two friends reminisced about the raids they had flown with 77 Squadron RAF. Jim turned to peer out the tiny window and saw below him the dancing red and yellow lights that signaled the approach to the target area. He was just about to remark, as he usually did, that the fires had a certain beauty about them when he was blinded by the stabbing glare of a searchlight. With brilliant white light streaming in the window, Jim and the crew braced themselves for the inevitable flak to hit. They did not have long to wait.

The first burst threw the Hallie on her back, and by the time the pilot managed to pull her out of the dive, she had lost thousands of feet in height. To make matters worse, the ailerons had jammed in the left turn position, leaving the pilot powerless to control the aircraft. He ordered the load dropped on the secondary target and struggled madly to free the controls. As he worked feverishly, the Halifax was carried deeper into Germany by strong westerly winds. She passed over flak posts, barely escaping further damage, before the pilot was able to free the controls and steer for England. It looked as if things were going to work out after all, so Jim Wernham relaxed a bit and set about working out a course back to base. He had come a long way from a normal upbringing in Winnipeg, Manitoba, to the navigator's chair in a stricken Halifax over occupied Europe.

*

James Chrystall Wernham's early days were typical of those of a generation of young Canadian men. His parents immigrated to Canada before the First World War but returned in 1914 to their native Scotland, where Jim was born on January 15, 1917. After the Armistice the family came back to Canada and eventually settled in Winnipeg. The elder Wernham worked for the Canadian Pacific Railway, and young Jim and his older sister, Florence, grew up in a young and bustling city in the Canadian West. On summer holidays Jim and Florence often went to Mine Centre in northern Ontario, where their aunt and uncle operated a general store. The summers were a delight for the Wernham children; the days were long and warm, and there was no shortage of places to explore at the beach and in the fields and wilderness around Mine Centre.

Upon graduation from high school in Winnipeg, the reality of the Depression hit Jim Wernham. Unable to find work in his hometown, he went back to Mine Centre and helped around the store. He was an ambitious young man, though, and soon returned to Winnipeg, where he managed to find a job in the accounts department at John Deere Plough. When war came, it took Jim Wernham some time to decide which branch of the service to join but on October 10, 1940, he settled on the air force. In July 1941 he was commissioned as an air observer. Later that month Wernham flew to England, and by the end of October he was operational with 77 Squadron. He did sixteen raids with 77, and in April 1942, after converting to Halifaxes, he was transferred to 405 Squadron RCAF.

The first operation for Wernham with his new squadron was the 'Thousand Raid' on Cologne. Jim and his crew returned unscathed and the next day found their picture in all the daily newspapers. 'Home again,' the captions read, 'back from the biggest ever Cologne raid.' It was a nice bit of publicity for the crew and it kept them in drinks at the station mess for a few days. There were three more operations over the next week before the return trip to Essen.

As the wounded Halifax droned away from the Ruhr to leave Essen behind, Jim Wernham slowly began to believe that they might make it back for a third bash at the Krupps works. Over Holland, the crunch of cannon shells slamming into the aircraft convinced him otherwise. The gunners knocked down one of the German fighters, but not before the damage was done. The Messerschmitts had found the Hallie's fuel lines, and both port engines faltered and eventually stopped altogether. The pilot set about trying to keep the big bomber in the air as long as possible but it was a losing battle. Nothing seemed to keep the stricken ship from falling and before long it had dropped from sixteen thousand to a little over one thousand feet. The intercom had been shot away, so the captain reluctantly motioned for the crew to bail out. Jim Wernham clambered toward the escape hatch, his bulky parachute making it difficult to squeeze through the fuselage, turned himself around in the doorway, and fell out into the blackness.

The deafening rush of air seemed to stop almost immediately, and Jim watched in fascination as the bomber sputtered away from him. He came to ground heavily at the edge of a plowed field. German troops were already running toward him as he landed.

*

When Jimmy Wernham reached Luft III, most of the problems plaguing the new facility had been worked out. In the first few weeks the prisoners had made numerous complaints about inadequate facilities and poor conditions, and the camp staff had made every effort to correct the problems. The commandant, sixty-one-year-old Colonel Friedrich Wilhelm von Lindeiner-Wildau, was an ex-cavalry officer of the old school who had picked up seven wounds and an Iron Cross (First Class) during the First World War. He had once served on Göring's personal staff and had been specially chosen by the *Reichsmarschall* for his reputation as a firm but humane officer. He was given to tantrums whenever an escape occurred but was generally acknowledged to be a very reasonable fellow.

Of the rest of the camp staff, there were three who came into regular contact with the prisoners. Hans Pieber, one of the duty officers, was a former schoolmaster who had been with the airmen at Barth. An early member of the Austrian Nazi Party, Pieber had been awarded the Nazi Blood Medal but refused to wear it after the *Anschluss,* the German occupation of Austria. He was a cagey character, not above changing his color if it suited his needs. Still, he got along well with the kriegies and was liked by most of them.

The two other Germans who were regularly in the compound were the head ferrets, Corporal Karl Griese, dubbed Rubberneck, and Staff Sergeant Hermann Glemnitz, christened Dimwits. Griese was a thoroughly objectionable character with a shrewd nose for malefactors and absolutely no sense of humor. Heartily detested by all, including some of the camp staff, he was a dangerous man because of his almost pathological desire to uncover escape plots. He disliked the airmen intensely and was completely incorruptible.

Glemnitz, who had been guarding the airmen since July 1940, was a different sort of fellow altogether. As a young man he had worked with an engineering firm in Yorkshire and over the years had developed an acute understanding of the ways of the English. This, combined with his quick brain and powers of observation, made him a very worthy adversary, despite his inappropriate nickname. Glemnitz would wreck dozens of well-laid escape plans over the years, yet he was always respected and even liked by the prisoners.

Rubberneck and Glemnitz presided over a staff of ferrets known only by their nicknames. There was Keen Type, so dubbed because of the conscientious way he performed his duties, and Adolf, who received his nickname because of a striking likeness to the Führer. Rudi was another who spent much of his day wandering around the compound in search of troublemakers. From the beginning, the escape organizers knew they would have to keep a careful eye on these ferrets.

The rest of the guards were rather less dangerous. Despised by the ferrets, who regarded them as plodding oafs, they were also viewed with disdain by their superior officers. One of the camp's security chiefs described the guard company as 'a rabble of the halt, maimed, blind with a sprinkling of mentally deranged whose only interest was the obtaining of cigarettes from the prisoners.' They were mostly overage soldiers unfit for service elsewhere and, in some cases, unfit for service even in prison camps. As the war progressed, many of them became more and more determined to secure from the prisoners luxuries such as tobacco and soap, which were all but unobtainable elsewhere in Germany. For this reason the escape organization would find them easily corrupted.

After the first few weeks of settling in to the new compound, things began to take shape. A theater troupe was assembled, and various officers began to organize sports events, with equipment provided by the Red Cross or the YMCA. The Red Cross also shipped life-saving food parcels to the camp from depots in Lisbon and Geneva. A parcels office in the *Vorlager* handled distribution of the packages, under the watchful eyes of Lawrence Reavell-Carter and Keith Ogilvie, a Canadian fighter ace who had flown Spitfires during the Battle of Britain. To give credit to the German staff, there was never any pilfering of parcels.

With the Red Cross food parcels, it was possible to produce some quite tasty meals. Still, one never had that lovely feeling of being totally satisfied after a meal. The German rations had changed little from Spangenberg days: black bread with margarine and a sort of chemical jam, known as ersatz (or substitute) jam; coffee made from roasted chestnuts or acorns; watery vegetable soup; and an odd 'luxury,' such as fish cheese, a pungent and practically inedible substance that bore no resemblance to the dairy product after which it was named. The Red Cross parcels provided enough raw materials so that decent meals could be whipped up each week. Sunday dinner might include soup, corned beef with chipped potatoes, peas, and fried macaroni and cheese, followed by pudding and coffee. Tea could include a cake made from powdered Red Cross biscuits, margarine, bread crumbs, powdered milk (called Klim), and raisins. Breakfast was rather less interesting, the kriegies making do with the rationed bread and jam and a brew of tea. However, there were times when the ingredients for porridge were obtainable.

When it came to making porridge, most of the kriegies consulted 'Sandy' Gunn, whose Scottish heritage had endowed him with the talents for concocting the dish. He was a well-built man, dark with a penetrating gaze, and could be dour and almost taciturn at times. However, he had a charming smile when provoked to show it and was kindly and humorous once his rather brusque exterior had been penetrated. He also had a deep sense of justice and fair play. Even as a young boy, he could never abide unfairness against himself or any of the other boys and was quick to act when he perceived an injustice.

The second son of a Scottish medical man, Alastair Donald Mackintosh Gunn was born on September 27, 1919, at the family home in Auchterarder, Perthshire. He was a fine athlete at school but left early to be taken on as an apprentice by Harland and Wolff, the shipyard that had built the *Titanic*, in 1938. The following year he applied to Pembroke College, Cambridge, and was accepted to study mechanical sciences with the intention of becoming a diesel engineer. His athletic prowess also secured him a trial for the rugby team, and he would have done well for the college had his education not been interrupted by war.

Sandy Gunn enlisted in the RAFVR on February 22, 1940, and when he left Cambridge for the holidays in March, he had a good idea that he wouldn't be back for some time. The hunch was correct, for on June 22 he was called up for training. In late September he began instruction and on January 18, 1941, was awarded his wings. A week later it was on to reconnaissance school before beginning his first tour of duty in June 1941 with 48 Squadron of Coastal Command. The squadron flew Ansons on reconnaissance and communications missions from airfields up and down the British Isles. It was not the most exciting flying, but at least Sandy was doing something useful. Then, on the first day of September, came a very welcome surprise in the form of a transfer to 1 PRU at Benson. No more flying the friendly but slow Ansons. Sandy Gunn was moving up to sleek blue stripped-down, unarmed Spitfires, specially modified to operate at high altitudes. Finally, he would get a chance to do some real flying.

In February 1942 Sandy got a week's leave and spent some time in Auchterarder, tooling around in his newly purchased 1928 Lagonda and fishing for salmon in the fast-running streams of Perthshire. It was an all-too-short break, though, and he was soon back in action, posted to Wick as part of a three-aircraft detachment assigned to monitor German naval units in the Norwegian fjords. With new modifications, the Spits now had more range than ever; they flew above the fighter cover, and their only enemies were flak and mechanical failure. Flying was tricky, though, in the terrible weather conditions that often prevailed in northern Scotland. Returning to base one day, Sandy found the entire area blanketed in thick fog and was unable to locate any landmarks. Thinking he was still far out to sea, he continued westward, hoping to pick up a radio fix once he reached Scotland. Suddenly, though, Gunn looked down and saw the outline of Cape Wrath, on the northwestern corner of Scotland. Quickly wheeling the aircraft around, he uttered a brief word of thanks to the break in the clouds. Had he not spotted land he would have continued to fly westward, eventually ditching in the North Atlantic when his fuel ran out.

Early on March 5, 1942, Sandy Gunn took off from Wick to photograph German shipping along the Norwegian coast. There was little dangerous flak in that part of Scandinavia, so Gunn could look forward to an uneventful flight. At about thirty thousand feet he spotted three Me 109s climbing toward him and decided to ascend a bit farther as a precaution. The Messerschmitts soon gave up the chase, but not before squeezing off a few rounds from an impossibly long range. Incredibly, one shell found its mark, and the Spit's engine started to overheat and cough alarmingly. When tongues of flame appeared from the engine cowling, Sandy decided it was time to abandon ship. He took to his parachute and came to ground in the deep snow on a mountainside not far from a small town. The first to reach him was a party of Norwegian villagers, and Sandy asked them to take him over the border into Sweden. Unfortunately, his descent had been watched by the small German garrison in the town; the troops arrived minutes after the villagers.

Sandy's captors were intrigued by his presence and, thinking that he had been operating from a secret airfield in northern Norway, subjected him to three weeks of questioning. When they finally decided that he wasn't worth spending any more time on, they shipped Sandy off to Dulag Luft, and from there to Sagan. He found a bunk in a room with a few other Scots, a Yorkshireman, and a Liverpudlian and slowly settled himself into the ritual of being a kriegie.

*

It was during the first summer in Stalag Luft III that Sagan's new escape committee scored its first success. Back at Barth, crewmates Henry Lamond and Bill Goldfinch had registered a scheme with the escape committee that involved three men burying themselves near the wire and burrowing to freedom; thus was born the idea of the famous mole escape. When they moved to Sagan, Bill and Henry co-opted a third man, Jack Best, and set about putting their plan into action. The first problem was to find some way to bury themselves close enough to the wire so that they could easily dig their way out. Clearly, they needed a good reason to be digging in full view of the goon boxes. They bandied about a few ideas, like a vegetable garden or digging pits for goalposts, but all were found wanting.

The three were silent for a moment and then Bill spoke up. 'How about this? We dig a drainage ditch for the wash hut, you know, to draw off the excess water – the goons would let us leave that open for a few days!'

'Sounds good,' said Jack, 'but where are we going to get all of this excess water? Hun plumbing isn't quite that bad!'

'It will be once I stuff up those drains,' replied Bill with an evil grin.

Jimmy Buckley approved the plan right away, and the next day, after a few hundred kriegies had performed their morning scrub-up, the hut was awash in a flood of biblical proportions. Pieber shook his head sadly as he surveyed the situation.

'Why should this happen? This is a new camp – there should be no problems of this sort,' he said despairingly.

Wings Day looked at Pieber without blinking. 'Probably those inferior German pipes you use. In any case, you've got to get this mess cleaned up – this hut is a breeding ground for disease with all this stagnant water lying around.'

'But I haven't the men to remedy this – watching you people keeps us busy enough,' moaned Pieber.

'Well, bring in the tools and we'll do it then – it would be good exercise for a few of the lads,' suggested Wings.

Pieber went off with a promise to discuss it with the commandant and returned the next day with a goon carrying an armful of shovels. 'The commandant thanks you for your offer,' he said, 'and wishes to remind you that we have taken a careful count of the number of shovels issued to you – all must be returned intact.' He bowed gravely and left the compound.

So as not to appear too anxious, Goldfinch, Lamond, and Best waited until after lunch to begin work. They planned to dig a deep ditch to act as a soakaway and push their tunnel from the bottom of the trench. For the first few days they went happily about their work, digging a bit and then pausing to wave to one of the tower goons or chat with a passing ferret. Then, when the staff was finally convinced that they were on the up and up, the molers pushed their shaft out from the base of the soakaway, a couple of feet below the surface. It was designed to pass halfway between the two seismograph microphones buried under the wire.

Their first day of digging brought a bit of a scare. The constant stream of prisoners who strolled past to report on the movement of ferrets evidently attracted some attention, and one of the German duty officers wandered up to see what the fuss was about. Best saw him coming and, with a word to Lamond, who was digging at the face, quickly began to fill in the tunnel. The hole was still not completely filled when the officer sidled up, so Jack threw himself over it and said *'Sehr heiss!'* (Very hot!), wiping his forehead with a dirty rag. The officer smiled politely, and Jack smiled back. They continued to smile at each other, and it was evident that the German was quite content to stay for a while. Putting on his best cheerful voice, Jack hailed a passing kriegie and called pleasantly, 'For Christ's sake, go find someone who speaks German and get this bastard out of here!' Playing along with the game, the other kriegie laughed and smiled at the goon before wandering off in no particular hurry.

A few minutes later, another kriegie strolled up and paused beside the officer. He gave a wink to Jack and began chatting with the German.

In time the two walked off, the German chattering happily and making expansive gestures toward the forest beyond the wire. The next day it was decided to drop the stooges because they attracted too much attention, and for a few days they were able to work without interruption. On Sunday, June 30, Henry, Jack, and Bill went down after lunch and dug another fifty feet; as they washed up for *Appell* (roll call), each knew that the next time they went down it would be for good.

After *Appell* they headed back to the hole and sealed themselves in. When he received their muffled okay, an accomplice let the water back into the soakaway and the three were entombed. They dug another twenty-five feet that evening and then stopped for the night so the sounds of their work would not be heard. They lay on top of each other for warmth, but sleep did not come easily. All three were glad when they were able to see daylight through the airholes made with a table knife. They began to dig again. The front man would scrape away at the face with the bowl of a coal scoop and then shove the sand behind him to the next man. The fellow in the middle pushed it around behind him to the last man, who packed it as tightly as possible behind him. They dug quickly, covering seventy-five feet that day, but conditions were hellish.

By nightfall they calculated themselves to be about twelve feet beyond the wire and decided to wait a few hours before breaking out. Nervous friends watched the compound and were startled to see little columns of steam rising from the airholes. A guard dog actually spotted one of these holes but showed no other interest than a good sniff. Finally, at 3:00 a.m., the molers looked up one of the airholes and decided it was dark enough. They burrowed to the surface and hared away into the woods.

The first day was spent hiding in terrible heat in a black glider trailer at a local airfield. Emerging after dark, they were disappointed to find nothing on the airfield they could fly. Momentarily discouraged, they mooched off to try something else. Wearing RAF battle dress, they traveled only by night and navigated by means of a large railroad map. They had brought a bit of food but got by mostly on potatoes scavenged from the fields.

After more walking the three reached the Oder River and combed its banks looking for a rowboat to steal. Eventually they found one that was unlocked and set off downstream, intending to row to the Baltic.

They made good progress that day, but in the evening it began to rain, so they headed to shore and sheltered under their overturned boat. Before too long the boat was lifted up and Jack, Bill, and Henry were confronted by its owner, who brought along a couple of policemen for emphasis. It was the end of a very plucky escape bid.

The three were congratulated for their effort by the camp staff; 150 feet in less than thirty-six hours was indeed an accomplishment, and the staff were willing to acknowledge a good job as long as it wasn't completely successful. However, alterations were made to prevent similar escapes in the future. The seismographs were doubled and, during the hottest week of the year, a squad of guards dug an eight-foot-deep 'antimole' trench near the warning wire. Best, Goldfinch, and Lamond got particular pleasure out of watching these goons sweat.

Of course, it wasn't long before the prisoners took advantage of the new security measures. Canadian 'Red' Noble and a friend tried a mole from the new ditch but had to return to their hut because they were completely exhausted after digging the first section. A few days later Tommy Calnan and Tony Barber tried the same thing, bringing along an extra pair of hands to help. This trio would have made it had not the guard dog figured out the meaning of the columns of steam rising from the compound. The Alsatian that sniffed the airhole set up a tremendous row of barking, and a party of ferrets trooped in to dig the three out. They were escorted to the cooler, filthy and exhausted. A few days later, the three original molers got some extra enjoyment. They watched as the same squad of guards returned to the ditch with shovels and proceeded to fill the whole thing in again. It was almost worth getting caught to see them work like that.

*

Not long after the mole escape, Roger Bushell returned. He looked a little leaner and more haggard, but his eyes were still as piercing and intense as ever. Some in the camp had already given him up for dead after his escape from the train. Others were convinced that he must have made it to freedom. The truth, when they got it out of Roger, was quite different.

He and Jack Zafouk had been wearing civilian clothes under their uniforms and had papers permitting them to travel by train to Czechoslovakia. Once there, Zafouk took over. They went to see his brother in Prague, who gave them a supply of money and a safe house to stay in. He then contacted the underground and tried to sort out an escape route for them. The waiting was the hardest part. Neither of them could leave the tiny apartment, Roger because he spoke no Czech and Jack because he couldn't run the risk of being spotted by someone who knew him. Day after day they sat inside, sometimes talking, sometimes reading, but mostly just sitting. Finally word came that their escape to Yugoslavia had been arranged, and Roger and Jack got ready to go. The day before their scheduled departure, though, the escape line was broken up by the Gestapo and the two were back to square one. More weeks of waiting followed until word came through that another route had been arranged, this time to Turkey. Again they prepared to go and actually made it as far as the Czech border before the line was infiltrated and broken up. Back to Prague they went.

Fate now took a hand. On May 27, 1942, Reich Protector of Bohemia-Moravia Reinhard Heydrich was attacked by Czech agents in a suburb of Prague; he died a week later. The Gestapo descended on Czechoslovakia and scooped up anyone who was remotely suspicious. Thousands were arrested, most of whom were never heard from again. To save their own lives, people turned in their friends and neighbors, and this was the downfall of Roger and Jack. The porter of the apartment block in which they were staying reported their presence to the police, and the two were immediately arrested. The family who had sheltered them were shot to the last member. Roger and Jack were separated, the latter to undergo severe interrogation and eventual transfer to Colditz. Roger never did talk much about his experiences. Some say that only his charm and skill as a barrister saved him, while others maintain that German skiing friends intervened on his behalf. It is also possible that the camp censor, who knew and liked Roger, asked his brother, a Luftwaffe general, to intercede.

Now in Sagan, it was clear that Roger loathed the Germans more than ever. Shortly after his arrival in the camp he was walking the perimeter circuit with Douglas Bader when they came to the molers' soakaway trench. Standing over it were an armed guard and a sign warning walkers away. Roger and Douglas ignored both the guard and the sign and went to step over the trench, whereupon the sentry unshouldered his rifle and screamed at the two to go a different way or face the consequences. Roger drew himself up and, in perfect German, shouted, 'If you speak to a British officer, you must first address him as "sir." Now let us pass!' With a dumbfounded expression the guard lowered his rifle and stood aside, and Roger and Douglas proceeded, continuing their chat as if nothing had happened.

Chapter 5

THROUGH THE WIRE

A s THE SUMMER OF 1942 wore on, the thoughts of many kriegies turned to the long-awaited second front, and betting on the date of the invasion was brisk. Tom Kirby-Green and a friend had ten pounds on the war being over by the end of the year, and Tom was giving even odds that if that failed to materialize, the invasion would take place the following June, and the war would be over by the end of 1943. In August 1942, the hopes of the optimists were fanned when Canadian troops and British commandos landed at the French coastal resort of Dieppe. The landing was a dismal failure, with the Canadians sustaining terrible losses, but news of the raid caused a spate of wagering on the date of the second front. If we were mounting this sort of operation, said the optimists, surely the big invasion must be near. They shortened their odds but at the same time, to hedge their bets, continued with the escaping game.

*

In late August, Australian Paul Royle pushed out a tunnel from Hut 68 that ran roughly parallel to Wally Floody's hole. For this effort Royle recruited a number of first-time diggers, such as a tall, slender South African with slightly thinning hair and a benign smile.

Born in London on February 17, 1919, Rupert John Stevens was raised in Cape Town, though his mother and father remained in England long enough for John to be baptized in St. Paul's Cathedral. The young Stevens had a typical childhood in the Cape, climbing Table Mountain and going horseback riding at Clifton on the Atlantic coast. He attended South African College School and became very interested in tennis, cricket, and rugby. When he graduated in December 1936 John took a position in the advertising department of the United Tobacco Company.

The young man had something else in mind, though, and in 1938 he enrolled in the newly instituted Pupil Pilot Training Scheme, receiving his wings just after the outbreak of war. On November 24, 1939, John was taken into the South African Air Force and immediately received his first assignment, flying Ansons out of Port Elizabeth. Just under five months later, he was posted to the Western Desert to join 12 Squadron. On November 14, 1941, Stevens and his crew were detailed with eight other Martin Maryland light bombers to carry out a raid on enemy aircraft at Derna. Just before taking off, the crews went over the emergency procedure should any of them have to make a forced landing in the besieged fortress of Tobruk. Friendly aircraft should approach the city at one thousand feet, with the undercarriage down and firing the colors of the day from their flareguns. John joked that he refused to land in such an undignified manner if he had a choice.

The raid was a success, but after crossing the coast on the homeward leg, the squadron came upon very heavy flak, and John's aircraft was hit in the port wing. The tanks were punctured and gasoline streamed from the wing, only stopping when the tanks were empty; seconds later the flow continued as the cross-feed valve funneled gasoline from the sound tanks into the holed ones, and straight out of the holes in the wing. Realizing what had happened, John's squadronmates tried to signal him to close the valve, but his control panels were badly damaged and nothing could be done. The Maryland continued to lose height and, as the squadron neared the enemy-held port of Bardia, the wounded bomber was seen to turn toward the city, with its undercarriage down and firing the colors of the day. It wasn't until the Axis flak opened up that the crew realized they had mistaken Bardia for Tobruk. The first burst of flak entered the cockpit and wounded John, who lost consciousness, so the navigator took control of the aircraft and guided it in for a crash-landing. He brought the Maryland down on a salt pan but could not avoid a small sand dune in the bomber's path. Striking the dune, the Maryland's undercarriage collapsed and the navigator was killed when the nose was crushed. John and the two gunners were rescued with serious injuries and shipped off to a German hospital.

Stevens recovered quickly, and just a month after the crash found himself in Barth. He later arrived in East Compound with the first group from Luft I. His first venture into escaping came to nothing, the Hut 68 tunnel going the way of most of its predecessors. But John was not to be put off; he merely doubled his resolve to try again.

*

Just after lunch one day in the fall of 1942, a crowd began to gather on the sports field to take advantage of the bright sunshine and a warm, gentle breeze. It was a beautiful September afternoon, and the kriegies looked forward to a bit of excitement in the form of a boxing match that had been scheduled. By 2:00 P.M. the field was buzzing with activity as the pugilists, George McGill and Eddie Asselin, appeared. They pulled on their YMCA gloves and climbed into the makeshift ring, bobbing around to limber up. When the bell clanged, the two warriors leaped out of their corners and started into each other wholeheartedly, much to the delight of the assembled crowd. Gradually the guards in the towers turned their attention to the ring and, before long, were smiling broadly as the two Canadians whaled away at each other.

A short distance off, Wings Day and Jimmy Buckley sat in the shade of one of the huts, glancing occasionally toward the ring with nothing more than casual interest. After scanning the scene for a few minutes, Jimmy gave a barely perceptible nod toward the hut. Within seconds, two figures wearing old khaki shorts, windbreakers, and soft cloth caps appeared. They walked along the circuit for twenty yards or so and then suddenly, without a look in either direction, stepped over the warning wire and lay down beside the main fence. The taller of the two looked toward Buckley, who gave another slight nod. Out came a pair of wire cutters and a handful of strong wooden pegs. Slowly and carefully, the men cut each strand of wire, crawled through the hole, and then propped up the rolls of barbed wire in the middle with the wooden pegs. They wriggled under the rolls and set to work on the outer fence, pausing only when one of the patrolling sentries approached the spot where they were working. As they cut the last strands of wire, a kriegie ambled past them on the circuit to give the all-clear. The final strand was cut and the two crawled through the gap, dusted themselves off, and walked calmly toward the woods. The whole operation had taken no more than ten minutes and had looked ridiculously easy as it unfolded.

It had not seemed that way at the beginning, when Irishman Ken Toft and William 'Red' Nichols, an American in one of the RAF Eagle squadrons, told the escape committee that there was a blind spot at the fence created by the density of the wire and the positioning of the guard towers. The surveyors checked the claim and soon proved that a man could in fact stand at a certain point along the fence and not be seen from any of the towers. If the organization could arrange a diversion,

Ken and Red wanted to try cutting their way to freedom. The boxing match was chosen over a choir practice because it was thought that the goons would be more interested in watching their enemies hurt each other than listening to them sing. This was the major diversion to hold the attention of the sentries in the nearest towers. The patrolling guards were to be covered by individual prisoners, who would engage them in conversation until the escapers were clear of the camp. It all had to be orchestrated down to the last second, or Ken and Red stood a good chance of catching a burst of gunfire.

Under the capable direction of Jimmy Buckley, the first part of the escape went like clockwork, but as Ken and Red strolled toward the forest, the first sign of danger appeared. One of the tower guards turned his head, noticed the two figures, and raised his rifle. Wings Day started to get up, but Jimmy raised a hand in caution as he watched. After what seemed like an age, the guard slowly lowered his rifle and turned back to watch the fight. Buckley's icy nerves and infallible intuition had won out again. Later he explained to Wings that the guard, rather than fire and risk a reprimand for not seeing the escape sooner, probably chose to ignore the incident and avoid being blamed for anything. At least that was the chance that Jimmy was willing to take, and there were few men who would have done the same.

It was a brilliant escape but, like so many others, it ended in failure. Walking through Frankfurt-an-der-Oder, Ken and Red were stopped and arrested because their papers didn't meet with the policeman's approval. When they arrived back in Sagan they were tossed into solitary, but in a chivalrous gesture, von Lindeiner recognized their daring by presenting them with a bottle of whiskey.

*

At the same time that Toft and Nichols escaped, it was decided that three other kriegies should go into hiding – or 'ghost,' as it was known – so that the Germans would be convinced that five men had actually escaped. Then, after the fuss had died down from the first escape, the other three could slip away from the camp unnoticed. In this way, the usual dragnet that trapped so many escapers could be avoided and the three would have an excellent chance of getting away.

Volunteers for the job were found in the persons of Mike Casey, Norman 'Conk' Canton, and a warrant officer named Johnson. Things went fairly well for the first five weeks. Because of the number of kriegies in the camp, the three merely had to remain as inconspicuous as possible and, above all, avoid any goons who might recognize them. But halfway through their second month of ghosting, Mike Casey was spotted by one of the ferrets. He wasn't caught immediately, but the Germans became convinced that all three of them were still in the camp. There was no general search, but during the period of increased watchfulness, Mike was surprised by the same ferret in one of the barracks. After a rather farcical chase around the huts, he was finally taken into custody. Canton and Johnson, however, remained undetected and managed to cut the wire after crawling through one of the camp's tomato patches. They got away but were caught within a week and brought back to the camp.

*

These attempts were all part of what was becoming a very bad September for the camp staff. Shortly afterward, a Dutchman in the RAF walked out of the gate in a goonskin, only to be recaptured at Heidelberg and packed off to Colditz. Then, just weeks from its completion, Wally Floody's tunnel was discovered. It stretched more than three hundred feet, and the Germans were stunned when they realized how close it had come to succeeding. They were also amazed at how well engineered it was. The discovery of Floody's tunnel convinced the camp staff that the first six months of Göring's 'perfect' camp had been, to put it mildly, less successful than they had hoped. Faced with an increasing number of escape-related disruptions at Sagan, those in authority began to wonder if putting all of the airmen in one place had been such a good idea after all. It had apparently just encouraged the kriegies to greater mischief. Under the rationale that any change would be for the better, the Luftwaffe elected to shift a load of prisoners to an army camp, Oflag XXIB at Schubin.

The group that left Sagan in November 1942 included some of the historic troublemakers, such as Wings Day, Jimmy James, Peter Fanshawe, Dick Churchill, Tommy Calnan, and Jimmy Buckley. Johnny Dodge also wangled his way into the purge, though he had no intention of seeing the destination on the other end. When the train slowed to crest a hill, the Dodger climbed out of a small window and made his leap. Since it was broad daylight, Johnny was spotted immediately, and a search party quickly escorted a grinning Major Dodge back to the train at gunpoint. 'No harm in trying,' he said innocently.

*

At first sight, the camp at Schubin looked quite pleasant. Until 1940 it had been a girls' school, and it retained a country estate atmosphere; there were playing fields, trees, a greenhouse, and various other amenities. The prisoners lived in twelve brick barracks in a separate compound near the playing fields and looked through the wire at a varied expanse of fields instead of an impenetrable wall of black fir trees as ringed the camp at Sagan. All in all, the first group to arrive were pleased. The barracks, however, turned out to be little more than barns. They had no ceilings or partitions, and the men had to use the sparse furnishings to create living cubicles. This was all overlooked, though, when the kriegies began to realize that the camp was ideal for escape. Despite Glemnitz's warnings, the German Army staff seemed to have little concern for security and arrogantly brushed away all suggestions. Prospects were excellent, and Jimmy Buckley took over the escape committee with hopes of big things.

The new arrivals from Sagan, and another group of airmen from Warburg, soon set about seeing what disruptions could be caused. One of the first attempts was made by Tommy Calnan and Robert Kee, who planned to dig a sixty-foot mole tunnel from an asparagus patch near the wire. To assist them in their labors, they recruited a compact and muscular squadron leader named Ian Cross, who had already made two escape attempts from Sagan. The three began by puttering around in the garden, moving piles of earth back and forth until the guards tired of watching them. Calnan then sank a four-foot shaft, and the tunnel was soon on its way toward the wire. The three took turns digging, passing the spoil up to the surface and spreading it around. Within a few days they had completed about fifteen feet and only needed to dig the same distance again before closing themselves in.

While working at the face one day, Tommy Calnan unearthed a faded scrap of paper and, his curiosity piqued, decided to inch back along the tunnel to read it in the dim light that filtered down. He was halfway back to the shaft when the tunnel caved in. At the base of the shaft, Ian Cross heard the muffled thud and immediately wriggled up the tunnel, only to come face to face with the soles of Calnan's boots sticking out of a solid wall of earth. He grasped Tommy's feet and heaved, but the weight of the sand and the closeness of the tunnel worked against him. Realizing that time was critical, Ian backed out of the tunnel and clambered up to Robert, who had been peering nervously down the shaft.

'There's been a fall,' said Cross with a gasp. 'We'll have to dig him out because we'll never pull him out.' He grabbed a shovel and started to dig while Kee conscripted passersby to help with the rescue effort. They dug furiously and, after a few minutes, Tommy's legs were unearthed. Ian and Robert each grabbed one and started to pull. On the fourth heave, a blue and sputtering Tommy Calnan was hauled out, and his rescuers sprawled in the asparagus around him. The perimeter guard, who had been watching the entire operation, simply stared in amazement.

Looking at the sturdy and well-built Ian Cross, one would never know that he hadn't always been that strong. The son of a London real-estate agent, Ian Kingston Pembroke Cross was born in East Cosham near Portsmouth on April 4, 1918, the youngest of five children. He was a frail and sickly child whose constant ill health cast a gloom over the entire household. It was even necessary to engage a private tutor because the lad lacked the stamina to spend time in school. It was not until the age of eight or nine that Ian's health began to improve and he was able to join in all the fun of childhood.

After the First World War, the Cross family moved to Hayling Island near Southampton. It was there that Ian and his siblings were raised, and there that he found one of his favorite spots on earth: the wide, soft beaches and extensive beachlands of the Sandy Point area. Many times Ian would return to Hayling while on leave, and the days spent wandering through his childhood playgrounds never failed to rejuvenate him. Eventually Ian was deemed strong enough to go away to school and was enrolled at Churchers College, Petersfield, as a boarder. He loved the years spent at the school, and his physical condition improved enormously. When he left Churchers in 1936, Ian had made quite a name for himself as a sprinter and jumper, and especially as a rugby player. Though still small in stature, what he lacked in size he more than made up for in power.

Since Ian had spent some time in the Officers' Training Corps at Churchers, it was no surprise to the family when he decided to follow his elder brother, Kenneth, into the RAF. On October 12, 1936, Ian took up a short service commission and was posted to the civil flying school at Hanworth, soloing less than a month after his first flight. In the summer of 1937 he was assigned to 38 Squadron at Marham, equipped with Hendon medium bombers. When war began, Ian Cross had reached the rank of flying officer and had been on Wellingtons for nine months.

The first months of the war were ones of great uncertainty for Bomber Command. Squadrons were alerted and briefed for missions, only to have them canceled at the last minute. Other days they spent hours on standby, waiting for the call to operations that never came. For Ian, they were very trying months. He had little patience with what he saw as dillydallying by the commanders, and he longed for a crack at the enemy. All the time he kept himself in peak physical condition by running and captaining the station's rugby team, and he got in his share of golf for relaxation. He also spent quite a bit of time developing a beam gun for the Wellington. Though the Air Ministry rejected his plans because of inadequate resources, Ian nevertheless kept the prototype for his own aircraft.

Finally, after three months of false starts, Ian flew his first operation, a strike against shipping in Heligoland, on December 3, 1939. In the months that followed, air activity for the squadron picked up considerably. Returning from Heligoland one night in early 1940, he and his crew had a close shave when they reached England to find the entire country blanketed in fog. They circled for hours looking for somewhere to land, but visibility was nil in every direction. Finally, after nearly ten hours in the air, they were forced to abandon the aircraft and parachute to safety. Through these early months in action, Ian was under no illusions about the longevity of Bomber Command crews of the time: 'It is unlikely that I shall see the end of June or July,' he recorded in his diary in January 1940.

Ian Cross did indeed see the end of July and on the twenty-sixth was taken off operations and posted to 11 OTU at Bassingbourn near Cambridge; he had completed thirty-four missions, more than half of them as first pilot. The adjustment to instructing was difficult at first, largely because of Ian's temperament. He set very high standards for himself, and he had little patience with people who expected less from themselves. However, in spite of two accidents during his first week at Bassingbourn, he soon began to enjoy instructing. In September

1940 word came that Ian had been awarded the DFC (at the same time as his brother, Kenneth). With his usual humility, Ian professed to being unexcited for his own sake. 'The thing that gives me the greatest pleasure,' he wrote, 'is how pleased the family must be.' Even the modest Cross felt a strong swell of pride when he found himself face to face with the king at the investiture.

In August 1941, after much coercion, Ian finally secured an assignment back to an operational unit, 103 Squadron at Elsham Wolds. His only disappointment was that the squadron flew two-engine Wellingtons instead of the four-engine bombers he had hoped to fly. Operations were now much more frequent than they had been during the first months of the war, and the targets had also become more demanding. There was a long trip to Turin in northern Italy (a raid that Ian thoroughly enjoyed because of the excellent views over the Alps), and a solo run to photograph the docks at Stettin.

Operations over the winter months consisted mostly of raids on harbors in occupied Europe. The targets of a number of these missions were the battle cruisers *Scharnhorst* and *Gneisenau*, sheltering in the French port of Brest. When these warships finally began their long-awaited dash up the Channel to Germany, the RAF was ordered to make a maximum effort to stop them. In the midafternoon of February 12, 1942, Ian Cross, with four other Wellingtons, took off from the cold and sodden Elsham Wolds for a strike against the ships. Each bomber carried a load of 500-pound bombs, sadly inadequate for the task, and headed off in atrocious weather to the reported location of the enemy. Icing immediately became a problem and, to make matters worse, the Wellingtons encountered thick fog soon after leaving the English coast. In an attempt to solve both difficulties, Ian ordered the flight to descend but at three hundred feet they were still in thick clouds.

They never did find the cruisers, and after fighting the clouds for what seemed like hours, the Wellingtons gave up and returned to base. Back at Elsham Wolds, 103 Squadron waited for the return of their aircraft, which eventually appeared out of the fog one by one. Only four came back, though. After fifty completed ops and over 1,330 hours as a pilot, Ian Cross had failed to return. A couple of weeks later, the Cross family was overjoyed to learn that Ian was a prisoner. His aircraft had ditched in the sea off Rotterdam and all of the crew had evacuated the aircraft safely, though two of the five were unable to get to the life raft and were lost. The others were picked up by a German ship after nearly twenty-four hours in the dinghy. All had a touch of frostbite but were otherwise unhurt.

*

Now Ian Cross was continuing his war against the enemy, although the escapade in the asparagus patch took on comic opera overtones when the three talked about it a few nights later. The failure of this effort merely freed them up for other plans, though, and they were soon recruited into a new and ingenious scheme being worked out in Schubin. The plan involved sending a tunnel out from the *Abort* (latrine) block, which was fairly close to the outside wire. The *Abort* stood on a large concrete platform and was divided into two halves, one with urinals and the other with stalls. A quick survey of the block revealed that there was a huge sewage pit under the stalls, but that the floor of the urinals room sat on solid earth. Here was the secret of the plan.

The tunnelers selected the end stall and cut the bench so that it could be raised sideways on hidden hinges. Then, a trap was made through the brickwork on the side of the waste pit, just above the level of the sewage. To cut the trap, an unlucky worker was suspended by his ankles through the hole in the stall bench and worked until so much blood had rushed to his head that he could no longer see straight. When the trap was completed, a large chamber was excavated under the floor of the urinals, with the bottom of the concrete slab acting as the roof of the chamber. From this chamber, to be used for storage of tools and materials, the tunnel would push toward the wire. Two of the scheme's originators, Eddie Asselin and William 'Tex' Ash, would be responsible for the construction of the tunnel, while the other two, 'Prince' Palmer and 'Duke' Marshall, would take care of shoring, traps, ventilation and lighting, and organization and supply. Tommy Calnan would control security.

All five were concerned that the number of workers be kept to a minimum for security reasons. One of their first contacts was an American named Fessler, an engineer who never went anywhere without his slide rule. Fes was responsible for the surveying, and he calculated that if the tunnel was angled upward at about thirty-five degrees, it would break in a drainage ditch that ran at right angles to the wire and led straight to the woods. This would make the task of exiting the tunnel much less risky. Next, it remained to select the digging teams and, fresh from their venture in the asparagus patch, Robert Kee and Ian Cross were natural choices. To shore the tunnel, the planners recruited a fair-haired man named 'Dutchy' Swain.

*

Born on December 15, 1911, in Wem, Shropshire, Cyril Douglas Swain was the odd man out among his two brothers and two sisters. As a child, he was not easy to get to know, tending to be rather moody and somewhat of a loner. As a young man he was inclined to be impatient and reticent, preferring to bottle up his problems inside rather than discuss them. He didn't care much for the academic life at Mill Hill School, which he attended between 1922 and 1929, because of the rules and regulations, which he viewed as petty and annoying. The only thing that appeared to interest him at school was rugby.

Still, there was much about Cyril Swain, or Sid, as he was known in the area, that was special. He was sensitive and sincere and even as a child was relied on by his friends, who knew they could count on him if they got into trouble. He had a typical boy's love of adventure and when he wasn't tooling around on his motorbike he could sometimes be found at the top of one of the taller trees around Wem. Sid was also the only one of the siblings who had any time for his younger sister, Sylvia. The two used to go swimming or walking together and spent hours arguing over the relative merits of horses and motorbikes. When finally persuaded to try riding Sylvia's favorite pony, Sid's only comment was that the brakes were far better on his motorbike.

In 1929, Sid's father decided that Sid should learn a trade and arranged a job for him at an engineering works in Birmingham. Unfortunately, Sid hated the job and was glad when an uncle convinced Sid's father to let him work on his farm in western Canada for a summer. The job lasted only a few months but the evenings spent listening to Uncle Frank's tales of flying with the RFC in the First World War put Sid on a different road. When he returned to England, he immediately applied to join the RAFVR and was sworn into the service on September 17, 1934, despite his father's objections.

Training began at Bristol and continued at Netheravon once Sid had been granted a short service commission. On January 11, 1937,

Pilot Officer Swain was posted to 83 Squadron at Turnhouse. The weather there wasn't the best for flying, and on the many days when practice bombing and air firing were canceled, Sid played rugby or golf or went to local motorcycle races. July 1937 brought some more interesting assignments. Swain flew one of six aircraft that staged a very successful bombing demonstration for the Staff College at Camberley, and later in the month he traveled to Northern Ireland to take part in a flypast marking the king's visit to Belfast. On the way back from this engagement, though, Sid force-landed at Thornaby, injuring his eye in the crash. The eye was quickly patched up, but the blurred vision took longer to correct and Sid was classified as unsuitable for flying duties. Cursing his luck, he left Turnhouse in November for navigation instruction duties at 10 FTS at Tern Hill.

Though classified as fit for flying duties within a couple of months, Sid languished at Tern Hill, hating instructing and longing to get back in the air; he hadn't joined the RAF to be a schoolmaster, he told his family. Finally, in February 1940 Swain was posted to Benson for operational training. The sting of being subordinate to younger men whom he had instructed at Tern Hill galled him, but he put up with it in the hopes of being sent to an operational unit. On May 10, 1940, his patience was rewarded with orders to proceed to France. Sid was flown to Nantes, but his time on the Continent proved to be a series of moves and confusions. Having transferred to 105 Squadron on May 14, he chased the unit all over the south of France, getting bombed in the process, before catching up with it at Echemines. After further training there the unit was ordered back to England. It was August 25 before Sid began his first mission, a photo reconnaissance of the Gelsenkirchen oil refinery, only to have the mission scrubbed due to lack of cloud cover. Two nights later, a trip to the Rennes airfield was aborted for the same reason. Not until September 15 was he finally able to complete a mission, a raid on gun emplacements on Cap Gris Nez.

Over the next few months, Swain flew eight further operations, three of which were aborted due to bad weather. Toward the end of November he had another bit of bad luck. While at Drem to study the new night landing system, Sid taxied his Blenheim into an Anson that had been left on the field without lights. There were no injuries, but both aircraft sustained considerable damage. By November 28 Sid and his crew were again ready for operations. In the late afternoon they took off for Düsseldorf. When dawn brought no sign of the aircraft, it was listed as missing. A couple of weeks passed before news was received at the squadron that the Blenheim had been shot down and that Sid was a prisoner in Barth. Eventually he was moved to Sagan and from there went with the first purge to Schubin.

*

Swain would be one of a team of carpenters working in the underground chamber, cutting and prefabricating the bed slats so they could be assembled in the tunnel. They had plenty of space in the chamber (it was about fifteen feet long by ten feet wide by six feet high), but initially they were hindered by a shortage of bedboards. However, the supply problem was solved when a couple of the workers broke into the German storeroom and discovered a huge stock of boards, more than enough to shore the entire tunnel. With this difficulty out of the way, the tunnel was pushed ahead. The earth was very hard, so progress was slow, but at least dispersal was a simple matter. The soil was passed up into the stall section in metal jugs and then dumped into the sewage pit through different holes so that the spoil wouldn't pile up. At regular intervals, a Polish workman came in with a tanker cart and pumped out the pit. The arrangement was a disperser's dream.

Unfortunately, the early success of the *Abort* tunnel was marred by two tragedies. Just a few weeks after arriving at Schubin, a young officer named Edwards succumbed to the pressures of captivity and tried to climb the wire in broad daylight, in full view of a guard tower. Despite the pleas of horrified onlookers, the guard opened fire, and Edwards was killed instantly. Then, less than two months later, Peter Lovegrove, another young airman, fell to his death from the top floor of Schubin's main building. Both Edwards and Lovegrove were only twenty-two, and their deaths cast a pall over the camp for quite some time.

Chapter 6

AN INTERNATIONAL COMMUNITY

BACK IN STALAG LUFT III, Roger Bushell had taken over the escape organization after Jimmy Buckley's departure. Many of the old escape leaders remained in Sagan, though, so Roger was able to gather around him an experienced committee. Crump Ker-Ramsay was given overall charge of tunneling operations, while security was put in the hands of recently arrived American 'Junior' Clark, a tall, rangy colonel. Tim Walenn took care of forgery, Nick Tindal resumed his superintendence of contacts and intelligence, and Conk Canton became the expert in charge of wire schemes.

Ralph Abraham took over the manufacture and distribution of clothing, ably assisted by a staff of Continental officers. They did most of the measuring, cutting, fitting, and pressing, while Ralph took care of the actual sewing. He also got occasional help in the Red Cross parcels store from Lawrence Reavell-Carter, who was happy to pick up anything useful he found lying around. One day in September he happened to find the German clothing storeroom unlocked and helped himself to four complete civilian suits and three raincoats. Of course, luck like this didn't come every day. Most of the time Ralph had to rely on Ivo Tonder and his other hardworking tailors to provide the necessary gear.

*

For Flight Lieutenant Ivo Tonder, escape work was nothing new; much of his adult life had been a series of prisons and escapes. Born on April 16, 1913, in Prague, Ivo joined the Czech Air Force to fulfill his national service obligations and completed his pilot training before being posted to an air display team. Ivo's two-year service term expired in May 1938, but he extended his commitment and remained in the air force. Later he was almost shot down when Hungarian anti-aircraft gunners pierced his fuel tank but escaped unscathed. It was, however, an omen of things to come.

Tonder's first escape of many was in November 1939, when he and two other airmen fled German-occupied Czechoslovakia. They were captured by the Hungarians and imprisoned, but a week later were taken to the Austrian border and released, with a warning not to re-enter Hungary. The three lay low for a few days and then recrossed the frontier and hired a taxi to Budapest, where they were sheltered by a family of Jews. Ivo and his friends were able to get papers allowing them to enter Yugoslavia, so they took a train to Subotica and crossed the frontier on foot, picking up a later train for Belgrade. Once there, escape was easy. They traveled in luxury to Salonika and Istanbul, then on to Beirut, where Ivo was taken on as a sergeant in the French Foreign Legion.

A few weeks later he continued his odyssey, finally reaching France via Morocco. Immediately upon arrival, though, Tonder was clapped into a refugee camp at Agde and got out only because he contracted jaundice and was transferred to a hospital in Paris. During his six-week convalescence, Ivo came down with a serious case of appendicitis and was moved to a clinic on the Riviera to recuperate. He was still there when France fell and the Vichy regime took over the southern part of the country. Viewing him as a possible enemy, the new rulers were not keen to release Ivo Tonder, so he escaped from the hospital and walked back to Agde, only to find the refugee camp deserted. He then stole a car and drove to Port Vendres in southern France, where he managed to get on a ship bound for Liverpool, arriving in August 1940. He immediately applied for and was accepted into the RAF and was posted to Benson for conversion to Spitfires. Ivo then transferred to 312 (Czech) Squadron and began operations almost immediately.

On June 3, 1942, after eighteen months on operations, Ivo took off from Warmwell with his squadron for escort duties. They were bounced by four FW 190s; one fell to Ivo's guns, but the Czech also took a few hits in sensitive parts of his aircraft. Halfway across the Channel on the way home, flames suddenly erupted in his cockpit, and Tonder took to his parachute. He pulled the ripcord and began his descent, catching a last glimpse of his pilotless Spitfire, all fires now out, flying bravely on toward England. Ivo floated in his dinghy for about five hours until a pack of 190s spotted him. An hour later a German seaplane landed to pick him up and ferry him to Cherbourg. When he finally got to Sagan in mid-June 1942, he could claim to have made three escapes already.

Another of the tailors was a balding, mustachioed Pole, Flight Lieutenant Jerzy Tomasz Mondschein. Born in Warsaw in 1909,

Mondschein served in the Polish Air Force before the war and earned his country's Cross of Valor and two bars. Aside from tailoring, Jerzy had another talent that was to become very useful. During his youth, he had worked with a building firm and had developed an unusual skill with concrete. He could cut out a section of almost any shape and fit it back perfectly, so that it was impossible to tell that there had ever been a hole. Somehow this bit of expertise came to Bushell's attention, and he duly filed it away in his encyclopedic store of useful bits of information.

When he was not cutting and sewing, Mondschein often could be found poring over German newspapers in his capacity as collator of intelligence from newspapers. All papers coming into the camp were collected by the organization and carefully studied by a trained staff of readers. Any detail that could possibly be of use, from the appointment of a police official in Munich to the name of a factory foreman in Stettin, was noted and passed on to officers responsible for collecting intelligence on various areas of Europe. Details on conditions in Germany were Roger Bushell's specialty, while the Low Countries and the Baltic coast were the province of a Lithuanian flight lieutenant named Romualdas Marcinkus.

Rene, as he was known, was born in Jurbarkas on July 22, 1907, and in 1927 entered the Lithuanian Military Academy from high school. After finishing the two-year course, he was posted as a lieutenant to the 5th Infantry Regiment. Rene had loftier aspirations, though, and six months later requested a transfer to the school of military aviation. In time he got his observer's wings and was posted to the 2nd Reconnaissance Squadron at Kaunas. He rose quickly and before long had qualified as a pilot, holding the rank of captain and the honorary badge *Plieno Sparnai* (Wings of Steel).

In 1934 Marcinkus was chosen to take part in the famous Flight Around Europe. Flying three little fighter aircraft, Rene and two other pilots traveled more than six thousand miles and visited dozens of cities in Europe. Always inquisitive and interested, Rene saw as much as he could and stored away vast quantities of detail in his incredible memory. After the tour, Rene moved back to the school of military aviation to become its chief administrator. At this time he was making a name for himself with his stunt parachuting; he was the first stunt jumper in Lithuania, and he taught parachuting at the military school.

Rene was also a star with the Lithuanian national football team and visited many more European cities during his time with the side.

In 1939 Marcinkus decided to retire from the military, for reasons that aren't entirely clear. Later, he may have been involved in a scheme to supply a squadron of Lithuanian pilots to assist in the defense of France. He eventually joined a French fighter squadron and had some success during the German invasion of France, downing three enemy aircraft and winning the Croix de Guerre. When France fell he was on the move again, escaping to North Africa, where he was demobilized from the French Air Force on August 12, 1940. He immediately went to see the British attaché in Tangier, expressing his desire to join the RAF. He was sent to Gibraltar with a group of Frenchmen and sailed for Liverpool in October. With 1,480 hours of flying, Rene was immediately taken into the RAF, although he had to shave three years off his age to meet the age standard.

For conversion to RAF aircraft, he was sent to 55 OTU at Usworth, and on May 4, 1941, was posted to 1 Squadron, flying Hurricanes from Redhill. The unit was operational for most of the summer, doing Channel patrols and bomber escort missions, but in August they began training for night-fighter duties. Though his time was well occupied, Rene was lonely in England. There were no other Lithuanians at the squadron's new base, Tangmere, and Marcinkus missed talking about his homeland. So it was with great delight that one day he received a letter from a Lithuanian stationed not far away. 'I was overjoyed at receiving your letter,' Rene wrote, 'because here in England I feel unspeakably lonely . . . throughout this period of almost three years I have had no news from home.' The two Lithuanians planned to meet, and Marcinkus eagerly looked forward to this contact with home.

It was not to be. On February 12, 1942, Marcinkus and five other squadron pilots were assigned to fly a low-level operation against the warships *Scharnhorst* and *Gneisenau*, the same targets Ian Cross had tried to attack. Just after lunch, the Hurricanes rendezvoused with their covering Spitfires and headed toward the French coast. The first line of ships they came across turned out to be friendly, but the second, a group of destroyers, opened fire on the Hurris, which quickly formed up to strafe the ships. Rene's wingman fell to the flak, but the rest emerged unscathed and set course for home. Having survived the difficult part of the trip, though, Rene's Hurricane ran straight into a flock of seagulls, which smashed his cockpit cover and brought his engine to a coughing halt. He made a forced landing on the French coast and was picked up by German troops. His forty-second sortie had proved to be his last.

In Sagan Rene became known as an expert linguist and acted as language adviser in the forgery workshop. His German was indistinguishable from that of a Prussian, and he also spoke Polish, Russian, French, and English fluently. Rene often joked that he could eat and make love anywhere from the Balkans to Scandinavia. He had enormous charm, and he carried himself in the best tradition of the Lithuanian nobility from whom he was descended. He was also very particular about his appearance, especially his thinning head of hair. Each time he washed it, Marcinkus used a small portion of his Red Cross lemon extract as a rinse. 'One must always look one's best in front of the Huns,' he would say.

The accurate information provided by Marcinkus and the rest of the intelligence organization was, of course, crucial, but it was equally important for the escaper to know where he was going, and where he was once he got there. For this he needed a map. Men who escaped by train could make do with a general map of the major travel routes and enlargements of sensitive areas such as border crossings. For the 'hardarser' – the man who intended to travel on foot – though, a much more detailed map was required, one that showed all of the tiny villages, watercourses, forests, hills, passes, and other landforms. A clear picture of the surrounding countryside could mean the difference between success and failure for a hardarser.

The mapping department was the domain of Desmond Lancelot Plunkett, a colorful character with flaming red hair and a great sense of humor. Working with a Fleet Air Arm lieutenant named Alexander Desmond 'Sailor' Neely and a few others, Des could provide a map of almost anywhere, and he was equally well known for his eccentric behavior. He tended to be absentminded and accident-prone. His roommates often joked that, while washing up, he was likely to dry the same cup six times and then break it. He was stocky, very strong, and always seemed busy, rushing around the camp in a cheerful flurry.

*

Born in 1915, Des Plunkett got his first taste of flying in the summer of 1925, when two biplanes landed on a field near his parents' home. They advertised rides for five shillings a trip, and the young lad pestered his father for the money. It was a good sum in those days but, despite his mother's objections, Des finally won out. The lad got on the last ride of the day and was up for a good thirty minutes with no straps or goggles. Even when he came back to earth, Plunkett's mind was still in the clouds.

In 1933 he got a job as an apprentice aircraft engineer, and for the next four years he moved around the aircraft industry, learning to fly and working for various companies before landing a job as a draftsman in 1937. Plunkett joined the RAFVR in the same year, and in May 1939 he qualified as an instructor and left aircraft engineering to teach flying at Hanworth. In November 1941 he converted to Wellingtons to become operational. He was posted to 218 Squadron, flying Short Stirling heavy bombers.

On June 20, 1942, with more than twenty-two hundred hours' flying under his belt, Des Plunkett was assigned as co-pilot for a raid on Emden. After leaving the target area, the aircraft was hit by a night fighter and the starboard wing tank was set alight. With the intercom useless, the pilot signaled to the crew to bail out. Plunkett came down outside the town of Spierdijk in Holland and went into hiding for the next day, planning to make his escape at night. It was Sunday, so he figured that the roads would be fairly deserted. However, soon after setting out, he realized with alarm that the entire village seemed to be out for a Sunday stroll, and within minutes he was surrounded by locals inquiring when the invasion would come. Des delicately broached the subject of escape, only to be discouraged by the villagers, who maintained that the area was crawling with Germans. Perhaps mistakenly, Des took their advice and gave himself up. He never did see more than a couple of Germans in the town.

Shortly after arriving at Sagan, Des was asked by Roger Bushell to take charge of the mapping department. Plunkett had done quite a bit of aerial survey work before the war and immediately began planning a system for the rapid and easy reproduction of maps. Fortunately, Des's absentmindedness miraculously disappeared whenever he worked on his maps.

*

The fall of 1942 brought some new additions to the ever-growing intelligence network as well, including a much-needed authority on Denmark. Though a New Zealander by birth, Arnold George Christensen was as much a product of his ancestors' Danish homeland as of his father's adopted country. A decade before Arnold's birth on April 18, 1922, his father, Anton, left the family home in Randers, Denmark, to begin a new life in faraway New Zealand. By 1920 the elder Christensen had married a young widow, and the couple bought a small house in Hastings. Anton was proud of his heritage, and young Arnold and his half-sister, Hazel, were often treated to tales of Anton's homeland, tales to which the boy listened with great interest.

From an early age, Arnold demonstrated a keen intelligence and quickness to learn. At school he showed a great love of sports and excelled academically, passing his examinations with distinction. During his youth Arnold also gained high honors in the 2nd Hastings Scout Troop, for which he edited and printed a little magazine titled *The Totem*. With Arnold's interest in journalism, the Christensens were not surprised when he took a position at the *Hawkes Bay Daily Mail* after graduation. The pale but always jovial young man loved his work, and his diligence and keen sense of humor slowly brought him respect in local press circles. He began to spend time with a pretty and cheerful young lady named Joan Rivers, and many who knew the couple began to wonder when the two would become engaged. The well-wishers would have to wait, though, for on June 19, 1940, Arnold Christensen applied for service with the RNZAF. He had only just celebrated his eighteenth birthday.

It was June 14, 1941, before Arnold was called for preliminary instruction. He finished the course with excellent results and was posted to New Plymouth, where flying instruction began on Tiger Moths. On October 20 Arnold left for Canada to continue training. The Christensens and Joan (who had become privately engaged to Arnold shortly before) were saddened to see the young man go, his five-foot, six-inch frame cutting a fine figure in his airman's uniform, but Arnold looked forward to his service with pride and excitement, speaking confidently of the day when he would return home. He was still only nineteen, and this was to be his first big adventure.

Arnold's letters from the ship revealed his youthful exuberance toward a trip he enjoyed as a luxury cruise. The food was marvelous, the accommodations were splendid, and the films shown onboard were the latest releases. Shore leave was even more exciting. The exotic natives sold quaint souvenirs and at Honolulu the Kiwis were treated to a display of hula dancing and a picnic of hot dogs, soft drinks, and fresh fruit. When the ship reached Los Angeles, Arnold and the others were feted by Warner Brothers Studios, which provided free ice cream and cigarettes, showed off their latest starlets, and even let the airmen try the cameras. The VIP treatment was short-lived, though, and the men were soon on another ship, bound for San Francisco, where they entrained for Canada. Two nights later, they arrived in Vancouver and were quickly shuttled off to 4 Service Flying Training School (SFTS) in Saskatoon, Saskatchewan.

November is a depressing time to reach the Canadian prairies; the days are dull and cold, and the nights are long and even colder. Arnold's enthusiasm, however, was unshaken, for it was all new to him. He enjoyed the continuous movies, archery at the YMCA, and Saturday night ice-skating. The food left a bit to be desired, but the Canadian hospitality made up for it. Arnold was invited to Christmas dinner by a kindly policeman and was glad to return, if only briefly, to a family setting. Flight training was rigorous, but the young man loved it all. He flew to Prince Albert and Moose Jaw and learned to gauge the size of towns by the number of tarred roads and grain elevators. The young New Zealander did well, and when the examination results appeared in January 1942, Arnold emerged at the top of his section. Signs of a growing maturity began to creep into his letters home. He wrote more of the long cross-country runs and the aircraft on which he trained, and less of the social life and the food. His youthful exuberance remained, but it was tempered with a more sober and serious outlook. Finally, on February 27, 1942, Arnold received his wings and commission. He was not yet twenty years of age.

In early March, Christensen left for England. He was intrigued by his first taste of the country; with more leave, he explored the sights and theaters of London, the cycle routes of the Lake District, and the cathedrals of the southern counties. He was most impressed by the sense of history around him, having spent his entire life in comparatively young countries. It was while in Bournemouth that Christensen received word of the death of his father. His first concern was for the welfare of his mother, and Arnold anxiously awaited news of the situation back in Hastings. A move to Harrogate provided a welcome change of scene and, between lectures, he found solace in the great landmarks of Yorkshire, such as Ripon Cathedral and York Minster. Tennis, boating, and garden parties at local estates also helped to ease the anxiety.

On June 2, 1942, came the long-awaited assignment to a single-engine training station, and soon Arnold was posted to 41 OTU at Old Sarum in Wiltshire to upgrade to Harvard single-engine trainers and Mustang fighters. As the prospect of seeing action grew, Christensen threw himself into his training. He enjoyed the navigation exercises, which proved more challenging in England than they had been in Canada, and took extra training in photo reconnaissance. At last, on August 13, the Kiwi received his operational posting to 26 Squadron at Gatwick in Surrey. He was the first dominion officer posted to the unit, and he was elated at finally reaching an operational squadron.

On August 19 the squadron was assigned to fly reconnaissance missions over the beaches of Dieppe. Normally a new pilot would have been given a few days to settle in before being sent on ops, but a maximum air effort was needed, and Christensen was sent into the fray. He and another pilot flew the last mission of the day and, during the brief twenty-minute tour of the battle area, both aircraft took hits from German small-arms fire. Arnold's wingmate caught the worst of it and went into the water a few miles offshore, leaving the New Zealander to nurse his damaged Mustang home alone. Halfway across the Channel, the faltering engine finally gave out and Arnold was forced to ditch the aircraft, a tricky maneuver that he performed quite handily. Furious but uninjured, he pulled himself into the dinghy and sat down to await assistance. His air war against Hitler's Germany had lasted just over thirty minutes. It was almost two days and nights before the dinghy drifted to the French coast, where Arnold was picked up by German soldiers. After a couple of days in a Paris jail cell, he was moved to Dulag Luft and then to Stalag Luft III. In his own words, that was to be his 'permanent address' for the rest of the war.

Soon after arriving in Sagan, Arnold re-established contact with his relatives in Denmark, and he eventually began receiving parcels from his father's homeland. Books and letters were carefully combed for details about life in Denmark, while a couple of food items were saved from each parcel and added to the escape organization's stores. The possession of a package of Danish crackers might someday be sufficient to convince a police official that the escaper he was questioning was actually the Dane he claimed to be.

*

Also knocked down over Dieppe was Per Bergsland, a Norwegian who served under the name Peter Rockland to protect his family in Oslo. Per began as a sailor but gave up after making the unfortunate discovery that he was prone to seasickness. He returned to school, first in Norway and then at a German commercial academy. While in Germany in 1938, he saw firsthand the burning of the synagogues and protested against the persecution of the Jews, only to be expelled from school for his outspokenness. Rather than tell his parents of his expulsion, he took a job in a sports shop before returning to Oslo to settle.

When the Germans invaded Norway on April 9, 1940, Per immediately left his job in a shipping office to join the army. But the campaign lasted just six weeks, and at the end of the brief struggle Per found himself idle. By late 1940 he had worked out a scheme to get back into action and with six others escaped to the Shetland Islands in a small boat. He joined the Norwegian Army at Dumfries in Scotland but was frustrated by inactivity and applied for transfer to the air force. For training, Per went to Little Norway in Toronto, Canada, the reception center for Norwegian airmen, and from there to the flying school at Moose Jaw, Saskatchewan. After a short refresher course on American-built fighters at Little Norway, Bergsland returned to England to train on Spitfires and was eventually posted to 332 Squadron, in the north of England.

Within a month the unit moved south to take part in operations against the French coast. On August 19, 1942, Bergsland took off for Dieppe with another pilot, but soon lost his wingman in the melee over the beaches. Per found himself chasing an FW 190 around a cloud and, after a couple of circuits, decided to wheel his Spit around and meet the 190 head-on. The two aircraft, all guns blazing, passed within yards of each other, but the Spitfire got the worse of the fracas. Oil spurted over the windshield and Bergsland realized that his only hope was to abandon the aircraft. Turning the Spit on its back, he calmly dropped out and pulled the ripcord. Per thoroughly enjoyed his descent and was soon picked up by a German vessel. With a brace of automatic weapons pointed in his direction, Per climbed the ladder to the rail, pausing just long enough to drop his pistol into the Channel, and was ordered to accompany the captain to his cabin.

'*Setzen Sie sich*' (Sit down), barked the captain, his stern eyes boring holes in the bedraggled airman. Then in the same tone he rapped, '*Was wollen Sie, Cognac oder Likör?*' (What do you want, cognac or liqueur?)

Per laughed as the captain's face broke into a grin. A sailor's uniform was fetched for the soggy Norwegian, and the two men began a lengthy conversation that was broken only by an attack on the ship by Allied aircraft. When the vessel docked, Per was put into a temporary cage at St. Omer, where he ran into Arnold Christensen, and after a week in less-than-palatial accommodation at Versailles, was shipped to Dulag Luft. His interrogators were anxious to discover his squadron number, which had not been recorded because no one had seen his aircraft crash. After two weeks of varied forms of persuasion, a German officer sat down on Per's bed and kindly offered to convey a message to his family in exchange for his squadron number. With his family in Norway protected by his false identity, Per looked blankly at the officer and lied through his teeth, saying that his parents had been killed in an air raid on London. In no time at all, he was out of Dulag Luft and on his way to Sagan.

The Stalag Luft III to which Per Bergsland and Arnold Christensen came was running fairly smoothly as a community. There was amateur theater, with the camp's version of a play based on *The Dover Road* in production, and any number of sports were available. The library was building up a good stock of books, so there was rarely a shortage of reading material. Some, however, took the library more seriously than others. One day, Des Plunkett was boning up on his Russian grammar when he glanced up to see dozens of tiny bits of paper floating around the library. Fascinated, he watched as they flew around his head and, at last, one dropped on the table in front of him. Looking closely, he realized the paper was tied to the back legs of a fly with a piece of thread. Turning the paper over, he saw that someone had written 'Deutschland Kaput!' on it.

Des looked around the room and spotted a flight lieutenant standing on a chair and catching flies at the window. After carefully tying a drogue to each one, he released them to carry their messages around the camp, in the hopes that one of them would alight on Pieber or Rubberneck. Just as the air was starting to get thick with little scraps of paper, a senior Allied officer strolled in and, noticing the snowfall of messages, reprimanded the fellow for showing cruelty to insects.

'Not at all, sir,' came the quick reply. 'After all, they are Hun flies!'

*

To newcomers, the camp seemed to be an enclave of comparative civilization in the Silesian woods. However, this was hardly what they were expecting as they made the trip to Sagan. So the first few days in the camp were something of an eye-opener. Everyone was friendly enough but because of the danger of German plants, the senior officers asked that newcomers be treated cautiously until someone in the camp verified their identity. Then the entire reception changed. The newcomer was given a feast and asked to tell all he could about things back home: the new plays and films, the latest sports scores, and even the exploits of the comic strip heroine Jane. From this point, the new man was a full-fledged member of camp society.

Flight Lieutenant Harold John Milford of Streatham arrived in Sagan in October 1942 after having been downed in a Boston medium bomber while attacking Chocques power station on September 22, 1942. The crew bailed out, buried their parachutes, and split up. Navigator Milford and the radio operator–air gunner went one way, and the pilot went the other. As it turned out, the pilot made the right choice. He evaded capture and eventually returned to England, while Milford and the gunner were pulled out of a haystack and placed in captivity. Now Milford stood just inside the gate at Stalag Luft III, wondering what would happen next. Having received his room assignment, Milford was about to make his way across the compound when a voice hailed him. It came from a slight officer with thick black hair and a mustache who looked vaguely familiar.

'Harold Milford, isn't it?' he inquired cheerily. 'You may not remember me – Flight Lieutenant John Francis Williams. I spent about a month with your squadron back in January, when I was right out of 13 OTU.'

The light dawned. 'Of course – good to see you again. I was hoping to see a familiar face,' Milford said honestly.

Williams laughed. 'Yes, we all feel that way at first! So what brought you here?'

Harold recounted the story of his last trip and then asked about Williams's misfortune. The latter had been downed by 190s over the Lille-Sequedin power station on April 27, 1942. It was only the second operation for Williams, the observer on a Boston. As they talked, they found they had more in common. Like Milford, Williams was a Londoner, born in Wandsworth and a resident of the South London suburb of Ewell. He was an only child and had worked with an engineering firm before joining up.

'Well, enough chatting – we'll have plenty of time for that!' joked Williams. 'Let's see about getting you settled. That's your hut over there, the one with the pants hanging out of the first window. Just go on in – I'm sure the boys will make you feel at home. I'll pop over in a little while and see how you're getting on.' With a wave, John Williams wandered away, leaving Harold to meet his new roommates.

The scene that greeted Milford as he entered the room was one of immense confusion. Clouds of steam billowed from a pot on the stove as a short, stout kriegie stirred a violently bubbling mixture. In the far corner, two bearded prisoners were engaged in a heated debate on the validity of various fertilization techniques in the cultivation of roses. In another corner, a seemingly oblivious squadron leader was making repairs to a homemade hammock and loudly humming airs from *Carmen* while, from above, a shower of wood shavings fell from a rough carving of a bison in the hands of a lean Canadian. No one seemed to take any particular notice of the new arrival, and Milford made his way to an empty bunk at the end of the room. As he emerged from the cloud surrounding the stove he noticed another prisoner who was seated at the table, hunched over a sketch pad. He was tall and slender, and a lock of thick, dark hair fell over his brow as he concentrated on his drawing. He seemed so out of place that Harold stopped and watched him. After a moment the young man looked up.

'Afternoon!' he said cheerfully, 'and welcome to the Madhouse Cells! I'm Hayter – Tony Hayter. Have a seat, if you think you can stand this place. Don't worry – it's not always like this – sometimes it's worse!' His face broke into a wide smile, and the two started to chat. Then the newcomer noticed the drawing that Tony had been working on. It was a splendid and carefully detailed sketch of a Wellington in flight.

'Your ship?' asked Milford.

Tony nodded. 'Although she didn't look quite like that when I left her. Actually I really can't recall what she looked like then. We were about two thousand feet over Sicily when the flak opened up. We must have taken one right in the bomb bay, because the next thing I remember is floating through the air, surrounded by bits of aircraft. It might have been rather comical if it hadn't happened so suddenly. My crew didn't even have time to get into their chutes. I guess it pays to be the pilot – mine was already clipped on and we both got blown out together. Everything seemed to be falling so slowly, and there wasn't a sound. I don't know how long it was before I realized what was happening and pulled the cord. It must have been a long time, because I came down a trifle more roughly than I might have wished.'

Harold noticed that Tony's expression had darkened. 'Awfully good sketch you've done,' he said quickly. 'Are you an artist by training or by nature?'

'Well, I really can't take all of the credit,' he said cheerily, 'because it's probably genetic. My great-uncle passed his time as court painter to old Queen Victoria, and his brother, my grandfather, did portraits of many of the great titled ladies and gentry of the day. We've all sorts of architects and painters of various description hidden in the family tree. I suppose I'm just utilizing a family talent!' Tony had been aimlessly working his pencil as they talked, and he suddenly picked up the drawing, strode over to the wall beside his bunk, and tacked the sketch in a blank spot. He stood back, stared intently for a moment and then smiled approvingly. He said nothing, merely letting out a satisfied grunt before returning to the table where Harold was sitting.

'That should turn out quite nicely once I get some color on it. Yes . . ' He paused thoughtfully. 'Well, I must dash now – I've a football match in a few minutes. Glad to have you with us – this room could use some livening up!' Harold looked up to see the same wide grin on Hayter's face, and the latter let out a laugh. With that, Tony threaded his lean frame through the confusion and vanished up the corridor. Harold Milford liked his new roommate immediately, and the more he learned about him, the more his respect grew.

Anthony Ross Henzell Hayter was born on May 20, 1920, at Farnborough in Hampshire and was only two when his father retired and the family moved to Burghclere Grange, a large rectory and small farm in Berkshire. Tony and his brothers and sisters grew up in a sporting atmosphere provided by their father, who was an enthusiastic and able horseman and yachtsman, and the children followed in his footsteps. Tony became very interested in golf, tennis, swimming, and yachting and eventually developed into an exceptional squash player. Like many boys, he had a fondness for sports cars and certainly enjoyed a party. There was a sensitive side to Tony, though, that only those close to him saw. He had a deep love of nature and spent much time in the fields and hedgerows around Burghclere Grange watching the flora and fauna. An artistic side became more apparent as he matured, as did a decidedly romantic streak. He was keenly aware of the beauty of nature around him, and his later letters confirm that he never lost that appreciation for his surroundings.

In 1929 Tony had his first flight, in a small biplane owned by his stepbrother. The little aircraft bumped and bounced off a field near the rectory and, as it circled the house, the lad waved excitedly to his brother and sisters on the ground. It was the beginning of a passion that was to grow as he did. Tony entered Marlborough College in 1933 and at the same time became friends with Cynthia Henstock, the daughter of a neighboring family. They kept in touch while Tony was at school and wrote lighthearted letters telling of walks in the country, champagne balls, and canoeing on the river. Tony had a great sense of humor and could always see the funny side of things, whether it be the strain of exams or scrambling to escape hostile swans on the river. His letters are as charming as they are innocent and reveal a sensitive soul blissfully unaware of the gathering storm clouds.

Hayter graduated from Marlborough in 1938 and, already bitten by the flying bug, accepted a short service commission in the RAF, beginning flight training in March 1939. He was an enthusiastic pilot and a quick learner and looked forward to a long and successful career in the peacetime RAF, enjoying the good company and travel between far-flung air force stations. The long, desperate, and bloody war couldn't be foreseen in that warm summer of 1939, when romance with Cynthia was blossoming further.

Tony was transferred to the Advanced Training Squadron at Hullavington and, after the war began, proceeded for conversion to Blenheims. After a winter of intensive training with his bomb-aimer/navigator Sergeant Midgeley, Pilot Officer Hayter was posted to 57 Squadron at Montdidier in northern France on April 13, 1940. The unit moved frequently but Tony had no complaints. He quite enjoyed his billets, especially one with a gruff old farmer who spoke no English. 'Whenever he sees us,' Tony wrote, 'he insists on us going into the parlor, where his wife and daughter are sitting. As we come in, they get up, rush about the place, and finally make us some coffee, bring cognac, biscuits, and cigarettes. The old man gets out his maps and starts explaining to us about the last war, ending up with his life story!'

On May 10, Hayter and Midgeley flew their first operation, a photo-reconnaissance sweep of the German-Dutch frontier. Tony was pulling away from a bridge when Sergeant Midgeley shouted a warning: Three Messerschmitts were bearing in on them, forcing Tony to throw the Blenheim into a spiral dive. Just managing to pull the aircraft up, he was screaming away on the deck when 'the only tree in Holland,' as he put it, appeared in front of them. Unable to avoid it, the Blenheim hit the tree, lopping off the top five feet, and continued on, unchecked. The 109s managed to get around the tree and fired burst after burst before being forced to return to base. Hayter and Midgeley didn't realize how many hits they had taken until they landed and counted the holes in the Blenheim; there were 237.

It was an exhausted Tony Hayter who returned to England on May 20 'after having a very hectic time for the last week,' as he wrote to Cynthia. 'I got exactly five hours' sleep the whole week. As it is, I am here with what I stand in only. A lot of our kit has been burnt and I don't know where the rest of mine is.' There was little rest for Tony, though, for two days later he was detailed to fly an extremely sensitive mission. His orders were to transport a certain major to the last remaining airfield in the British Expeditionary Force's area of retreat; a dispatch carried by the major contained plans for the retreat to Dunkirk, where an evacuation would be undertaken. Tony landed the Blenheim safely on the badly cratered airfield and was efficiently directed to taxi the aircraft under the cover of some trees. The major was whisked away, leaving Tony under attack by German bombers that had been alerted by the Blenheim's approach. Sheltering in a shallow ditch, he awaited the major's return patiently and then skillfully took his Blenheim off down the well-perforated airstrip. The mission was a success and, for his skill and courage, Pilot Officer Hayter was awarded a mention in dispatches. 'No one was more surprised when I heard and I didn't really believe it until I happened to see it for myself,' he wrote to Cynthia.

On June 24, Tony was posted to Scotland for a stint with Coastal Command. He had been there only a month when disaster struck. While he was waiting to take off on a practice flight, his Blenheim was struck by a taxiing Wellington, and Sergeant Midgeley's arm was severed by a propeller. Fighting his way through the shattered aircraft,

Tony reached his gravely wounded navigator and managed to secure a tourniquet to the bleeding stump, probably saving the sergeant's life. Both aircraft were write-offs, and Midgeley's flying war was over.

Tony was assigned a new crewmate and for the next few months flew training missions and reconnaissance sweeps over the North Sea. Though he occasionally got in a burst at a German bomber or a floating mine, the trips were uneventful. Over the winter of 1940–41 he converted to Wellingtons, and on March 18, 1941, he flew his first Wellington mission against an oil facility at Rotterdam. It was a fairly calm trip, but a raid on Cologne on March 27 proved to be less successful. The crew braved the intense searchlight activity and heavy flak as far as Antwerp and then were forced to return to base with equipment failure. On April 9, 1941, they took their Wellington through a cloudless sky to Berlin; it was to be Tony's last completed mission against a European target.

In late April word came that Tony was to be posted to the Middle East for three months, and on April 23 he left for Gibraltar. The crew was delayed there for five days owing to repairs in progress on the runways, and the time allowed Tony to sample the treats of a city free from the inconveniences of war. 'We are eating oranges, lemons, etc to our hearts' content here,' he wrote to Cynthia, 'and of course there is no butter ration or blackout.' The respite was brief, though, and on May 6 Tony took off for Malta. Three days after arriving on the beleaguered little island, Tony flew his first operation in the Middle East, a diversionary raid on Tripoli.

On July 12 he was posted to 253 Wing Communications Flight in Egypt and a month later received the worst possible news. His letter to Cynthia tells the story: 'I am afraid I have been posted out here now, which means I shall probably be here for three years. It was a bit of a dirty trick as they did tell us when we left England to leave most of our stuff behind, as we were returning right away.' It was a cruel blow for the two, but their letters provided a constant link. Tony was fascinated by the desert and wrote of the thunderstorms and sailing on the Mediterranean. He sent drawings of himself as a shaggy, tanned figure in baggy desert uniform, or as a bewildered pilot trying to communicate with a hairy Arab waiter. Through it all, he retained his charming sense of humor and talked much of their plans for the future.

By September 1941 Tony had been promoted to commander of the communications flight and was chiefly involved in transporting men and spare parts between various landing grounds. After three months of this, however, he was anxious to get back into action with a Wellington unit, and on January 10, 1942, he was assigned to 148 Squadron. A week after his first op, he ran into trouble. On February 8, on the way to the base at Kabrete, one of the engines lost power and Tony had to put the aircraft down on the desert floor. As the crew piled out of the bomber, Tony noticed a group of Arabs on camels approaching. Unsure of their sympathies, he pulled out his revolver and thrust it into his sock, leaving the butt clearly visible. The Arabs were obviously undeterred by this and retaliated with an offer of eggs, which Tony gratefully accepted. In fact, the crew had a pleasant stay with the Arabs before being picked up by their unit.

Operations continued through February and March, mainly against Benghazi, and on April 18, Tony Hayter's logbook records a trip from Kabrete to Faiyum to pick up three aircraft. It is the last entry. Six days later, Tony's Wellington fell over Sicily. He was unhurt, and the Germans lost no time in sending him to a permanent camp. By the first week of May he was in Sagan, acclimatizing himself to the life of a prisoner.

Chapter 7

THE PLAN IS HATCHED

For some POWs, the first few days in Sagan were not just strange, but downright disconcerting. Roger Bushell had long told his fellow prisoners to ignore anything odd or out of place that went on. As he put it, 'If you see me walking around with a tree trunk sticking out of my arse, don't ask any questions because it'll be for a damn good reason!' In September 1942 one of the new kriegies was treated to a perfect demonstration of this piece of advice.

Les Harvey was an Australian pilot officer whose Halifax was knocked down in August 1942. He arrived at Sagan from Dulag Luft just in time for a bowl of soup. Though he didn't know it at the time, his roommates were some of the most notorious troublemakers in Luftwaffe hands. Wearied by the long train ride, Les sat down at the table and began to eat his soup. No sooner had he lifted the spoon to his mouth than two figures clad in long woolen underwear trotted in; each wore the leg of a pair of long underpants over his head. Without a word, Mike Casey and another airman lifted the table and moved it to one side; then Guy Griffiths and Bill Goldfinch pulled up one of the floorboards to reveal a dark hole underneath the hut. The two mystery men clambered down into the hole, the plank was replaced, and the table was shifted back. It all took less than a minute, and Les was able to get back to his soup before it went cold.

Les Harvey saw for himself that he was surrounded by all sorts of escape activity, while others got the message after seeing guards hauling small groups of kriegies to the cooler or hearing shots and guttural shouts coming from the direction of the wire at night. Some of the newcomers decided to wait a while before involving themselves in nefarious deeds, while others jumped immediately into the fray. Flight Lieutenant Bram (Bob) van der Stok was one of the latter.

*

Van der Stok, the son of a Dutch engineer, was born in Pladjoe, Sumatra, on October 30, 1915, and spent much of his youth in exotic locations around the world. Bob and his three brothers and sisters were raised in Balikpapan in Borneo and, after a few years in Rotterdam, moved to Curaçao. For high school the boys were sent back to Holland, and Bob later went to Switzerland for postsecondary education. He graduated in 1934 and entered the school of medicine at the University of Leiden. However, Bob found that he wasn't yet ready for the sort of work needed to succeed in medical school; he was more interested in sports, and he devoted his time to hockey and boating. Before he knew it he was a year behind with little hope of catching up. Discussing his future with his father, Bob mentioned the prospect of playing professional ice hockey in Canada. The elder van der Stok quickly rejected the suggestion and ventured that some form of military training might be just what Bob needed. He could always try one of the more sporting branches of the service, such as the cavalry, or even flying.

Flying. Now, there was something Bob hadn't considered – there were certainly worse ways to spend a couple of years. As it turned out, his father had already made a few inquiries in the right places, and in no time Bob was on his way to begin training. His two years in the service were great fun. Bob developed a passion for stunt flying but unfortunately found it difficult to indulge his love while in the military; he was once put up on charges for flying under a bridge. After a year with a fighter unit, Bob's service term ended and he returned to medical school, this time at the University of Utrecht. Older and more mature, he threw himself into his studies – no more athletics and begging off classes. He worked hard and did well. Bob began to see what medicine was really about, and he liked it. This time he planned to make it through to the end.

Then came 1939. When the Dutch armed forces mobilized, Bob was called up and posted to a fighter squadron, flying Fokkers from the Den Helder airfield. For months they stood by, doing patrols over the German–Dutch border and occasionally getting a look at an enemy aircraft. And they waited to see what would happen. On May 10, 1940, the wheels began to turn. Flying dawn patrol that morning, Bob and his squadronmates were jumped by Me 109s, and a fierce battle ensued. Bob claimed one destroyed and one damaged, but the weight of numbers told. Air attacks continued for the rest of the day, and by nightfall all but seven of the little Fokkers had been destroyed.

The Dutch resistance lasted a mere five days. On May 15 Bob and his squadronmates flew the Fokkers to Schipol and set them on fire to keep them from falling into German hands. A few hours later the German conquest was complete. Without the space to hold all of the Dutch servicemen as POWs, the Germans ordered their demobilization and told them to go home. Bob van der Stok went back to medical school, but things had changed. One always had to be on guard, for it was impossible to tell who was loyal and who was a German sympathizer. Friendships and even families were torn apart as people took sides. Among the students at the university there grew up resistance cells ready to act. Within thirty minutes a secret message could reach up to eight hundred people through a cell organization. Bob and others went on with their studies but remained ready to continue the fight.

In the fall of 1940 two Dutch airmen stole an aircraft and flew it to England. The next day Hitler ordered that all other Dutch military pilots be arrested and held as POWs. When the Gestapo came to get Bob van der Stok, they found only an empty apartment; he had been warned by the underground chain. He went into hiding in Rotterdam and began to plan a way to escape to England. His first scheme, cycling to Belgium and making his way south to Spain, ended in a hail of gunfire at the Belgian border. His second plan, an escape in a boat built by a friend, was ruined when the boat was destroyed by Allied bombs while in the friend's garage. Later Bob joined four others in a plan to reach England in a gravel barge. Everything went well until they ran aground on a shoal, and the plan was scrapped when they had to ask a German patrol boat to pull them off.

On June 2, 1941, van der Stok was on his way again. He swam out to a neutral freighter in the harbor at Rotterdam and, with the help of a crewman, hid belowdecks. A few days out of Holland the ship was stopped by HMS *Devonshire*, which sent over a boarding party and ordered the ship to proceed to the Faeroe Islands to be searched. The British authorities were skeptical when Bob and a few other Dutchmen on the ship came out of hiding and announced their intention to join the Allied forces, but they were all taken to London to be cleared by British intelligence. Bob was told that, since the Dutch government had never officially demobilized him, he was still an air force officer.

In time van der Stok was sent to 91 Squadron, based at Tangmere. The Spitfires flew primarily defensive missions against German intruder aircraft, and the squadron had good success. However, it had been in action almost continuously since the Battle of Britain and needed a rest. When it was moved to Liverpool to regroup and refresh, Bob was transferred to 41 Squadron. Before long he was flying Spits on offensive sweeps over the Continent. Again Bob had some success, adding to the tally sheet he had opened in 1940, but on April 12, 1942, he was rudely brought to earth. Flying a sweep over northern France, Bob's unit ran into a pack of 190s. After knocking down a couple, the Dutchman found himself on the receiving end of a line of tracer bullets. His trusty mount gave out, and Bob hit the silk and was captured.

*

Once he was in Sagan, van der Stok's ideas quickly turned to escape, and in this he had one distinct advantage over many of his fellow kriegies: He had actually lived under the German occupation. Many prisoners had traveled through Germany on previous escapes, and others knew Europe well from prewar travel. But, useful though this was, it was not the same. Bob had lived for more than a year in an occupied country. He knew what the occupiers were like, how they were organized, what sort of people they were likely to question, and what they would ask. Perhaps most important, he knew what was acceptable behavior for the average European traveler in wartime. Many escapers had been tripped up in the past on little points of etiquette because a guard or police official spotted something they did or didn't do. More than one escaper had been arrested after offering his seat to an elderly woman, something that was never done in occupied Europe. Bob van der Stok knew all of these little points; more than most, he could blend in with the population. If he ever got out of the camp, he would be a difficult man to catch.

For his first attempt, he and a Canadian officer planned to sprint toward the wire and burrow under after dark. Roger Bushell approved the scheme but told them to listen for his whistle, which would signal danger and summon them back to the hut. On the big night the pair got to the wire without incident and began to dig. Suddenly they heard a terrible commotion and, in the midst of the racket, Roger's warning whistle. Reluctantly abandoning their rough hole, they darted back to the hut and climbed back into bed. The next day they discovered they had not been noticed at all; the commotion had been caused by an Irishman trying to retrieve a guard's stolen cap from the roof of his hut.

For his next scheme, van der Stok paired up with a Dutch naval officer. They had bribed some Russian workmen to leave a couple of shovels leaning against the wall of the shower block in the *Vorlager* and planned to slip away from a shower party, change into Soviet uniforms, and hang around the *Vorlager* until it was safe to make a try at the wire. The first part of the plan went smoothly but the prisoners were unable to fake the count at roll call and the Germans were alerted to the escapers' absence. The Germans immediately searched the area around the shower block, and the two Dutchmen were found.

*

November came to Sagan, and the prisoners prepared for another winter in the bag. The theater company's production of *French Without Tears* had just started, and the first dustings of snow were appearing on the compound. Escape plans continued, though, in an attempt to get a few more schemes under way before the weather made traveling impossible. Des Plunkett and Ivo Tonder had been keeping their eyes on a cart used to remove trash from a storage bin in the compound. They believed that if they could hide inside the cart, it would be possible to make a getaway from wherever the trash was dumped outside the wire.

With the help of Crump Ker-Ramsay, the two climbed into the cart late one afternoon and were covered with a solid layer of garbage. Unfortunately, it proved to be too solid a layer; every time one of them moved, the garbage settled down more heavily upon them and before long they found it impossible to breathe. Regretfully, they decided to vacate the cart and face the consequences. Accompanied by a great amount of noise as cans and bits of refuse clattered out of the bin, Des and Ivo pushed themselves upward and discovered to their surprise that no one had heard the commotion. They rearranged the heap and made their way back to their hut, vowing to try again the next day.

This time Crump covered them with just the right amount of garbage, but unfortunately someone dumped a load of hot ashes on top of the heap, and within minutes the two leaped out of the bin with their clothing smoldering. The Germans still appeared to take no notice of the incident but Des and Ivo were fed up with being entombed in garbage and decided to scrap the plan. Later that day the cart in which they had hidden was pulled to a spot between the warning wire and the main fence, where its load was dumped. Had the two stayed in the wagon, they would have been no further ahead.

*

After Toft and Nichols's bold attempt at the wire, the goons had made modifications to eliminate the blind spots. Extra guards were put outside the wire to patrol the perimeter, and the platforms on the guard towers were enlarged so that the sentries could step outside the boxes to scan the wire between the guard posts. However, for all their thoroughness, the Germans merely succeeded in creating different blind spots. With the larger platforms on the guard towers, there was now a fairly safe area directly below each box. It was simply a matter of diverting the attention of the guards in the adjacent towers while some brave soul climbed the wire right under the Germans' noses.

The brave soul this time was Flying Officer John Gifford Stower, a small, mustachioed sugar planter from Argentina. Born September 15, 1916, in Buenos Aires, Stower was educated in England but lived most of his early life on a huge farm in South America. He returned to England when the war began and enlisted in the RAF. By August 1942 he was flying 142 Squadron Wellingtons from Waltham. Operations were frequent during the late summer months of 1942, but there was a break in the action in October, and Stower took the opportunity to make a radio broadcast in Spanish back to Argentina, recounting some of his experiences over Germany. For his many friends in Buenos Aires, it was a treat to hear of the contribution of one of their own to the war effort. On November 16, 1942, Johnny's crew was assigned to join a minelaying operation to the North Sea coast. It was to be the dark and cheerful pilot's twenty-sixth operation. In the gloom of the late afternoon, the Wellington lifted off from base and droned toward the rendezvous point. The squadron waited for word on its progress, but nothing was heard. Months later, Johnny's aunt received a card from her nephew telling of the unfortunate end to their trip in the cold waters of the North Sea. 'We were eleven hours drifting in the dinghy,' Johnny wrote. 'We thought we were being washed onto a neutral coast but it was Germany and we were captured.'

A wanderer at heart with a pronounced adventurous streak, Johnny chafed more than most men at captivity. Though a newcomer to Sagan, he lost no time in asking to be considered for this next assault on the wire. Covered by the necessary diversions, he managed to get over the fences and was bolting across the open ground toward the woods when a sentry noticed him. As the guard let out a yell, Johnny's boot caught on a tree root and he went head over heels on the ground. By the time he gathered himself up again, he was well covered by quite a few rifles. As it happened, it was fortunate that Stower had stumbled and fallen, for the guards would not have let him get too much farther before opening fire. A protruding pine root may well have saved the little flier from a bullet in the back.

*

In the weeks following Johnny's attempt, the weather got progressively colder, and the snow began in earnest. The long *Appells* became more unpleasant as the temperature dropped, and one morning, while the Germans dawdled more than usual, at least one kriegie's patience wore a little thin. 'Now is the winter of our discontent,' intoned a stentorian voice from the back of the ranks, 'made more ghastly by this bastard from Bavaria!'

The deteriorating conditions didn't stop Danny Król and a cheerful reconnaissance pilot named Sydney Dowse from having a go at the wire. The London-born Dowse joined the RAF in July 1937 and was downed on August 20, 1941, while photographing the *Scharnhorst* and *Gneisenau* in a 1 PRU Spitfire. Wounded in the leg, Sydney came down off Brest and hoped to make his way quietly ashore and contact the Resistance. As he neared the beach, though, he was dismayed to see a crowd of young French women waving to him and shouting welcomes to *l'aviateur anglais;* they drew the attention of everyone within earshot, and Sydney was quickly captured.

Despite his injury, Dowse had already made two escape attempts. On December 1, 1941, he climbed over the gate of a prison camp hospital near Leipzig and traveled all the way to Roermond before being captured by a frontier guard three days later. Then, on January 21, 1942, he swapped places with a Canadian prisoner at Stalag IXC Bad Sulza and got out of the camp with a party of Belgian POWs. Sydney slipped away from the group in the German compound and hid in a latrine, where he peeled off the Belgian uniform to reveal a suit of civilian clothes. Playing the part of a workman, he pretended to inspect a waterwheel near the wire and, after a suitable amount of poking and peering, walked straight out of the gate. Sydney was without papers, maps, or a compass, but he did have a fair amount of German money and walked to the local station, where he boarded a train for Erfurt and, from there, to Cologne. With plans to cross into Belgium, he took a local train to a border town and began walking in the direction of Stavelot, in Belgium. After twenty-four hours of plodding, Sydney took refuge in a wood and, the next morning, found himself completely disoriented. He finally arrived at a small station and realized that he had been heading in the wrong direction. Undaunted, Dowse got a train back to his starting point and got set to try again.

However, the exertion of traveling was beginning to tell. The snow was two feet deep in places, and Sydney soon began to feel the effects of exhaustion and snow blindness. He wandered around in a daze for the next day and, when he finally regained his senses, he was in a railroad station attempting to buy a direct ticket to Brussels. Quickly realizing the folly of his action, Dowse beat a hasty retreat and hid in a wood for a few hours before starting to walk again. By the late evening of January 26 he had reached the German–Dutch frontier, where he was fired upon and arrested by border guards. Except for a case of frostbite, Sydney had nothing but experience to show for his troubles.

In spite of his experience as an escaper, Sydney's command of German was not good. He covered this up by learning a few stock phrases and bandaging his throat; then, if approached by anyone, he would reduce himself to paroxysms of coughing and spluttering in an effort to speak, and the inquisitive were usually scared off. By linking up with Danny Król, he could rely on the Pole's language ability.

Their assault on the wire at Sagan was simple. They would scale the unlit and unguarded wire between the officers' and NCOs' compounds, crawl across the latter camp using blankets as camouflage and then cut through the less well patrolled fence separating the NCOs' camp from the *Kommandantur*. The first half of their journey went without incident, but on their way through the wire into the *Kommandantur*, the pair was spotted by a guard, who opened fire on them. It was into the cooler again for Sydney and Danny. Their attempt marked the end of the 1942 escaping season at Sagan and, just like schoolboys, the kriegies took a break for Christmas.

*

It was a milder Christmas than the previous one, with little fresh snow to brighten the barren compound, but the airmen made the best of a bad situation. Red Cross parcels provided the necessary ingredients for a rather good Christmas cake, and there was also a beautiful midnight Mass featuring the Polish choir to bring a little seasonal spirit to Sagan. The New Year brought snow, and temperatures dropped enough to allow the prisoners to build another ice rink. It was officially opened on January 17, 1943, by the new SBO, Group Captain Herbert Massey, and there were enough Red Cross skates for every prisoner to have thirty minutes' skating time each day. The first day of the rink was reserved for a hockey tournament that saw two Canadian teams battle to a draw. Then an English team played the Americans, with the Brits narrowly winning by a goal.

For those who were more partial to indoor activities, the theater started again after Christmas and opened its production of Emlyn Williams's *Night Must Fall* at the end of January. Study increased in popularity during the cold months of early 1943, too. Peter Fanshawe's class in celestial navigation was well attended, and a number of kriegies took exams. Brian Evans passed his intermediate exam for auctioneers and real-estate agents, while Jack Grisman successfully completed examinations in English and math through the University of London. Meanwhile, Cookie Long had made a start on his new life by taking up economics, with textbooks that his family had sent from Foyle's in London.

Of course, language classes were as popular as ever. One could study Spanish with Tom Kirby-Green or Johnny Stower, and Des Plunkett learned Russian from the multilingual Wally Valenta. German lessons were available from any one of a dozen prisoners. Those given by Rene Marcinkus were very popular and drew officers from all nations. Marcinkus often gave each class in five or six languages, switching back and forth to answer the questions of his students.

In fact, just about every language imaginable could be learned in Luft III, from Chinese to Norwegian to Urdu. One fellow who tried his tongue at the Nordic language was a smiling Australian squadron leader named Jimmy Catanach. Jimmy always had to be doing something. His older brother said that he had more energy than a piece of radium, and his squadron commander remarked that he had never seen so much superfluous energy in anyone over the age of twelve. Jimmy never smoked or drank, and he talked at an incredible speed. Even in conversation he couldn't keep still for a moment but kept fidgeting and hopping around all the time. It would have been a most annoying habit if he hadn't been such a delightful fellow.

*

James Catanach had been an unexceptional child. Born on November 28, 1921, to a respected family of Melbourne jewelers, he was indistinguishable from the other boys at Geelong Grammar School, which he entered in 1932. Friends remember him as smallish and not outstanding in any way – he was an enthusiastic athlete and scout but rarely reached the first teams or troop leadership, and he usually obtained passes rather than honors. All enjoyed the company of the pleasant, blue-eyed boy, but few noticed anything remarkable about him.

Still, there was something special about Jimmy that came out when he was away from school. He had the laughing eyes and dazzling smile of his mother, and the ready sense of humor and delightful personality of his father – it was a combination that many found irresistible. During the summer vacation, Jimmy often went to stay with his aunt and uncle, the Cooleys, and their children, Alan, Barbara, Margery, and Helen. It was common knowledge that Jimmy was the one to ask favors of Mrs. Cooley for the rest of the children, for she found it difficult to refuse him. He was an imaginative and daring boy, and he loved to explore Mount Macedon and Hanging Rock with the Cooley children. The five spent many long hours together during those summers, and Jimmy grew very fond of his cousins.

Upon graduation from Geelong in 1938, Jimmy followed his elder brother, Bill, into the family jewelry business and started in the repair department at Catanach's. He was always a favorite with the staff, even before he joined them in the store. His childhood nanny even went so far as to take a job with the firm so she could be with him. When war came, the two Catanach boys were quick to enlist, Bill in the army and Jim in the air force, and both prepared to leave Melbourne for training. Before leaving, Jim spent a few of his final days at home with his cousins. As a parting gift, he gave his favorite antique engraved watch to Barb Cooley. 'Take care of it,' he told her as he left, 'and I'll fix it for you when I come home.'

It was August 1940 before Jim was called up for preliminary training, and in February 1941 he left Australia for Canada. By April he had earned his flying badge and commission and was posted to England, becoming operational with 144 Squadron in October. After nine missions with 144 Squadron, Jimmy was transferred to 455 Squadron RAAF, the first and most famous Australian bomber squadron, in December. If there had been any doubt about Jim's potential, it was finally dispelled in 455 Squadron. He and his crew quickly made a name for themselves on the Hampdens flown by the squadron. Their first operation was on December 27–28, 1941, when the squadron joined in a raid on Düsseldorf. Over the next few months they completed various bombing and minelaying operations and on March 13, 1942, flew their last mission as a bomber crew, to Cologne. Soon after leaving the target area, the Hampden took a burst of flak that ripped into the nose of the aircraft and partially blinded Jim; his only words to the crew were 'Boys, I think we'd better be going home now.' It was the third time he had brought back a badly damaged aircraft, and on April 11 he was rewarded with a promotion to flight lieutenant.

At about the same time, 455 Squadron was transferred to Coastal Command and posted to Leuchars in Scotland to begin training as a torpedo bomber squadron. Jim's reputation as a pilot continued to grow, and in June he was promoted to squadron leader, becoming the youngest to hold that rank in the RAAF and the RAF. On June 26, 1942, he was awarded the DFC. Still only twenty years of age, Jim seemed assured of future success in the air force. The work at Leuchars consisted mostly of training exercises, with odd sweeps over the North Sea to keep the crews sharp. Jimmy described one of these missions in the fall of 1942: 'The other night we were ordered to investigate a big merchantman off the Norwegian coast. Within ninety minutes, the squadron was briefed and airborne, heading over the moonless sea toward a 350 miles' distant dot on the ocean. We reached Norway as dawn was breaking, searched the shipping lanes, saw nothing, and headed for home. Mostly, it is just like that.'

In late August the crews learned the details of the mission for which they had been training. Sixteen aircraft from 455 Squadron, as well as sixteen from 144 Squadron, each carrying an extra ground crewman, were to fly to Sumburgh in the Shetlands, and on to Murmansk in Russia. From there they would fly torpedo missions against a German naval force that was operating against the Allied Arctic convoys. In all respects it was a dangerous mission. The distance to be flown approached the flight limit of the Hampden, allowing little or no room for errors in navigation or fuel consumption calculation. Maps of the area were unreliable, and radio aids for navigation and landing were nonexistent. To cap it all off, the meteorologists predicted awful weather for the entire flight. The prospects were not at all encouraging for what was to be the last operation of Catanach's tour.

The squadron left Leuchars on September 2 and, after final preparations and refueling, flew from Sumburgh at 9:00 P.M. on September 4. In typical fashion, Jimmy couldn't restrain himself to wait his turn to take off. He taxied into the first gap in the line and roared down the runway. Each crew drew up their own route and, like the others, Jimmy's navigator had elected to turn north near Trondheim, make height to clear the mountains, and hopefully pick up their bearings at first light. It wasn't much of a flight plan, but it was the best anyone could do.

The flight across the North Sea was uneventful and, passing Trondheim, Jimmy wheeled his Hampden north toward Narvik. As dawn broke, the aircraft was over Finnmark, the crew searching for some recognizable feature to pinpoint their position and guide them the rest of the way to Murmansk. With less than an hour's flying time to go, it looked as though they would reach their destination with fuel to spare.

As they flew over Vadsø, things began to go wrong. A burst of ground fire holed the tanks and damaged the control panel and one engine, leaving Jimmy with the difficult task of crash-landing the aircraft. Fortunately there were a few available open spaces and he was able to bring the Hampden in wheels-up on a heather flat not far from a beach. The crew piled out of the plane, only to find themselves trapped between a small gunboat offshore and a party of soldiers in white coveralls. They were unsure of which way to go, but a few rounds from the boat's light gun convinced the airmen to try the soldiers. Since they had no visible insignia, Jimmy hoped that they might be Norwegian and called out, '*Sprechen Sie Deutsch?*' (Do you speak German?) only to receive the disheartening reply, '*Ja, ich spreche Deutsch – ich bin Deutsch!*' (Yes, I speak German – I am German!). The crew's fate was sealed.

Their first days in captivity were spent in a muddy labor camp for Soviet prisoners, but they were soon sent south in the company of a party of guards on leave. From Rovaniemi, the five were flown to Helsinki to spend the night in a civilian jail. The next day they were flown to Frankfurt and tossed into solitary confinement. By mid-September Jimmy was in Stalag Luft III. Like Arnold Christensen, Jimmy Catanach was still only twenty years of age.

*

Shortly after the New Year, the prisoners noticed signs of activity in the woods beyond the wire. Parties of workmen were felling trees, and soon a rough compound had been cleared. When questioned, Pieber revealed that the airmen would be moving as soon as the compound was ready, probably in March. Immediately, Roger Bushell's mind went to work. Ever since arriving at Dulag Luft, he had been planning for a big escape, one that would really throw Germany into a panic. Individual attempts were fine as minor irritants, but Bushell knew that a big escape would tie down thousands of soldiers and auxiliaries and really make a difference to the war effort. Now, with an impending move to a new compound, Bushell saw his chance.

That afternoon, Roger called together his lieutenants. 'We know that the goons are putting up a new compound and Pieber says that most of us will be moving. I want to decide on a plan of action now, so that we can start work as soon as we move.' He looked around at his cohorts – Wally Floody, Johnny Bull, Conk Canton, and Johnny Marshall – who all nodded in agreement.

As he went on, it became clear that Roger had done a fair bit of thinking on the subject already. 'I'd like to try some new ideas this time. First of all, I want to start three tunnels instead of just one. That way, if the goons find one, or even two, we still have one in reserve. Now, this will require a pretty massive organization, so to keep things under control I'm going to outlaw any private tunnels. I don't want the main scheme competing for resources with half a dozen other efforts. Besides, there's going to be enough sand coming out of the three main tunnels that we won't need any more from smaller holes.'

Roger continued, sounding all the more determined as he spoke. 'Finally, we're not going to work to a deadline. Security is going to be paramount – if the goons get in a snit over something, I'm quite prepared to close up shop completely for a couple of weeks until the fuss dies down. Oh, and by the way, I don't want to hear the word 'tunnel' again – we'll call the three Tom, Dick, and Harry. Any questions?'

'How soon can we decide on the directions?' asked Bull.

'Well, being the philanthropic people that we are, I thought we'd volunteer to send over a few work parties to help with the new compound. They can make a preliminary survey of the layout, so we should have a pretty good idea of the best locations before we even move,' answered Roger.

'You said there would be no private tunneling,' brought up Conk, 'but what about other schemes – will you still allow the odd wire job?'

'Yes, I think we'll have to – if we stop attempts altogether, even the goons will figure out that something's up. But they'll be more tightly controlled than before. I want an overall planning committee in charge of individual attempts. Conk, you'll be the wire expert, and Norman Quill will handle gate escapes. If anyone has a plan, they'll have to go through these chaps first. Once they get the okay at that level, they'll come before the whole planning committee. What I don't want are efforts that will rile the goons for no good reason. That's not what we're here for.'

'By the way,' went on Roger, 'we're going to have a bigger escape committee than ever before as well – we'll be needing a hell of a lot of gear to put this plan into action. Once we get into the new compound, I'll thrash out the details with the individual department heads on the circuit. The main thing is to get the plans set now. Well, if there are no more questions, I thought I heard Johnny Marshall invite us all to tea!'

'I must have missed that,' said Marshall with a groan, 'not that that will stop you hungry bastards! But one more question, Roger. How many do you think we can get out?'

'The first night, I plan to put two hundred through. Then we can close up the hole, and if it survives the searches, we can send out another lot later.' In a mood of buoyant confidence, the group left Roger's room to claim their tea.

*

As the new compound progressed, parties of kriegies went over to lend a hand. They moved piles of wood from here to there, stacked bedboards, and pulled up tree stumps. They carried around sacks of concrete, shifted bales of tar paper, and filled in holes. They were being, by all appearances, exceedingly helpful.

However, they also paced off distances from various huts to the perimeter wire and made notes of exactly where the guard towers stood. They drew up a detailed plan of the new compound and scouted around individual huts to see where tunnels might be started. And, in a moment of weakness, one of the prisoners stole a blueprint for the compound's underground drainage system. He carried it back crammed down his trouser leg and proudly presented it to Roger later in the evening. When he saw it, Bushell's face lit up with an evil smile. He showed it to his lieutenants, and they discovered that there were a couple of perfectly placed drains. They started in convenient huts and ran very close to the perimeter wire. If the drains were big enough, they might provide the escape organization with a prefabricated tunnel. An examination of the drains would be the first item on the agenda, Roger said.

It was still quite cold for spring, and prisoners coming to Sagan from the North African campaign found their desert kit entirely unsuitable. One who came from the fighting in Tunisia was a Canadian pilot named George William Wiley, whose boyish face made him look incredibly young. His first letter home spoke about the cold, and his parents were quick to assemble a parcel of warm clothes. They still had in their minds the voice of their son, heard just a few months before.

Each Christmas Day it was customary for the traditional message from the king to be prefaced by personal greetings from a number of Allied servicemen. On December 25, 1942, as the radio crackled to life in the home of the Wiley family, they listened expectantly for the voice of their son George, speaking from a Cairo hospital where he was nursing a broken leg. The voice seemed full of life and hope, yet so muffled and distant that the Wileys were saddened by the reminder that their only son was spending another Christmas away from home.

Born in Windsor, Ontario, on January 24, 1922, George Wiley developed at an early age a marked happy-go-lucky streak. At school the young Wiley displayed academic potential but often found other pursuits more to his liking. The alleys around his home provided no end of fun, and George spent many hours lost in play with Johnny Jones and the other kids on the street. During the winter they would skate at a nearby park or wander around the yards heaving snowballs at one another. The worst effects of the Depression were still around the corner, and it was a good time to be a kid.

While still a boy, though, George was struck by rheumatic fever, which confined him to bed for months and caused him to lose a year in school. It also left him with a slight limp, which he eventually lost, though his leg never regained its full strength. He wasn't about to let the fever interrupt his boyhood fun, and as soon as he was well enough to see friends, Johnny Jones was allowed to visit with his American Flyer electric train. The two boys screamed with delight as George's engine raced Johnny's around the little metal track, and Mrs. Wiley soon gave up admonishing them for their noisiness.

When he started high school, George Wiley decided to try his hand at football and swimming but was still more partial to extracurricular activities. He and John Jones often went fishing together, baiting with worms they had coaxed from their holes with mustard solution. They also spent their share of afternoons in the theater, gorging themselves on peanuts and making a bit too much noise, as boys usually do. George had a knack for carrying a tune and could always pick out the musical numbers on his trumpet after the show.

As he grew older, George's fun-loving streak became more pronounced. One day, he and a couple of buddies decided to cut class and hitchhike out of town for the day. Once out of the city, the wanderlust caught them and they didn't return for almost a week, having hitched over five hundred miles to Montreal. They were brought up for disciplinary action before the principal, who was already familiar with George and his pals. He had spoken with them once before about their Model T Ford, painted in the school colors of blue and gold, for which they had each chipped in five dollars. Apparently the principal didn't think that this type of publicity was suitable for the school parking lot.

As he had in the past, George spent the summer months of 1939 with his older sister at Port Stanley on Lake Erie. This year he had arranged to meet John Jones there, and the two were to hitch back to Windsor together. John arrived on the first day of September to find his buddy fishing off a pier, 'for our food,' as he put it; the Depression was in full swing, and with no money left, the family was literally surviving on what remained in the cupboards. That night George and John went for a walk in the country, ambling off down the road carrying an empty suitcase. A few hours later the boys returned, their suitcase stuffed with fresh vegetables. 'It'll get us through the weekend,' George remarked nonchalantly. It was a significant weekend, the last normal one before the lights went out.

On the way home, the boys noticed armed guards at one of the hydro stations and talked about joining up. They took their medicals for enlistment but, because of the number of recruits signing up, it was December 4, 1940, before George was taken into the RCAF in Windsor. He left for training shortly after and, in September 1941, received his wings and commission at Summerside, Prince Edward Island. Later in September Wiley arrived in England, sailing for North Africa in May 1942. In August he was posted to 112 Squadron near Alexandria to fly Kittyhawk fighters on armed reconnaissance sweeps, ground support missions, and cover for bomber raids. He reached the unit during a period of calm, but it wasn't long before the squadron was back in action.

His first two months with the squadron went without incident but on October 7, 1942, George's aircraft was jumped by fighters and forced to land just behind Allied lines. He circled to put the Kittyhawk down but had the misfortune to land in a minefield. The fighter hit a mine that blew off one wing and fractured George's leg and ankle. At the hospital in Cairo, a pin was inserted in the leg, but the limb, weakened by rheumatic fever, took longer to heal than usual. His parents hoped that their son would be invalided home, but in his Christmas greeting Wiley firmly stated his intention to get back to the squadron as soon as he was fit.

He returned on January 13, 1943, despite the fact that his leg was still weak, and was operational again almost immediately. Bad luck continued to plague George, for soon after getting back to combat, he had another run-in with German fighters and returned to base with more than forty holes in his aircraft. The ground crew were amazed that a Kittyhawk with such extensive air-conditioning still could fly.

Through the early months of 1943, the squadron moved west through Egypt, Libya, and Tripolitania and by March had reached Tunisia, where it was assigned to fly support missions for the Eighth Army's assault on the Mareth Line. On March 10, 112 Squadron was assigned to fly cover for a Free French force that was crossing the Sahara to join the Allies. With two other fighter squadrons flying top cover for 112, it should have been a routine mission, but the supporting squadrons somehow lost touch, and 112 was jumped by enemy fighters. The Kittyhawks simply couldn't hold their own against the superior Me 109s and six machines were shot down, including

George Wiley's. It was third time unlucky for George. Unable to find his direction, he wandered the desert for two days before being picked up by a German patrol. It was just as well that he was found, for his weak leg probably would not have carried him much farther. After spending a couple of days in a German compound in North Africa, he was transported to Italy and, from there, to Luft III. He arrived just as big things were happening.

Chapter 8

NORTH COMPOUND OPENS

By THE SPRING OF 1943, the Luftwaffe had decided to move all of the NCOs out of the Sagan complex and convert the camp into an officers' facility. In preparation for the influx of new prisoners, labor battalions had been hard at work constructing new compounds around Luft III's *Kommandantur*, which was gradually becoming an administrative island in the middle of a sea of POWs. The inmates of the camp had watched the construction with considerable interest, and in March they learned that the new facility was ready to receive them. It was clear from conversations with guards that the camp staff intended the new compound to be more escape-proof than their old home. For their part, the escape leaders had chosen it as the battleground for their largest escape offensive.

*

Sagan's new compound was finally ready in March, and the prisoners began trailing over on the twenty-seventh. An advance party went first, followed by the Poles, the Americans, and finally the rest of the group. In all, 850 kriegies made the move to what became known as North Compound. A couple of weeks later, another fifty were moved in from Warburg.

North Compound was essentially the same as East, as their old camp became known. It was roughly 350 yards square, with perimeter fences nine feet high and five feet apart and the warning wire fully thirty feet from the main fence. Every 150 yards or so, there was a guard tower. The fifteen barrack blocks were arranged in three rows. Nearest to the gate were Huts 101 and 103 to 106; then came 107 to 110 and 112, and finally 119 to 123. In the middle of the compound was a firepool, and the main kitchen block was situated between Huts 110 and 112. A small *Vorlager* adjoined North Compound and contained the guard room, the hospital, the coal store, and, of course, the cooler.

Each block had eighteen rooms, that accommodated four officers each, and three or four designed for two men. There was also a washroom with a concrete floor, a lavatory, and a small kitchen equipped with a coal stove with two burners and an oven. All in all, the rooms looked quite comfortable. Each was equipped with bunk beds, a dry sink for washing up dishes, and a large table that became the center of activity in the rooms. Upright lockers were provided for the prisoners to store their kit, and there was also a small stove for cooking and heating. The Germans allowed the kriegies to make changes in the rooms to make them more comfortable. All of the furniture was movable, and could be shifted around quite easily. Some rooms moved their stove out from the wall a bit and put a bench behind it, while others took their bunk beds apart and made single beds. Later, when the number of prisoners in each room increased to six, eight, and more, some of the upright lockers were moved into the corridors to leave extra space within the room itself.

If you could find the materials, you could make your own furnishings. Some fellows made rather nice armchairs from Red Cross packing cases, while others made stools, bookcases, and shelves. Nearly every room had a large map of Europe on the wall; the course of the war was charted and discussed at length. Whenever the day's BBC news came in, received on a radio made from parts bribed from guards and read in the huts by a staff of 'newscasters,' the kriegies could be found clustered around their maps, shifting the pins and bits of string that marked the front lines.

True to his word, Roger's first act in the new compound was to send Henry Lamond down to look at the drains. Eventually the little New Zealander reappeared, covered with grease and with a sour look on his face.

'Not a hope,' he said disconsolately and formed a circle about six inches across with his hands. The assembled diggers groaned.

'Hardly surprising, really,' put in Roger. 'The goons have been very careful with this compound – we shouldn't really have imagined they would slip up on something like that. Not to worry – we can start on the real work as soon as the lads settle down and get the moving jitters out of their systems.'

Faced with a new compound and a whole new batch of possibilities, escape fever hit the men to such an extent that X Organization (the Stalag Luft III escape organization) had to waive its traditional right to authorize all attempts. Roger was happy to pass on his blessings (along with a map and a compass) to any game kriegie who approached him, but most were content to have a bash at the first opportune moment.

The most popular means of escape was the trucks used to carry out branches from the pine trees that were being felled in the compound. As the trucks drove past the huts, dozens of POWs leaped from the roofs into the evergreen boughs and burrowed down as far as they could. It was such a popular method that it became difficult to find a truck that didn't already have a number of would-be escapers hiding in the branches; Johnny Stower was pulled off a truck with four other fliers. Red Noble managed to get a truck all to himself and made it through the gate unseen. Unfortunately, he had been advised by the escape organization to vacate the truck as soon as possible, and he clambered down into the hands of a row of guards lining the road away from the camp.

Some were spotted even before they got into the trucks. Les Harvey was just about to hop into one of the trucks when he noticed that Rubberneck was watching him with a half-amused smile. Luckily, Harvey was able to clear out quickly enough to avoid a spell in the cooler. Others were not so fortunate and fell prey to the pitchforks wielded by the guards. They limped to solitary, nursing nasty puncture wounds to go along with their wounded pride.

Australian Geoff Cornish and Czech Ivo Tonder were a bit more creative and decided to take advantage of the parties of Soviet prisoners who came into the camp to cut down trees. Wearing Polish Army greatcoats and a few days' growth of beard, they slipped into opposite ends of a group of Soviets shuffling toward the gate and were all set to amble to freedom when Tonder heard a call from one of the tower goons. Realizing that the game was up, Ivo slipped out of the borrowed greatcoat and made a dash for the nearest bunch of kriegies. Cornish, however, didn't hear the guard's cry until it was too late and soon found his entire party surrounded by rifle-toting sentries trying to locate the interloper. Ever game, the Soviets pushed forward one of their own number, who, despite his protestations, they claimed was the Englander. By this time the gate guard was a little suspicious and called for Pieber, who recognized Cornish and pulled him out of the group for a stretch in the now-bulging cooler. There he was given a nickname by a couple of guards amused by his bedraggled appearance. They christened him Ivan der Schrecklich (Ivan the Terrible).

Out of all these attempts, only one worked: two Americans of the RAF Eagle squadrons, who succeeded because of their diminutive size. Instead of jumping from the roof of a hut, they climbed into one of the remaining pine trees and dropped onto the truck canopy from the cover of the upper branches. The two burrowed under the canopy deep enough to avoid discovery and soon found themselves outside the wire. Ill-equipped as they were, though, they didn't get far and were picked up the next day to join their fellow intrepids in the cooler.

Shortly after this, Red Noble decided to tackle the ash cart, which collected the refuse from the camp incinerators and deposited it outside the wire. With a staged brawl as a diversion, Noble climbed into the wagon and buried himself in the ashes, ready to dig his way out when the cart was out of sight of the camp. However, when the time came, he discovered with dismay that he had buried himself too deeply and couldn't get out from under the heavy mass of damp ashes. Cursing heartily, he waited helplessly as the cart trundled past the planned escape point and straight into East Compound, where the filthy Canadian was pulled out by a guard who noticed him struggling under the ashes.

*

Two who missed the first days in North Compound were Canadian Kingsley Brown and a strongly built fighter pilot named Gordon Brettell. While construction was going on in the new compound, Gordon and Kingsley swapped places with a couple of orderlies from one of the work parties and concealed themselves in a hut near the wire. Pieber made a cursory search of the barrack but did not spot the two, who were hidden in a pile of palliasses. When night fell, it was easy to slip away through the unguarded wire. By way of disguise, Gordon and Kingsley, both fluent in German, decided to go as Bulgarian steelworkers traveling between factories and were fully equipped with passports, maps, money, and safe addresses in Mulhouse and Strasbourg. They were to make the first part of the journey west on foot and then pick up a train for the rest of the trip to the French frontier.

The two left Luft III on March 27, 1943, and doubled back to the south before heading west. It was a crisp and clear night, ideal for traveling, and they made good progress through the pine trees. Once or twice they had to take cover while patrolling policemen cycled by on a narrow logging track, but apart from that, the first night went without incident. After another day's walking through forests, broken by an occasional bold stroll along a secondary highway, Gordon and Kingsley decided they were far enough away from Sagan to risk the train and made for the station in the town of Sorau. They bought third-class tickets for Kottbus, where they got off and had a hot meal in the station restaurant before boarding a train to Leipzig.

An odd incident occurred on that leg of the journey. Gordon and Kingsley found themselves in a compartment with five German soldiers and were eventually joined by a sixth, who was proudly wearing the uniform of the Afrika Korps. He looked haughtily at the gray-clad soldiers before sitting down and, after a brief pause, began to recount the glories of his own unit. Egged on by the obvious envy of the other soldiers, he became ever more animated and described not only his army's equipment, but their present whereabouts and impending movements as well.

The escapers listened with interest to the monologue, for, ironically, the young soldier was sitting directly beneath a large and lurid propaganda poster that screamed, 'BEWARE THE THIRD PERSON!! THE ENEMY HAS EARS!!' This incongruity tickled Gordon's sense of humor, and he rustled a newspaper in front of his face so he could whisper to Kingsley.

'You know,' he breathed, 'I have a good mind to tap that lad on the knee, point to that sign, and say: "Be careful, old boy, for all you know we might be British officers."' The comment was completely in character, for to say that Gordon Brettell had a touch of daring was an understatement. Indeed, he had already come through his fair share of close scrapes, most of which were due to a powerful inner voice that prodded him into attempting some rather dangerous deeds. Though he never took foolish risks, he was never one to shy away from a challenge.

Gordon once had occasion to visit an attraction at London Olympia known as the Wall of Death, in which a rider named 'Tornado' Smith drove a motorcycle around a steep metal bowl until, at the end of the display, he was riding around the inside of the vertical wall of the bowl. His sense of adventure piqued, Gordon decided to investigate further and asked if Smith took passengers on the ride. An oily mechanic said he certainly did, but that he would have to sit on the gasoline tank with his legs flopped over the handlebars and no other means of support.

Brettell had never felt comfortable on motorcycles at the best of times, and the prospect of this type of ride was more than he could take; he melted off into the crowd and wandered away.

As soon as Gordon left Olympia, his conscience 'stood up on its hind legs and never left me alone,' as he later wrote to his sister. An inner voice began telling him that he had funked the Wall of Death, waking him up in the morning and hounding him when he went to bed. 'You consider yourself game to try most things once. You proclaim in a loud voice that if there was a war you would join the air force,' it told him mercilessly, 'and you funked the Wall of Death.' Brettell could take it no longer. He bought a ticket to London and headed straight for Olympia. The crew was surprised to see him back but helped him onto Smith's motorcycle, and the two started their trip around the Wall of Death. It wasn't a very good ride, for as soon as they reached the vertical portion, Gordon shifted on the handlebars and Smith had to slow down or lose control. Nevertheless, the Wall of Death had been conquered, and Gordon and his conscience were reconciled. 'I must go again for a proper run sometime,' he wrote, 'but there's no particular hurry!'

Born on March 19, 1915, in Pyrford, Surrey, Edward Gordon Brettell grew up with his younger siblings, Cynthia and Terence, in Chertsey. He had his first serious scrape at age fifteen, when he underwent surgery for mastoiditis. The infection spread over the left side of his face and, even with several more operations, it was feared that he might not live. The lad was a tough fighter, though, and pulled through eventually, in spite of occasional blackouts. In time, all that remained of his illness were the scars on his face.

Like many boys of the era, Gordon early in life developed an interest in flying, but that was soon overtaken by another love. In 1932 an uncle took Gordon to a motor race at nearby Brooklands, and the boy returned home bubbling with enthusiasm. When he and Terence went again later in the year, it was enough to get them hooked. The two brothers went to every possible race, but it wasn't until Gordon entered Clare College, Cambridge, in 1936 that he was able to get involved in motor racing. He became secretary of the Cambridge University Motor Club and converted a little Austin Seven into a two-seat racing machine with a top speed of seventy miles per hour. Though his promising entry in the last race of 1936 came to nothing because of mechanical problems, Gordon's appetite was well and truly whetted. He moved up to a faster car, an Austin Ulster, which he converted into a very narrow single-seater, and in the Easter Monday races of 1937 took a first and a third, to the amazement of the organizers. His next race was the prestigious British Mountain Handicap and, because of his fine but rather cheeky showing at Easter, the organizers slapped Gordon with a heavy handicap. In an effort to overcome the deficit and secure a place in the final, he pulled out all the stops and drove hell bent for leather in the heats. Brettell was on the verge of winning a place when he took one of the corners too quickly and soared over the high banking of Brooklands. In the words of a reporter, he 'arrived in *crescendo* when *pianissimo* would have done' and came to rest upside down in the trees over the banking. His left arm fractured in six places, Gordon was sidelined. At the speed he was traveling, he was lucky to be alive.

Remarkably, he was fit to race again by early July, and he continued to do well through the rest of the 1937 season. The following year saw further success and, in what would be his last race, Brettell overtook a number of newer and faster cars to take fourth place. Unfortunately, the racing budget had always been tight, and in late 1938 the money simply ran out. Gordon hoped to team up with a friend for the 1939 Donington Tourist Trophy Race, but his plans were interrupted by the coming of war.

Refused entry into the Cambridge University Air Squadron on medical grounds in 1936, Gordon now saw his chance to get into flying, and he and Terence volunteered for service in the RAF. Much to their surprise, they were received with less than open arms by a brusque recruitment officer who simply took their names, told them to await further notification, and bade them good day. The two dutifully waited for the promised communication, but when no word came, they decided to take jobs at the Vickers factory at Brooklands to make themselves useful.

It wasn't until June 18, 1940, that they were called up for medicals, and Terence promptly failed because of a bout of flu. Gordon, however, passed the medical and began training in September. It was well worth the wait, though, for he loved the training exercises and obviously enjoyed flying as much as motor racing. On one occasion he took Terence up in a Miles Magister trainer and, after flying around for a spell, decided to buzz the family home. As the little aircraft screamed earthward, Terence watched the airspeed indicator with delight as it nudged past 145 miles per hour and approached 150. Back on the ground, Gordon later apologized for a rather tame flight. 'I didn't go very fast,' he said to Terence. 'I'm told the wings are apt to come off at 140!'

By February 1941 Brettell had completed his training and was commissioned, spending a month with 58 OTU before being posted to the venerable 92 Squadron at Biggin Hill on March 31. For the rest of 1941 he took part in many sweeps over the Continent and was once wounded in action. On that occasion, in September 1941, Gordon became separated from his mates and was on the way home alone when he spotted two Messerschmitts winging in the other direction. As he craned his head around to check the sun for marauding 109s, nine of the enemy came out of the glare and harried him all the way to the French coast. He was faring quite well when, turning to avoid one fighter, he strayed into the path of another and took some cannon shells in the wing and cockpit. Badly wounded in the head, Gordon radioed to Biggin that he was going down into the sea and blacked out. As the Spitfire spiraled down, he slowly came to and, in his own words, 'my black world was turning red and I could dimly see the red nose of the Spitfire pointing down to the deep red sea.' He found the Spit sluggish and was still unable to shake his attackers, who continued to come at him 'like a ton of bricks, shooting so prolifically that it was almost funny.' Again, luck smiled on Gordon, for the 109s soon had to turn back, and Brettell was left alone to nurse the wounded aircraft to England. He picked the first flat land that appeared and made a decent landing before passing out.

Brettell was awarded the DFC for his gallantry and received a well-deserved rest from flying duties to heal his injuries. On January 6, 1942, he went back into action, this time with 124 Squadron, and flew with them until late July. On August 2 the newly promoted Flight Lieutenant Brettell arrived at 133 Squadron, one of the famed RAF Eagle squadrons.

The Americans quickly took to Gordon, whom they regarded as a typical English gentleman. It wasn't long, too, before Gordon was making his mark in the squadron. Over Dieppe on August 19, he had a share in destroying three German aircraft and damaging seven more. However, he also made his mark in another way. At one boisterous party on the base, Gordon persuaded a young WAAF to remain a little longer with the promise that he would fly her back to her station after the party. In the early-morning hours, he squeezed the girl into the cockpit of a Spitfire and, as promised, scooted her home. Unfortunately, she left her cap in the aircraft, and embarrassing questions were asked. It was a seemingly harmless act, but Gordon was reprimanded by the station commander and told to await court-martial for ferrying an unauthorized passenger in a squadron aircraft. He was never to see that court-martial.

On September 26, 1942, 133 Squadron was ordered to escort a flight of USAAF B-17s to the Focke-Wulf plant at Morlaix on the Brittany peninsula. With the unit's commanding officer away in London, command of the squadron fell to Gordon Brettell, who was to lead what should have been a fairly straightforward mission. Instead, tragedy struck. A headwind of thirty-five knots had been forecast but, at 18,000 feet, the aircraft were in a tailwind that approached one hundred knots. Unbeknownst to them, they were being carried far south above a thick blanket of clouds, and it wasn't until the bombers reached the foothills of the Pyrenees that they decided something was amiss and turned for home. As they turned north, so, too, did the Spitfires of 133 Squadron.

Gordon and his squadronmates retraced their path until they neared the English coast and then dropped down to break through the thick cloud cover. The Spits came into clear sky at 3,000 feet and saw ahead of them a south coastline with a large city. Assuming it to be either Plymouth or Portsmouth, they swung around toward it and tightened up in close formation to make an impressive fly-by for the townsfolk. Tragically, they were still unaware of the meteorological blunder and didn't realize that they had been flying into the teeth of a hundred-knot headwind. Below them was not Portsmouth but Brest, on the south coast of the Brittany peninsula, the most heavily defended city in western France.

With the Spits in close formation, the German flak gunners couldn't miss. They shot down every single aircraft from 133 Squadron. Gordon Brettell's Spitfire received a direct hit in the wing root that jammed the cockpit cover and sent the fighter careening. It was all he could do to keep the aircraft close to an even keel as it plowed into the ground. When German soldiers reached the wreck, they were astonished to find the pilot still alive and dragged him from the twisted aircraft. With multiple fractures in both legs and a host of other injuries, Gordon was rushed to a hospital. He recovered with his usual speed and reached Stalag Luft III in time for Christmas.

*

Now, just four months after arriving in Sagan, Gordon was on the run on a train headed from Leipzig to Chemnitz. With any luck, he and Kingsley might make it to Nuremberg by nightfall. By a stroke of misfortune, though, that city had recently been heavily bombed, and travel into it was severely restricted. The ticket clerk at Chemnitz main station became suspicious and, in spite of their forged papers and prepared stories, Gordon and Kingsley were detained for questioning. They were clapped into a tiny cell at the train station, where Gordon scratched on the wall Rupert Brooke's lines: 'If I should die, think only this of me: that there's some corner of a foreign field that is forever England.' He was the archetypal romantic.

Things took a turn for the worse when the pair were turned over to the Gestapo for questioning. The fellow who interrogated them from behind a huge desk covered with telephones demanded to know their exact movements for the entire trip. Next, they were shown a series of German soldiers and were instructed to identify each man's rank, presumably to determine whether they were familiar with military rank. Having passed that part with honors, the interview suddenly took a different tone. The Gestapo boss asked why they had escaped in the first place. When they replied that it was the duty of every prisoner to attempt to return to his unit, the German leaped out of his chair, beat the desk with his fist, and barked, 'Yes, it is your duty to escape!'

While Gordon and Kingsley tried to figure out what he was driving at, the chief smiled and told them that he had been captured during the First World War and had escaped and returned to his unit. Then he left the room for a minute and returned with a man of roughly the same age. 'This man,' he said proudly, 'was my comrade in that prison camp in France. He, too, escaped, but like you, he was recaptured.' The two Germans were obviously quite pleased with their own achievement, and the conversation continued in a friendly manner for a few minutes. Then the Gestapo chief said they were being sent back to the camp and ordered the guards to escort them out. As they were leaving the office, he called toward them, 'Better luck next time!' It was probably the most pleasant Gestapo interrogation of the war.

Back in the camp, Gordon was pressed for details about the escape but told the story in his typical understated fashion. He had always been known as a modest man, very quiet and self-effacing, and never wore or even mentioned his DFC in the camp. He told the tale of their escape in his quiet, measured voice, giving Kingsley most of the credit for their success.

*

During those first few days in North Compound, Roger Bushell met many times with his new escape committee, both individually and as a group. It was a committee made up of both old and new faces. As usual, there was Tim Walenn the forger; Des Plunkett the mapmaker; and Conk Canton, in charge of food and wire schemes. Overall security was the responsibility of Junior Clark. The tunnel committee, as before, was made up of Crump Ker-Ramsay, Johnny Marshall, and Les Bull. Tommy Guest was again in charge of the tailors, while Bob Stanford-Tuck became the new custodian of escape supplies. Information received from the ferrets was passed on to the head of contact intelligence, Czech Wally Valenta.

Because of his previous military service, Flight Lieutenant Arnost 'Wally' Valenta was anxious to avoid German scrutiny, choosing instead to carry on the fight behind the scenes. Born on October 25, 1912, in Svebehov in northern Moravia, a partly Germanized region of Czechoslovakia, Arnost Valenta grew up an ardent patriot, thanks to the linguistic strife around him. Disturbed by events in Germany in the early 1930s, Valenta applied to become a cadet at an infantry reserve officers' school in 1933. The following year, he was accepted into the Czech military academy at Hranice. In July 1936 he graduated from the course and was commissioned in the 39th Infantry Regiment at Bratislava. At the same time, Valenta applied to study military history at Comenius University in Bratislava and soon became a recognized authority on the subject. For the benefit of the other officers in the regiment, he gave lectures, organized discussion groups, and arranged exhibitions on subjects ranging from the Peace of Pressburg to the doctrines of Clausewitz. His studies were interrupted by a bout of jaundice, but Valenta had nearly finished the requirements for his degree when events intervened.

When the Nazi Party branches in the Czech border districts began to cause trouble, Valenta, who was fluent in German, was dispatched to western Bohemia with a picked platoon of men. He remained there, attempting to keep order, until September 1938, when he returned to his unit in Bratislava. Later, when Hitler offered parts of southern Slovakia to Hungarian Admiral Miklos Horthy as a sop for his support of Munich and the *Anschluss*, Valenta helped with the evacuation of the Slovak population. In the months before the Nazi invasion of Czechoslovakia, Valenta worked at demobilizing the reserve troops and bringing his company back to a peacetime footing. Ordered to swear allegiance to Hitler's puppet state of independent Slovakia, Valenta and four of his fellow lieutenants refused because it was contrary to their original officers' oath to the Czech Republic. Fearing arrest for their action, they planned to escape to Yugoslavia, the nearest friendly country, but instead headed north through the Tatra Mountains to Poland. They arrived on March 15, 1939, the date of Hitler's invasion of Prague.

Since the border between Poland and Czechoslovakia had been closed, the Poles knew little of what was happening to the south of them and were eager to hear the news from the five Czechs. Passed quickly to Warsaw, they went immediately to the Czech embassy to see what the military attaché could suggest. Given the choice of joining the French Foreign Legion or the Soviets or throwing in their lot with the Poles, the five decided on the latter. After debriefings by the Polish Army and the Foreign Office, it was proposed that they return to Czechoslovakia to gather information on the Germany Army in occupation. They readily agreed and, after rudimentary intelligence training, were smuggled back into occupied Czechoslovakia on April 9, 1939. They remained in the country for nearly five months, escaping back to Poland on August 28, 1939.

Valenta and his comrades joined the Czechoslovak Legion near Cracow and, after the German invasion of Poland, were evacuated to northeastern Poland. Caught between the advancing German and Soviet armies, the legion traveled over the Prypet marshes to Lwow in the hopes of reaching Romania, the nearest safe haven. The 850-man column was easy to spot, and south of Lwow their luck ran out. They were overtaken by the advancing Red Army, disarmed, and led to the Soviet border at Husiatyn. The date was September 17, 1939. Valenta and his fellow Czechs were eventually taken to Jarmolince, where they occupied a ruined monastery. The winter of 1939–40 was one of the most severe of this century, and the Czechs suffered many hardships. However, they did manage to make Christmas a happy occasion. Sunflower oil was smuggled in so the men could make toast, and a Christmas tree, complete with decorations, was drawn on the wall in charcoal. Then the men gathered in the ruined, roofless chapel of the monastery for a midnight Mass.

In the spring, after prolonged negotiations, those men with valid passports were given permission to leave the Soviet Union. On March 12, 1940, Valenta and the first group of Czechs left for Odessa to board a passenger liner bound for Istanbul. There the Czech consulate arranged transport on the next French cargo ship to Beirut, where the Czechs officially joined the French Army. They were sent via Alexandria to Marseilles and were then allowed to proceed to the Czech Army depot at Agde.

Valenta was assigned to the 3rd Infantry Regiment but worked instead for the military administration of the Czech National Committee in Paris before transferring to the air force on June 15, 1940; he was evacuated from Port Vendres to England later in the month. On July 29, Wally was posted to 311 (Czech) Squadron, receiving his commission in the RAFVR a few days later. Classified as a radio operator, Valenta got along well with his new crew. He was the most reserved among them, was usually very quiet, and never drank or smoked. He often talked about his mother but rarely mentioned his father, who had been killed on the Eastern Front during the First World War.

Valenta was kept busy with his duties as official squadron chronicler, but it wasn't until December 9, 1940, that the crew flew their first raid, on Boulogne. There followed four more operations before they were assigned to make the return trip to Boulogne on February 6, 1941. The crew left East Wretham in their Wellington just after six in the evening and bombed the target successfully, but on turning for home, the pilot discovered that his navigator had lost consciousness. With the weather rapidly worsening, Wally Valenta tried to get a course heading from base but could only pick up one transmission. Flying on this course for about an hour, the pilot concluded that they must be nearing England, and when he spotted land below, decided to force-land because of the bad weather and lack of fuel. Unfortunately, they were still over France, and the crew was captured as soon as they piled out of the wrecked bomber near Flers.

While in Barth, Wally Valenta had been discouraged from escaping because his intelligence activities in Czechoslovakia might put him in great danger if he fell into police hands; for the time being, he was happy working behind the scenes. He took up the study of Chinese, taught Russian to Jimmy James, and gave periodic lectures on military history.

Most important, Valenta ran the contact network, one of the most sensitive and ruthless branches of X Organization. Much of the material needed for escape purposes could be manufactured within the camp, but certain things (such as cameras and film, to make photographs for identity documents) had to be brought in from outside. Some guards were willing to smuggle virtually anything into the camp in exchange for Red Cross chocolate, cigarettes, or soap. In other cases, guards were carefully blackmailed to ensure that they did X Organization's bidding. The process of rendering a guard useful to the escape organization was known as taming.

Each of Valenta's men had one goon to tame, and none of the other prisoners was allowed to speak to that German. The process of taming a goon was quite simple. It might be as easy as inviting him in for an occasional cup of coffee and offering him a bar of chocolate now and then until you gained his confidence. Or it might entail downright blackmail. On one occasion, a goon was persuaded to smuggle in a pair of pliers in return for some chocolate. Foolishly, he consented to signing a receipt on the grounds that his contact's entire mess had contributed the chocolate and needed some sort of chit. Once the organization had this receipt, the unfortunate guard had to bring in what was asked of him or face court-martial. Another time, Bob van der Stok was asked to cultivate an elderly guard from Vienna. He did so by stuffing the goon's pockets with Red Cross food and then threatening to report him as a thief unless he returned with six buttons, a field cap, and some embroidered shoulder patches. The poor guard could only agree.

The only qualification for Valenta's department was a reasonable knowledge of German. However, even the language qualification could be overlooked in certain circumstances. The ferret known as Rudi struck up a friendship with Kiwi Billy Griffith, who became his contact man. Though nothing of great value was ever obtained from Rudi, it was just as important that Billy keep him occupied during the times when he was supposed to be patrolling the compound. One of the best contacts was Corporal Hesse, the duty interpreter at the *Vorlager* gate, who developed a friendship with Sydney Dowse. Sydney was able to get no end of information and material out of Hesse, including two full civilian suits, complete with hats, food coupons for five weeks, and more than two thousand Reichsmarks.

*

Of the other key escape planners, four held particularly sensitive positions. The design and construction of the tunnels were controlled by Wally Floody, the lean ex-miner from northern Ontario who headed the tunnel committee. The second member of the executive was George Harsh, an American in the RCAF, who was put in charge of the security of the three tunnels.

Harsh's story was unique in Sagan. He was the son of a wealthy Georgia family and, in the days of Prohibition, he and four other teenage friends from college decided after a night of drinking that it was possible to commit the perfect crime, with careful planning and intelligence. They embarked on a series of minor holdups, taking turns pulling the heists with a handgun, and indeed had the police stumped. Then, one rainy night in October, things went wrong. It was George's turn to carry the weapon and one of the clerks in the grocery store panicked and produced a revolver from under the counter. He came up shooting, and when the firing stopped, both clerks lay dead.

Two weeks later, George Harsh was arrested and charged with the murders. There was a trial, and after only fifteen minutes' deliberation, the jury found him guilty; he was sentenced to hang. But, as Harsh wrote in his memoirs, 'You can't hang a million dollars.' Faced with the wealth and power of Harsh's family and of the other man charged in the case, the judge allowed the death sentence to be set aside in exchange for guilty pleas. Instead of the gallows, George Harsh was sent to a Georgia chain gang. He spent twelve years in prison, most of it on the chain gang, where the prisoners lived in steel cages and shoveled dirt for fourteen or fifteen hours a day. Life was cheap, and the death of a convict was neither mourned nor investigated. Harsh himself once stabbed a man to death in a fight over a bar of soap. Eventually he was transferred out of the chain gang and became a trusty in a prison hospital. There he performed an emergency appendectomy on another prisoner and earned his pardon. Within a year he was an officer in the

RCAF. Wally Floody was the only person who knew the truth about George Harsh's past. Floody knew that if anyone had the guile and the ingenuity to safeguard his tunnels, it was Harsh.

*

The third member of the executive was Peter Fanshawe, recently returned from Schubin, who would control the dispersal of sand from the tunnels. Past experience had shown that careless dispersal was usually the reason for the discovery of a tunnel. Once the goons found fresh earth, they kept searching until they found the tunnel. The fact that there would be three tunnels made the dispersal problem even more acute, and it was obvious that Fanshawe's job would be a big one.

With Roger Bushell, code-named 'Big X,' at the top, Wally, George, and Peter made up the executive of X Organization, which would be responsible for marshaling all available resources and manpower to further the cause of escape. As a preliminary step, Roger met with the department heads to give a brief outline of the plan as it stood. Fuller instructions would be given once the sites of the three traps were finalized, a task that all agreed was top priority.

Based on the surveys made by the work parties and more exhaustive studies done by X Organization's engineers, the three sites were chosen by April 11. Tom would go west from Hut 123, which was judged by the planners to be the least desirable of the locations. Granted, it had a comparatively short distance to go before reaching the woods, but this fact also made the hut a natural target for German searches. It was hoped that, since 123 was the farthest from the gate, operations could be closed up well before any parties of ferrets reached the hut. Dick would run parallel to Tom from Hut 122, the advantage being that the Germans were less likely to suspect a tunnel to begin in a hut so far from the wire. Harry, to be in Hut 104, was the closest to the main gate and therefore presented the greatest security problems. However, the committee decided that, since it was toward the center of the compound and separated from the woods by the hundred-foot-wide *Vorlager*, the goons were unlikely to suspect it as a starting point.

The next matter was to find a way to marshal the workers needed for the escape plan. Roger's solution was to appoint an officer from each hut to act as 'Little X's.' This officer was responsible for vetting all escape plans before they were submitted to the committee and then assisting with planning, timing, and supplies if the plan was approved. Little X was also responsible for canvassing the men in his hut to see what talents they had. Those with an aptitude in drawing, metal- or woodwork, cartography, or any of the other necessary skills were slated for the relevant branch of the organization. Those without a particular expertise or who were new to escaping were added to a card file of general helpers to be used wherever needed.

Before any work could be done on surveying for the tunnels, a large-scale map of the entire compound had to be made. The organization's mathematical types set to work and soon produced a plan that showed every block, building, and guard tower, along with any other notable features, such as the firepool, a large pool of water to be used for fighting fires in the compound. Then, by sketching in the lines of sight from the guard towers, they were able to mark the locations of any blind spots in the compound. However, none of the spots was completely safe from the ferrets who roamed the compound, so the job of keeping tabs on these goons fell to the security branch of X Organization.

*

Bushell's first instruction to his Little X's was to find people with experience in surveying or mathematics. With three large tunnels about to begin construction, Roger wanted to have exact figures for the distances required. The difficult job of surveying for the tunnels was left to a number of different teams, each working independently. In this way, each team's calculations could be checked against those worked out by the others, thereby ensuring a greater degree of accuracy. One of the teams was made up of Brian Evans and Emmet Cook, a bombardier from Fort Worth, Texas. Emmet had gotten an engineering degree from Texas A&M University before the war and had an excellent knowledge of drafting, while Brian's work with the real-estate agent had given him a good grasp of surveying.

In the absence of a real transit, X Organization's workshops had built transits out of bits of wood and tin. Because they used a crude V and post sight instead of a scope, it left a lot to be desired in accuracy, but it was the best that could be done. Under the watchful eye of the stooges, Brian and Emmet took their measurements quickly but carefully, usually by leaning out of the block windows after receiving the all-clear.

Though they were only providing the initial measurements for the final computations, it was still a very tricky job. They worked with a baseline of about 128 feet, which meant that they had to take naked-eye azimuth shots of more than 300 feet. To complicate matters further, they were targeting not a surveyor's rod but a tree roughly 20 inches in diameter. With a target of that size, a 1-degree error in shooting could mean a difference of 20 feet or more in the distance computed for the tunnel.

It was precisely because of this possibility that the organization had more than one pair of workers providing the initial measurements. It was hoped that exhaustive cross-checking would eliminate any mistakes.

Brian and Emmet each took numerous sightings at various times, and then they compared all the measurements until both were certain that the distance they had arrived at was as accurate as possible. Both took their work very seriously, albeit for different reasons. Brian Evans, after nearly three years in captivity, had done his share of escape work and had developed a very businesslike attitude toward it. Emmet Cook, on the other hand, had been in the bag just over three months, and the workings of the organization were new to him. This was the first big escape scheme he had been involved in, and he was determined to do a good job and to learn all he could. Evans and Cook discussed little but their work when they got together for tea.

*

The surveying complete, the only other major task to be accomplished before the actual digging could begin was the establishment of a security system in the compound. Junior Clark had a makeshift system in place, but as he prowled around the compound with his deputy, Tom Kirby-Green, and George Harsh, it became apparent that a better security web would have to be set up. Harsh chose Canadian George McGill as his deputy, and the four of them immediately got down to work. Roger gave them a week to do the job.

To start with, they divided the compound roughly in half, with a line running north to south through the firepool. The side nearest the gate was called the safe, or S, zone, while the other side was called the danger, or D, zone. It was decided that work on the traps could progress safely if there were goons in the S zone, but as soon as they crossed into the D zone, everything would be closed down.

Furthermore, if any three ferrets entered the compound at once, operations would also be stopped.

To monitor the movements of individual Germans, the planners created a position called the duty pilot, a man who sat near the main gate and recorded all incoming and outgoing traffic. He was assisted by a runner, who conveyed periodic status reports to the department heads. Also devised was a system of innocent signals so that anyone could tell at a glance how many goons were in the compound. For example, a Red Cross box and a coal bucket might be lying casually on the ground beside the duty pilot; if the lid was on the box, it might mean that two guards had entered the compound; if the bucket was on top of the box, it meant that the compound was clear. All security men in the camp were trained to recognize the meaning of various combinations of articles.

Since Huts 122 and 123 were not in direct view of the duty pilot, a relay station was put in the south end of 110, using the shutters of the lavatory windows as a sort of semaphore. If both shutters were open, it meant that the compound was clear; one shutter closed meant one goon in the compound; both closed signified two. If three or more had entered the gate, a handkerchief was hung on the closed shutters. The watchers in 122 and 123 were told to keep their eyes on 110's lavatory at all times so the traps could be shut if a party of goons entered the compound.

The watchers – or stooges, as they were known – had a tedious but crucial job. Slipups were inevitable but usually only resulted in a rather embarrassing situation. One day, one of the stooges missed a ferret, who walked straight into the corridor where another watcher was furtively peeking around a corner. The stooge was understandably startled when he came face to face with the goon but recovered quickly and pretended he had been looking outside to check the weather. The ferret must have wondered, but he said nothing. Another time, a stooge was lounging on the steps of 101, trying to look innocent, when one of the ferrets strode right up to him and said that he would be visiting a prisoner in Hut 107 for ten minutes. The fellow did his best to appear unconcerned, but all he could muster was a wan smile.

However, because a slip in the stooging operation could have disastrous consequences, individual shifts were kept as short as possible so that the workers remained alert. As a result, it became one of the largest organizations in the camp. Most of the kriegies did their share of stooging under the supervision of Junior Clark, Tom Kirby-Green, and a committee of block security officers known as 'Little S's.' Each Little S was responsible for searching every inch of the hut after *Appell*. He would climb all the way through the attic and then under the hut to ensure that no ferrets had hidden themselves in the block during *Appell*. Only after the all-clear was given by each hut security officer would work begin.

Chapter 9

SINKING THE TRAPS

WITH THE DUTY PILOT and stooging system in place and tested to Roger Bushell's satisfaction, it was possible to start work on the traps. Though the huts had been selected, it remained to choose the specific locations and, in this, the engineers were limited in their choices. To provide maximum camouflage, the traps would have to be sunk through solid foundations, which were found only in the washrooms. Sitting on a log outside his hut one day, Wally Floody realized that it might also be possible to dig through the brick supporting the chimneys. With these two possibilities in mind, the engineers got to work.

For Tom, they selected a spot at the end of a short corridor leading to a room next to the kitchen. Beside the stove chimney, there was a poorly lit corner that would be perfect for a trap. Its construction was left to three Polish officers, who used stolen cold chisels to cut a two-foot-square section out of the concrete floor. Beneath the floor they found a layer of loosely packed rubble over the sand. The square they had removed was smashed up and replaced with a piece cast from stolen concrete. Once it was replaced and the cracks filled with cement and dusted with sand, it was impossible to tell the trap from the rest of the floor. Only those who knew where to look could find the two metal hooks with fine strands of wire attached that were used to lift the trapdoor. The officer placed in charge of Tom's trap was Mike Casey.

Next, the Poles moved on to Hut 122 to begin work on Dick's trap. In the washroom there was a drain eighteen inches square and about three feet deep. The drain-off pipe was only two-thirds of the way down, so there was always at least a foot of water in the bottom of the sump. This would be the spot for Dick. The engineers removed the iron grate, bailed out the water, and then chipped away one of the sidewalls of the sump. Behind the wall was virgin sand, perfect for digging. The sidewall was replaced with a slab made by Jerzy Mondschein and the cracks sealed with a mixture of blue clay, soap, and cement. Then the grate was replaced and the water let back in. It was one of the most ingenious traps ever constructed.

Dick's *Trapführer* (as the controller of the trap was known) was Flying Officer Leslie Charles James Brodrick, who had spent his first year of war in the 92nd Heavy Regiment of Coastal Defense. Born in London on May 19, 1921, Les entered the military in early 1939, choosing the Surrey Yeomanry of the Territorial Army because he liked the uniform. In August 1939 he took a leave from his job at an insurance company to attend an army training camp; he was called up on September 1 and eventually was transferred to the RAF in late 1940.

Les was part of one of the first courses to train in the United States, at a flying school in Texas. His instructor was a typical cowboy, or bush hopper as he preferred to call himself, whose only fear was flying in the dark. He stuck with Les for the first night-flying circuit and then hopped out at the end of the runway. 'You're okay, aren't you?' he said before walking off and leaving Les to fend for himself. In spite of this, Les survived training and returned to England, first serving with the Air Transport Auxiliary. He eventually converted to four-engine bombers and in February 1943 was posted to 106 Squadron, commanded by the legendary Guy Gibson of Dambusters fame.

There followed an extremely busy period, in which Les and his crew flew twenty missions in five weeks. On the night of April 14–15, 1943, they were out again, on their way to Stuttgart. However, because of heavy cloud and icing, Les couldn't get his Lancaster to the recommended height of 20,000 feet, so he elected to observe Gibson's maxim that it was safest to fly either very low or very high. Accordingly, he dropped down to low level, only to find it impossible to keep up with the rest of the bombers. Consequently, when Brodrick's aircraft arrived late over the target, it had the undivided attention of the ground defenses.

The Lancaster was peppered by shrapnel but, since nothing vital appeared to be damaged, Les roared away at treetop height. Unfortunately, they strayed over a small airfield, where a single machine gunner fired a short burst that hit the port wing tanks and started a serious fire. Seeing an open flat area ahead in the distance, Les decided to crash-land. However, the aileron and elevator controls chose that moment to fail, so when Les cut engine power to land, the nose dropped sharply and the Lanc crashed.

Only Les, the mid-upper gunner, and the navigator, who was unconscious, survived the crash. The first priority was to find medical attention for the injured crewman. Brodrick and the gunner made their way to the nearest village, just east of Amiens, and gave themselves up to the German authorities. The three were taken to a nearby hospital, and from there Les and the gunner were shipped to Dulag Luft. When Les Brodrick arrived in North Compound in May 1943, he was just in time for the start of tunneling operations. Mike Casey was looking for someone to take over the second trap, and Les seemed just the fellow.

*

The last of the traps completed was Harry's, in Room 23 of Hut 104. The Poles removed the stove from its base and took up the floor tile by tile, cleaning each tile and saving it to reuse. The fabrication of Harry's trap was not so easy, though. The four-foot-square wooden frame that supported the stove had to be rebuilt and, in the meantime, the area had to be left open. Working as quickly as possible, the carpenters built the wooden frame, and then the Poles got to work at resetting the tiles. However, five of them had been cracked, and none of the other stoves in the compound had similar floor tiles. After a few days of panic it was decided to smuggle a supply over from East Compound, and the requisite number duly arrived secreted in the battle dress of one of the kitchen orderlies. The Poles worked in the kitchen hut and completed the trap in seven hours. To get it to Hut 104, they mounted carrying poles on it, loaded it up with empty crates so it just looked like a load of scrap wood, and carried it across the compound. It fit perfectly, and once the cracks were filled with cement and sprinkled with dust, the stove was put back in place. For the next eleven months the little stove in Room 23 was never without a fire, to discourage the goons from exploring it too closely.

Custody of Harry's trap was given to a Canadian named Pat Langford, who adopted it as one would adopt a child. Over the coming months he would develop a love–hate relationship with his charge. Controlling a trap was no easy job, but Pat gave it all his energy. In time he was able to perfect his routine so that in an emergency the trap could be closed and sealed, complete with blankets to avoid a hollow sound, in less than twenty seconds.

*

Patrick Wilson Langford was born in Edmonton, Alberta, on November 4, 1919, the son of an English-born forest ranger in Jasper National Park. The eldest of three children, he was a quiet and conscientious student who spent much of his free time skiing, hiking, or horseback riding. Upon graduation from high school in 1937, Langford took a job as a chauffeur with Brewster Transport. This was a prestigious position and involved picking up tourists at the local train station and driving them in a big Packard touring car to Emerald Lake, Takakaw Falls in the Yoho Valley, Lake Louise, and Banff, where they could board another train or stay in the luxurious Banff Springs Hotel. It was great fun to rub shoulders with the wealthy tourists, and Pat thoroughly enjoyed telling them about the mountains he had loved since boyhood.

He was quick to enlist when war came and was one of the few accepted into the first batch of recruits to be trained as flying instructors. Pat was delighted at being one of a select group and was beaming when he reported for the course on January 29, 1940. He did well in training, learned quickly, and, when he finally won his wings on August 19, was ranked third in his class. After further training, it was on to 6 SFTS at Dunnville to begin a sixteen-month stint as a flying instructor. It took Langford a little while to adjust to teaching on the single-engine Yale trainers, and in the first month he was involved in two taxiing accidents that were put down to carelessness. However, he was quick to settle in and soon became a favorite with the students. He was more approachable than many of the other instructors and was always anxious to bridge the gap between teacher and student with a few friendly questions about hometown and family.

After a year of instructing, Pat was getting restless and put in for an assignment to a heavy bomber squadron when his tenure at Dunnville ended. His request was granted, and on April 7, 1942, he left Gander, Newfoundland, for the twelve-hour flight to Prestwick in Scotland. On arrival, Pat entrained for the reception center at Bournemouth, where he spent a month before being posted to 16 OTU at Upper Heyford. After a few refresher flights Pat was ready to try his hand at Wellingtons. He took to the aircraft well and by the end of June was deemed ready for his first mission, the 'Thousand Raid' on Bremen on June 25–26, 1942.

For the next month, Flight Lieutenant Langford was back on training runs, but on July 28–29 he finally got the chance to fly an operational mission again, to Hamburg. The city was always a tough proposition and was especially so this night because much of the attacking force couldn't leave their airfields due to bad weather. Pat's unit managed to get off the ground, but the weather worsened on the flight out and the OTU aircraft were recalled to base. The Wellington carrying Pat Langford and his crew was one of four aircraft from 16 OTU that failed to receive the signal and continued toward the target. As the force neared Hamburg, it became even more dispersed, and only sixty-eight bombers found the target to drop their loads. Most of the rest jettisoned their bombs on anything they could see through the clouds. Pat's aircraft stayed with the remains of the bomber stream, but over Lübeck the Wellington took a number of flak hits and caught fire. Pat bailed out with his parachute alight and landed heavily in the suburbs of Lübeck with serious burns to his upper body. Though he had more than a thousand hours as a pilot, Pat Langford had done only two operations. The wounded Canadian was quickly moved to a German military hospital, and it was two months before his burns healed sufficiently for him to be transferred to Stalag Luft III.

*

May came, and again the camp began to feel the warmth of summer. More and more prisoners began sunbathing on the compound, and the sports equipment was dusted off for another season. While most of the kriegies enjoyed the warm sun, the first few teams were beginning excavations in the three tunnels. Only the most experienced diggers worked on sinking the shafts, since this was one of the most difficult parts of the operation. The old hands were divided among the three tunnels, Johnny Marshall going to Tom, Wally Floody to Dick, and Crump Ker-Ramsay to Harry. They were assisted by other experienced diggers, such as Johnny Bull, Conk Canton, and a Canadian named Hank Birkland, who came in as a friend of Floody's.

They didn't come much tougher than Flight Lieutenant Henry Birkland. The son of a carpenter, he was born on August 16, 1917, in the small town of Spearhill, Manitoba, where he and his six siblings were raised. The family was not well off and moved around to wherever work was available. From Spearhill they went to Calgary, and then to Winnipeg, where Hank finished high school. With the Depression in full swing, Birkland went to work to help out the family. He began as an odd-job man at local farms, a career that ended with a serious accident.

While towing a car to a neighboring town, Hank ran his truck off the road and sustained a severe concussion in the crash. In the hospital it was discovered that, in addition to the concussion, Hank also had scarlet fever and an advanced case of blood poisoning in one arm. Hank's father brusquely refused the doctor's suggestion that the limb be amputated, so slits were cut down Hank's forearm to let the poison drain out. The survival of the arm hung in the balance for several weeks, but it eventually healed and Hank was able to return to work.

Finding work was easier said than done, though. At first the only job he could get was as a door-to-door salesman, but this hardly suited Birkland's temperament. He then picked up work at a meat-packing plant, only to lose it months later when the firm went bankrupt. Convinced that there were no immediate prospects on the prairies, Hank jumped a freight train bound for northern Ontario in the hope of finding work in the mines. This area, too, was badly depressed, so he hopped another train and went in the other direction, to British Columbia. Finally he found work in a gold mine in the town of Sheep Creek and was at last able to settle down. He got back to the sport of lacrosse, a passion he had discovered while at school, and acted as playing coach for the Sheep Creek Bombers. With his powerful physique and immense strength he was known as the Big Train.

Soon after the war began, Hank Birkland enlisted in the RCAF; he was called to Toronto to begin training in September 1940. The following month he was posted to Cap de la Madeleine, Québec, for elementary instruction, and then to Summerside, Prince Edward Island, in January 1941. On April 10 he received his wings and commission, proceeding overseas shortly afterward. He went first to 57 OTU at Hawarden in Wales and then spent a month with 122 Squadron before being assigned to 72 Squadron on September 19, 1941. Hank was in action almost immediately, flying Spitfires on cross-Channel sweeps and convoy patrols but had completed just twelve sorties when the squadron was assigned to fly a diversionary operation over Dunkirk on November 7. While sweeping down the French coast, Birkland's Spitfire passed directly over a flak tower and took a full load of anti-aircraft shells in its belly. With his aircraft blazing, Hank was only just able to put her down on the beach before blacking out.

The flak gunners pulled Hank from the wreckage, and he spent some weeks in a hospital before being shipped to Barth. There he met up with fellow miner Wally Floody and the two became firm friends. They made a rather odd-looking pair, the tall and lean Floody and the compact and broad Birkland, but few could work harder or longer underground than they could. And judging by the first week's digging, they would all have to work pretty hard.

*

Dick posed few problems but both Tom and Harry presented difficulties. Under Harry's trap was a layer of solid brick and concrete foundation that had to be chipped away using a stolen pickhead mounted on a baseball bat. To disguise the noise of the operation, Roger stationed a bunch of kriegies outside 104, innocently bashing out baking dishes and other bits of hardware for use in their kitchens.

Tom proved to be the most difficult. The engineers discovered that the rubble they had removed supported the concrete floor, so head craftsman Johnny Travis, a ruddy and immaculate fellow who had once been a mining engineer in South Africa, had to design and build a wooden frame to act as a brace between the floor and the sand. Then he mounted a tray on top of the frame that could be packed with sand. With this in place, the trap wouldn't sound hollow if anyone stepped on it.

The diggers worked on the shafts from after morning *Appell*, at 8:00 A.M., until about 5:30 P.M., with a short break for lunch. At first, they worked with coal scoops, but these proved so fragile that Travis engineered stronger shovels using iron plates stolen from the stoves. They dug about five feet at a time, then installed a shaft frame made from the corner posts of dismantled bunks. Bedboards were wedged behind the frames for shoring, and a strong ladder was built on one side. Slowly, all three shafts approached their intended depth of thirty feet.

When this level was reached, the tricky job of enlarging chambers at the base of each shaft got under way. Just how tricky a job it was became apparent when Ker-Ramsay, Floody, and Canton set to work on Dick's chamber. The three had just started when Canton looked up the shaft and spotted sand leaking from between the boards near the top. In the few seconds that he watched, the trickle grew to a flood, and in a flash he and Crump were on their way up the ladder, closely followed by Floody. Conk and Crump scrambled out and turned to heave out Wally, whose legs were already buried by sand. Cursing softly, the three stood back to survey the damage. In less than half a minute, the thirty-foot shaft had filled nearly to the top. Pausing only to regain their breath, they quickly got down to digging it out again. Days later, the same thing happened in Harry, and again Crump stood sadly at the trap with Johnny Bull, pondering the tons of sand that had obliterated all their hard work. Once again they got right back at it, adding a double layer of bedboards on the shaft in the hope that such a fall wouldn't happen again.

With the shafts duly reinforced, work could proceed more safely on the chamber at the base of each tunnel. One was to be used for dispersal and temporary storage of sand, and another as a manufacturing workshop. Also in this chamber was a small can filled with pebbles and attached to a string running up to the barrack above. Whenever the men in the chambers heard the pebbles rattle, they immediately stopped work and waited until the all-clear was received. Even though they were thirty feet underground, there was always the chance that some sharp-eared goon might hear the sound of activity below.

The third chamber was the most important, for it contained the vital air pump. Because of the length of the tunnels, extra-strong air pumps had to be installed to get enough oxygen to the face. Various methods had been tried in the past, including a gramophone-like device that blew air when the turntable was revolved, but these were rejected in favor of a pump that had been used in East Compound. In fact, the original idea came from a mechanics magazine that somehow found its way into the camp.

The men who crafted the air pumps were twenty-six-year-old Jens Einar Müller, a tall, slender Norwegian with a serious face and clear blue eyes who was downed on June 19, 1942, while flying with 331 Squadron, and Yorkshireman Thomas Robert Nelson, captured in North Africa in September 1942 when his Wellington suffered engine failure.

To begin with, Jens, Bob, and others made large, tubular bellows by sewing two kit bags together and strengthening them with wire hoops. Then the whole affair was mounted on runners on a wooden frame, and a strong handle was attached to one end. Intake and exhaust vents were fitted, and leather flap valves controlled the movement of air through the kit bags. Operating the pump was not unlike using a rowing machine; the pumper sat on a sliding seat and pulled the handle toward him to draw in the air and then pushed back to blow it up the tunnel. The intake vent was concealed in the hut above, while the exhaust was connected to the main air line of the tunnel. There was also a bypass valve in the pump to permit natural ventilation when the tunnel was shut. To test it, the engineers held a burning rag over the intake vent and pumped until the thick, black smoke started to issue forth from the exhaust vent. It worked well, and the whole process of construction and assembly took only ten days, done in a workshop in 104 under the cover of a choir practice.

With the air pumps in place and functioning, it was possible to work underground with the traps sealed, thereby greatly reducing the risk of discovery. As the tunnels were pushed ahead slowly, all of the other services were prepared and installed. Electric lighting was provided by tapping into the mains. Fixtures were removed from corridors, and sufficient cable was procured by a rearrangement of the camp's electrical system by qualified electrician-kriegies. Though fat lamps still had to be used at periods during the day when the current was turned off, the electric lamps made the tunnel air much less stifling.

For the air pipe, the Little X's collected empty Klim tins that the prisoners received in Red Cross parcels. The tin-bashers carefully removed the ends and fitted the cylinders together into a long pipe; the tins were slightly narrower where the lid fitted, so they nested together perfectly. Then, each joint was wrapped tightly with greased paper, and the air pipe was laid in a nine-inch-deep channel dug in the floor of the tunnel. It was covered with earth and floorboards and was ready for use. At the tunnel face, an angled nozzle to direct air upward toward the digger was attached to the end of the air pipe. The nozzle was removable and could be shifted along as the pipe was extended.

For ease of travel up and down the tunnels, railroad lines were installed. The rails were made from battens stripped from the huts. They came in sections an inch wide, half an inch thick, and a few feet long and were nailed securely to frames on the floor of the tunnel. Johnny Travis and Bob Nelson were responsible for crafting the trolleys themselves. To make the wheels, they glued together three disks of wood, with the outside one being larger to form a flange. The flanges were lined with metal strips to protect against wear, and the wheel hubs were secured firmly to a rotating axle that ran on margarine-greased hardwood bearings on the trolley. For the axles, Travis and Nelson removed the front rails from cooking stoves and split the ends before bolting them to the wheels. Each trolley could carry two boxes of sand or one worker at a time and was pulled with ropes made of plaited string from Red Cross parcels. The railroad soon became indispensable, allowing a digger to arrive at the face without having exhausted himself in the long crawl up the tunnel.

*

Perhaps the most important bit of engineering to be done in those first days was the design and fitting of the shoring frames. The frames were not perfectly square, being twenty inches wide at the bottom and eighteen inches wide at the top, and consequently it was possible to install them without nails. The boards were cut with tongue and groove joints and, once they were in place with the sand packed above and behind them, the weight of the earth pressed down on the frames and made them solid. As the carpenters set to work at cutting a supply of frames and boards, the tunneling shifts began digging.

At first there were three digging teams, with each ten-man team divided into two shifts. Johnny Marshall led the team in Tom, Crump Ker-Ramsay led the group in Dick, and Johnny Bull was in charge of Harry's diggers. On their teams were the most experienced diggers, such as Danny Król, Conk Canton, Muckle Muir, and Henry Lamond, who would excavate the first fifty feet or so and keep a close eye on sand conditions. The tunnel committee knew that the sand at Sagan was very unstable and decided to leave the first section of tunnel to the old hands before bringing in any new workers.

Each day's digging went pretty much the same. After morning *Appell* and once the all-clear had been received from the block security men, the first shift went underground. The traps were then sealed, and one stooge was left to watch the entrance. The pumper took his position at the air pump, and the disperser went right to the dispersal chamber, where he was also responsible for preparing the shoring frames for installation. The first digger climbed onto a trolley and pulled himself up to the face; then his number two pulled the trolley back and climbed on, to be hauled up by the first man. The worker at the face lay on his side on one elbow and scraped the sand away and back to his number two, who lay facing the opposite direction. The number two gathered the sand and put it in the boxes on the trolley, signaling to the disperser when the trolley was full. It was hot, grimy work made even more unpleasant by the fact that the diggers were instructed to wear heavy, woolen long underwear to protect the skin against sand scars. And when it came time for number one and number two to change jobs, they had to travel all the way back to the base of the shaft, for there wasn't enough room in the tunnel to switch.

Despite these challenges, progress was good. Because the diggers didn't have to worry about dispersal, they were able to clear seven or eight feet each day. Then, with the dispersal chamber bulging with bags of sand, the first shift prepared to come up for afternoon *Appell*. The workers changed into their uniforms at the base of the shaft and then went up to shower away the telltale sand that got into every pore of one's body.

After *Appell*, the second shift went down to get rid of the spoil, and for this job the tunnel had to be left open. Blankets were spread around the trap to catch any sprinkles of sand, and the heavy kit bags and aluminum jugs full of earth were passed up to the *Trapführers*; after heaving up seventy or eighty hundred-pound loads of sand, the *Trapführers* were completely worn out.

Waiting near the tunnel room were the dispersers, each carrying a number of canvas bags. The bags were filled with sand and then hung around the neck under the fellow's battle dress. He then wandered out into the compound to one of the designated dispersal points, took off his tunic or greatcoat, and emptied out the bags. The many pine trees left in the compound served as an effective screen for the operation, and the various blind spots discovered by the surveyors also came in handy. Consequently it was possible to get rid of tunnel spoil in the sandy patches where excavations had been made during the construction of the compound. There, the bright yellow tunnel sand could be mixed in and camouflaged. Under normal circumstances the dispersal operation was confined to lunchtime and mid-evening, when there were few Germans in the compound.

While the dispersal was proceeding, the engineers went down to inspect the air pump, which had to be checked daily in the damp conditions underground, and extend the air pipe, lighting cable, and railroad. Another supply of wood was stacked in the dispersal chamber and the tunnel was closed, ready for work to begin again the next day.

Periodically the surveyors made checks to ensure that the tunnels were proceeding according to plans. Travis crafted a spirit level to verify that they were pushing ahead on a level plane, and the engineers also had two stolen German prismatic compasses to check the direction of the tunnel. The length was gauged with a cord that had been premeasured with a ruler from a parcel of Red Cross school supplies. The cord was taken to the end of the tunnel and pulled tight, and the distance from the face to the entry shaft was calculated by one of X Organization's mathematical types. As Tom, Dick, and Harry progressed, these measurements would become crucial.

*

The tunnels had been going very nicely for a couple of weeks when Roger summoned his lieutenants for a meeting.

'Very shortly,' he began, 'we're going to run into a problem with dispersal. The method we're using now is just not satisfactory – the bags are too difficult to fill, and it's far too risky with the dispersers having to take off their coats to unload the sand. Besides, in the warm weather, chaps wandering about in greatcoats are going to look rather suspicious.'

Peter Fanshawe was the first to speak. 'Perhaps this might be suitable,' he said, pulling from his battle dress an odd-looking device consisting of a pair of Red Cross suspenders connecting two long sausage-shaped bags, made from German towels, with pin-type closures at the bottom. Two strings hung from the pins. 'Now, if I may demonstrate. You hang this contraption around your neck and run the strings into your pockets. Each bag is filled with a load of sand, and the bags put down your trouser legs. Then, looking as innocent as you know how, you just stroll out into the compound, pull the pins, and the sand drops down your trouser legs onto the ground. You just kick it in a bit and wander away.'

The plotters stared at Fanshawe for a moment and then broke into wide grins as his idea sank in. 'It's brilliant!' exclaimed Roger. 'It has to work!'

'It does,' said Hornblower quietly. 'I tried it earlier. Unless you're a complete idiot, it's foolproof.'

And so was born the idea of the penguins, so called because of the way they waddled when carrying eight pounds of sand down each trouser leg. In fact, the name soon became inappropriate because the dispersers were able to walk so naturally that it was often impossible to tell, even at a distance of a few feet, that a man was loaded with sand. Fanshawe began recruiting workers and constructing trouser bags immediately and within a week had a force of two hundred penguins ready to handle all the sand that Tom, Dick, and Harry could provide.

*

Like the camp as a whole, the dispersal organization was made up of a tremendous variety of people, from all of the Allied nations and from every conceivable background. There would be six separate teams (British, Commonwealth, American, Polish, South African, and other Allied officers), each working independently.

The British team included some of the original kriegies, such as Lieutenant Douglas Arthur Poynter, a naval aviator who had entered the Royal Navy as a midshipman in November 1938. He qualified as an observer in the Fleet Air Arm the following year and was later posted to 825 Squadron in HMS *Furious*. On September 22, 1940, Doug and his pilot took off in their Swordfish torpedo bomber to attack German ships in Trondheim Harbor, but bad weather forced them to land on an island north of Trondheim. They found a boat and set off for the Orkney Islands but came ashore on another part of the Norwegian coast and were captured soon after.

Almost all of the members of the Polish team were prewar regular officers whose years of service, on average, far exceeded those of any other national group. There was the balding and fatherly Flight Lieutenant Kazimierz Pawluk, a Warsaw native who served in the Polish Air Force before the war and escaped to England in 1940, to be posted to 305 Squadron at Lindholme. In March 1942, navigator Pawluk was downed and captured during a raid on Lübeck. Another Pole, Flight Lieutenant Paweł Wilhelm Tobolski, was born in Bydgoszcz in 1906. He was a blond and poker-faced chap with heavy features and a cheery smile who had joined the service in October 1927. He served in the ranks for ten years before being commissioned as an observer lieutenant. On June 26, 1942, Tob's 301 Squadron Wellington fell to a German night fighter after the 'Thousand Raid' on Bremen.

The elder statesman of the Poles was Flight Lieutenant Antoni Kiewnarski, a charming and enthusiastic man with graying hair and an odd, quizzical expression. Born in Moscow in 1899, Tony had entered the service in August 1917 and since then had risen through the ranks, fought in three separate wars, and gained a chestful of Polish and foreign decorations along the way. Tony was captured after a raid on

Kassel on August 27, 1942, while flying as navigator in a 305 Squadron Wellington. He was respected and liked throughout the camp and was strikingly childlike in his kindness of heart and simple goodness. At one time or another Tony had instructed many of his fellow Polish POWs, who regarded him as something of a father figure.

In contrast, the head of the South African team, a mustachioed Afrikaner named Johannes Stephanus Gouws, was young enough to be Kiewnarski's son. Born in Bultfontein in Orange Free State on August 13, 1919, he was the eldest of four children who grew up on the family farm. The young Johannes was a cheerful and happy boy who always seemed to be on top of the world. His greatest ambition was to become a policeman.

Johannes began his education at the local farm school before going on to Bultfontein High School. There he was an enthusiastic athlete and captained the school rugby team when it toured Cape Province in 1937. He graduated the same year and entered the Special Service Battalion, a select training course for prospective soldiers. A new interest had taken hold, though, and Johannes applied for the SAAF, failing only because his English was poor. Undeterred, he returned to his old dream and secured a transfer to the South African Police. After a year with the police, the young Gouws decided to return to school and entered the University College of Orange Free State to study science. With this came the opportunity to get into flying through the university training program for students. His English continued to improve, and he was sure that the air force would accept him upon his next application.

His confidence was well founded, and Johannes was taken into the service on May 14, 1940. He loved the training exercises and talked about them at great length whenever he was home. Once, he even dropped in unexpectedly, landing his Tiger Moth on the rough ground of the Gouws farm while on a cross-country training flight. He could stay only a few minutes, but the unannounced arrival caused quite a sensation.

As soon as he received his wings and commission, on March 29, 1941, Johannes began to talk about putting his training to good use. He soon got his wish, and on May 7, Lieutenant Gouws was posted to 41 Squadron, flying Hartbee fighter-bombers in Abyssinia. The family saw him off at the railroad station for the first leg of his journey north, and Johannes was obviously delighted at the prospect of getting into action. 'Wish me luck as you wave me good-bye,' he sang excitedly and then led the group in a chorus of the South African national anthem. With a cheery wave, he boarded the train for Pretoria to fight the foe.

The operations flown by 41 Squadron were largely low-level reconnaissance missions, and the aircraft often carried a few bombs to beat up the enemy trenches. One such raid took place on August 18, 1941, when Gouws and his crewmate, 'Buster' Keeton, took off from their base at dawn with two other aircraft. Well before they reached the target, in Abyssinia, Buster noticed that oil spewing from the engine had fouled his front machine gun, rendering it inoperable. Unable to strafe the enemy, they could only release their bombs and do a few aerobatics while waiting for the rest of the flight. On the way home, oil began to seep onto the floor of the cockpit and Keeton turned back to his pilot, to see Gouws's face covered with oil. Moments later the engine gave up and Gouws motioned to his wingmates that he was going to force-land. Diving down, Johannes and Buster were dismayed by the lack of a suitable landing ground. The only option was a plowed field about sixty yards square. Their two wingmates watched in horror as the tiny biplane touched down in the field and immediately flipped over on its back in a cloud of dust. Buster disentangled himself from his cockpit and struggled to free Johannes, who was still trapped under the fuselage. Unable to open the escape hatches, he finally had to dig Gouws out.

As the two walked away from their machine, a local resident, presumably the owner of the field, wandered up and offered them a bowl of milk and a pail of water to wash the oil from their faces. He read with interest the multilingual note that offered a hefty reward for the safe return of the fliers and decided it was worth his while to take them to his hut. The South Africans were fed and allowed to rest and the next morning set out on the trek back to civilization. Carrying supplies dropped by their flight commander, Gouws and Keeton made good progress with their native guide and by late afternoon had reached a larger village, where they were handed over to the Abyssinian police. Now with official escorts, the two were led to Sakota the next morning and marched between a double file of policemen, to be met by a guard of honor at the outskirts. After a ceremony of welcome they were taken to the chief of police's house for a banquet and then settled into a bed shared with a herd of irritating insects. The pattern of walking most of the day and sleeping in the huts of friendly locals continued, and on August 23 they finally reached their destination, the town of Quoram, where they were feted again. The Abyssinians clearly enjoyed entertaining Johannes and Buster, and it was with some regret that a boisterous Abyssinian colonel drove them back to their squadron.

Gouws was back in action almost immediately and on August 25 flew as wingman to Captain S.F. Du Toit (the leader of the mission on which Johannes and Buster had force-landed) for a raid on the bridge at Gondar. This time it was Captain Du Toit who was downed, and Lieutenant Gouws circled the wreck, looking for a place to land and effect a rescue. After almost touching down two or three times, he decided against attempting an emergency landing and scooted back to base to alert the squadron of Du Toit's whereabouts. Thanks to that information, the captain and his observer were eventually returned to base.

In September 1941 Lieutenant Gouws was transferred to 40 Squadron and proceeded north to Egypt. He flew with the squadron until April 9, 1942, when he took off on a reconnaissance of the Ras Chichiba–El Ezzeiat area. His Tomahawk was jumped by two Me 109s, and Gouws was captured after belly-landing on fire south of Mteifel Chebir.

*

Over the course of a few days, Gouws, Poynter, the Poles, and the rest of the dispersers were brought together in small groups so that Fanshawe could explain the operation to them. The routine was simple and, since the traps had to be left open during loading, was carefully planned to eliminate any delays. Blankets were spread around the trap to catch any sprinkles of sand, and the bags were filled using funnels crafted out of thick cardboard. The penguins picked up the loaded bags from hooks in the tunnel room and wandered off into the compound to disperse. In time the system became so sophisticated that four penguins could be loaded every minute. If there was an alarm, all the equipment could be stowed away in two minutes. Finally, because freshly dug sand gave off a very distinctive odor, a tin of the most pungent tobacco was left smoldering in the corridor to camouflage the smell of the spoil.

Because the tunnel earth was bright yellow, it had to be mixed thoroughly with the topsoil or covered completely so it was not visible. Paths were good for dumping because the dirt was constantly being kicked and trampled. Similarly, sand could be dumped during athletic events and would be mixed in by dozens of pairs of feet. There were still many areas that had been excavated for the drains, lavatories, or the firepool, or where tree stumps had been pulled. There, sand could be dumped and mixed in, using homemade wooden rakes. In all there were twenty-three such dumps, of which as many as seven might be in use at once. The prisoners' gardens were also excellent for dispersal. A deep trench would be dug and then filled with yellow sand. The darker topsoil was then replaced and sown with seeds. In other areas, where the pine trees had created layers of peat, the soil was dug out in sods and the bottom half of the sod was scraped off to be used as topsoil in the gardens. Then the hole was filled with sand and the remainder of the peat sod was replaced.

Careful planning went into the routing of the penguins, so the goons would not notice streams of men coming from a single hut at regular intervals. Thirty airmen staged diversions to cover the movement of the penguins, and any mass movement of men, such as an *Appell* or a line for something, was taken advantage of. For example, if an *Appell* was called, the penguins would use the four or five minutes when prisoners milled around the compound to carry their sand to various huts, where it would be hidden in boxes under the bunks. Then, after roll call, the penguins could work from a number of different huts instead of from the same block.

Using the slung bags was the most common method, but other means of dispersal were used as well. The sleeves of greatcoats could be filled with sand and the ends tied shut with string. Draping the coat over his shoulders, the carrier then walked to his dispersal area. The South African team favored another method. They wore two pairs of trousers, with the inner pair being tightly fastened around the ankles. Then sand was poured into the inner pair and shaken into place around the fellow's legs. The outer pair was then put on and the carrier walked to his dispersal area, where he loosened the inner trousers and dumped his load. This method enabled each carrier to transport about thirty pounds of sand per trip, but the greater capacity was offset by the length of time it took to load each carrier.

Chapter 10

THE DELOUSING PARTY

W HILE THE THREE TUNNELS were putting out huge amounts of sand, they were at the same time consuming vast quantities of wood. The first thirty or forty feet of tunnel were shored with solid box frames made from bedboards, but because there was a limited supply of bedboards, it was decided to space the frames about a foot apart. To fill the gap, the carpenters used floorboards, which were available because all of the huts had been built with double floors.

The spacing of the frames certainly saved wood, but it also increased the danger of falls. With the new system, the man at the face had to dig two feet unshored before he could put in a frame. Consequently, falls at the face became almost a daily occurrence. And to make things more inconvenient, when repairing a fall it was impossible to jam more than two-thirds of the collapsed sand back behind the shoring frame. As a result, each fall not only produced extra unwanted spoil but also left a weak spot where the repacked sand was more liable to cave in again. Still, in spite of the many falls, all of the tunnels were well past the sixty-foot mark by the end of May.

Even with the new shoring system, wood remained the most immediate need. Roger Bushell talked it over with the tunnel committee and decided to order a levy on bedboards. Responsibility for the collection was put in the very capable hands of Squadron Leader 'Willy' Williams, a big, curly-headed Aussie who attacked the job with all the zest his countrymen were known for.

*

John Edwin Ashley Williams was well known in the camp as a big, bluff joker who was typically Australian in his outlook and demeanor. Willy was born on May 6, 1919, in Wellington, New Zealand. His family moved to Manly, Australia, while he was a child, and Willy and his three brothers grew up in the Sydney suburb. He attended the Sydney Church of England (Shore) Grammar School from 1932 to 1936 and then opted to try medical school at the University of Sydney. It wasn't to his liking, however, and in December 1937 the young man left Australia for England to join the RAF.

Willy enrolled as a pupil pilot on January 17, 1938, and was posted to the flying school at Ayr. Two months later he was granted a short service commission. He completed the customary pilot training and was then posted for training as a flying instructor. Eventually Williams was sent to Rhodesia for instructional duties. He later went to Durban, South Africa, to test aircraft that had been reassembled there after reaching Africa by sea, and it wasn't until April 1942 that Williams was posted to an operational unit, 112 Squadron.

For the next two months Willy went through three different squadrons to gain experience before reaching 450 Squadron on June 14, 1942. He quickly made a name for himself. He had a strong and vibrant personality and was a very aggressive pilot. Most of his squadronmates, though, remember Willy for his good humor and quick wit. Many a newcomer was jokingly threatened with an assignment to Chad or Lake Titicaca if he failed to stay in line. The squadron flew Kittyhawks in fighter-bomber raids against Axis airfields in the Western Desert, and Willy's personality seemed ideally suited to this type of mission. In place of service issue, he always flew wearing the same ensemble: baggy khaki shorts and shirt, and leather sandals. His unorthodox gear, however, didn't seem to hamper his combat effectiveness. His first kill was an Me 109, downed over Gambut on June 18. In September Willy led the squadron into a formation of Stukas and emerged with two more victories to his credit. Later that day he pursued an enemy aircraft almost to Tobruk before bringing it down, boosting his total to four. He became an ace a few days later when he downed an Me 109 after a long and tough dogfight over El Adem.

In October the focus of 450's operations shifted. Fitted with long-range tanks, the Kittyhawks were now sent against any available target in enemy territory. Willy, promoted to squadron leader on October 18, prepared to lead his pilots against anything that moved, from trucks to trains to aircraft. Though many of his pilots were new, Willy was confident they could do the job. On October 31 he took the squadron to attack Abu Haggag railroad station. The reported ammunition train turned out to be a hospital train, so the squadron decided to strafe El Daba instead, to make the trip worthwhile. Unfortunately, a wicked piece of bad luck overtook Willy. On the way over the airfield, his own wingman accidentally fired on him, scoring numerous hits with a very difficult full-deflection shot. Williams's Kittyhawk was badly damaged but he was able to crash-land it near the coastal road. He climbed out unhurt and was captured immediately.

Now, still wearing his baggy summer shorts and a decrepit khaki shirt, Willy canvassed the entire camp for bedboards, and within days his haul was safely hidden away, ready for use in the tunnels. By taking a couple of planks from each bunk in the camp, he had collected about two thousand board feet of wood, enough to keep Tom, Dick, and Harry satisfied for quite some time.

*

While work continued underground, the other branches of X Organization were gearing up as well. Soon after the move to North Compound, Bushell gathered the department heads, outlined his plan, and allotted their tasks. Then they were allowed full latitude in the way they chose to accomplish them. Roger asked for frequent progress reports and occasionally offered suggestions but never forced an opinion on one of his lieutenants. He viewed them as experts in their own individual areas and deferred to their judgment.

When told by Roger that at least a thousand maps would be needed, Des Plunkett gave a rather preoccupied 'No problem,' and Tim Walenn merely smiled when Bushell gave him the order for 240 sets of forged documents. If either of them was at all fazed by the request, he certainly didn't show it.

Next, Roger turned to a strongly built chap of medium height with thick brown hair and bushy eyebrows. Al Hake was well known to most kriegies as a tinkerer who loved to design and build things with bits of scrap scrounged from various places. Once again his talents were to be put to the production of escape gear.

'Al, the compasses will be up to you,' said Roger softly, 'and we're going to need at least two hundred.'

There was no comment from the phlegmatic Australian, who raised his ample eyebrows to signal his comprehension. 'I'll see about getting a production line going,' he said at last.

That was about all one usually got out of Warrant Officer Al Hake, one of the few noncommissioned officers involved in the escape preparations. He was a quiet and sometimes stolid fellow but could always be depended upon. Meticulously neat and well organized, he brought these habits to his work in X Organization.

*

Albert Horace Hake was born in Sydney on June 30, 1916. As a youngster, he showed more of a predilection for the sea than for the air. The Hakes lived close to Sydney's Parramatta River, and Al and his brother Les spent many pleasant afternoons in a canoe they had been given. Later Al yearned for something bigger and began constructing a sailboat in the family basement. When it came time to launch it, Al and a friend realized that the boat was a little larger than the door to the basement, but they managed to overcome the difficulty and set out for a sail in Sydney Harbor. Unfortunately, they were becalmed on the way home and had to spend the night in the harbor while the authorities sent out search parties. Coincidentally, Al's friend later escaped from a Japanese POW camp and made his way to freedom by boat.

Hake's greatest talent was in technical drawing and metalwork. He showed sufficient proficiency at school to be selected for a special course for future manual arts teachers at Sydney Technical High School. Al was a serious student, painstaking and conscientious, and really took to the training. He had a passion for drawing in three dimensions and creating little gadgets and, upon leaving school, put his skills to good use as a draftsman and apprentice engineer with an air-conditioning firm. The position was fine for a few years, but Al aspired to bigger things. He hoped one day to start his own air-conditioning company.

Early in 1940 Al's life received a boost thanks to an outing at a local ice-skating rink. A friend from work introduced him to a striking brunette named Noela Horsfall, and Al was instantly taken by her gay smile and cheery eyes. They started going out together immediately and spent every weekend hiking, surfing, or picnicking. More frequently, though, they returned to the skating rink where they had first met. On March 1, 1941, they were married.

Sadly, the couple's time together was all too short. In July 1940 Al had joined the RAAF Reserve and on January 4, 1941, he was called up to begin training; it was on a four-day leave that he and Noela were married. Eventually, Hake was posted to Wagga Wagga, the training center that brought together fledgling fliers from courses around Australia. It was a tense environment, with the trainees struggling to measure up to their comrades while trying to conquer the courses and examinations. Soon after arriving at Wagga Wagga, Al made friends with John Hannan, another young recruit, and when they graduated from the course on August 20, 1941, Al and John were firm friends.

The new pilots were given leave upon graduation but almost immediately were recalled to the embarkation depot at Sydney. Al and John were told that the camp was restricted and that no calls were allowed. They had a pretty good idea that something was up, and Al decided he had better slip out to see Noela, just in case there wasn't another chance. He, John, and another recruit scaled the fence at the rear of the depot and slunk away, planning to return by the same route later in the evening. Unfortunately, it was more difficult to get back into the depot than it had been to get out, and the three were caught by a disgruntled senior officer, who threatened them with all sorts of dire punishment. Al was unimpressed. 'I think they'll be a bit too busy tomorrow to worry about us,' he said quietly.

He was right. The next day, September 7, 1941, the airmen were put aboard the *Athlone Castle*, an old luxury liner bound for England. As he climbed the gangway, Al felt more thankful than ever that he had made the trip to see Noela. Though he assured her that they would not be long separated, Al had no idea when he would see Australia again. The airmen lived a life of ease aboard the huge liner, and Al and John found a roomy first-class cabin and settled down for a pleasant cruise. Arriving in Scotland, the airmen were then moved to the reception center at Bournemouth.

On November 18 a draft of fliers, including Hake and Hannan, boarded a train for 53 OTU, at Llandow in Wales, to begin instruction on Spitfires. This was the dream of many Allied airmen but the reception at Llandow turned out to be less than appealing. It was late at night when the group reached the camp, and Al and John groped around the damp, dark compound, searching for an empty barrack to claim. After a miserable stumble in the mud, they found a room with three beds and a small iron stove in the corner. With droplets of water clinging to his eyebrows, Al looked grimly at the sad little stove. 'From now on,' he said resolutely, 'that thing is going to work overtime!' The next day he climbed up into the attic and pulled down a few beams, which he hacked into kindling with a heavy hunting knife. From then on, their room was always warm and their clothes always dry.

The weather at Llandow was foul, especially for Australians accustomed to clear conditions. Apart from the apparently continual fog and rain, they also had to contend with barrage balloons over Cardiff and Swansea. Training was not without its dangers, and the course lost six pilots out of sixty in the first three weeks. Luckily, Al and John adapted well to the Spitfires and thoroughly enjoyed flying them.

The food also left a lot to be desired, but Al and John made do. They purloined a couple of pounds of margarine and took it back to the room in their gas mask cases. With a few loaves of bread liberated from the sergeants' mess and a toasting fork crafted by Al, the two treated themselves to hot toast each night before retiring.

Their stint at 53 OTU finally ended on January 14, 1942, and Al was judged to be one of the top three pilots in the course; he acknowledged this honor with a very meaningful raising of the eyebrows. They were then posted to operational squadrons, Al to 72 at Biggin Hill and John to 64 at Hornchurch. Hake had requested an assignment to the Pacific Theater, where he would have had a chance to see Noela while on leave, but the authorities turned him down. The two chums had few chances to see each other, what with the pressure of operations, but John did drop in at Biggin Hill one night, ostensibly because of bad weather. He and Al spent an entertaining evening at a disreputable little club called Daniel's Den before he returned to Hornchurch the next morning.

On April 4, 1942, 11 Group was detailed to carry out a massive escort mission, sending three hundred fighters to shepherd twelve Bostons to St. Omer in northern France. It was a perfectly clear day with unlimited visibility, and the bombers completed their attack on railroad installations without loss. The escorts, however, were less lucky. They were jumped by masses of Focke-Wulfs over the target and, at 20,000 feet, couldn't match the performance of the German fighters. Ten Spitfires fell to the FW 190s, but Al fought his way out of the battle, only to have a chance anti-aircraft shell smash his propeller and send him careening.

He regained control and set his sights on the English coast but was bounced by five Focke-Wulfs. Al fought like a wildcat in his crippled aircraft and managed to knock down one of his opponents before realizing that the damage to his own machine had caused him to lose thousands of feet in height. As he descended farther, tongues of flame begin to appear from under the engine cowling and Al decided it was time to evacuate his burning Spitfire. With some minor burns and a few shrapnel wounds, he clambered out of the cockpit at the minimum height for a safe parachute jump and plummeted to a heavy landing not far from a German troop depot.

As he was being trucked off to a hospital to have his wounds tended, Al noticed that the rank insignia had been burned off his battle dress; let's just see if they decide to promote me, he said to himself. As Al expected, the Germans who picked him up assumed that anyone flying one of the venerable Spitfires must be an officer, and they slated him for an officers' camp. The unofficially commissioned Australian was not about to disabuse them of their mistaken notion.

Back in Australia, Noela heard the news of her husband's capture in a rather disturbing way. In mid-April German radio broadcast an alleged interview with Pilot Officer Albert Hake, who had reputedly been shot down in a Wellington on Easter Sunday. According to the interview, the airman complained of the 'hypocritical and unfulfilled promises' made by England and expressed satisfaction with his new surroundings. Of course, no one took the interview seriously, as John Hannan wrote to Noela, and Al would have laughed had he heard the broadcast, for his new accommodations proved to be less than satisfactory.

His burns had healed quickly, and a month after being shot down, Hake was in East Compound, a fact that pleased him little. 'Well, "here ah is, boss" in a bloody zoo,' he wrote to John, 'and I don't feel proud of the fact.' Since the camp was still relatively new, there were few amenities, but Al looked forward to starting his own vegetable garden. Soon other pursuits were found to occupy his time. His particular manual talents were noticed by one of the woodworkers, and Al was glad to be put to work making any little gadgets that were required. Johnny Travis soon discovered that Hake had a knack for crafting compasses, and mentioned the fact to Roger Bushell. Big X could think of no one better to run the compass line.

*

The late spring also brought a new member to the Sagan family in the form of a pregnant cat that turned up one day and attached herself to Tom Kirby-Green. She bore a litter, nursed them and then disappeared whence she had come, leaving Tom with a brood of hungry little mouths to feed. He gave a few away to other kriegies but kept three, which he christened Tweeny, Group Captain Prune, and 2/6. Soon they were getting more visitors than he was. Kaz Pawluk, a dyed-in-the-wool cat-lover, came over almost every day to see the kittens and would sit with them for hours as they chased around bits of string or balls of paper. Watching them play, one could almost forget the barbed wire. But as the kittens got older, they wandered off one by one until the day when Tom had to tell Kaz that the last of the litter had mooched off through the wire and into the woods. Pawluk smiled sadly and gazed off toward the pine trees. 'If only it were so easy for us to get away,' he said quietly to Tom.

*

If there was one thing that made the Germans nervous, it was lice. The merest mention of the little creatures was usually enough to send the average ferret packing. Of course, their phobia was not entirely unfounded. Lice often carried disease, and many a Soviet camp had already been ravaged by epidemics. So occasionally a scare went through Stalag Luft III, putting the Germans into a temporary panic while they rushed to organize parties to the delousing station in East Compound's *Vorlager*.

During the first week of June, another lice alarm was raised, and the Germans quickly set about assembling groups and marching them out of the camp for the short walk to the delousing block. The second day of the operation, June 12, was a beautiful summer day, warm and calm, and there was a hint of excitement in the air. Everyone enjoyed the delousing parties, especially on a pleasant day, for it was a nice walk through the pine woods, and any break, no matter how short, from the dullness of the camp was very welcome.

At about two in the afternoon, another party of kriegies began to form up outside one of the huts. They carried small packs of clothing to be deloused and, as they waited in the sun for their escorts, a few of the younger chaps engaged in some rough but harmless horseplay. Shortly, a couple of German NCOs appeared and started to form the twenty-four kriegies into ranks of three. Eventually they got things organized and marched the straggling mob toward the front gate, where the guards waved them past, paying little attention to the passes that were presented. The prisoners ambled through, whistling tunelessly, chatting, and laughing noisily. No one paid any particular attention to them as the column wound around the corner toward the delousing station.

Part of the reason for the guards' lack of interest was the impressive party of senior officers approaching the front gate. Led by an officious-looking goon corporal, Bill Jennens, Bob Stanford-Tuck, Junior Clark, and three other officers were on their way to an emergency meeting with von Lindeiner. The guard at the first gate looked at the escort's pass with little interest, but the second gate guard decided to have a closer check and began turning the pass over and over in his hand. He looked up at the corporal, then back down at the pass, and eventually asked to see the escort's sidearm. The NCO shrugged his shoulders and raised his hands. It was Bob van der Stok.

When Bob slowly put up his arms, Roger Bushell, who had been watching the scene intently, took a deep breath and waited for the storm to break. He knew that it would be only minutes before the goons realized that the first party had not arrived at its destination. Their escorts had been less than conscientious in their duties – hardly surprising, since they were a couple of German-speaking Belgian airmen. By now the entire party was scattered through the woods around the camp. Were it not for a new identification mark on the back of the passes, the second party would have gotten through as easily as the first. Even with the failure of one group, though, the delousing party escape was still a major success.

The original plan had been hatched during the first days in North Compound, when Roger and a few others realized that the paper checks at the gates were not as rigorous as they had been in East Compound, or as they were likely to become in time. If the organization could get hold of a gate pass, it could shepherd out a fairly large group of escapers at once. The pass was provided by Sydney Dowse's contact, Hesse, the duty interpreter at the *Vorlager* gate, and Tim Walenn soon made a few typically excellent copies. Now all they needed was an excuse to use them, and that's where the lice came in. There had been delousing parties from East Compound before, so Roger decided to create their own lice alarm. After sending out a few genuine delousing parties, he believed that another group, escorted by kriegies in German uniform, would not appear amiss to the sentries on the gate – that is, if the escorts looked convincing enough to fool the guards.

The uniforms were relatively easy to fabricate. Tommy Guest had made goonskins before and now set to work at making a few more. The badges and belt buckles were made by Jens Müller, who cast the eagles for the lapels out of melted silver foil. The soap molds in which they were cast either were carved by Jens himself or, in the case of the buckle, were impressions taken from the real thing. To make the insignia for the jackets, Tom Kirby-Green reluctantly sacrificed the tail from a very well-worn shirt.

The difficult part would be the rifles carried by all escorting guards. It was to be a daylight escape, so they had to look practically perfect. The task of building the weapons fell to Johnny Travis, who in turn conscripted Jens Müller and Flight Lieutenant Ian Alexander 'Digger' McIntosh, a prewar RAF officer who had been downed and badly burned at Maastricht in 1940. Bushell gave them a week to finish the job.

Before doing anything, Jens and Digger needed the correct dimensions of the rifles, and for this they called on Henri Picard, who was happy to do anything for X Organization. Besides, some outdoor work would be a welcome change from the closeness of the forgery factory, thought the dark-haired little Belgian.

*

One former kriegie recalls that his first impression of Flight Lieutenant Henri-Albert Picard was of a sloppy, heavy-featured, lethargic dullard. He is quick to admit, though, that first impressions are so often wrong. Very soon one realized that Henri was a charming fellow with a keen intellect and a well-stocked mind. He had a flair for languages and possessed a remarkably wide English vocabulary, often being able to come up with the meaning of a word that had stumped his English roommates. But most appealing about Henri was his sparkling sense of fun and nimble wit, qualities that kept a smile on his face most of the time.

Henri was born on April 17, 1916, in Etterbeek, the third of four children, and was a diligent and capable student whose real love was drawing. Like most boys, he was fascinated by airplanes and cars and spent hours sketching them. Henri was even fonder of nature, drawing colorful and highly realistic sketches of birds and animals from around his parents' home. Upon finishing high school, Henri was admitted to the École Royale Militaire in Brussels, arriving at the school on November 28, 1936. Henri made friends quickly with the other recruits and students at the school. One young man, Roger De Wever, would pop in and out of Henri's life over the next few years. Another, Louis Rémy, would also become a POW and would escape successfully from Colditz.

One of Picard's greatest joys at the school was sports, and he excelled in gymnastics, riding, and fencing. He was also an excellent diver and helped his swim team to win the school's challenge tournament in 1938. He enjoyed the military life so much that in November 1937 he enlisted for a three-year term. At first, Henri was attracted by the infantry because he wanted to be in the front lines if Germany attacked Belgium, so in December 1938 he was commissioned in the Chasseurs Ardennais. Before long, though, Henri's boyhood interest in flying took over, and he asked to be posted to military aviation. His request was granted, and Picard was sent to Evere for observer training. In January 1940 he started as a student pilot. Henri loved the freedom of the skies and on training flights often buzzed his family's home, an old sawmill on the road to Bastogne. As soon as the locals heard an airplane engine approaching, they would spill out into their gardens and wave at the little biplane, for they were immensely proud of their aviator son.

On May 10, 1940, the day of the German invasion of the Low Countries, Henri and his classmates were stationed at Gossoncourt. They didn't even get off the ground before their aircraft were destroyed. That afternoon, as they surveyed the havoc wrought by the German bombing, the class vowed to continue the fight. Five days later they were on their way out of Belgium, intent on regrouping and making themselves into a fighting unit somewhere else. After orders and counterorders, the squadron gathered at Caen–Carpiquet airfield in northern France and entrained for Marseilles. On May 31 they arrived at Oran, in Algeria, with the intention of re-forming the pilot school at Oujda in Morocco. However, with no supplies or aircraft, there was little they could do but sightsee. Henri was fascinated by the strange and intriguing North African animals and often went on day trips to seek out wildlife to sketch. All in all, his first days in Morocco were very pleasant.

After a month of inactivity, the Belgians became restless. Anxious to get into action and make themselves useful, Henri and another pilot traveled to Casablanca and managed to arrange passage to England through the British consulate. On July 17, 1940, Picard was officially taken into the Belgian forces at Gloucester. On December 22 he was posted to Peterborough for training in Tiger Moths, and instruction went well until January 1941. Then, while taxiing for takeoff, he failed to see a parked aircraft in front of him and struck it, cutting into a wing with his propeller. There was a fire, but luckily the aircraft was empty and Henri got away with only a mild reprimand from the station commander. When he left Peterborough for the flying school at Tern Hill, that was the only black mark on his slate.

At Tern Hill Henri was reunited with Roger De Wever, and the two remained together when they were posted to 58 OTU at Grangemouth in July 1941. There they both converted to Spitfires, and on August 30 Henri was posted to the Belgian flight of 131 Squadron, flying Spitfires from Tern Hill. On September 28, disaster struck again. In much the same circumstances as before, Henri was taxiing his Spitfire but failed to see a stationary aircraft on the runway in front of him. His propeller slashed into the little Magister trainer and completely destroyed it. But this time, the other aircraft wasn't empty. In it were two squadron pilots, and both were killed in the crash. The accident was put down to gross negligence, and a grief-stricken Picard was placed under open arrest, the RAF's mildest form of punishment.

No further action was taken against Henri, and on November 14 he was reassigned to 350 (Belgian) Squadron, based at Valley in Anglesey. From there the unit did sweeps over the Irish Sea to protect convoys coming into and out of Blackpool and Liverpool. In April 1942 the squadron rejoined 11 Group at Debden and re-equipped with newer Spitfires in preparation for sweeps against the Continent. The squadron moved around quite a bit that spring, but the confusion didn't affect Henri. On June 29, 1942, he got his first two kills while escorting a squadron of Bostons to Hazebrouck. The following month, Henri was awarded the Croix de Guerre with palms.

August was a dramatic month for the young Belgian. On the sixteenth, while pulling out of an attack on a train, his wing caught a high-tension wire and he was only just able to limp home. Three days later, over Dieppe, Henri and another pilot claimed an FW 190 destroyed. Then, on the twenty-seventh, the squadron was assigned to escort twelve Bostons to bomb the Abbéville–Drucat airfield. It sounded like a straightforward operation, but the Spitfires were bounced by 190s and the Belgians found themselves fighting for their lives. Henri got one of the enemy but was shot down himself and seriously wounded in the leg. He came down near the mouth of the Somme estuary and was carried into the English Channel by the current. Searches were undertaken by his squadron and others, but they failed to spot Henri's dinghy. He drifted for five days and five nights.

For most, the ordeal would have been a nightmare, but for Picard it was something of an education. In a letter to his brother, he described his experiences: 'The second night was magnificent. Dolphins played around me and two of them came up beside my dinghy to rest . . . they sounded like locomotives and when they blew off their air, it was a real sound of an explosion!' With nothing else to do, he watched the birds and fishes intently, although the longer he drifted, the more he began to view them as a means of sustenance. Finally, on September 2, Henri came ashore, exhausted and semiconscious. The Germans picked him up immediately, and he spent a week in a hospital with his leg in plaster before he was well enough to be sent to Dulag Luft. Ironically, as he was passing through Belgium on his way to Oberursel, his family and friends were holding a little celebration in a workshop at the old sawmill. They had only just learned that Henri had been awarded the Croix de Guerre.

*

Henri continued to indulge his love of drawing in captivity and asked his family to send drawing paper and colored pencils to the camp for the caricatures that he did so well. For his other pastime, forging documents, it was less easy to get supplies. But now Henri had a chance for a break from forgery. Reunited with his old friend Roger De Wever, Henri was to sketch the rifle that Roger would carry in the escape. Armed with a pair of homemade calipers, Henri followed Jens Müller out into the compound and on to the circuit, where Jens sidled up to one of the guards and engaged him in conversation. While the two chatted away happily, Henri ducked in and out behind the guard, taking measurements with his calipers and then dropping back to jot them down on his notepad. Jens had chosen a guard who was roughly his own height, so Henri just had to note where the butt and muzzle came on the guard's thighs and head and then take the measurements on Jens later. It was a slow job, but after a couple of days of inane conversation and careful observation, Henri had an accurate and detailed plan of the carbine used by the guards.

To make the gun, Travis hunted down all of the very few beech bedboards in the camp. Each rifle was cut and roughly carved in two halves, which was then glued together (using an adhesive obtained by boiling German bread) and clamped with vices taken from table tennis nets. After careful sanding, the metal parts of the gun were laboriously rubbed with a piece of graphite until they were indistinguishable from the real thing. The wooden sections were colored with boot polish so that they, too, looked authentic. For the fittings, Jens used bent nails and small strips of metal and even cast a realistic-looking barrel end out of silver paper. Once completed, it was impossible to tell that the rifles were fake without touching them.

Selecting the escapers was the easiest job. The senior officers were chosen almost entirely on their demeanor and impressiveness of carriage, while the guards were selected from among the most fluent German-speakers in the camp. To make up the delousing party, Bushell picked the workers who had put in particularly good service for a couple of years. He wanted to go himself but was talked out of it. Wally Floody was another who wanted to go, but Roger quickly torpedoed that idea. Wally was much more useful to the organization underground than he would be in the cooler.

Within a week, the guards' disguises were complete, their German had been checked by Rene Marcinkus, and the escapers were starting their final briefing. The forged passes had come out of Tim Walenn's workshop and were, as usual, letter perfect. Everything waited for the word to go. At the last minute, though, one of the kriegies noticed that the NCOs who escorted prisoners out of the camp were wearing pistols instead of rifles. A new order from above had discontinued the carrying of rifles.

When he was given the news, Roger blew up, as did Johnny Travis and Jens Müller, and everything was put on hold while one of Tommy Guest's workers, who had made handbags before the war, fabricated some holsters. He scored a few pieces of cardboard to give them a leathery look, cut and bent them to resemble holsters and then rubbed them with black boot polish until they shone. Bits of paper were stuffed into the ends of the holsters, and Digger McIntosh crafted some wooden pistol butts to stick out of the top of the cardboard. As with the rifles, it was almost impossible to tell the holsters from the real thing.

The escapers knew that limited supplies could be carried without creating suspicion, so the odds against making a home run were heavier than usual. However, the confusion that would be stirred up was also considerable, and this was the primary value of the escape. The thought of twenty-six kriegies strolling out the front gate was sure to ruffle a few feathers in the *Kommandantur*. And that it did. There was an emergency *Appell* and every available member of the camp staff, from the doctor to the parcel-room orderly, was mobilized to search for the escapers.

*

After leaving the compound, the main party straggled up the road for a hundred yards or so; then the kriegies broke off into the woods in ones and twos. Roger De Wever and Otto Geesinck, the two escorts, ducked behind a bush and peeled off their goonskins, which they gave to Walt Morison and Lorne Welch. The others dove into their packs and pulled out, not lice-ridden blankets and jackets, but roughly tailored civilian clothes, little packets of concentrated food, maps, and small amounts of German money. Within five minutes of leaving the camp, the escapers were on their way out of the area, some making for the railroad station and the rest heading for the deeper woods.

Because they had very little head start, most didn't get far and were rounded up within a few miles of the compound. Hank Birkland was picked up while trudging through the forest south of the camp. Red Noble, traveling to the Baltic as a Norwegian workman, had better luck. He lost no time in getting to the station and managed to board a railroad car that was just pulling away. By the time the guards got to the platform to round up the other escapers waiting for trains, Red was gone. He had a bit of a shock when a Luftwaffe officer showed more than a casual interest in his RAF trousers but arrived in Posen without further difficulty. Having reached the one-third mark of his journey, Red was feeling confident. However, just as the train was about to leave the station, the police pulled off a few dozen people at random, including Red and another escaper whom he recognized, and detained them in the waiting room. It was obviously a hit-and-miss search, but when they got to Red, the police became suspicious. They were about to telephone the firm listed as his employer on his *Ausweis* (identity card) when Red decided to give himself up. He and the other escaper were shuttled off to the civilian jail and then back to Sagan.

Digger McIntosh, hoping to get to Switzerland via Bohemia, followed the railroad line south for about fifteen miles and then jumped a southbound goods train. At Siegersdorf he found the station full of police and was immediately stopped and questioned. He was about to be released when one of the policemen noticed that the official who had signed Digger's identity card had died weeks before the pass was supposedly issued. That was it for Digger.

At least two of the escapers fell afoul of the camp doctor. Roger De Wever found the railroad station after a few unintentional detours, only to learn that he had missed the train to Leipzig. Opting for the next train heading away from Sagan, he bought a ticket to Berlin and was waiting in the booking hall when the doctor appeared and asked to see his papers. That ended Roger's attempt.

Conk Canton had even worse luck. He boarded a train in Sagan station and, just as the train was leaving, a German officer climbed on and sat down in Conk's compartment. Realizing with horror that his new traveling companion was the camp doctor, Conk quickly hid his nose behind a newspaper and prepared to hold his breath for the entire trip. After a few minutes of terrible waiting, Conk felt a tap on his knee. He ignored it, and also the second tap, but he couldn't ignore the third, so he peeked rather nervously around the edge of his paper. The doctor was regarding him apologetically and said, 'I am so sorry, Mr. Canton, but I am afraid you will have to come with me.' He, too, ended up cooling his heels in solitary, along with most of the other escapers.

In fact, only three of the original group managed to stay at large more than a couple of days before being dropped back in the bag. Lorne Welch and Walt Morison, two of Travis's engineers, headed for a nearby airfield to look for something they could fly to Sweden. (X Organization had sketches of the instrument panels of dozens of German aircraft, provided by airmen who had flown captured machines before being shot down.) When they got to the airfield, they set their sights on an old trainer and nonchalantly strolled up to it and began cranking the engine. Just as the engine caught, a hefty German pilot appeared and fired a couple of phrases at the two escapers, neither of whom spoke German. Baffled, they could only salute and back away from the trainer in deference. This seemed to satisfy the German, who climbed into the cockpit and roared off. They were able to find another airplane but discovered that the starting crank was missing. Not to be put off, the two wandered into the hangar and rummaged around until they found a crank in one of the lockers. Returning to the tarmac, they were just starting up the trainer when another German appeared. Again, Lorne and Walt listened politely as the sergeant barked at them, but this time he wasn't so easily assuaged with a salute. Realizing the game was up, the two raised their hands and were trundled off for questioning. Their interrogators were understandably upset about two British prisoners wandering around their airfields, and Welch and Morison were left sweating in cells for a couple of weeks while charges of sabotage were thrown around. Eventually the Germans settled for packing them both off to Colditz.

Of the twenty-six, little Johnny Stower had the worst luck. He was stopped about a mile from the compound but was saved by papers identifying him as a Spanish worker and he continued on his way to Czechoslovakia. Walking cautiously through fields and forests, he made good time and covered the eighty-odd miles to Czechoslovakia in about a week. Once there, he contacted the underground through a friendly innkeeper near the Prague airport and, for the next three weeks, was kept in safe houses while the Resistance tried to get papers for a train trip to Switzerland. When this failed, they outfitted him in new clothes and gave him a ticket to a small station near the German border, and Johnny was able to cross back into Germany on foot.

He then caught a train heading toward Switzerland and got off about forty miles from Lake Constance. X Organization had given him a detailed map of the Schaffhausen area, and Johnny hoped to cross into neutral territory there, where the border followed a dry riverbed. At that point the frontier looped around, leaving a small pocket of Swiss territory between two parts of the river. Having brought him this far, Johnny's luck now deserted him, for he misjudged the distance on the map and passed over the dry riverbed frontier without knowing it. Walking through Swiss territory, he came upon the other part of the river loop, which marked the frontier back into Germany, and, excited at being so close, stumbled right into a guard patrolling the German side of the frontier. It was cruel misfortune.

The Gestapo held Johnny for a few weeks to pump him about the Czech underground, but he preferred to discuss his walk in the woods and was eventually returned to Sagan. Stower's family was alarmed at the sudden halt in letters from Germany, and it wasn't until October that they learned what had happened. 'I am longing to see you all again,' Johnny's letter began. 'I nearly managed it in June, but just failed by less than a hundred yards . . . will tell you all about it when I see you, so near and yet so far.'

*

The Germans reacted to the escape with the customary measures. They doubled the number of *Appells* per day to four and cut off the issue of Red Cross and cigarette parcels. They were also very anxious to discover who had played the parts of the guards in the escape. They came into the cooler at regular intervals and asked every single kriegie if they had worn the goonskins. Not surprisingly, everyone, including De Wever and Geesinck, denied everything. Eventually the goons gave up and sentenced everybody to the same stretch of solitary. However, it wasn't really all that solitary, because the escapers were packed into the cooler three to a cell so they would all fit.

As soon as he came out of the cooler after the delousing party escape, Dougie Mellor was tracked down by Neville McGarr, his well-built South African roommate, who had lost none of his strength in two years of captivity. Neville wanted to hear all about the break and listened to the story of Dougie's short-lived freedom with undisguised fascination. When the tale drew to an end, Neville was quiet for a moment and then began to speak in a soft voice. 'Doug,' he said, 'I'm going to escape from this camp before the war is over. Then I'll have an escape story to tell as well as you.' Having said that, Neville allowed his round face to break into the smile that was always waiting on his lips. Dougie Mellor knew then that his pal's mind was made up, and from that day on there was never any question of Neville McGarr reneging on his promise, whatever the odds against him might be.

Of course, it wasn't the first time that Clement Aldwyn Neville McGarr had found the odds stacked against him. Born in Johannesburg on November 24, 1917, Neville was the second child in a family of five that lived in the Transvaal before moving to Durban in 1923. The young McGarr began school there, but at age twelve was stricken with polio and completely paralyzed from the waist down. He spent eight months in the hospital, doing constant therapy to learn to walk again. A lesser boy might have given up, but Neville's determination saw him through, and he was left with nothing more than flat feet and a slight numbness in the legs. By September 1930 he was well enough to start high school and, by the time he graduated in 1935, he had received awards for academic achievement and played on the school rugby team. Neville was a very solid player, and his strength made it difficult to imagine that he had ever been paralyzed. He was known for hard tackles and was occasionally on the giving or receiving end of a concussion. In one particularly crunching tackle, his hapless opponent was knocked unconscious and hospitalized for a couple of days. Neville was so concerned for his well-being that he rode to the hospital every afternoon to visit the lad.

With the help of his father, McGarr secured a job in the laboratory of Lever Brothers and was later taken on as a clerk in the Treasury Department of the Durban Corporation. He lived a busy life before the war, tooling around on his Rudge Special motorcycle and later in his BSA Scout motorcar, or playing drums in a small dance band he had put together with three friends. He spent some time in the naval reserve and cut quite a dashing figure in his uniform. His six-foot frame was broad and very powerful, and Neville was meticulous about his clothes and hair. He also took great pains to look after his beautiful white teeth. It was a real blow when one had to be removed in camp.

Neville had left the naval reserve by the time war came, but there was no doubt in the McGarr family that he would re-enter the service. In May 1940 Neville and two friends happened to see an advertisement requesting applicants for pilot training and immediately decided to join up. The three passed their medicals, wangled rail warrants to Pretoria, and appeared unannounced at SAAF headquarters on May 23. Unsure of what to do with these eager stalwarts, the authorities mustered them as air mechanics until the next pilots' course started. Just under a year later, on April 26, 1941, Neville was commissioned, and he was posted to Egypt on July 21. In early October he was transferred to 2 Squadron, flying Curtiss Tomahawk fighters over the Libya–Egypt frontier region.

On October 6, in the first week of Neville's operational assignment, the squadron was detailed to patrol the Sidi Omar area. The first half of the sweep went without incident but as the twelve Tomahawks were about to turn for home, they were set upon by a dozen Messerschmitts. In the ensuing melee, Neville and a squadronmate were shot down. The other pilot was killed, but Neville took to his parachute and watched the rest of the battle from a front-row seat as he drifted down to the desert floor. Missing a shoe that had been lost in the descent, he set out toward Allied lines and after three days without food or water had walked to within a few miles of safety. As he paused to grab a few minutes' rest before the last leg of his trek, McGarr heard the sound of vehicle engines in the distance. With success so near, he had no desire to risk capture and searched for a place to hide on the barren desert. The tired South African spotted a slight depression from which he could watch the approach and hared off toward the gully. As the trucks crested the hill, one of the German soldiers saw Neville and let out a yell. He was just a few hours' walk from freedom.

After spending a couple of days in a makeshift compound in Libya, Neville was moved to Dulag Luft. He arrived at Barth just as winter was settling in and, once equipped with something more suitable than desert service kit, rather enjoyed the snow of the Baltic coast camp. From Barth, Neville went to Sagan's East Compound and, as he wrote to his family, it was a trip that he thoroughly enjoyed: 'I passed through some beautiful country getting here … Spring is in her stride, must write to Göring to see if a tour can be arranged.' Later he was part of the first purge to the North Compound in April 1943. He didn't know much about X Organization before the delousing party escape, but after that, he made it his job to find out. From Dougie Mellor he learned about the tunneling department and decided that his strength might best be used underground. Cheery Neville McGarr offered his services to the diggers but instead was asked to work with George Harsh and George McGill in supervising the tunnel security men. That suited Neville just fine.

*

There was a minor sequel to the delousing party escape. A few days after the original escape, three kriegies donned German uniforms and, carrying the rifles that Travis had so carefully crafted, marched toward the gate, thrusting forward forged passes bearing the identification mark that had tripped up van der Stok's party. Both gates swung open, and the three breezed through to freedom. By a nasty stroke of luck, two of them happened upon Glemnitz on the road to the train station and were immediately recognized and arrested. The third was Clapton native Dennis Herbert Cochran (born Cockram), a twenty-one-year-old radio operator–air gunner who had developed a reputation as one of London's premier table tennis players before the war. Downed in October 1942, Cochran had been at large for more than a month before being captured. This time his luck was even worse. In spite of his excellent command of German (which he had been studying intensively since he was a schoolboy), Dennis was pulled off a train a few hours after leaving the camp. The brevity of his escape was something the young officer accepted stoically, and it only deepened his resolve to do better next time. The already reserved young man became even more preoccupied with escape work and when not actually involved in some nefarious pursuit could be found on his bunk, poring over a volume of German grammar.

Hank Birkland, while in training in Canada (Hans Birkland)

Gordon Brettell, in his motor racing days (Terence Brettell)

Les Bull, early in his captivity (Kathleen Anstey)

Jimmy Catanach (W.A. Catanach)

Dennis Cochran in happier times before the war (Beryl Fitch)

Ian Cross, in 1938 (Sir Kenneth Cross)

'Winters Drawers On': from left, Des Plunkett, unknown, Dudley Davis, Wally Valenta, 'Digger' Carter, Tim Walenn, John Boardman, unknown (Alex Cassie)

Jack Grisman (Stan Grisman)

Noela and Al Hake (Noela Hake)

Halldor Espelid (Ingrid Espelid Hovig)   *Brian Evans* (Noel Evans)

Johannes Gouws (Sheila Oberholzer)   *'Sandy' Gunn* (Hamish Gunn)

Tony Hayter, after starting operations on Wellingtons (David Hayter)

Reg Keirath in Cairo, 1941 (Peter Kierath)

Kaz Pawluk (left rear) and Tony Kiewnarski (right front) (Polish Institute and Sikorski Museum)

Pat Langford in 1941 (Dennis Langford)

Adam Kolanowski in his Observers class photo, July 1942 (Polish Institute and Sikorski Museum)

A room in Sagan's East Compound in 1942; at rear, Lawrence Reavell-Carter, unknown, Dickie Edge, unknown, Jack Grisman; front, unknown, Henry Lamond, 'Conk' Canton (Judith Maidment)

Les Long as a new POW in 1941 (Dorothy Gallop)

'Johnny' Marshall, at Mersa Matruh, June 1931 (Vera Hamer)

Neville McGarr, at Barth in 1941 (Athlene Stevens)

George McGill (left), relaxing in his room in Sagan (Betty Gillies)

A room in Sagan's North Compound in early 1944: standing, from left, Purvis, Jeffries, and Mullins; sitting, from left, Harold Milford, John F. Williams, Tony Hayter, Chaz Hall, and Tom Whiting (Cynthia Cruickshank)

Norwegians in Sagan: from left, Jan Staubo, Per Bergsland, Halldor Espelid, and Jens Müller (Ingrid Espelid Hovig)

(above, left) *Sotiris Skantzikas (left) with his brother Sarandis* (Sarandis Skantzikas)

(above) *Henri Picard contemplates the skies* (Mimi Martin-Picard)

(left) *John Stevens showed a love of flying early in life* (Unity Price)

(below) *'Tommy' Thompson (third from left) and 'Wank' Murray (right) shortly after their capture* (Nora Thompson)

Sagan's East Compound at Christmas 1942: from left, Des Plunkett, 'Digger' Carter, Tim Walenn, Dudley Davis, Wally Valenta, John Boardman, and Guy Griffiths (Joy Troughton)

(right) *Paweł Tobolski* (Polish Institute and Sikorski Museum)

(below) *Jimmy Wernham with his cousin Marie Charleson, just before going overseas* (Marie Charleson)

(below, left) *George Wiley* (Jacqueline Broome)

Chapter 11

TUNNEL SUCCESS AND FAILURE

A FTER A COUPLE OF weeks, the restrictions were relaxed and life returned more or less to normal in Sagan. The sports field was always in use during those hot summer months as soccer squads squared off against one another. New Zealand had a narrow victory over Australia in a hard-fought contest, while the British Isles and the Dominions battled to a draw. For those who preferred more sedentary diversions, there was a bridge tournament that Gordon Brettell and Pat Leeson entered. Neither had played before, but that didn't deter them. They procured a copy of Culbertson's *Golden Book on Bridge* and studied it intensively for two days. Their hard work paid off and Gordon and Pat finished second, ahead of dozens of experienced pairs.

Fortified by the soil from Tom, Dick, and Harry, the camp's vegetable gardens prospered. The men grew potatoes, lettuce, spinach, radishes, and mustard cress to supplement their diet, and the gardens soon became a source of great pride. However, one prisoner went a bit too far for his roommates' taste when he had a load of sewage dumped on the garden outside his window. He was told in no uncertain terms that if he continued to use that form of fertilization, he had better find another room.

In fact, life in the camp appeared entirely normal, which was exactly Roger's intent. Work in the tunnels went on, and while the diggers were toiling away underground, the various workshops in X Organization continued to iron out their own wrinkles and get production rolling. And all the time, private escape ideas were being dreamed up and approved by the organization. In fact, there was such a volume of schemes that many prospective escapers had to wait in line. Twice, Canadians Pat Langford and Bill Keech approached the committee with plans, the first time to get out in the garbage cart and the second to use a trench dug by Soviet prisoners. Both times they were informed that others had already registered the plan and therefore had priority.

After careful observation during the first month in the new compound, Lawrence Reavell-Carter noticed that sacks of wastepaper from the compound were taken by horse cart through the main gate and deposited in the *Vorlager* of East Compound. He believed that he could hide in one of the sacks and cut his way out while the cart rumbled down the two-hundred-yard path between the two gates. The old driver didn't appear to be too bright, so Reavell-Carter thought he could dash to the woods unobserved. The plan was duly presented to Norman Quill, in charge of approving gate escapes, who watched the operation one day and was satisfied there was a reasonable chance of success. He and Reavell-Carter then went to Roger Bushell to seek final approval. Big X listened carefully, with furrowed brow and downcast eyes, as Reavell-Carter outlined his scheme. At the end, Bushell was silent for a moment before looking up.

'You know,' he began, 'it's an awfully good scheme, but I've got to be honest with you. You're a bloody big fellow and I just don't think you're the best man for it. Once we get you in that sack, there'll be no room for any paper to cover you! I'm going to have to suggest we send someone better suited.'

Reavell-Carter smiled. 'I was afraid you'd say that, Roger – you're quite right. But I'd still like to run the show.'

'Good,' replied Roger. 'We'll let you know when we've found a couple of willing victims.'

It was a couple of weeks before the substitute escapers, a New Zealander and an American who were small enough to fit in the sacks, were briefed and ready to go. On the appointed day in mid-July, Reavell-Carter and Dennis Cochran, fresh out of the cooler after his last escape, mingled helpfully with the orderlies shifting the sacks. They had been warned that two would be heavier than usual and were able to heave them onto the cart without any noticeable extra exertion. They gave a wave to the ancient driver of the cart, who trundled off toward the gate, where the guard halfheartedly poked a few of the sacks with a metal rod before waving the driver past. Reavell-Carter and Cochran watched the proceedings with great satisfaction. The plan worked perfectly. The two escapers cut their way out of the sacks as soon as the cart was out of sight of the first gate and then dropped noiselessly off the back of the wagon. The American had terrible luck and was recaptured not far from the camp but the New Zealander got clean away, only to be picked up on the island of Rugen in the Baltic a week later.

*

By far the biggest excitement during the weeks following the delousing party escape was created by the return of the last batch of kriegies from Schubin. With them came the full story of the latrine tunnel, which had pushed ahead through the early spring of 1943. Everything had gone exactly according to plan. As the cold and damp of February slowly subsided into the thaw of March, Eddie Asselin's tunnel neared the wire. At the same time, a rival tunnel was pushing west from under the night latrine, located in the barrack closest to the perimeter wire. The brainchild of Dickie Edge and David Strong, it was a full-service tunnel, complete with shoring and electric lights tapped from the mains, and had a cunningly concealed trap that resisted dozens of security searches. In fact, it was sheer carelessness that finally resulted in the tunnel's discovery.

In March 1943, rumors began to circulate that the kriegies in Schubin would be moved to Sagan sometime in April and, since the night latrine tunnel had farther to go than Asselin's hole, Edge and Strong decided to speed up work in an effort to break their tunnel before the POWs were moved. No sooner had they picked up the pace than they were shifted to another hut while the Germans turned the barrack upside down looking for a tunnel that had registered on their seismographs. The search lasted a full week but turned up nothing, so the tunnelers were allowed to return to their hut and to work.

Purely for reasons of time, Dickie and Dave made the difficult decision to begin working in the daylight hours, confident that their stooging system could pick up any German who might pose a threat. The system worked well for a time, but literally as the last boxes of sand were being dumped out of the window and spread on the ground, a misunderstanding between stooges allowed one of the guards to pass unnoticed. He wasn't picked up until a disperser noticed him standing outside the perimeter wire watching the dumping operation. The tunnel had been on borrowed time for weeks, and this search was far too thorough to miss it. The Germans found the trap eventually and, much to their astonishment, discovered that the tunnel was more than 110 feet in length and reached a full 60 feet beyond the wire. It would have been ready to break in less than a week.

The usual searches followed the discovery of the Edge/Strong tunnel, but the ingenious trap in the *Abort* escaped the Germans' eyes. By the beginning of March, it was ready to go. A meeting of the organizers was held and it was decided to make the break on the night of March 5–6, 1943. In fact, the tunnel was the largest part of a coordinated escape scheme involving a number of attempts. On the day of the break, two officers would escape from the camp in the muck cart; the count at *Appell* would be faked to conceal their absence. Then at the same time that the tunnel was breaking, ten officers would secrete themselves in the attics of various huts. These ghosts would wait until the fuss died down and hopefully slip away from the camp unnoticed.

The day started on a good note. Czech Joe Bryks and an English squadron leader got clean away in the muck cart, and the guards never missed them on *Appell*, thanks to the diversions of a few of the POWs. (The squadron leader was caught after a few days, but Bryks walked all the way to Warsaw, where he remained at large for three months before recapture.) That night, the thirty-three escapers assembled in huts near the *Abort* to wait for the go-ahead. The ten ghosts had already been hidden and had arranged for enough food to be brought to them so they could remain concealed for a few weeks. Eddie Asselin, Tex Ash, Prince Palmer, and Duke Marshall gleefully looked forward to missing morning *Appell*, when the Germans would discover that dozens of prisoners had escaped.

With everyone lying uncomfortably in the tunnel, Asselin dug the last few feet and was delighted to see that their navigation had been dead accurate: The tunnel broke in the bottom of the drainage ditch, so the escapers could crawl to the woods unseen. However, getting out of the tunnel proved to be a bit more difficult than first imagined. The hole was very narrow at the exit and, though the shaft was only a couple of feet high, each escaper had to lie on his back and gradually struggle up into a sitting position. Then it was a matter of muscling himself up through the hole. The first four out – Asselin, Ash, Marshall, and Palmer – were able to make the exit without too much difficulty. However, by the time Wings Day, thirty-third and last, made it to the end, the exit had filled with so much soil that he was barely able to clamber out.

As dawn broke over the camp, it became apparent to the prisoners that the Germans were still unaware of the escape. Seizing the opportunity, a South African wing commander gathered his escape kit, made his way casually to the *Abort*, and vanished up the tunnel. He was the last escaper to get away from Schubin before all hell broke loose. In the commotion that followed, the goons tore the camp apart, and it didn't take them long to find the ten ghosts. They took an almost ghoulish delight in that discovery, but it didn't change the fact that they had thirty-six kriegies missing and a long, empty hole under the *Abort* block.

Most of the escapers were back within two weeks. The walkers, many of whom were heading for the Baltic, started trickling in first. Wings Day and his partner, armed with only a few Polish phrases scribbled on the back of a cigarette package, had set out along the railroad line toward a small town eighty miles south where they had a contact, but they were picked up on the second day, hiding in a barn. Tex Ash and Eddie Asselin had found the woods full of soldiers and went to ground for a day or two before pressing on. They were caught on the fifth day in the Hohensalza area. A group of six was making for Warsaw, where they hoped to link up with the Polish underground and be smuggled to the Balkans. From there they would steal a German bomber and fly it to the Middle East. One pair was recaptured at Hohensalza, but the other four made it all the way to the Polish capital before being picked up.

The train travelers had marginally better luck. Tony Barber's disguise as a Danish businessman got him as far as Schneidemühl on the way to his destination of Bornholm, while Tommy Calnan and Robert Kee covered a good distance before being caught by the police at Cologne. Prince Palmer and Mike Wood hopped a freight train not far from the camp and sat in it for the better part of a day, waiting for it to move. Finally they climbed down and into a different train, only to see the first one leave a few minutes later. Now thoroughly discouraged, they decided to make their way on foot but were picked up not far from the train.

One by one, they all filtered back to Schubin – Fes Fessler, Ken Toft, Ian Cross, and the rest of the airmen. However, three weeks after the escape, two others were still missing. The venerable Jimmy Buckley and his running mate, a Danish airman, were believed to have been heading for Denmark, where they intended to find a boat and sail to Sweden. They managed to steal a small canoe, but the story had a tragic epilogue. Weeks after the escape, the Dane's body washed up near Copenhagen, and it was assumed that their canoe had been hit by a larger vessel while crossing the Kattegat. Jimmy Buckley's body was never found.

Back at Schubin, the escapers were clapped into the cooler, four men to each single cell, but were moved again after Prince Palmer crafted a skeleton key and went up and down the corridor letting everyone out of their cells. They were shifted to the top floor of the old girls' school building and kept in large rooms to await questioning. This time it was Ian Cross's turn to have a bit of fun. Every few minutes, a guard would poke his head in the door to make sure there was no trouble. On one occasion, Ian jumped to his feet, yelling, *'Ein Mann aus dem Fenster!'* (Man out of the window!) and gesticulating wildly toward the window. The guard let out a bleat of agony and rushed to the window, only to find it securely locked and bolted. Ian, meanwhile, was doubled over in laughter at the unfortunate goon. Over the next few days Cross pulled the same stunt periodically, and it never failed to send the poor goon into momentary panic.

There was very close questioning after the escape, and the prisoners were accused of sabotage on various occasions. The Gestapo couldn't seem to understand that they just wanted to get home. An interesting incident occurred during the questioning, too. A police party visited the camp to check up on security measures and, during the visit, the senior official spotted one of the barrels of heavily watered beer that was issued to the prisoners. He immediately began extolling the virtues of German beer and accepted readily when offered a glass. However, he insisted on paying for it and handed over a few coins. Finishing his glass, he went back to his investigation, one of the aims of which was to discover how the prisoners obtained real German money. It was only a small sum, but it did show that even the professionals slipped up now and again.

Only a few of the Schubin group, such as Day and Dodge, were transferred to North Compound; the rest, including Ian Cross, Prince Palmer, and Mike Wood, went into East Camp. There, some of them joined the enterprise that would become famous as the Wooden Horse. Under South African John Stevens, a number of the Schubin lads took their turns vaulting over the horse that concealed a tunnel entrance, and many of them had barked knees to show for it. However, when Oliver Philpot, Eric Williams, and Michael Codner finally broke the tunnel on October 29, 1943, and got clean away to Sweden, the vaulters soothed their wounds with the knowledge that they had helped in one of the most successful tunnels of the war.

*

The summer months were marvelously hot and sunny, and again North Compound was dotted with little groups of kriegies doing calisthenics, having a lively debate, or just sprawled out enjoying the sun. Even this was not as innocent as it seemed, though, for many of these sunbathers had carried blanketloads of sand out with them and slowly worked it into the surface sand as they tanned. Another popular event was a mock parliament. In one unforgettable session, Labour Party leader John Casson and his deputy Roger Bushell, an inveterate distruster of politicians, tabled a bill proposing the nationalization of all private wealth. John and Roger surprised even themselves when their oratorical skills pushed the bill through the mock house.

Johnny Dodge's recently formed international relations group was immensely popular and became a forum for many varied viewpoints. There were always heated discussions, and frequent guest speakers lectured on their areas of expertise. Tom Kirby-Green spoke about the need for the British Empire to come to terms with the black majority, while Johnny Stower discussed the experiences of the British community in Argentina. One of the most popular speakers was Wally Valenta, who gave periodic lectures on the military situation. It was always standing room only when Wally spoke, for he was able to analyze correctly and predict the outcome of almost every great phase of the war, especially on the Eastern Front. After the Battle of Kursk in July 1943, one listener asked Valenta if there was any way the Germans could still win the war.

'Yes . . . yes,' said Wally slowly, 'there is a strategy that would allow them to win, but I refuse to discuss it.' He paused and then added with a smile, 'I don't want to give them any ideas!'

*

There was one place in the camp where madness reigned supreme: a room in Hut 120 inhabited by Alex Cassie, Tim Walenn, Gordon Brettell, Des Plunkett, and Tony Hayter – three forgers and two mapmakers. Because they all did important work in the escape organization, Alex, Gordon, Tim, Des, and Tony had been able to keep their room to five men for some time, under the rationale that it was better for security. Eventually Roger Bushell decreed that they could no longer play this card and that a sixth man had to be brought in. Alex suggested his old roommate Henri Picard and from then on, the six got along famously. They all shared the same zany sense of humor and soon earned a reputation around the camp for being a bunch of good-natured madmen.

Their room was usually abuzz with activity. Picard often had a subject in for one of his caricatures, while Hayter and Plunkett could often be found around Tony's plans for a revolutionary sailplane that he hoped to construct after the war. Cassie always had a story to keep his roommates in stitches, while Brettell, the quietest of the lot, was modest to a fault. A warm-hearted and gentle man, he lived a very austere life, having few possessions when the lockers of most prisoners overflowed with various bits and pieces. And there was Tim, always courteous and cheerful, always with a smile under his big, Pilot Officer Prune mustache.

One morning, Wing Commander Dicky Milne, a young, cherub-faced, and much-decorated fellow who had once been Gordon's CO, popped in for a cup of coffee. He found things pretty much as they always were, in apparent disarray with kriegies bustling this way and that. Something in the collective insanity of the room's behavior prompted Dicky to call them a bunch of amiable lunatics. For the six, the gauntlet was thrown. They vowed to show Dicky just how lunatic they could be when they stopped pretending to be normal.

Over the next week, intricate plans were laid for an elaborate dinner party to be held in Dicky's honor. The long-awaited night arrived, and Milne was ushered into the room and given the best seat, a spot in one corner behind the stove. The first few minutes should have given Dicky a clue as to what was to come. On the wall beside his seat was a very ornate notice that said, 'Senior officers are respectfully requested not to damage this notice.' Above him, tacked to the ceiling, was another note that read simply, 'Bored?' The predinner chat was interrupted by the occasional low moan coming from an upright locker beside Dicky's seat. Inside it, the lunatics had installed Frank Knight, who was also in on the scheme. Frank's groans gradually got louder and louder, until Dicky finally began to take notice.

'What's that noise?' he asked after one particularly prolonged moan.

'What noise, sir?' came the deadpan response, and the conversation quickly resumed. Milne accepted rather dubiously that he might have been hearing things, but eventually, with Frank bellowing inside the locker, Dicky spoke up again.

'It's in that bloody locker!' he shouted. 'Let me have a look!' But despite their best slapstick efforts, the others seated around the stove couldn't seem to shift themselves to allow Dicky out of his corner spot. The squirming and shuffling went on for several minutes; then Dicky finally gave up and sat down again.

Minutes later, there was a knock on the wall and a voice called from the next room, 'Lads, tell Frank that dinner's ready.'

The locker door was opened and Tim said cheerily, 'Dinnertime, Frank.' Out stepped Knight, immaculately dressed. 'Good evening, sir,' he said politely to Dicky and left the room. The wing commander gaped at the scene and asked what Knight had been doing in the locker.

'Oh, not much,' came the vague reply. 'He just likes the peace and quiet. But let's sit down to dinner now . . .' and Milne was hustled off to the table in the center of the room.

The feast was as sumptuous as possible with the limited resources and had been beautifully prepared by Brettell and Hayter. However, the entire meal was punctuated by entirely inexplicable incidents. People came in singly or in groups, some just standing in silence for a few minutes, others passing on strange and cryptic messages. One bunch stood around the table and laughed, while a group of Canadians serenaded the dinner party with a folk song. The Amiable Lunatics ignored all this, behaving as if it was perfectly normal, but Dicky found that the constant, bizarre interruptions diverted him from enjoying his very tasty meal.

Dinner concluded, and Dicky was ushered back to his seat of honor for a mug of coffee. On the other side of the upright locker and hidden from his view, Des Plunkett and one of the orderlies, Private Ryan, did the washing up. However, this night it wasn't Private Ryan but Flight Lieutenant 'Funf' Watson, putting on a broad Cockney accent and impersonating the orderly. With Milne safely ensconced in the corner, Watson began playing the role of the garrulous gossip.

'And another thing I've heard,' he continued, after passing on to Des a few slightly off-color rumors, 'is about that new young Wing Commander Milne. You know who I mean, sir. The one with a face like a baby's bum . . .'

'Be quiet, Ryan,' hissed Des loudly, playing up the part.

'No, really, sir,' continued Watson, 'you'll love this one.'

All the while, Dicky sat in the corner, out of sight of the gossipers. He was torn between a desire to hear the scurrilous rumor, which in fact never came out, and pretending to carry on a conversation with his hosts. All in all, Milne maintained his composure well and quite enjoyed himself in the lunatic mood of the evening.

*

Early in June, construction started on a new compound to the south of the camp. A few weeks later, word came through a tame goon that the new compound was being built for the Americans, who would be moved as soon as possible. This created a dilemma for Roger.

'A lot of Yanks have put hard work into these tunnels,' he said to Johnny Bull. 'It will be a bloody shame if they're purged before everything is ready. I think we'll try and speed things up a bit.'

'Fine, Roger, as long as security can be kept up,' cautioned Johnny. 'It would be a damn sight worse if some idiot blows the lot because he's in too much of a hurry.'

'Of course, but I think it can be done without taking any chances. Right now, Tom's the farthest ahead. What if we close up Dick and Harry and concentrate on Tom with picked teams of diggers? That way there'll be no more activity in the camp and we'll have our best men doing the work. There should be no reason for security to suffer.'

Johnny nodded, and Roger went on. 'Have Wally get the tunnel committee together and we'll bounce this off them. Unless anyone has a big problem with it, we'll go ahead.'

The idea was thrashed out with Floody, Canton, Marshall, and the others, and they were able to overcome all objections. So, over the next few days, Dick and Harry were sealed and a roster of experienced digging teams was drawn up. The teams included seasoned tunnelers such as Henry Lamond, Danny Król, Cookie Long, and Shag Rees, as well as a few Americans so they could take some experience with them to their new home.

With the diversion of resources to Tom, the tunnel shot ahead. When it reached the warning wire, a halfway house measuring ten feet long and six inches higher and wider than the rest of the tunnel was built. There were no rails in the halfway house, but two extra workers were stationed there to ferry men and supplies between the face and the shaft. With this addition it meant that the diggers no longer had to go all the way back to the shaft to change positions.

Another suggestion, but one that failed to gain approval, was that the tunnel be angled upward, leaving a shorter distance to dig for the exit shaft. Arguments on both sides were heated, but finally the idea was rejected as too risky. All necessary precautions could be taken, but there was always the chance that someone might lose hold of a rope and send a cart rolling down the tunnel. In that event, it could dislodge shoring frames all along the way and bring down thirty or forty feet of tunnel.

With progress as it was, the compound took a well-deserved rest to celebrate the Fourth of July. Morning *Appell* set the tone of the day when two Americans appeared on the parade ground dressed in a horse suit that had been made by some Polish officers. The horse took up a position in the front row and, as Pieber made the count, the fellow in the front of the suit nodded his head in time with Pieber's counting. Not even the Austrian could restrain a chuckle. At evening *Appell*, after a day of plentiful homemade alcohol, another American appeared on the parade ground stark naked but was quickly chased off by one of the guards. Wings Day and Johnny Dodge, soaked to the skin after having been tossed into the firepool and swaying from the effects of the hooch, tried to focus their bleared eyes to identify the offending kriegie. They couldn't manage it.

As the pace of work picked up, it was perhaps inevitable that slipups would be made. Because the evening shift was digging as well, dispersal went a little less smoothly than it had before, and it was only a matter of time before someone goofed. One of the penguins jettisoned his load while standing on the fringes of a volleyball crowd, and Glemnitz spotted the yellow sand before it could be kicked in. This, combined with the discovery of sand in some of the gardens, convinced the goons that something was up. Over the next few days, little happened. Glemnitz and Rubberneck turned over a few more gardens and found more yellow sand, but there was no general search. Then someone spotted a tower guard scanning the compound with binoculars, evidently trying to pick up a pattern of traffic in the camp. When he heard this, Bushell immediately put a restriction on the amount of traffic in and out of Hut 123 during dispersal hours.

Finally it came. A party of goons trooped into the compound and started searching the huts on the west side of the camp. The first day they turned over 106 and 107, allowing the engineers enough time to seal Tom completely before 123 was searched. The next day Rubberneck and his ferrets spent five hours going over 123 but emerged with nothing. Rubberneck was not a happy man. A day later, two Little S's found ferrets hiding in their huts, and it was three days before Roger felt it was safe enough to start work on Tom again. That day they dug a record ten feet but could disperse only three-quarters of the sand. Things were still too hot to do any more.

The chess game continued. Ferrets were spotted spying on the camp from behind piles of brush in the forest, and then the goons tried a snap search of Hut 101 at 2:00 A.M. Luckily X Organization avoided digging at night since having been caught at Barth in a similar search. Later Glemnitz found more sand in the gardens beside 119. He left the compound quickly and came back in force. With a hundred soldiers and a local Kripo official in tow, he kicked everyone out of 106, 107, and 123 and searched them thoroughly. Then, he put his men to work digging a four-foot-deep trench between 123 and the wire. When this was completed, a pack of ferrets with long metal probes were let loose, poking down in the bottom of the trench in hopes of finding the roof of a tunnel. Knowing they had another twenty feet to go, Roger and the other plotters looked on in amusement. Eventually one of the goons hit something and let out a cry of triumph. Quick as a flash, they were back to work with the shovels, digging madly and sweating furiously. When they sheepishly produced a large rock from the trench, Canton nearly peed himself laughing.

Though they failed to find anything that time, it was obvious that the goons would keep the pressure on. With this in mind, the top men of X Organization were faced with a dilemma. Tom was only fifty feet from the planned completion length but was hampered by two major drawbacks: the trap was set in a flat concrete floor, making it much more vulnerable; and, because both doors to the hut were in view of the guard towers, the routing of the penguins presented major security problems. Furthermore, it was obvious that the goons' attentions were now focused on the huts on the western side of the compound. According to the general policy, the operation should have been shut down until the situation improved, but there was no doubt that the Germans would keep searching until they found something, whether or not work was proceeding. After a long discussion it was decided to accept the risks and press on with Tom.

As expected, the ferrets kept up their tricks. One day someone spotted Glemnitz hiding under a hut, so a senior wing commander was sent around to invite him out for a cup of tea. A grimy and sheepish

Glemnitz appeared and slunk off to the *Vorlager*. On another occasion, the duty pilot noticed that Rubberneck had been marked into the compound but not marked out. A search was instituted and he was found in the kitchen block, peering out of one of the windows. Rather than confront him, Roger ordered that all the windows of the block be shuttered from the outside. Within minutes, Rubberneck skulked from the compound with an evil scowl on his face.

As Tom pushed ahead (now using lamps made from fat and pajama cord because the electric cable had run out), the game continued. The rest of the trees in the compound were taken down, removing the very useful camouflage they had provided for the dispersers and necessitating the closure of a number of dispersal areas. Another halfway house was built for Tom, which now reached the edge of the woods and was just twenty feet from the planned exit point. Then, work parties began to cut back the forest outside the wire, and the leaders of X Organization watched gloomily as Soviet prisoners cleared thirty yards in three days. It was purely coincidental that the area had been chosen as the site for another compound, but it suddenly meant that Tom had another hundred feet to go. Clearly, a new dispersal system would be needed to deal with the extra sand.

To begin with, Fanshawe altered the operation slightly. Previously, each penguin had been responsible not only for delivering his load of sand but for concealing it as well. From now on, each disperser would have an assigned area, with a dispersal officer in charge of concealing the sand. This method served to break up the streams of penguin traffic and brought more dispersal areas into use. It also allowed for more careful camouflaging of sand. Then someone suggested that the sand be stored in the thousands of Red Cross boxes that lived under people's bunks. They got away with this for five days; then Glemnitz noticed an inordinate number of people coming from 123. A couple of days later he found dozens of sand-filled boxes in 103. He brought in a couple of heavy wagons to drive around the compound in the hopes of collapsing the tunnels but only succeeded in wrecking a few gardens.

By now Tom was at the 260-foot mark. It was still forty feet from the woods, but it was deemed safe enough to crawl that distance from the exit to the forest. With this in mind, Roger closed Tom, planning to finish it after things cooled down. To divert the goons' attention, Bushell assembled strings of POWs and had them carry around empty Red Cross boxes. Glemnitz figured that something must be up and searched 119, which turned up nothing. At the same time, some of the kriegies passed the word that the entire thing was a joke to pull Glemnitz's leg.

Luckily, there were occasional diversions to allow the POWs to let off steam. In August word came that Willy Williams had been awarded the DFC, an occasion that was marked with a hearty celebration. The following month the camp's attention was diverted by the opening of the brand-new theater, designed and built by the prisoners themselves. The grand opening featured a production of Gerald Savory's *George and Margaret,* with Roger Bushell in the cast.

A small group from a purge in East Compound came over in September, too. John Stevens was on it, and so was a pilot officer named Bernard Green. 'Pop,' as he was known, was a short, bulky fellow with a benign smile and a balding head. At age fifty-seven, he looked more suited to a library desk than a prison camp. In spite of his appearance, though, Pop Green was a tough and determined fellow. The holder of a Military Cross from the Great War, Pop joined the RAF in 1940 when they were recruiting experienced air gunners up to age fifty-four. His first operation on July 19, 1940 was also his last. Hit by flak while laying mines, the Hampden gradually lost height and crashed into the sea off Denmark, killing two of the crew.

Ian Cross also came over from East Compound and immediately let his presence be felt. A tireless goon-baiter, he was quickly in trouble with Rubberneck for throwing cigarettes through the wire to a group of Soviet workers. 'I'm not going to stand by while the finest fighting army in the world is treated like this!' he yelled as two guards escorted him to the cooler.

Shortly after the purge, Brian Evans was able to secure permission to visit the NCO compound to see Sergeant Pilot Richard Hutchison, his fiancée Joan Cook's cousin. It was a welcome get-together for both of them and brought back many memories of life at home. Their time together was short, but they made an appointment for after the war. Hutchison, however, was not to see the end of the war; he would later die on one of the forced marches of 1945.

*

There was a new Little S in Tom Kirby-Green's fold in the fall, too. In September New Zealand Squadron Leader Len Trent took over the all-important job in Hut 104. Having worked for a few months as a penguin, Len was anxious to do more in the organization, and the job of taking care of 104's security was just the ticket.

Leonard Henry Trent was twenty-two when he joined the RAF in 1937 and, throughout his operational career, he always seemed to draw the tough missions. In May 1940 he flew one of the Blenheims for the disastrous attack on the bridges at Maastricht, and for the first trip of his second tour, Len drew another tough nut: the Phillips factory in the Dutch city of Eindhoven. Again the casualties were heavy, and Trent's 487 (New Zealand) Squadron took a beating; but again, Len was fortunate and got home safely.

Perhaps it was third time unlucky for Trent, for on May 3, 1943, he led another difficult mission, a raid by twelve Lockheed Venturas against a power station on the outskirts of Amsterdam. Events were to conspire against the New Zealanders, for on that very day there was a state visit of the Nazi governor of Holland to Haarlem and a meeting of top Luftwaffe fighter pilots at Schiphol Airport. Furthermore, a diversionary fighter sweep designed to draw the Germans away from Amsterdam arrived ahead of schedule, so that when the Venturas approached the coast in tight formation, the cream of the Luftwaffe was already up and waiting for them.

The German pilots slipped between the Venturas and their fighter cover and had a field day. Six of the bombers were shot down in the first four minutes, and by the time the target area was reached, there were only two Venturas – those of Len and his wingman – still in the air. Soon the number 2 disappeared, leaving Len alone to continue to the target. Doggedly concentrating on his instrument panel, Trent pressed home the attack and dropped his bombs. He was about to put the nose down and peel away home at low altitude when a terrific burst shook the aircraft. The controls dead, Len ordered the crew to bail out before fighting his way out of the cockpit himself. The navigator had bailed out first, and Len was pleased to see him when they were both captured; the other crew members perished. Back at 487's base at Methwold, the squadron was in mourning. One Ventura had turned back early with mechanical trouble and a second limped home badly damaged. Ten of the eleven aircraft that had crossed the enemy coast were missing.

*

In time, Len Trent found his way to Sagan, where he and the rest of the Little S's had to stay on their toes while the goons kept up the pressure. Glemnitz had decided on one more day of searches on September 8, focusing on 104 and 105, but at the last minute changed his mind and opted for 123. If nothing was found this time, he would give up. For what seemed like ages, the ferrets poked around 123 while Roger and the tunnel committee watched with as much disinterest as they could muster. It was late in the afternoon before the ferrets started filtering out of the hut, and Big X was ready to heave a sigh of relief when he heard a shout from within 123. Tom's trap had finally been found.

It was later discovered that the ferrets were on their way out of the hut when one of them dropped his metal probe. By a cruel stroke of ill fortune, it fell on the corner of Tom's trap and dislodged a piece of the cement camouflage. Getting down on his hands and knees, the ferret turned on his flashlight and picked out the faint outline of the trapdoor. Tom's entrance had always been the riskiest because it was sunk in a flat floor, but it was a crushing blow that it was found purely by chance.

However, no one in Sagan will ever forget the last revenge of Tom. A German engineer was called in to explode the tunnel, but he was obviously something of an amateur at demolition. The explosion roared up the tunnel and blew Hut 123 off its foundations, leaving it sitting on a crazy angle. Still, the cheers of the assembled prisoners did little to soothe the disappointment of the escape workers.

Though Tom was discovered, it was still a remarkable success for X Organization. At twenty-five feet deep and 260 feet long, Tom was one of the largest tunnels the kriegies ever built and was completely shored and fully serviced with ventilation, electric power, and railroads. Even more incredible was the amount of sand that had been dispersed by the penguins. Each 3½ feet of tunnel produced roughly one ton of sand. So, allowing for falls and halfway houses and considering that the shaft and chambers of each tunnel produced twelve tons, the workers disposed of at least 165 tons of sand between April and September 1943. During that period, the record rate of dispersal was 1½ tons in a single hour. By any standards, Tom was an incredible achievement.

*

In the weeks following the discovery of Tom, the German POW camp system as a whole was rocked by a number of other major events.

On September 18, 132 French officers escaped through a tunnel at Oflag XVIIA, and the next night, forty-seven Polish officers broke a tunnel from a camp at Dössel. To deal with the growing number of escape-related disturbances, the Germans co-opted more and more men into the system. By late 1943 it was estimated that more than 400,000 men were directly involved in the supervision of POWs, while 100,000 more might be mobilized to deal with a mass escape. The problem, from the German point of view, was clearly getting out of hand.

The RSHA, Himmler's security headquarters, placed the blame squarely on the heads of the military authorities, saying that they were not doing enough to stop the escapes. Himmler advised that the camps be turned over to the police, so that escapers could be dealt with more harshly. This was clearly unacceptable to the military, but steps were taken to increase the involvement of local police officials in the internal security of the camps. At the same time, another major change took place when the RSHA absorbed the Orpo, the regular uniformed police, and finally gained full control of the local Kripo offices. With this, the two services most directly involved in the recapture of escaping POWs came under the direct control of Himmler and the RSHA. Unbeknownst to the prisoners in Luft III, escaping had suddenly become a much more dangerous game.

Chapter 12

X ORGANIZATION REGROUPS

AFTER THE DISCOVERY OF Tom, X Organization's immediate goal was to regroup. During the inspection of Tom, someone had overheard Glemnitz say that he doubted there would be another tunnel because all available wood must have been used up. Roger immediately ordered a huge levy of two thousand bedboards, leaving an average of five or six four-inch slats per bunk. The boards were hidden behind walls and down Dick. That way, once Glemnitz got around to keeping tabs on the number of bedboards, there would be no further disappearances.

The Americans left for the newly opened South Compound at the end of the first week in September, although those who served in the RAF or the RCAF remained in North. With them went Glemnitz, and the escape organizers were glad to see the back of him. Also in September, a party of POWs arrived from camps in Italy. They had had a rough trip, packed in boxcars with very little food and water and no sanitary facilities. One of the few bright spots of the trip was a short stop at the huge stalag at Moosburg, near Munich. There the kriegies cleaned up and had their first half-decent meal in quite a while, and were even serenaded by a massed chorus of Soviet prisoners when they left the camp. At Nuremberg the airmen were separated from their army comrades and forwarded to Sagan.

The new theater also helped to divert the kriegies' attention. A revue entitled *Between Ourselves* featured a large cast that included Canadian Jimmy Wernham, and the first batch of English-language films, including Fred Astaire and Ginger Rogers in *Shall We Dance*, came to Sagan. At the same time, the sporting types were trying to cram in more matches before the weather turned against them. There were some very competent cricketers and soccer players in Luft III, and track-and-field days were held occasionally as well. For some, these 'mini-Olympics' were a reminder of the RAF Athletic Championships of the prewar years, when many of the kriegies had first met on the playing field. For Tom Kirby-Green and Ian Cross there were memories of the 1938 Championship, when Tom had competed for Mildenhall and Ian for Marham.

On a cool September night, a New Zealander and a Canadian made the first escape attempt after the loss of Tom. They decided to try cutting the fence on the far side of the *Appell* ground, where the goons would never expect an attempt to be made. It took them seven hours to crawl the 250 yards across the open space, but they were caught getting through the wire and put in the cooler. Unfortunately, the Canadian was claustrophobic, and after suffering through solitary for a couple of days, he finally cracked and made a dash for the door, dressed only in his pajamas. A guard fired, wounding the airman in the shoulder; it was months before he came out of the hospital and returned to the compound.

*

Work on Harry and Dick resumed shortly after the loss of Tom but stopped again on September 15. With the goons still on the alert, it was far too dangerous to disperse the sand. So Roger Bushell decided to leave Harry sealed for a couple of months, both to give the workers a rest and to let the commotion blow over. In the meantime, all energies would be concentrated on the manufacture of escape gear.

Al Hake, just recovering from a mild bout of diphtheria, had set up the compass factory in his room in the northern end of Block 103, a location that had given the workers a ringside seat for the delousing party escape. With his roommates, the phlegmatic little Australian ran a model assembly line that turned out hundreds of compasses, each fully waterproofed and proudly bearing its place of origin embossed on the bottom.

Each compass started as a piece of Bakelite phonograph record. The records were cracked into small pieces about 3 inches across, and the pieces were heated over a candle until they became malleable. The Bakelite was then placed over a 1¼-inch hole in a board and pushed into the hole with a wooden peg. A metal disk at the bottom of the hole imprinted the inscription 'Made in Stalag Luft III – Pat. Pend.' neatly on the bottom.

For the magnets, X Organization's procurement team collected razor blades, which were affixed (using glue made from powdered milk) in two rows on a bedboard. Then a worker spent an entire afternoon stroking a horseshoe magnet, also scrounged by the procurement team, over the rows of blades, making sure that the magnet always went in the same direction. After a few hours he had a bunch of magnetized razor blades, which were broken into bar magnets with a scavenged window hinge.

To make the compass cards, Al Hake hit upon a brilliant idea. Among the items made available by the Germans were little black cardboard slates that turned out to be just as good for making compass cards as they were for drawing or writing. Using a precision instrument of his own construction, Al marked perfect circles on the slate, cut them out with a razor blade, and punched a hole in the center.

The most important and delicate part of the compass was the bearing point on which the card was to rest; Al always insisted on doing this part himself. A tiny drop of heated Bakelite was placed over the hole on the back side of the compass card and pressed through with a specially shaped pencil point that pushed out a little knob on the top side of the card. The resulting pocket balanced admirably on the phonograph needle support. Two bar magnets were then glued to the underside of the card, one on each side of the bearing point, and the card was balanced with tiny drops of powdered milk on the underside.

To paint the figures on the cards, Al used high-quality white paint (again courtesy of the procurement team) and a tiny brush made from human hair, of which he had no shortage. The reference points were first sketched on in pencil and were then done over with white paint. Because it was oil-based, the paint took time to dry, so Al built a little hiding place that could take six cards at once. Later some of the compasses even came equipped with luminous north points, the luminous chips taken from an alarm clock that had been stolen from the *Kommandantur*.

While Al was working on the cards, another kriegie cut cardboard slate circles, each with a hole in the center for the supporting phonograph needle, to fit into the bottom of each casing. A third piece of cardboard slate was cut for the interior wall of the casing, to act as a support for the glass face. The glass for the faces was taken from broken barrack windows and, under water, pressed against a metal disk of the exact size needed. It was broken into a rough circle with a liberated pair of German surgical scissors. The edges were smoothed out by stroking the circle against a brick until it would fit snugly into the casing.

When all the component parts were completed, the factory went into its production line stage. For each compass, the phonograph needle was placed on the base card, which was then put into the casing. The card to support the glass was fitted around the inside of the casing, and each compass card was balanced on its needle and tested for clearance and stability. For the final step, sealing the compass with the glass face, Al constructed a blower out of a can about 5 inches high and 2½ inches in diameter. Using metal chipped off the lids of corned beef cans, a narrow tube was soldered onto the can as a steam outlet. One-half inch of water in the can was heated, and the steam escaping from the tube was used to warm the top lip of the compass casing. Al used a spoon to mold the lip on the casing over the glass, sealing it in place. As a finishing touch, a bit of old, dried putty that had been taken from barrack windows and mixed with sardine oil was forced under the lip as a sealant. With this putty in place, the compass was waterproof. Working at a leisurely pace, the workshop could assemble about twenty compasses in an afternoon. They were not often bothered, but when a warning was given, Al put everything away, picked up his banjo, and led his workers in a song until the danger passed.

It was an ingenious operation that turned out high-quality, easily concealed, and accurate compasses, which were all inscribed with the place of origin, as defense against being branded a spy. But the compass factory wasn't all that Al Hake turned his considerable talents to. He also lent a hand in the tin-bashing shop when it was needed. The tin-bashers were led by Digger McIntosh and Johnny Travis, who used to be a digger until Roger pulled him out of the tunnel on account of his claustrophobia. Around them they gathered a team of craftsmen who could fashion almost anything with their hands.

To craft their tools, the tin-bashers bribed guards to bring in old scraps of file or useless lumps of metal. Little did they know that these harmless bits and pieces were turned into cold and wood chisels, screwdrivers and augers, planes and spokeshaves. Teeth were cut in broken gramophone springs to make saws, and table knives were transformed in a similar way. To make wire cutters, they removed tie bars from the huts and riveted them together like scissors. After notches were cut in the blades, Johnny Travis hardened them in his homemade forge. He heated the metal to red hot and then sprinkled a few grains of sugar around the notches. Again the cutters were heated in the forge until the carbon in the sugar was baked into the metal. Finally they were plunged into cold water, and the process was complete. Cold chisels were also made this way. When the tin-bashers' fingers were wearing ragged from the work, Tommy Guest's tailors made special gloves for them. When they needed a strong hammer, they stole a spike from the wheel hub of the muck cart. The wheel came off before it left the compound, but the hammer was well worth the nasty stench that lingered when the load of waste spilled.

*

The woodwork shop, after months of moving around from hut to hut, found a home in the main chamber at the base of Dick's shaft. Unfortunately, the cramped conditions did not make for the best of workshops, as only one person could work there at a time. It was a lonely and tedious job. Every day after morning *Appell*, the trap was bailed out and a worker clambered down the ladder to begin his shift. As soon as he was down and settled, the trap was closed, sealed, and filled with water again; the worker could then toil undisturbed for seven or eight hours. For most of the time the chamber was lit by electric lights, but for a short period each day, the power was shut off and the chamber had to be illuminated by fat lamp. Fortunately, the electricity was never off for long, for the lamps gave off a terrible stench and a suffocating, oily, black smoke.

Most of the work done in the shop was in constructing fittings for the tunnels. Using saws and chisels crafted by the tin-bashers, and scrapers and smoothers made from pieces of broken plate or glass, the workers cut and fitted all of the shoring frames (to be assembled once they reached the face) and carved the bedboards into male and female sections roughly two feet in length; these, too, could easily be fitted together by the digger in the tunnel. For some jobs there were real carpentry tools that had been 'borrowed' from various sources. They were, however, used sparingly, for they were impossible to replace. After hours of slogging away at bedboards and shoring frames, the worker was glad to hear the sound of water being bailed out of the trap above him. He handed up his day's work to be conveyed to the tunnels and emerged for a much-needed stretch. After a bit of cleaning up, he was ready for evening *Appell*.

Because of the size of the workshop chamber, Australian Willy Williams, who took over the operation in September 1943, kept the number of workers to a minimum and usually recruited from among his own countrymen. One Australian who found his way into the carpentry department was a cheerful fellow named Kierath, the camp's cricket convener, who sported a reddish mop of hair that had earned him the obvious nickname of Rusty. Kierath was a powerful chap whose years in combat and captivity had given him a hardened and almost haggard appearance. He never lost his broad smile, though, not even after a long shift in the cramped confines of the carpentry shop.

*

Born on February 20, 1915, in Narromine, New South Wales, Reginald Victor Kierath was the youngest of nine children (his eldest brother had fought in the Great War) and was descended from German grandparents who immigrated to Australia in 1855. His family were merchants, operating the general store in Narromine, and Reg often helped out in the shop after school. In 1929 he left Narromine to attend Shore School, the same school attended by Willy Williams, and he graduated in 1933 after an average academic but excellent athletic career. After a little urging from his father, young Reg took a clerk's position in the Narromine branch of the Bank of Australasia while he decided on his future.

Though he had spent a year in the 17th Battalion of the Australian Army, flying seemed to be in Reg's blood ever since he helped his eldest sister, Hope, and a family friend site an airfield at Narromine. The government had asked for suggestions for an airfield location, and the three had taken up the challenge. Once they had cleared away the local farmer's sheep and lit a fire to determine the wind direction, they knew it was the perfect spot. When war came, it was hardly surprising that Reg decided to join the RAAF.

Shortly after enlisting on August 2, 1940, Reg learned that he was one of six hundred Australians selected to take their flight training in Southern Rhodesia. He did only preliminary instruction in Australia before leaving for Africa, and by December 1940 had finished initial training. It wasn't until he reached the flying school at Cranborne that Reg really started to enjoy training, and then his mischievous streak began to show through. One day in early May, he was flying as passenger in a Harvard for a low-level bombing practice run. The pilot dropped four smoke bombs and then wheeled around to look at the results. As he swooped over the target area, he heard Rusty's disgusted voice through the intercom: 'Can't you do better than that? I can't see a bloody thing from this height!' After a few more circuits and further caustic comments from Rusty, the pilot took the Harvard back to Cranborne, where he realized just how low Reg had goaded him into flying. Before leaving the aircraft, he had to pluck a few handfuls of grass from the bomb racks.

Reg Kierath graduated as an airman pilot on June 10 and was posted to 71 OTU. Two months later, he was transferred to 33 Squadron, flying Kittyhawks from Amriya in Egypt. Reg's first month of operations was not as smooth as it might have been, and in those weeks he aborted twice with mechanical problems, was strafed while taking off, and crash-landed after being jumped by a gaggle of Me 109s. That trying first month did not go unrewarded, though, for in November he was given leave in Cairo. The diversion did him a world of good, for he soon started to have more success. On November 22 he damaged a couple of Ju 88 medium bombers, and two weeks later he attacked and burned a column of Italian vehicles. On December 20 he scored his first confirmed kill, sharing an Italian troop carrier with another pilot.

The new year saw a change for Reg, who was transferred to 450 Squadron RAAF on January 8, 1942, and commissioned at the end of the month. He continued with fleet patrols and sweeps over the desert and on July 31, with one tour of duty under his belt, was posted to the flying school at Belvedere for an instructors' course. Upon completion of that course he went to Guinea Fowl in Southern Rhodesia for a five-month stint as flying instructor beginning in September 1942. Instructing was not what Reg had in mind, for he had joined up to fight the enemy. He wished nothing more than to get back to operations and avenge the death of his brother Greg, who had been killed in action at Tobruk.

However, Reg was never one to bemoan his own fate, and he made the best of the circumstances. He was popular with the young recruits, and there was plenty of time for rest and relaxation on weekends or on leave, when he and some of the other instructors would head down to Durban for a few days. Reg's company was much sought after, for his great sense of humor, cheerful demeanor, and general outlook on life. Whether it was an afternoon of tennis with local young ladies or a raucous night at some disreputable nightspot, Reg could always be counted on to provide a good time.

On February 23, 1943, Flying Officer Kierath finally got out of Southern Rhodesia and returned to 450 Squadron for a second tour. However, it was two months before he flew the first sortie of that tour, an antishipping patrol on April 23. About fifteen miles off Cap Bon, the squadron was hit by some light anti-aircraft fire from a German vessel, and Reg's Kittyhawk took a couple of shells in the oil system. When the engine seized, he turned the aircraft toward land and glided as far as possible before being forced to bail out. In a letter home, Reg described the experience quite dispassionately: 'Stepped over the side, pulled the rip-cord and had a very pleasant journey down to the water. I spent about two hours in the water during which time I drank a flask of brandy and then a boat-load of Germans came and picked me up.'

Though Reg was uninjured, the sailors took him to a hospital in Tunis and later to a temporary camp outside the city. His troubles were far from over. On the way to Sicily, the transport ship was strafed by Allied aircraft and later narrowly avoided being torpedoed. Throughout the voyage, Reg felt a sickening sense of powerlessness and later wrote to his brother that the journey was the worst nightmare he had ever experienced. The lean Australian could not have been happier to see a safe POW cage.

*

One of the more important jobs for Rusty Kierath and the rest of the woodworkers was the construction of hides for sensitive materials. The huts were prefabricated, and the prisoners soon discovered that there was a space of about five inches between the walls. Using the real tools, five or six wall boards were removed and fitted with tiny clips. Once replaced, they could be quickly removed if you knew where the clips were but were invisible to the uninitiated. Under the supervision of Mike Casey, whose previous job was made redundant by the discovery of Tom, hides were built all over the camp to hold forged papers, compasses, clothing, and any other escape gear that needed safekeeping. Roger even had his own personal hiding place in his room (international law stipulated that senior officers be housed in single or double rooms instead of dormitories), although he was discouraged from keeping too much in it because he was an obvious target for investigation.

Because of the bulkiness of their products, though, Tommy Guest elected to keep most of the tailoring department's goods in the attic of the lavatory block; only suits under construction were kept in the more convenient wall hiding places.

The tailoring shop was the most decentralized of X Organization's operations, their cutters and fitters working in rooms all across the camp. There were various sources of material for the tailors, the most fruitful of which was military uniforms. Some uniforms were taken to pieces and recut as civilian suits; Polish Army uniforms and RAF other ranks battle dress, both of which were made of a heavy serge, were particularly useful for this. Once taken apart, the various pieces of material were shaved with a razor blade until they were smooth and were then colored with beet juice, boot polish, or a dye made by boiling the covers of books. Another source of material was the guards, who could sometimes be convinced to bring in odd scraps of cloth. This material, along with the heavy linings from some military greatcoats, could be sewn into very passable suits.

Tapping all of these sources, Tommy and his crew were able to produce an incredible amount of clothing: six pairs of overalls; twelve German uniforms; two hundred civilian jackets and pants; one hundred complete civilian suits; forty overcoats; two hundred and fifty caps; forty ties; and ten haversacks. The tailors also taught others how to convert their own uniforms by shaving them smooth, rounding the corners, removing the pockets, and attaching pocket flaps. Guest was also willing to lend his newspaper patterns to prisoners who wanted to recut their own uniforms.

Most of the sewing and delicate work was done by Tommy, while other kriegies helped with taking apart old uniforms. The rest of the measuring, cutting, and fitting were done by Ivo Tonder and a staff of tailors. The operation was very decentralized, so they had very little problem with security. Only once was there an emergency. On that occasion Glemnitz happened to stumble on a beautiful suit that Ivo had just finished. He carried it triumphantly from the compound, while Tonder could only shake his head and curse.

*

October came to Sagan, and what few leaves still clung to the pathetic little birch trees around the camp fell disconsolately. Inside the stalag, the mood was somewhat brighter. There was an excellent production of *Macbeth* in the theater, with Lawrence Reavell-Carter as Menteith, and many of the kriegies turned from sports to study. Jimmy Catanach finished his course in Norwegian and was awarded a first-class certificate from the Institute of Linguists, and Henri Picard and Arnold Christensen traded English and French lessons. With an eye to the completion of Harry, German was still the most popular language to learn. Leonard Hall studied with Paweł Tobolski, who was looking forward to taking his English proficiency exam in June 1944, while John Casson was instructed by Rene Marcinkus. Tony Hayter and Ian Cross also concentrated on the subject.

One of X Organization's most capable language instructors, and one of the few with any sort of formal training, was a quiet and studious Canadian named Gordon Arthur Kidder. The son of a cannery manager, Kidder was born on December 9, 1914, in the small city of St. Catharines in southern Ontario, where he received his early education. After graduating from high school, Gordon went on to the University of Toronto to study French and German. The academic world seemed to suit Gordon's temperament, and in 1937 he was accepted at Johns Hopkins University in Baltimore to do an MA in German. However, Kidder had a change of heart and decided to try his luck in the working world, first as a clerk in the Ontario Department of Education and later as a translator with a Toronto insurance company. He was well respected in the office as a conscientious and capable worker, and would have gone far had he not joined the RCAF when war broke out.

After completing his training as a navigator, Gordon was posted to the operational training unit (OTU) at Pershore for crew assignment. He did two operations there before the crew was posted to 149 Squadron, flying Short Stirlings. Upon arrival at 149, though, they learned that the squadron hadn't enough aircraft for them, so they were given the choice of joining a Pathfinder unit. The lads jumped at the chance and on September 8, 1942, were sent to join 156 Squadron at Warboys. The first few trips with 156 Squadron took the crew to the Ruhr, but on October 13, 1942, they were assigned to take part in a raid on Kiel; it would be Kidder's ninth operation.

The first half of the flight went without incident, but over the target area the Wellington was coned by searchlights. The pilot immediately went into a steep dive, which broke them out of the beams, but one of the engines died as he tried to pull out. Now with fairly substantial flak damage, the Wellington began limping back across the North Sea but before long the second engine gave out and the pilot ordered the crew to take crash positions.

The aircraft came down hard. Radio operator–air gunner Earl Macdonald found himself trapped in his position and was knocked unconscious as the aircraft broke apart in the heavy swells. When he came to, he was free of the wreckage and floating, apparently alone, among bits and pieces of the Wellington. He called out to see if anyone else had survived and was relieved to hear Gordon Kidder's voice answer from the darkness. Kidder had been able to inflate the aircraft's dinghy, which, though leaking, was adequate for the purpose, and Earl heaved himself aboard. He was uninjured, but Gordon had broken an ankle and lost his flying boots in the crash. In great pain as the dinghy heaved and pitched, Kidder was grateful when Macdonald offered his own flying boots, which the navigator promptly strapped on as tightly as possible.

The two survivors floated in the dinghy for the rest of the night and then, just after dawn, were relieved to see a ship on the horizon. The fact that it was a German minesweeper was unfortunate, but nevertheless a preferable alternative to dying of exposure. Being uninjured, Earl was sent immediately to Barth from Dulag Luft, while Gordon had a short stint in the hospital before arriving at Sagan just before Christmas 1942.

Gordon Kidder was known around the camp as one of the more reserved prisoners, something that definitely could not be said of the Amiable Lunatics of Hut 120. Two of them, Alex Cassie and Des Plunkett, were rehearsing for a Victorian music hall production as members of a death-defying acrobatic team called the Royal Raviolis. With the help of a harness and lifting gear provided by a guard who had been a professional acrobat, Alex was balanced on various members of the team, drawing suitable oohs and aahs from the rest of the cast. At rehearsal one day, Alex was being pulled up to do a spectacular handstand on Plunkett's outstretched arm when the piano wire suspending him broke. Only Des's strength and quick reflexes saved Cassie from a nasty fall. Luckily, the public performances went without a hitch, and the sight of Alex doing a handless headstand on Des's head brought cheers from the audience.

Pleased with the success of two of their members, the Amiable Lunatics planned a party in celebration and decided to make a brew for the occasion. They began saving raisins and other fermentable foodstuffs and set about making a jerry-built still. First, they dumped their raw materials, including a few bits of bread, into a wooden bathtub filled with water and added some yeast that had been scrounged from the Poles. After about a week of fermenting, the brew was ready to be distilled. The still itself was a large kettle with a three-foot pipe attached to its spout. The pipe led down to the condenser, which was actually a trombone that had been stretched out and laid in a wooden trough lined with tar. The component pieces were joined with solder taken from Red Cross cans and flux made from the resin of the few remaining fir trees in the compound.

A taster was needed to monitor the distillation process, so Kingsley Brown, who had a certain expertise in these matters, volunteered and worked a full twenty-four hours tasting the various substances that came off. Early in the process, he dubbed the brew Eau de Dunlop, because of the taste imparted by the rubber connections in the system. Once, he was interrupted by a bang on the window.

'*Was ist los?*' (What's the matter?) called a guttural voice.

'*Ruhe, bitte*' (Quiet, please), replied Kingsley, who went to the window, opened the shutters, and spoke to the two guards who were standing there. '*Wohlen Sie ein klein Schnapps trinken?*' (Would you like a little drink of Schnapps?)

'*Ja, danke*' (Yes, thanks), said the guards, and they quickly drained the mug that was passed out to them. The second helping went down a little more slowly and, after a few more samples, the two guards staggered back to the main gate, feeling the effects of the extremely pure alcohol.

'Lucky those guys came along,' said Kingsley after they had left. 'We needed to make sure the hooch wasn't poisonous!' It may not have been poisonous, but it was very strong. Alex Cassie collected a few drops of the brew in a tin spoon and set it on the table to cool off before tasting it. When he got to it he saw that the hooch had etched a neat cavity in the bowl of the spoon.

When the Amiable Lunatics threw their brew party, the resultant drunkenness provided some memorable moments. The Irishman Paddy Byrne overindulged a bit and dashed out of the room, saying he was feeling rather sick. Later, he returned to the party with a bruised forehead and a bleeding nose.

'I was walking to the toilet when the floor came up and hit me in the face,' he said quite earnestly.

Paddy had also been sick on his trousers and, rather than facecleaning them, drunken logic told him it would be wiser to discard them. So, at the earliest opportunity, he cast the trousers into the main *Abort* and thought no more of them. Weeks later, when the *Abort* was being drained by a local contractor, the trousers emerged, and the entire sewage pit was dragged in an attempt to find the body that went with the trousers.

Later still, the compound reverberated with gales of Irish laughter. Byrne had been sitting outside his hut when he spotted the drainage operator. Looking closely at him, Paddy was amused to see that the man was wearing his trousers. Evidently he had not wanted to see a good pair of pants go to waste so he cleaned them and wore them himself. The poor German never did find out why Paddy and the other partygoers laughed at him whenever he came into the camp to pump the tank.

Since September, X's expanded intelligence section had been led by Wally Valenta, the apparently omniscient Czech who coordinated a team of experts covering all parts of Europe. As before, Roger Bushell was the authority on Germany, and Tom Kirby-Green took care of Spain. Bob van der Stok collected details on conditions in the Low Countries. Valenta himself was responsible for Czechoslovakia and military affairs, while Dennis Cochran acted as general consultant. And, of course, there was the indispensable Rene Marcinkus, who, apart from acting as the authority on the Balkans and the Baltic ports, was also the general expert on all things European. Rene had stored away in his incredible memory everything he had seen during his tour of Europe in 1934 and in the course of his travels as an international soccer player. Now the supervisor of the camp newspaper readers, Rene supplemented his knowledge with details gleaned from every German publication that came into the camp legally and many, including a Baedeker and a railroad timetable, that came in illegally.

The Scandinavian section of the intelligence network consisted of Arnold Christensen, still covering Denmark, and a cheerful Norwegian named Halldor Espelid. He was born on October 6, 1920, in Askøy near Bergen, and like many Norwegians was fond of outdoor activities such as soccer, cross-country running, and hiking in the hills around his home. Every summer in his childhood, Halldor went hiking in the mountains around Hardangerfjord, which he always maintained was the most beautiful spot on earth. Even with his passion for the outdoors, though, the young lad liked school and especially enjoyed his musical training. He played the organ and was an enthusiastic member of the school orchestra.

When the Germans invaded Norway in April 1940, Halldor made plans to escape, and in mid-September, just after starting his final year of high school, he and a few friends fled to England in a small boat. They applied to join the Royal Norwegian Air Force, and at the beginning of September 1941 Halldor was posted to Canada for training at Moose Jaw, Saskatchewan. His ready smile and good humor made him a favorite with the locals, and when he left Moose Jaw with his wings on November 21, a large contingent of new friends was at the station to see him off. Halldor proceeded to Little Norway in Toronto to complete his training and in April 1942 returned to England to become operational.

On July 15 he joined 331 Squadron, flying Spitfires from North Weald. Sadly the eager young Norwegian had a short operational career. He and another pilot claimed a damaged FW 190 on the last day of July, but on August 27, 1942, Halldor's aircraft was hit by light flak just east of Dunkirk. The damage appeared slight at first, and Espelid was able to keep up with his wingmates, but as they turned for home at Gravelines, he suddenly wheeled his aircraft inland and began losing height rapidly. He crash-landed in the Pas de Calais and was picked up immediately.

Aside from a short stint in Schubin, Halldor had spent all of his captivity in East Compound. There he became known as a very useful intelligence contact by providing Wooden Horse escaper Oliver Philpot with all the details he needed to carry off his disguise as a Norwegian businessman. When he made the move to North Compound in the late summer of 1943, Espelid's reputation preceded him, and he was called upon to be the resident authority on all things Norwegian.

*

Halldor was soon joined by a compatriot, Nils Jørgen Fuglesang, who was born on October 7, 1918, in Rasvåg, Hidra. The only son of a customs official, Nils and his four sisters were raised and educated in

Florø, on Norway's rocky and beautiful western coast. In September 1935 Nils moved on to the Lycêe Corneille in Rouen, France, and then in 1939 took a course at Bergen Commercial College, which he completed just before the outbreak of war. In September 1939 the young man was taken on as an apprentice with a shipping firm in Oslo, only to lose his job in a mass dismissal after the German invasion. He found work on a relative's farm and eventually went back to Florø, where he and a few friends began to plan their escape to Great Britain. On March 12, 1941, Nils and eleven other young men left Florø in a motor cutter, arriving in Scotland two days later. They immediately applied for entrance into the Royal Norwegian Air Force.

A month later, the group left Scotland for Toronto to do their preliminary training at Little Norway. Six months later they were back in England as fully qualified pilots and were posted to their final training courses. On June 9, 1942, Nils finally reached an operational unit, 332 Squadron, also flying Spitfires from North Weald. Unlike Halldor Espelid, Nils had a long operational career, and his reputation as a reliable and steady pilot earned him Norway's King Haakon VII medal and a promotion in March 1943.

On May 2, 1943, Nils was piloting his Spitfire over Flushing when misfortune struck. He followed his number 1 for a head-on attack on an FW 190 and, as the opposing aircraft approached each other at tremendous speed, Nils's Spitfire was hit by cannon shells aimed at his section leader. It was immediately apparent that there was little life left in the aircraft, and Nils beat a hasty retreat from the smoke-filled cockpit. He came down close to a German Army training unit, an inauspicious end to his eighty-fifth sortie.

After the customary week in Dulag Luft, Nils came to Sagan, where he met up with Halldor Espelid, whom he had last seen in Little Norway more than a year earlier. The new kriegie expressed a desire to get into escape work and was quickly taken into X Organization as a part-time disperser and part-time intelligence expert. He soon found out what an important job the latter was.

*

Within the escape organization, the intelligence experts fulfilled a dual function: They provided potential escapers with information about the countries through which they would travel, and they assisted with the creation of background stories to be used by escapers. Of course, they had to keep their information as up to date as possible and did so by supplementing their own knowledge with details passed on by Marcinkus's staff of newspaper readers.

Once an escaper made a decision about the identity he was going to assume, his first stop was the intelligence expert for that country. The expert would recommend a hometown and could perhaps provide a list of the firms that were large enough to send traveling businessmen, but small enough that he was not likely to encounter someone actually employed by the company. He would talk about the city itself and mention a few landmarks and names of restaurants or cafés to use in case an interrogator knew the area. There was nothing so discouraging as escaping disguised as a native of Budapest and running into a police official who knew more about the city, despite the fact that he had spent only a summer there in 1937. Finally, the area expert could pass on details on any of the little local idiosyncrasies, such as the way to wear a beret or the sort of greeting that was customarily used. These little points so often made the difference between success and failure.

Once the escaper had his assumed identity down pat, it was time to find out about the countries through which he would be traveling. This might involve seeing as many as four or five different people, or perhaps only one. It was essential to know the best route to take to get from the camp to neutral territory, what places to avoid, whether there were any curfews, and whether travel through a certain area had been restricted because of Allied bombing or other factors. When planning a route, it was always a good idea to have a chat with Rene Marcinkus, who had a remarkable facility for describing almost every major European railroad station. He knew how to get to the stations, and what regions they served; he could even describe where to look for the ticket hall, and what time the various trains left. Having been given all of this information, it only remained to memorize it, not forgetting such trivial details as one's date of birth and the spelling of one's assumed name.

*

Of course, an escaper could have the best cover identity and supplies in the world, but without a good set of forged papers, there was little chance of making a successful escape. It was the job of the Dean and Dawson Travel Bureau, headed by the charming Tim Walenn, to provide those forged papers. Dean and Dawson produced three types of documents: actual forgeries; invented documents; and typewritten documents. There were many different kinds of actual forgeries: the *Ausweis*, or identity card, that had to be carried by every civilian; the *Solbuch*, a German soldier's paybook; the *Urlaubsschein*, which authorized a foreign worker to return home on leave; the *Ruckkehrschein*, the final release of a foreign worker to return to his own country; and countless others. These documents were the most time-consuming to produce; an *Urlaubsschein* took one forger working five hours a day an entire month to complete.

Invented documents were official-looking cards or papers, with a suitable number of impressive rubber stamps and signatures. It was hoped that if a document looked convincing enough, it might be accepted by a less-than-bright interrogator. One of Tim's proudest creations was a Lithuanian *Ausweis*, invented with the help of Rene Marcinkus. Typewritten documents were last-ditch papers, used primarily by hardarsers. They were supposed to be temporary documents issued while the genuine item was in for renewal or updating. No one knew exactly what form these documents took, or even if they really existed, but Dean and Dawson made some pretty convincing guesses.

Once an escaper had decided on his cover story, he went to see Tim Walenn, who would determine what documents the fellow would need. If he was traveling as a Danish businessman, he would need an *Ausweis*, at least one travel permit, and perhaps a letter of introduction from his company to add a bit of extra weight. Once Tim had the personal information needed for the documents, Dean and Dawson could go to work.

The first order of business was to obtain originals of the documents that were required. The forgers would work directly from the originals and could refer to them frequently to ensure that their copies were exact. Thanks to the contacts and others, Tim Walenn was able to build up a collection of documents. Many were bribed or blackmailed from guards, but others could be obtained from foreign workers during escape or stolen from any vehicle that appeared in the compound. Various papers and passes were obtained from the *Hundführer*, the goon in charge of the camp's patrol dogs, while Sydney Dowse was able to get two real Dutch workmen's identity cards and numerous other passes for copying from Corporal Hesse.

The next matter was procuring the supplies necessary to make the copies. Paper came from various sources, such as the guards or YMCA and Red Cross drawing sets, but it was sometimes difficult to get the right thickness and quality. Tim Walenn took to examining all new books that came into the camp to see if the endpapers could be used for anything. Watercolor paper from overseas parcels was also useful if tinted to the right shade with hot sand, tea, or coffee.

For ink, it was sometimes possible to use watercolors but, because they did not stand up well and had a tendency to change color, it was better to get real ink from tame guards. Bob van der Stok tried making ink with the help of a Polish chemist in the infirmary. Using a mixture of soot, glycerine, ether, and mineral oil, he was able to produce a black ink that could be applied with a brush and was waterproof when it dried. After the ink, the forgers needed something with which to apply it. The contact organization was able to extort a selection of pen nibs from various tame goons, so Dean and Dawson was well equipped on that score. Some of the forgers preferred to use paintbrushes, also easily obtainable from Red Cross or YMCA parcels; they trimmed down the brushes so that only four or five bristles were left.

The process of forging was time-consuming, finicky, and hard on the eyes. The number of forgers was kept to a minimum, partly for security reasons and partly because there was very little room around the window table where they worked. And the fact that they had to work beside the window for the best lighting created great security problems. Early on, Tim took to hanging a piece of muslin over the window, ostensibly to keep the flies out but really to make it more difficult for prying eyes to see in.

The documents were at first entirely produced by hand, and each was the work of a single forger; it was thought that a keen eye might be able to detect slight differences in style and print, possibly bringing to an end a very good escape. For letterpress, used in the forgeries of actual documents, a fine pen or brush with India ink was used. Gordon Brettell, using a fine pen nib, became a master at the print needed for these documents. Other documents required the ornate, Gothic script; this was the specialty of Alex Cassie, who used a very fine brush to achieve the desired effect.

Once the print on a document was complete, it remained to add the finishing touches. Many forms of *Ausweises* and travel permits required photographs, so a small studio was set up by Geoff Cornish and Chaz Hall. The camera, films, paper, and developing chemicals all had to be brought in by hooked goons, and the studio was also equipped with a couple of suits of civilian clothes for use during a photo session. Then most documents required some sort of seal, and for this, Jens Müller cut a mold of the stamp from a piece of soap and cast a replica using silver paper. Johnny Travis crafted a little stamping machine with a centering device that made perfect imprints on documents. Rubber stamps also had to be improvised. Tim Walenn painted the stamp in reverse on a boot heel or an ice hockey puck; then an Australian squadron leader did the carving. The Aussie often worked in the open compound and looked like any other kriegie pursuing a hobby. If there was any trouble, he only had to bury the goods in the sand beside him and pull out a book. A blank space was left on the stamp for the date and city name, to be painted in when required.

Finally, the document needed a cover. For a long time, the stiff linen covers on some documents gave the forgers problems. Many methods had been tried, but none had produced an effect that satisfied Tim. Then Walenn found in the camp a fellow named Lusty, who had worked in the publishing trade before the war. He took over the production of the stiff covers, which he made out of etched and tinted tracing paper glued over cardboard; the finished product looked exactly like a linen cover. In all, Lusty produced twenty-two of these covers for use by many of the train travelers.

The document was now complete and only remained to be signed. This was done at the last possible minute, to get the greatest use out of a document's life span and to ensure that information about the signing official was up to date. There was nothing like being stopped by a policeman and learning that the official who was supposed to have signed your leave pass last week had been killed in an air raid a month ago.

Most of the other documents required were handwritten. One might have a letter of introduction, signed by the president of one's company. The elegant embossing was applied with a carved toothbrush handle, while the name of the company president had been gleaned by one of Marcinkus's newspaper readers. Or one might have a small bundle of love letters from an ardent fiancée. Anything that helped to strengthen an escaper's disguise could be prepared by Dean and Dawson.

Eventually the typewritten forms to be carried by many of the hardarsers were taking so long to produce that Tim began to search for another method. He had already sent a coded request back to England for a miniature typewriter, but since no one knew when it would arrive, another solution was needed. The contact organization was able to find a tame goon who was willing to take drafts of the necessary documents to his wife in Hamburg. She typed them out on stencils, which were then smuggled back into the camp. To reproduce them, Tim crafted a printing press out of a wooden roller covered with blanket material. Using ink made from a mixture of mineral oil and soot from fat lamps, very decent typewritten forms could be run off by the hundred.

The forgers started work in an empty room in Hut 120 but soon moved to the kitchen block, beside the orchestra's practice room. There was one main advantage to this: If any of the dangerous goons came too close, the work would be stuffed into a violin case and carried from the building by a kriegie who merely appeared to be returning from rehearsal. If any of the less dangerous goons came by, the forgers just tucked their work away and became prisoners transcribing sheet music.

In October 1943 Tim decided to move the operation to the church room in Hut 122 and, later, to the library in 110. At the same time, a modification was made to the stooging system. It had become apparent that the ferrets were beginning to lock onto individual stooges and instituting searches wherever there appeared to be lookouts hanging around. Tim experimented with dropping the stooges altogether, but one day Adolf got a little too close and was seen peering in the window of the forging room. Luckily he could see nothing because of the condensation on the panes. Realizing that it was too dangerous without stooges, Tim, Alex Cassie, and Paul Brickhill, the forgers' security boss, came up with a new system.

In this system, stooges were placed in the southern end of 103, on the eastern side of 109, and in the room beside the forgers. The stooges remained inside the huts, invisible to the ferrets but with a clear view of all angles of the compound. If goons approached from any direction, signals would be passed from either of the two stooging positions to the man in the room beside the forgers. He would knock on the wall, and the forgers could pack up in seconds. To anyone watching, it looked as if nothing had happened.

In the months before the escape, Tim also took to storing everything down Dick as a security precaution. Travis made four large waterproof cans with sliding lids to keep the documents dry, and everything was packed in them. Les Brodrick brought out all the papers in the morning and took them to Dean and Dawson, returning them to the tunnel at lunch. After lunch the process was repeated, and they were finally returned to Dick before evening *Appell*. It made for some extra work, but it was a whole lot safer.

Chapter 13

TRAVEL PLANS ARE MADE

NOVEMBER BROUGHT WINTER TO Sagan, with cold winds blowing down from the north. They carried sprinkles of snow, and soon the compound was covered with a light dusting of white. This didn't stop John Stevens from continuing his morning exercise group, though. For the past few months he had led calisthenics on the parade ground before *Appell*, putting a few of the kriegies through their paces. In the warmer months there were usually fifteen or twenty of the lads with him, in all manner of dress, from pajamas to shorts to towels. Some looked frightfully keen and energetic, while others seemed to be struggling to stay awake. Now, with temperatures dipping to zero, John was still out, clad in long johns and pajamas. His attendance had thinned somewhat with the coming of winter, and nowadays he usually had only two or three eager souls. Despite that, he led their exercises with the same vigor and enthusiasm with which he led a larger group.

John's fellow South African Johannes Gouws was a bit less enthusiastic about the winter weather. He hated the cold and remained bundled up for much of the period between October and March. There was always some good-natured chiding, but his roommates soon got used to Johannes's nightly ceremony of undressing, putting on his pajamas, and then putting on every scrap of clothing he owned before climbing into bed and cocooning himself in his blankets.

*

By now Des Plunkett and his men had perfected a system for the easy reproduction of maps. The keys to the operation were slabs of jelly, which arrived in great quantity in Red Cross parcels, and onionskin or cellophane page dividers from Bibles. With these innocuous materials, Plunkett, Tony Hayter, and the Pole Adam Kolanowski turned out thousands of maps of all parts of Europe.

The first step was to obtain maps of the necessary areas. These were either copied from German maps obtained legitimately, bribed from guards (for sensitive areas such as border crossings), or sent to the camp in phony parcels. One lot of maps, showing the route from Sagan to Prague, came into the camp hidden in a pair of old gym shoes. The maps were constantly updated with new information, and Plunkett's collection was expanded whenever possible. Eventually he accumulated a series of twelve maps covering the route from Sagan south to Turnau in Czechoslovakia. Another coup for Des was getting a good map of the area around the camp, blackmailed from a contact and supplemented with information obtained from various guards.

Once the master maps were on hand, supplies of green, black, red, blue, and gentian violet ink were procured. Some came from Tim Walenn, who had a good supply of extorted stamp pads, while others were produced by scraping lead shavings from indelible pencils and boiling them in water. Then, using a sharp wooden stylus, the maps were drawn on the onionskin. This job was the specialty of Adam Kolanowski, who had been a cartographer before the war.

While the maps were being drawn, another worker watered down the jelly powder to dissolve the sugar, which was poured off and discarded. The jelly mixture was then strained through a handkerchief to remove any last remnants of sugar. Finally it was heated and poured into a pan, about the size of a sheet of legal paper, made from Klim cans. When the jelly was firm but still warm, the onionskin master copy, its ink still wet, was laid on the jelly pan. When it was removed several minutes later, an impression of the map remained on the jelly. Then, using thin paper scrounged for the purpose, it was merely a matter of laying a sheet on the jelly, pressing lightly, and drawing off a perfect color reproduction. Each master produced about twenty copies and then had to be redrawn and placed on a fresh pan of jelly for the next run. It was possible to reuse the jelly once or twice by reheating the mix and straining it again, but the quality deteriorated after the second or third use. Similarly, each pan might yield more than twenty copies, but as more imprints were done, the colors became fainter and had to be touched up.

When the maps were completed, they were divided into numbered sets, with each set showing a different part of the Continent. Des Plunkett made careful notes in a small book of which escapers required which sets. The maps were then stored in sealed canisters made from Klim cans and put away in Dick for safekeeping. Plunkett's vital notebook never left his person.

The mainstays of Plunkett's operation were Adam Kolanowski and Tony Hayter, the former involved with the drawing the maps and the latter working with techniques of reproduction. It was Tony who developed the method of producing five-color maps, and he was constantly trying to find ways to improve the process. He spent hours working with various jelly mixes in the hopes of one day producing a jelly that would yield thousands of imprints.

*

As for many of the other Continental officers, captivity was nothing new for Wlodzimierz Adam Kolanowski, who was a POW for the second time in the war. A thin fellow with a tapered face and dark, straight hair, Adam was a career military man who joined the Polish Army in September 1934 at age twenty-one. He rose up through the ranks and was commissioned in the 66th Infantry Regiment, stationed at Chelmno, in October 1937. Just over a year later, Kolanowski decided to transfer to the air force and trained as an observer, receiving special instruction in aerial surveying. In August 1939 Adam was attached to 222 Squadron, flying light bombers from Biala Podlaska.

Kolanowski saw little action during the September campaign and on September 17 his unit was evacuated southward, crossing into Romania three days later. He and his fellow airmen were housed at an army camp at Drăgășani, and in October Adam finally received authorization to travel to France via Yugoslavia and Greece. Soon after beginning his journey, though, he was stopped by Romanian police, who confiscated his passport and interned him in a camp at Turnu-Severin. It was nearly two weeks before he was able to retrieve his travel documents and continue his journey. He managed to get to the Polish embassy in Bucharest, where passage was arranged via Malta to Marseilles. There Adam rejoined the Polish Air Force on November 13, 1939.

During the Battle of France, Kolanowski was attached to 11 Squadron but, since no equipment was available, the unit remained inactive. Finally, after much toing and froing, he returned to Marseilles to embark for England, arriving on June 30. Adam was taken into the RAF and, after training, was posted to 301 Squadron at Hemswell on October 10, 1941. He flew only three operations with the unit and was captured on November 8, 1941, when his Wellington was shot down during a raid on Mannheim.

Once they learned a bit more about Adam Kolanowski, the escape organizers were delighted to have him onboard. Not only did he have extensive experience in mapping techniques from his prewar service, but he was also born in Pawłowice, about sixty miles from Sagan. Pawłowice was in the border region between Germany and Poland, an area that was a target of escapers seeking to gain the comparative safety of occupied but friendly Poland. When an escape drew near, Adam Kolanowski would be a valuable man to consult.

*

In early December heavy snow came, as well as a welcome shipment of chocolate parcels just in time for the Christmas season. There was also a wealth of entertainment available. Another American film, *Bringing Up Baby* with Cary Grant and Katharine Hepburn, had arrived in Sagan, and the theater company was about to open their production of Leslie Storm's *Tony Draws a Horse*. The cast included Arnold Christensen, playing a maid 'with about a dozen words to say,' as he told his family.

Christmas Day brought another light snowfall, and the officers relaxed and celebrated the season. For some, such as Wings Day, Mike Casey, and Tommy Thompson, it was their fifth in captivity; others were experiencing the unwelcome novelty of their first behind barbed wire. Some rooms got together to collaborate on Christmas dinner, and a few even employed white-gloved waiters and cooks to be in attendance. After the New Year, the cold spell broke, though it remained just cold enough to freeze the camp ice rink. In the first game of the New Year, a team of early prisoners beat a team of newcomers, with George McGill scoring the second goal for the old-timers. The newcomers immediately demanded a rematch but were beaten again.

*

Late in the month, a full discussion of the future of the escape plan was held. At this time, five of the Little X's, elected by a popular vote of all X workers, joined the four-man executive to take part in the decision-making process. Such a move would allow a full hearing of all opinions before any decisions were made. As things stood, Harry was approaching one hundred feet long, while Dick was only at sixty feet. Furthermore, the removal of the pine trees to the west of the compound meant that Dick would have to be nearly five hundred feet long to reach the woods. It was fairly obvious, then, that work should concentrate on Harry, and it was also decided that digging should resume as soon as possible, since the Germans were less likely to expect tunneling in the winter months. Security would have to be stepped up when work began again, though, for there was now a constant ferret patrol in the compound, another legacy of Tom.

On January 10, 1944, Roger Bushell decided to reopen Harry. Pat Langford had sealed the trap so well that it took a good two hours to open it, but when the engineers got underground, they found the tunnel in surprisingly good shape. The bypass valve on the pump had been left open so the air was still fresh, and there were only a few small sand leaks and four shoring frames that had twisted and needed replacing. All the trolley ropes were also replaced with new four-ply ropes. The air system required a bit more work. The kit bag on the air pump had rotted, the air line was blocked near the base of the shaft, and there were a few other small leaks elsewhere. However, because of the design of the shoring, it was impossible to remove the floorboards to get at the air line. The midsection of each floorboard had to be cut out and then replaced after the repair was made. It was four days before the ventilation system was passed fit for use.

Work progressed pretty much as it had before, with some new men on the digging teams. Ivo Tonder took a few shifts underground in spite of his claustrophobia, and Sandy Gunn, Cookie Long, Sydney Dowse, and Johnny Stower were regular diggers. Wally Floody found he had trouble with two of the Canadians, Scruffy Weir and Hank Birkland (who had never gotten used to Floody's order that he not work naked because of the risk of sand scars). Whenever they dug, Scruffy tended to veer sharply to the left, while Hank's work dove to the right; only by putting them on back-to-back shifts could Wally keep the tunnel straight.

*

Another of the diggers was a fellow who had still been flying when Harry's shaft was sunk the previous April. On the night of April 26–27, 1943, while the kriegies were settling into North Compound, Bomber Command's maximum effort was directed against Duisburg, and at the navigator's station of a 77 Squadron Halifax, Flying Officer Robert Campbell Stewart plotted a course toward the huge oxbow shape of searchlights and gun flashes that was the Ruhr Valley. The bombers came in from the northwest and were on course for the target indicators when the aircraft was caught by a blue master searchlight. Immediately, other searchlights picked up the Halifax and, just after the bombs were dropped, very accurate flak began to strike. Evasive action couldn't shake the searchlights, and when a direct hit shook the Hallie, the crew knew it was time to get out.

Bob Stewart grabbed bomb-aimer Doug Atter's shoulder and pointed to the escape hatch, and the two made their way toward the exit past ruptured hydraulic lines that burned like gas jets. After struggling with the hatch, they finally got it open and pushed themselves clear. Atter was free for two days before being captured, but Bob Stewart was less fortunate. He went through the roof of an apartment building and was still struggling to disentangle himself from the debris when the police arrived to take him into custody.

Bob Stewart was born on July 7, 1911, in Finsbury Park and was raised in Finchley and Golders Green. He worked for a road construction and tunneling firm before the war, but the firm closed its doors when war broke out, and Bob applied to join the RAF. He had no special interest in flying but found the whole atmosphere of the air force more congenial than that of the army. He had to wait to be called up, though, and in the intervening period was drafted as a special constable in the Metropolitan Police. It wasn't until December 1940 that Bob was summoned to Stratford to begin training. Ten months later, as a sergeant, he was posted to 11 OTU and became operational with 77 Squadron on March 5, 1942. Soon afterward 77 was attached to Coastal Command and flew Whitleys out of Chivenor in Devon. Bob completed eighteen operations, mostly shipping strikes and antisubmarine patrols, and in August was commissioned. A short time later 77 Squadron reverted to Bomber Command and re-formed at Elvington in Yorkshire.

At Elvington Bob lived off the station with his wife, Doris, whom he had met while golfing at Finchley Country Club in 1938, and each morning Doris would stand at the door and watch as Bob walked to the airfield. He always paused at the gate to wave good-bye and when he did, Doris knew he would return from the night's operations. On that morning in late April, he left the cottage as usual and paused at the gate to give a cheery wave to Doris. This time, though, on his twenty-seventh operation with 77 Squadron, the little good-luck charm failed to work. Eventually word came through that Bob was a prisoner. Then, in one of his letters, he made a casual yet meaningful remark to Doris. 'I'm getting my hand in again at my old job,' Bob wrote. Doris may not have realized it at the time, but Bob was telling her that he had turned to digging tunnels instead of roads.

*

By late January Harry had passed the hundred-foot mark, and the first halfway house, named Piccadilly, was built. Engineers calculated that it lay under the cooler, and sometimes, if you listened carefully, you could hear the guards' jackboots on the concrete floor above. However, the dispersal problem had once again become acute. With the frozen compound often blanketed in snow, it was no longer possible to distribute sand around the camp. In any case, the days had shortened considerably, and it was far too suspicious for kriegies to be shuffling around the compound in the dark. The solution, when it was finally reached, was not the most popular ever devised by X Organization.

The camp theater was built on solid brick foundations and, because of its sloping floor, there was a 2½- to 3-foot space underneath. There was no way the ferrets could get under to check for fresh sand, and it was calculated that the space could hold the spoil from two or three tunnels. However, the theater was a very jealously guarded privilege, and the acting troupe objected to their facility being used for escape purposes. It wasn't that they were anti-escape. They simply believed, and rightly so, that the theater was tremendously important for camp morale and objected to anything that might endanger its existence. Roger Bushell weighed both sides of the argument carefully and came to his decision: The theater it would be.

First of all, a trap was cut under one of the seats (seat 13, as it happened) and dispersal areas marked out underneath. There would be one trench running up the middle, with smaller trenches going off on either side for ease of movement. Then new shift bosses for dispersal were chosen. Jimmy James and Ian Cross were put in charge of the overall scheme, while others were appointed to control individual teams of workers. There were about eighty workers altogether: thirty-five carriers; twelve men working under the floor of the theater; fifteen helping shift sand at the trap and load up the carriers; and the rest acting as controllers. From the beginning, it was apparent that dispersal could proceed only during the evening hours. If they began at about 6:00 P.M., the dispersers would have a good four hours to work before the prisoners were locked in their huts promptly at ten. However, on fine nights when the moon was high, the operation had to be suspended; it was too easy for the carriers to be spotted from the guard towers.

When it was all in place, the system worked well. The sand was loaded into Red Cross kit bags, each weighing eighty to one hundred pounds, at the bottom of the shaft. The bags were then hauled up, carried to the room at the end of the hut, and taken across the path to Block 109, where the carriers were loaded. This was done to reduce as much as possible the traffic in and out of the tunnel hut. Two sacks of sand were suspended around the carriers' shoulders and covered with a greatcoat. Under the watchful eyes of the controllers, they followed various routes to the theater so that the amount of traffic didn't become too heavy. In many ways, the trip to the theater from 109 was the hardest part of the operation, as Pop Green found out. Carrying thirty-five pounds of sand one evening, his boot caught on one of the protruding tree roots that dotted the compound. He nearly took a header and spilled the bags of sand in full view of the guards.

At times when the ferret patrolling the compound could be coaxed away from his duties by his contact prisoner, dispersal could proceed much more quickly. At such times the sand was taken directly to the theater from 104. (In fact, the record for a single night's dispersal was set on one of these occasions, when the ferret spent two hours in his contact's room, which happened to be in Hut 104. On that night, nearly four tons of sand, representing thirteen feet of tunnel, were taken to the theater and dumped.) When they arrived at the theater, the carriers dumped their sacks down the hole beneath seat 13. The underground workers used basins to shift the sand, ferrying them up and down the trenches to the various dispersal areas. It was hot, dirty work, but it was much faster than the penguin method. The final step in the dispersal process occurred very early the next morning, when all routes to the theater were inspected for traces of sand. Any sand found was carefully swept up and hidden away.

Above all this, rehearsals were going on in the theater just as before. On January 20, the opening of *Hit the Air* wound up with the wail of air raid sirens as the RAF bombed Berlin yet again. Kriegies returning to their huts claimed to be able to see the glow of fires in the distance. After *Hit the Air* came a pantomime version of *Treasure Island*, complete with maidens in distress and swashbuckling pirates. It was all great fun.

*

With work on the tunnels once more under way, the mood in the camp became considerably brighter. Jack Grisman wrote home to his mother, 'We are all a little more optimistic than of yore so perhaps I may be in time to help you move.' Anxious to get a head start on the postwar world, Jack continued with his studies, passing his exams in French, mechanics, and advanced math in January.

The only ones apparently not infected with this optimism were some of the East European officers. Perhaps because they had seen so much already, they were less willing to believe that there might be an end in sight. Rene Marcinkus confided to John Casson that he expected the war to last until 1947, while Wally Valenta was sure that they would all be shot before it was over. Paweł Tobolski wrote to his wife, whom he had married in Marseilles in February 1940, and told her not to expect a quick reunion. Convinced that he would never see his wife and child again, Jerzy Mondschein suffered frequent bouts of depression. Late at night, the others in Hut 110 would hear him pacing up and down the corridors for hours on end.

*

By mid-February Harry had reached the two-hundred-foot mark, under the far wire of the *Vorlager*, and a second halfway house, called Leicester Square, was built. Because this coincided with the full-moon period, when it was too risky for the carriers to travel the compound to disperse, it was decided to shut down Harry until the period ended. During the layoff, the engineers again considered gradually digging upward to save time, but the suggestion was dismissed. Aside from the inherent dangers of the practice, it was believed that digging upward would make it even more difficult to keep the tunnel straight. They had only recently discovered that Harry was one foot out of line to the right, an error that had taken thirty feet of careful digging to the left to correct.

They were also running into problems due to a shortage of electric cable, but this was solved by pure providence. One day a team of electricians came into the camp to install loudspeakers so the POWs could enjoy German martial music and war communiqués. One lad noticed that they had two reels of wire, and the decision was immediately made to steal them. Canton had collected a team and begun planning elaborate diversions to pull off the heist when, from their vantage point behind a hut, they spotted Red Noble returning from one of his frequent spells in the cooler. He, too, saw the reels of wire and, changing direction slightly, passed right by them. In the blink of an eye he scooped one of them up and carried it nonchalantly to his hut under a blanket. Not to be outdone, Canton and his boys swiped the other reel with their carefully planned diversion, and the wire was hidden down Dick in anticipation of the inevitable search. However, nothing happened and after a couple of days Roger concluded that the electricians had been too frightened to report their loss.

With more than enough wire to light Harry, work continued but the number of searches was also stepped up, the ferrets concentrating on the huts nearest the wire. Special attention was paid to rooms with tiled stove bases, but nothing was found. Perhaps this was because a British airman named Marcel Zillessen had persuaded his tame goon, the once-vigilant fellow named Keen Type, to warn them of any upcoming searches in exchange for finding a few bits of escape gear now and again. The ferret Adolf, who was constantly snooping around and turning up in the most inconvenient places, was tamed by a big, red Scot named Jim Tyrie, who was able to keep him talking for hours. Chalk up another conscientious goon corrupted.

Down in Harry the workers were dogged by a spate of mishaps. On February 10 Wally Floody was buried badly but still managed to dig a record 12½ feet. Then a bedboard fell from the top of the shaft and hit Cookie Long squarely on the head, putting him in bed for two days. A couple of days later, Pat Langford dropped another board and nearly clobbered Ker-Ramsay. And then someone dropped a metal jug down the shaft; it glanced off Floody's head, leaving a wicked bruise.

Searches continued. Hut 104 was turned over with no result, and then Valenta's contact, Walter, the thin, bespectacled goon who helped Pieber count on *Appell*, warned that 110 would be the next target. Roger cleaned out his hide and waited for the ax to fall. The next day at *Appell*, he, George Harsh, Wally Floody, and Wings Day were pulled out of the ranks and strip-searched. By sleight-of-hand, Roger was able to pass a wad of important papers to the fellows around him. The goons then took apart his room and, by sheer luck, happened upon his hide. It was empty.

Perhaps in a fit of desperation, the Germans brought in a psychic, a weaselly little character who wandered around the camp waving a divining rod. He, too, had to admit defeat and was chased from the compound by hoots of derision. A snap *Appell* was next. The Germans had used this successfully once at Barth, but this time the organizers were prepared for anything. As the party of goons trooped into the compound and wasted time by lining up and numbering off before starting the count, Pat Langford called up his workers and closed the trap with scant seconds to spare.

*

By the early spring, noxious smoke produced by the fat lamps was beginning to take its toll on the workers, some of whom were coming down with minor respiratory ailments. Les Harvey, after long hours in the woodwork shop at the base of Dick's shaft, was hit by a bad bout of conjunctivitis and had to be taken out of the tunnel. To fill his place, the organization chose Porokoru Patapu Pohe, a jokey little Maori who usually went by the name Johnny, although he signed all the official forms with his full name to confuse the Germans. Johnny was one of the more recent arrivals at Sagan, but as soon as Willy Williams talked to him, he knew he could count on Pohe to be a tireless worker.

Born at Wanganui, New Zealand, on December 10, 1914, Johnny grew up on the family farm with six sisters. He was a popular boy in the local area and at Te Aute College and excelled academically (his only weakness being in the Maori language) and athletically, in rugby, cricket, tennis, and golf.

After leaving Te Aute, he returned to work on the farm yet still managed to indulge his love of sports and music. He even found time to spend two years in the Territorials with the Manawatu Mounted Rifles. It was an unexpected delight for the Pohe family when in 1937 another son, Kawana, was born. Though more than two decades separated him from Kawana, Johnny doted on the youngster and was doubtless glad to have another male ally in the midst of all those girls. Leaving Kawana was the hardest thing facing Johnny when the time came to go overseas.

Though he applied for pilot training on September 12, 1939, Johnny had to do a year of preparatory courses before being called for preliminary instruction in September 1940. Flying training began in November at Woodbourne, where Pohe received his flying badge on January 18, 1941, and in April he was ready to embark for Europe. Johnny left Auckland with mixed emotions, as his letters from the troopship RMMS *Aorangi* reveal. On the one hand, it was all terribly exciting and a bit suspenseful ('I am on the eve of a big adventure and perhaps may never see you again'), but on the other hand he hated to leave his family, especially Kawana ('I couldn't come into the carriage that night to say good-bye to him as I was weeping like a baby'). His greatest solace was the imminent opportunity to make his parents proud of him.

Johnny found the trip across the Pacific to Canada a delight. Fiji offered wicked native women ('these women were trying to drag us to some dark spot but nothing doing') and parties at the Grand Pacific Hotel, and Christmas Island provided shark fishing and pint after pint of coconut milk. The last stopover was at Fanning Island, and before long the *Aorangi* was putting into Vancouver. The New Zealanders didn't linger in Canada, and by late May 1941 Johnny had reached 10 OTU at Abingdon; instruction on Whitleys began immediately. By July 21 he was ready for his first operation, flying as co-pilot for a hit-and-run raid on Paris and Orléans, to become the first Maori to bomb a target in occupied Europe. On August 24 Pohe was assigned to 51 Squadron at Dishforth in Yorkshire.

Over the next eight months Johnny completed twenty-two ops, and men who had known him before recall that those raids changed him. Johnny lost none of his wit and good humor, yet he seemed much more mature and self-assured than he had been during training. Small wonder, given some of the experiences he had. Over Kiel, his Whitley took some heavy anti-aircraft hits in the belly and just managed to limp back to Dishforth in one piece. Another night, after bombing the submarine yards at Sylt, Johnny was so determined to get back to base quickly that he flew straight into Dishforth despite the fact that the base was completely fogbound. Only a series of threats from an old friend in the control tower convinced Johnny to head for another airfield instead of trying to dump the Whitley on the tarmac blind.

Johnny's ability did not go unrecognized, and he was picked for promotion and for a number of sensitive assignments. In October 1941 he became a flight sergeant and on February 27, 1942, was pilot of a Whitley that dropped paratroops on the German radar station at

Bruneval. The following month he flew operations in support of the commando raid on St. Nazaire.

With one tour of duty under his belt, Johnny was posted to 24 OTU at Honeybourne in late April 1942 to serve a stint as flying instructor. His commission came in May and he still flew in occasional operations, such as the 'Thousand Raid' on Bremen on June 25–26, but most of his time was spent instructing.

There was enough spare time to explore the local watering holes with his fellow instructors. They used to cycle from pub to pub, and Johnny imagined himself to be quite a drinker, taking pride in his ability to down a pint in four seconds – that is, until a Women's Auxiliary Air Force officer wandered into the pub and asked if she could have a try. No one was more surprised than Johnny when she downed her pint in 3½ seconds!

As much as Johnny enjoyed life at Honeybourne, he was clearly fed up with being off operations but got nothing more than an occasional trip with his OTU. He did have a bit of excitement in March 1943, when his Wellington crashed with the port wing on fire, but he couldn't seem to get posted away from his unit, where he spent almost a year on instructional duties.

Finally, in August 1943, Johnny was transferred to 1663 Heavy Conversion Unit (HCU) at Rufforth in Yorkshire for conversion to Halifaxes. He was quickly back on ops and was soon set up with a new crew. However, the transition to Hallies wasn't as smooth as it might have been. On September 8, after a cross-country training flight, Johnny got a red flare on landing approach and had to pull up and try for another circuit. Losing power quickly, he got most of the way around at treetop level but finally had to put the big bomber down wheels-up on the grass. Though no one was injured, the Halifax was a write-off and Johnny got chewed out by the station commander. A very experienced Flying Officer Pohe took it with a grain of salt, for with more than a thousand hours as a pilot, he was headed back to operations.

It was late evening on September 20 when the little Maori and his new crew reached 51 Squadron, based at Snaith in Yorkshire. The CO was glad to get a pilot of Johnny's experience and sent him on a diversionary operation to Brest the following night.

On September 22 Bomber Command targeted the industrial center of Hannover for the first major raid on that city in more than two years.

When 51 Squadron arrived over the area at 23,000 feet, they found the aiming point free of clouds but swept by stronger winds than forecast. Johnny was forced to remain longer over the city than usual. After maneuvering to avoid other aircraft below, they released their load and were leaving the target area when the Hallie took a couple of serious flak hits in the midsection, knocking out the intercom.

She fell into a steep dive and, in the confusion that followed, four of the crew bailed out, leaving Johnny and bomb-aimer Dave Wells with a stricken aircraft and their rear gunner, nineteen-year-old Tom Thomson of Alberta, Canada, trapped in his turret. After what seemed like ages, Johnny was able to pull the big ship out of the dive and level her off with two thousand feet to spare. Wells managed to free Thomson from the rear turret, and the two headed to the cockpit to work out a course for home. Everything went fairly smoothly for a while but the longer they flew, the more the three became convinced that something was dreadfully wrong. Suddenly they realized that, instead of flying across the Channel, they had been flying along it. It was a cruel twist of fate, for they had already used most of their fuel. The only option was to ditch.

The moon was fairly bright, and Johnny put the Halifax down in one piece on the water, no mean feat given the size of the aircraft. The three piled out of the sinking bomber and clambered into the dinghy that had released automatically from the wing. They floated for two days before being spotted by a German aircraft, which signaled for a torpedo boat to pick them up and convey them to Brest. The Luftwaffe lost no time in shipping them to Dulag Luft, and from there Thomson and Wells went on to Stalag Luft VI, while Johnny was transferred to Sagan, arriving on October 6. The following spring he was put to work in Dick's chamber.

*

One day in late February, Bill Jennens was waiting in the *Kommandantur* for a meeting with the SBO and a few members of the camp staff. For a few minutes he found himself alone in the commandant's office and, to his great surprise, noticed that the safe was open. Not wishing to miss an opportunity, Jennens quickly went over to the safe and leafed through a few of the files that were in it. Many were standard supply requisitions and personnel rosters, but there was one document, titled *Stufe Römisch III*, that alarmed him. It originated from OKW headquarters in Berlin and stated that every officer or NCO who escaped, with the exception of British and Americans, was to be turned over to the police upon recapture. Exactly what action was to be taken against them was not specified. Bill was about to dig deeper in the safe for further details when footsteps in the outer office signaled von Lindeiner's arrival. Bill quickly replaced the files and returned to his seat.

What Jennens had stumbled upon was the latest volley in the Nazis' harsh new policy regarding escaping prisoners of war. Had he found the safe open a couple of weeks later, he might well have seen another document, this one from Gestapo headquarters in Berlin, entitled *Aktion Kugel* (Bullet Decree). This order stated that all non-British and non-American escapers were to be transported to a concentration camp for liquidation. However, the decree said explicitly that British and American escapers were to be returned to the military authorities in all cases. The camp staff was evidently well aware of this order, for in the weeks before the tunnel break was scheduled, ominous rumors ran through the camp.

One afternoon, Sydney Dowse caught up with Roger Bushell on the circuit. 'Can I have a word, Roger?' asked Sydney.

'Of course, Dynamo. What's the news?'

'I've just had a little talk with Hesse,' began Sydney. 'He said that von Lindeiner and Rubberneck are sure there's going to be a big break – they don't know when, but they know it's coming.'

'Full marks to the goons then!' said Roger with a laugh.

'We also talked about you, Roger. You and I both know how well connected Hesse is – he seems to know the score pretty well. The thing is this: He says you're a marked man – he says the Gestapo's after you and they only need an excuse. I think you ought to consider staying behind. You can cause just as much trouble organizing things from inside the camp.'

There was barely a moment's pause before Bushell spoke again. 'Sorry, Dynamo, but I'm going. I've worked a long time for this. The fact is that this time, they're not going to catch me!'

Dowse chuckled. 'I hadn't really expected any other answer. I just wanted to let you know.' The pair continued around the circuit, saying nothing and lost in thought.

At the same time, other veiled warnings were circulating. Pieber privately told Johnny Marshall that they should avoid mass breaks because the Gestapo was looking for an excuse to take matters into their own hands, and similar warnings came from other goons. Because of these rumblings, there was some discussion in the camp about the dangers of the escape. Des Plunkett told his roommates that he didn't expect to come out alive but that he had weighed the risks against the nuisance value and the chance of getting home and decided it was all worth it.

'You're mad,' remonstrated Tim Walenn. 'The Germans would never be so unsporting as to shoot prisoners in cold blood!' Throughout the camp, Tim's view was the predominant one. The rumors and warnings were all very well, but there had been nothing concrete to suggest that the Germans would deal with this escape any differently than they had dealt with others. For all the kriegies knew, the rumors were just part of the war of nerves between the prisoners and the camp staff and had no real foundation. And the escapers had no intention of being put off by a few vague warnings.

Instead, they pushed ahead with the finishing touches on their travel plans. Having been out together once before, Gordon Brettell and Kingsley Brown teamed up again, this time using a brilliant cover of Brown's invention. They would go as Bulgarian forestry students and do most of their traveling through the woods, their notebooks and sketch pads giving them a plausible excuse for lurking around forests. Rene Marcinkus had recommended the identity because there were many Bulgarians working in Germany, yet few policemen were likely to speak the language. The assumed nationality would also explain their strange accent if Kingsley was called upon to talk about spruce budworms or pine beetles by curious Germans. Brettell and Brown hoped to reach Kolberg, on the Baltic coast, after about ten days of walking. Once there, they planned to steal a small boat and row to Sweden. To toughen themselves for the final leg of the journey, the pair built a small rowing machine, which they set up outside one of the huts. It must have puzzled the guards to see two apparently insane officers rowing themselves to nowhere for hours on end in the compound.

Len Trent had linked up with his old friend and fellow New Zealander Mick Shand, a tough Battle of Britain veteran with a DFC, and the pair planned to head south across the Czech mountains and contact a baker whom they hoped could arrange their passage to Switzerland. Cookie Long would travel with Tony Bethell, a tunneler and Mustang pilot who was one of the youngest men in X Organization. The two decided to make for Berlin, and then Stettin. They planned to travel as French workers, but to avoid using their rusty French, hoped to jump freight trains all the way to the Baltic coast. The two Norwegians Espelid and Fuglesang, with five languages between them, were hoping to get to Sweden via Arnold Christensen's relatives at Kolding in Denmark. Arnold and Jimmy Catanach, the latter fluent in German, were headed in the same direction. Earlier in the war, Rene Marcinkus had joked to Tim Walenn that if he ever escaped, he would take the forger along. Now, as the break drew near, Rene was good to his word. He teamed up with Tim, despite the fact that the latter's poor language skills could be a hindrance.

Wings Day and Paweł Tobolski had an unusual plan. Day had the address of an apolitical German couple in Berlin who had a young Danish lodger. With Wings traveling as a renegade Irish officer and Tob as his Luftwaffe escort, they would go by rail to Berlin and spend a few nights with the couple. Once there, they were counting on the young Dane to have some connections for an escape route out of Germany. If this panned out, Wings would get on the line as a Hungarian mechanic, while Tob would make his way to France in his Luftwaffe disguise. It was a dicey plan, but perhaps just audacious enough to work.

Jimmy James was being equally audacious. He planned to head south and follow the Danube Valley through Hungary and northern Yugoslavia. Then he would branch off and try to get to Turkey via Greece. He was going to make the long trek alone, but a few weeks before the escape, someone suggested that a Greek officer might be a valuable ally on the journey. The name of Sotiris Skantzikas was mentioned and when Jimmy met him, he knew he was just the ticket.

*

Sotiris – or Nick, as he was known in the camp – was born on August 6, 1920, the fourth of seven children, in the Peloponnesian port city of Calamata. When he was just two, the family moved to Athens, where Nick's father ran a coffee shop. They had a good-sized house with a yard and small garden for the children to play in, and Nick grew up a happy and boisterous child. In March 1940, after completing high school, Nick followed in his elder brother Sarandis's footsteps and enlisted in the Military Air Academy. Just over a year later, in April 1941, the Nazis invaded Greece, and the academy was evacuated to Crete, and from there to Gaza. Nick was sent to train at Salisbury in Southern Rhodesia and was delighted when his brother Sarandis turned up there in March 1942. The two had many happy times together before Sotiris was posted to an OTU near Cairo at the end of 1942. From there Nick went to 336 Squadron, flying Hurricanes from Sidi Barrani, on March 5, 1943. The unit flew operations in support of the Allied landings in Italy, and it was on one of these sweeps that Nick was downed. On July 23, 1943, while strafing enemy installations on Crete, Skantzikas's Hurricane was hit by ground fire and forced to pancake in. He was captured immediately, and he reached Sagan after a lengthy journey.

*

Jimmy James was pleased to have Nick along as a partner. The little Greek was always cheerful, usually sporting a broad smile under his bushy mustache. He would be a valuable asset on the way south, his olive complexion and dark, wavy hair lending credence to their story of being workers on the way home to Greece for a vacation.

Per Bergsland had been out once already, though with less than conspicuous success. His first escape was in 1943, in the wake of von Lindeiner's announcement that any prisoner escaping in a German uniform was liable to be executed. Never one to pass up a challenge, Per set about making a uniform and, armed with forged documents, he trudged toward the gate, only to be stopped for not having a photograph on his pass. In his impeccable German, Per replied diffidently that he was new and hadn't had a chance to get one yet. This seemed to satisfy the guard, who waved him on, but the Norwegian's luck was out that day. As he left the camp, he met Glemnitz on the road and, though it took the German a few minutes to make the connection, he finally realized whom he had just passed and ran back to arrest Per.

For the big break, Per decided against going in a German uniform and opted instead to travel as Norwegian Nazi Olaf Andersen, who was being sent from the Siemens factory in Frankfurt-an-der-Oder to do a job in a village near Sagan. For this part of the journey he had a permit allowing him to travel between Frankfurt and Sagan. Once Per reached Frankfurt he would destroy the first pass and use a second one, which ordered him to report to a certain office in Stettin.

The master pumpmaker, Jens Müller, had basically the same plan, so X Organization decided they should travel together. The two made a formidable pair. Both had traveled extensively on the Continent before the war, and between them they were fluent in six European languages.

While preparing for the escape, the two left nothing to chance. They carried nothing that could incriminate them, restricting the contents of their Norwegian suitcases to a change of socks and underwear, sandwiches made from German bread and margarine, Norwegian toothpaste and soap, Danish sausages from a Red Cross parcel, and a small can of concentrated meat. Each had about 160 Reichsmarks to pay for their trip.

Six of the escapers planned a reunion of sorts in Prague. Des Plunkett and his partner, Czech fighter pilot Bedrich 'Freddie' Dvorak, Ivo Tonder and Johnny Stower, and Wally Valenta and Johnny Marshall were all intending to head south by various means but had arranged to meet at Gbel in the Czechoslovakian capital a few days after the break. It was hoped that they could get help from the hotelkeeper who had assisted Johnny Stower after the delousing party escape.

Roger Bushell and Bob Stanford-Tuck, old mates from 92 Squadron, made up another pair. With Bushell's fluency in French and German and Stanford-Tuck's knowledge of Russian, picked up in his youth from his nanny, the pair could head either east or west, depending on conditions outside the camp. The two would travel by rail and looked like perfectly respectable businessmen in their civilian clothes.

Wally Floody and George Harsh had very different plans. Both were key figures in the escape organization, but neither had any fluency in European languages and so did not expect to get top places in the tunnel. They would be hardarsers, walkers who had little chance of making a home run but who could still create a nuisance, which was perhaps more valuable than a successful escape. If they got clear of the camp, Wally and George could look forward to some cold nights out in the open.

Chapter 14

THE FERRETS STRIKE

WITH THE BREAK DRAWING nearer, Jimmy Catanach, Alan Righetti, and a few other Australians got together over a homemade Ouija board and tried to unlock the secrets of the future. There were some feeble attempts at ventriloquism and a few knocks on the table that no one was willing to admit to, but the only information the board provided was that they would probably have bully beef fritters for dinner the next day.

At about the same time, Johnny Pohe was able to slip one past the censors. 'Glowing pictures of a POW's life have been published in England and perhaps New Zealand,' he wrote to his family, 'and you can believe them as being *tito*.' Since none of the camp censors spoke Maori, they didn't realize that *tito* meant 'lies.'

However, it was not smooth sailing everywhere. Dennis Cochran shared a room with a few Englishmen, a Canadian, and a Brit from Uruguay, not all of whom understood the importance of Dennis's work as a contact. Whenever his tame goon came around, it was understood that the rest of the lads would wander away and let Dennis talk to his man in private. Unfortunately, one of the roommates considered his bunk to be his own personal, inviolable space and resented having to leave the room whenever the tame goon came around. Gradually a deep resentment developed between Cochran and his roommate, and one afternoon they had a heated argument. After the words ceased, the roommate brooded for a while and then came up behind Dennis and tapped him on the back. When Cochran turned, the other fellow slugged him nearly unconscious and returned to his bunk. The others in the room returned a few minutes later and found Dennis lying dazed and bleeding on the floor, his eyes badly bruised and nearly closed. He was definitely not in the best of shape to be traveling inconspicuously around wartime Germany.

*

It was mild on the morning of February 20, as it had been for most of the New Year. Only for a short time had it been cold enough to freeze the camp ice rink. But that dull morning was even warmer than usual, for it was the day of the long-awaited draw for places in the tunnel.

There were 510 names in the draw altogether. The first 100 were specially selected by the escape leaders as those who had contributed the most or who had the best chance of escaping successfully, and the rest came from the complete roster of the organization's workers. In addition, eight names were put forward by the camp entertainment and administrative staffs. While these men hadn't assisted with the escape preparations, it was rightly decided that their valuable contributions to the running of the camp as a whole should be recognized.

The selection process consisted of a number of different draws. The first thirty names to be drawn for final exit order were those who, in the eyes of the organizers, had the best chance of escaping successfully. They would travel by train, without incriminating Red Cross food or large maps. After this group, the names of forty of the most prominent workers were put in, and twenty were drawn. Then the next thirty most prominent workers' names were put in and twenty drawn. To round out the first hundred, those names remaining from the earlier draws were put back in the hat and the last thirty spots allotted. Finally, the remaining four hundred ten names were put in and one hundred were drawn to complete the exit order.

Once the list of two hundred escapers had been established, it still had to be revised. On the night of the escape there would be men stationed at Piccadilly, Leicester Square, and the exit shaft to pull the escapers through the tunnel. These men were known as haulers, and each would pull through twenty escapers before going out himself. The final list had to be adjusted so that in each group of twenty, there were three experienced diggers to act as haulers. Red Noble and Shag Rees actually drew in the second hundred but were allotted numbers seventy-eight and seventy-nine so they could act as haulers. Ivo Tonder, Tony Bethell, and Bob Nelson were also assigned hauling duties.

*

With the escapers having been notified of their final exit numbers, they could press on with their plans. Bill Fordyce had planned to go with Tom Leigh, an Australian-born ex-Halton apprentice who had been downed in 1941, but the latter drew in the 40s, while Bill drew number 86. Consequently he teamed up with Roy Langlois, who had also drawn a later number. Paul Royle drew number 55 and, since he had no particular plans, got in touch with number 54, who happened to be Edgar 'Hunk' Humphreys, another Halton alumnus and a prisoner since December 1940. Others, believing that a single escaper would be less conspicuous, elected to travel alone. One of these was Flight Lieutenant Albert 'Shorty' Armstrong, a Bolton native and electrical engineer by trade who was shot down in North Africa in August 1942. Shorty was one of the few hardarsers traveling alone but the prospect of a solitary trek didn't bother him. On the contrary, he was anxious to get going.

When push finally came to shove, some of the escapers had attacks of nerves and asked to be removed from the list. Paul Brickhill had a spot in the second hundred and was allowed into Harry to get a feel for it. As soon as he got to the base of the entry shaft and looked up the tunnel, he knew he couldn't go through with it – his claustrophobia was just too strong. Rather sheepishly, he went to Roger Bushell and gave his reasons for asking to be dropped from the list. Someone panicking in the tunnel on the night of the escape could be disastrous.

'Thanks for being so honest, Paul,' said Roger. 'You're the eleventh man to come off the list this morning.'

*

With the draw completed, the idea of escape suddenly became more real for the prisoners, as they could actually see their chance to get out of the backwater of the prison camp. They had missed much over their years in captivity. Certainly prospects for promotion became dimmer with each passing month, and the more adventurous among them were missing combat action that they would likely never get the chance to see again. But more important, their lives were passing them by. The homes that each had left the day before his last operation were no longer the same. Dennis Cochran's mother had died during his time in captivity, Johnny Stower's mother was dangerously ill, and both of Bob Stewart's sisters had died. Those men who had left fiancées at home, such as Cookie Long and Tom Leigh, found the separation very hard to bear.

As pieces of their old lives dropped away for some, others waited helplessly while their new lives went on without them. Paweł Tobolski had never seen his son, being raised by his wife in Scotland. His roommates often joked that it would be difficult to wean the lad off wearing kilts once they got back to Poland. Jack Grisman's daughter, born on the last day of 1941, had just celebrated her second birthday and still had never seen her father. Her twin brother had died at birth, a loss that Marie Grisman had to bear alone. Things like this made up the real tragedy of captivity.

Others never stopped planning for the future. Brian Evans and Joan Cook had become officially engaged in 1943; Brian said that he would much rather have things for certain, rather than just an understanding. Tom Kirby-Green was looking forward to a new life with Maria in Tangier. He had inherited some land from a rich uncle and was planning to settle there after the war. He had no idea what they would do but was sure something would come along.

*

However, there were still a few feet of sand separating the prisoners from freedom, and removing it was the first order of business. When Walter told Wally Valenta that Rubberneck was going on two weeks' leave at the beginning of March, the organizers saw their chance to finish Harry and get him completely sealed before the hated ferret returned. Then, the day before his leave, Rubberneck struck a parting blow. Without warning, he and a security officer, Broili, brought a party of guards into the compound and began calling names.

In all, nineteen officers were summoned, rigorously searched, and marched out the gates to Belaria, an auxiliary camp about five miles away. Purges were standard procedure, but this time the Germans had struck it lucky, for they picked some of the most important men in X Organization: Wally Floody, chief tunnel engineer; Peter Fanshawe, chief of dispersal; George Harsh, chief of security; Kingsley Brown; Bob Stanford-Tuck; Jim Tyrie; and thirteen others. The goons could hardly have picked better had they known the entire setup of X Organization.

It was a cruel blow, but because of the progress of the escape preparations, one that could be endured. Ker-Ramsay took over as chief tunnel engineer, and the seconds-in-command of the other departments could supervise the operations for the few days until the scheduled break. However, the disruption of travel plans was less easy to overcome, and some men were faced with the prospect of quick improvisation.

Gordon Brettell turned to roommate and fellow forger Henri Picard and worked out a new plan that took advantage of Picard's native tongue. They would travel to Danzig as French workers and look for a ship to take them to Sweden. Danzig was known to be full of French workers, so the two hoped for some help once they reached the port. Tom Kirby-Green's partner had also been included in the purge, so he had to make other arrangements as well. Gordon Kidder had planned to travel with Dick Churchill as Romanian woodcutters, but X Organization decided that Kidder should team up with Kirby-Green, with the pair going as Spanish laborers. Dick Churchill agreed to the plan and linked up instead with Bob Nelson. The arrangement was satisfactory, though no one liked making such major changes at such a late date.

*

Without his Russian-speaking partner, Roger Bushell first elected to travel alone and then decided to team up with Lieutenant Bernard Martial William Scheidhauer, a soft-spoken Free French officer who wasn't quite so English in appearance as Bob Tuck. About five feet, nine inches tall with clear blue eyes and chestnut hair, Bernard was one of X Organization's intelligence experts, specializing in his native land. More important, he knew one area of the border particularly well. His father had commanded a battalion of the Moroccan infantry regiment occupying the Palatinate after the First World War, and it was in Landau, near Saarbrücken, that Bernard was born on August 28, 1921.

His father retired while Bernard was still young and the family returned to their hometown of Brest, where Bernard went to high school. He was a charming boy, full of exuberance tempered with a dignified and almost aristocratic mien, and became popular at the Brest *lycée*. The young Scheidhauer was finishing at the *lycée* when German troops reached Brest in the summer of 1940. He had planned to take pilot training after graduation, but his father recommended that he try to escape to Britain, so Bernard headed south for Bayonne, hoping to reach England via Gibraltar. He got no farther than St. Jean de Luz, though, and was forced to return to Brest.

Undaunted, Bernard arranged with five others to sail to England in a little boat called *La Petite Anna*. On October 19, 1940, they left the port of Douarnenez for Cornwall. A couple of days out, however, their craft ran into a gale, and they used the last of their fuel trying to ride it out. The storm passed, but the six were helpless and drifted for days. In time, their food and water ran out, and still they drifted. Finally, on the twelfth day, they were spotted by a Scottish freighter that picked them up, half dead from hunger, thirst, and exposure, and took them to England.

Less than a week after the ordeal, Bernard was accepted into the Free French Air Force. He completed flying training and in March 1942 was posted to 53 OTU. At the end of May he was hospitalized briefly after a flying accident, but on June 24 he was posted to the famed 242 Squadron, with which he flew his first operation. On September 4 Bernard was transferred to 131 (French) Squadron. The unit was busy with convoy patrols and cross-Channel sweeps that autumn, and Bernard completed more than forty sorties in only weeks.

On November 11, 1942, he and his unit took off from Westhampnett in their Spitfires for a patrol over the Somme estuary. They found nothing, but on the way home ran into a towering bank of cumulus clouds. The first section of three aircraft swung to port and missed the bank, but Blue Section, with Bernard Scheidhauer flying in the number 3 spot, plunged into the clouds in a line astern. It was a pretty rough ride but didn't get too alarming until Bernard suddenly saw a tailplane loom up in front of him. Putting the nose down, he dove away to port but not before hearing a tremendous crash as he hit the aircraft. Emerging from the cloud at two thousand feet, Bernard was counting his blessings when his engine gave out. Then he noticed that a good eighteen inches were missing from his propeller blades. Without hesitation Scheidhauer abandoned his mortally wounded Spitfire, made an easy parachute descent, and clambered into his dinghy. He was later picked up, damp but unhurt, by a Royal Navy Walrus flying boat.

A week later, on November 18, Bernard was back in action, searching for trains on the Caen–Cherbourg railroad line. He and his wingmate claimed hits on four locomotives, but on the way home, Bernard's Spitfire began to act up, likely damaged by debris from one of the trains. Realizing that he would never reach England, he turned toward the nearest land, which happened to be Jersey in the Channel Islands. He force-landed and was picked up by German soldiers.

His first interrogation was a bit hairy. Intrigued by the sound of his name, the interrogators became even more interested when they discovered that Bernard had been born in Germany. Making a note to that effect in their files, the Luftwaffe passed him on to Sagan.

Scheidhauer was glad to be of use to the intelligence section of X Organization, but it was his birthplace that attracted Roger's attention. As a boy, Bernard had played in the hills and fields around Landau and observed everything around him with the keen eye of youth. Something in his past might one day hold the key to a successful crossing into France.

*

Before Rubberneck's chair was cold, the organization had been altered to compensate for the purge. Now there were more men working in the tunnel than ever before: two at the face; two in each of the halfway houses; and one at the entrance shaft. During the first nine days of March, they excavated the last 100 feet of tunnel, including an eighteen-foot-long chamber at the base of the exit shaft. On March 4, the workers dug a record fourteen feet of tunnel. After the last chamber was finished, the surveyors went down and measured the tunnel carefully. They had calculated that the distance to the edge of the woods was 335 feet, and their measurements indicated that Harry was 348 feet long from shaft to shaft. The exit should be well inside the trees.

Now came the tricky part. It was decided to dig upward almost to the surface, leaving two feet of earth to be removed on the night of the escape. The most experienced diggers did this work, because the risk of falls was great. It was such a tricky job that it took until March 14 to complete. Just after *Appell* on that day, Johnny Bull and Red Noble disappeared down the tunnel to dig the last few feet and shore up the roof of the exit shaft. As they clambered up the exit ladder, a deep and loud rumble ran through the tunnel.

'Jesus, what the bloody hell was that?' whispered Bull. Seconds later another rumble rolled around them as the two looked at each other quizzically. Noble was the first to speak.

'Must have been something driving along that road. Either that was a helluva loud truck or we're awful damn close to the road!' said the Canadian. 'We'd better get this little job done and have a word with Roger.'

Before starting to dig up, Johnny took a broken fencing foil and poked it upward to measure the amount of soil they had to remove. It was then that he got the second shock of the day. The foil went no more than six inches before breaking the surface. He climbed back down to where Red squatted with the tools.

'There's maybe six inches of topsoil between us and the great outdoors,' he said hurriedly. 'It's bloody lucky I didn't start right in with the shovel.' Johnny climbed back up the ladder to wedge a couple of bedboards in as a ceiling and then packed the sand behind them. Red passed up the last of the braces, and the exit was made secure in the event of a wandering goon treading on it.

The two worked in silence, both thinking about the discoveries they had made. The fact that the tunnel came so close to the surface was worrying but not particularly dangerous. Six inches of dirt should be enough to prevent the trap from sounding hollow if a sentry stepped on it. The rumble of trucks was considerably more alarming, though. If the trucks were as close as they sounded, the tunnel exit was less than twenty feet from the road, in the middle of an open field. That meant that Harry could be at least thirty feet short.

That night the escape leaders discussed the discovery. Again, they went over the measurements taken by the surveying teams, and the mathematical types returned to Harry to confirm their calculations. Everything seemed to check out, and the loud rumble was put down to the properties of the sand.

After Johnny and Red left the tunnel, everything that was not absolutely essential was taken out and either burned or stored down Dick. Pat Langford sealed the trap and then scrubbed the floor around it so the boards would swell and close any cracks. He would do the same chore twice a day until the tunnel broke. The following day, Rubberneck returned from leave and announced his arrival by descending on 104 with a party of ferrets. As usual, they found nothing.

With the sealing of Harry, a mood of excited anticipation gripped the camp. Many prisoners couldn't help but let it slip into their letters home. 'The vital day for which we are all keenly waiting,' wrote Brian Evans to his fiancée, Joan, 'is even nearer than we actually think.' Tim Walenn wrote to his brother, 'We are all expecting to be home in a few months.' John F. Williams was a bit more practical and asked his parents not to send any more cigarettes or tobacco, while Henri Picard told his family that he wouldn't need any more drawing materials for the time being.

Still, it was crucial that a show of normalcy be kept up. Ian Cross took time out from tidying up the dispersal areas under the theater to go across to East Compound for a soccer match. There he chatted with his old friend and escape partner Robert Kee and talked excitedly about the coming break. *Arsenic and Old Lace* was playing in the camp theater, and Tony Hayter was planning the year's garden. There appeared to be nothing out of the ordinary at all.

New prisoners were coming into Sagan every day, and one of the purges from Dulag Luft included a recently captured Canadian named Freiburger.

'Freiburger . . .' intoned the duty officer approvingly. 'That is a good German name.'

'Well, I'm from Canada,' replied the newcomer without so much as a pause, 'and that's where all the good Germans are!'

*

The morning of March 20 was bitterly cold and windy and, as was often the case on mornings like that, early *Appell* was held not on the parade ground but in the open space between the first two rows of huts. The men piled slowly out of the huts and took their places; Alex Cassie, Des Plunkett, and the other Amiable Lunatics straggled to their spots between Huts 103 and 110, chatting and laughing while they waited for the duty officer. Tim Walenn wasn't with them that morning. For the past few days, he had been staying in his bunk during *Appell* to be counted on the sick list. The real purpose behind this was so he could keep an eye on the bulky bag of rubber stamps used by Dean and Dawson. Strictly speaking, they should have been stored down Dick at all times, and there would have been hell to pay had Bushell learned of the practice. But Tim was concerned with the amount of work still to be done and decided that the process of getting the stamps in and out of Dick consumed too much valuable time. All over the compound there were similar breaches of security, done solely for the sake of speed.

Plunkett and Cassie were chatting happily about the progress of preparations when a posse of guards doubled into the compound and encircled Hut 120. Obviously a search was planned.

'Well, that's a bit hard,' said Alex with a groan. 'Now I suppose we'll be standing out here for hours. At least we've got our showers on this morning – that'll give us a bit of a break!'

Suddenly, Plunkett went deathly pale and grabbed Cassie's arm, his other hand frozen in his tunic pocket. 'Oh, Christ,' he said with a gasp, 'my map book! I must have left it on my bed. It's got the names of everyone who's going out and the maps they'll need.' For a moment, Plunkett was frantic. If that little notebook fell into German hands, it would ruin the entire escape. And poor Des alone would be to blame.

However, Plunkett was nothing if not a realist and he collected himself quickly. His mind went to work, trying to arrange a plan to retrieve the valuable book. In a surprisingly short time, he was outlining his scheme to Alex. It all hinged on two things: the fact that Tim Walenn was still inside the hut; and their scheduled shower party. Soon Des had gathered a few others from the hut and put the plan in motion.

Very casually and with a jaunty whistle, he sauntered over to Hut 120 and called to the guard in their room. He politely told the goon that this hut was scheduled to go to the shower block that morning but hadn't taken their shower kit with them on *Appell*. Would the guard be so kind as to retrieve his from his locker and pass it out to him? All the way down the hut, others asked the same question, and soon various guards were passing out small bags and bundles.

As Plunkett's guard called his superior for permission, Des quickly whispered to Walenn, who was on his bunk directly under the window, about the book and asked him to pitch it out when the opportunity arose. The guard turned back to Des and said he would pass out the necessary supplies. Plunkett smiled his thanks and directed the guard to his locker out in the corridor. As soon as the guard left the room, Tim bounced off the bed and grabbed the map book. Thrusting it into the bag containing his rubber stamps, he tucked the lot into his shower bag and gave it to the guard when he returned from the corridor. The unwitting sentry then passed everything out the window to Des, who accepted the bundle gratefully and wandered back toward the firepool with the vital escape equipment stuffed safely inside his tunic. After that the Amiable Lunatics never mentioned the close call again; it was best forgotten.

*

With the tunnel now ready, the organizers had to decide on the best date for the break. Dark of the moon was at the end of the month, with the best days being the twenty-third to the twenty-fifth. The twenty-fifth was quickly dropped. Because it was a Saturday, the train travelers would have to contend with Sunday rail schedules. That left the night of the twenty-third or the night of the twenty-fourth. Since there was no difference between Friday and Saturday train schedules, either day would do.

However, there were still many final preparations to be made. On March 20, Crump Ker-Ramsay inspected all the cases to be carried by the escapers to ensure that they would fit through the tunnel easily. Some of them were pretty beaten up, having been acquired in the early days at Schubin.

Then began a seemingly endless round of briefings. Beginning on the twenty-second, Crump and Johnny Marshall lectured all the escapers on how to get through the tunnel.

'Lie completely flat on the trolley,' boomed Marshall, 'and for God's sake keep your head down. There's nothing to see so don't bother looking up, because if you do, you'll bash your head and bring everything down. Hold your cases straight out in front of you and keep your bloody elbows in or you'll tear down a frame. And whatever you do, don't tip the trolley!'

A hand came up timidly at the back of the room. 'What happens if the trolley tips itself, Johnny?' asked one of the listeners. Johnny smiled and spoke soothingly, sensing some nervousness in the room.

'That shouldn't happen if you do what I've told you to. But if it does, the first thing to remember is, don't panic – as soon as you panic, you're going to squirm around and knock a frame out. As carefully as you can, get off the trolley and crawl to the nearest halfway house. Don't try to get back on the trolley, and don't leave the trolley in the tunnel – pull it behind you! Any more questions?' Seeing none, Johnny wished the group well and cleared the room so that Crump could go over the whole thing again with the next lot.

*

One of the most important briefings was given to the marshalers, those men appointed to guide groups of ten escapers away from the compound. Most were to go west, but there were also some groups going south along the railroad line toward Tschiebsdorf. In some ways the marshalers were among the most vital cogs in the escape wheel. If they failed in their task and ran into trouble near the camp, the entire operation could be ruined. Because of this, Tony Bethell, Jack Grisman, Hank Birkland, Larry Reavell-Carter, and the rest of the marshals listened to the briefing intently and went over the drill time and time again.

Each marshal would wait in the forest until his ten men had arrived and then strike off into the woods. Keen Type had given Marcel Zillessen complete information on the paths through the woods and how far the trees stretched in all directions, so they were able to get a pretty good idea of where to go. They first had to navigate around a small lighted compound a few hundred yards from the camp. It was thought to be either an ammunition dump or an electrical installation, but the organizers were certain that it should be avoided at all costs. Then the group had to get past the other compounds in the Sagan complex, cross a narrow road, and hit a branch of the railroad line. They would follow this until they came to the main north–south line, where they would split up. The distance was just over a mile.

From there the escapers were on their own and had to find their own way around the various obstacles. Those continuing south would have to negotiate one main road and the small villages of Hermsdorf and Tschirndorf before coming to their first big hurdle, the main Berlin–Breslau autobahn. Escapers going west had to cope with Sorau, a largish town similar to Sagan in size, while those going east would have to deal with Sprottau, another good-sized town. Only those walking north had a relatively easy trip – that is until they reached the Oder River, roughly thirty miles north of Sagan. Information recently received in the camp revealed that the river was flooded and would likely be very difficult to cross.

Because of the importance of keeping to a schedule, the train travelers would make their own way through the forest and were given explicit instructions for the trek. They would have to walk northeast for about a quarter of a mile, and then look for a road that ran roughly northwest to southeast past the station. Beside this road was a fence that backed onto the station entrances. There were three possible entrances to the station. The most desirable was a path across the tracks to the east of the platforms, but if this proved impossible to use, there was an overhead walkway to the west of the station. Only if neither of these was available were the escapers to use the subway, which went under the tracks and came up in the main booking hall.

This route was the busiest and therefore the most dangerous and was to be used only as a last resort.

In addition, each escaper was given a special briefing by one or more of the area experts, depending on the individual's travel plans. For instance, those traveling south to Czechoslovakia would hear from Wally Valenta or from another Czech officer who came from the Riesengebirge, the mountains that straddled the Czech–German frontier, who knew them as well as anyone. They were also taught to say in Czech, 'I swear by the death of my mother that I am an English officer,' and were assured that this oath would cause them to be believed anywhere in the country.

They were also briefed by Wing Commander John Ellis, an expert on outdoor survival who passed on tips to make a hardarser's journey more bearable. Those making for Switzerland listened to Roger Bushell and Johnny Stower, who spoke of their experiences at the border, and were given information about the location of guard posts on the frontier that Zillessen had obtained from Keen Type. That helpful ferret had also provided a list of the foods that could be obtained without ration cards and directions to the berths usually reserved for Swedish ships in Danzig and Stettin.

Finally, Roger met with all the escapers in the lavatory of 104. He spoke confidently of the arrangements made regarding the marshalers and passed on some contact addresses. For those going south, there was the address of a baker just inside the Czech frontier and the name of the hotelier in Prague who had helped Johnny Stower the previous year. Roger also gave out the address, sent in code to Schubin in 1942, of a brothel in Stettin that was frequented by Swedish sailors. He wished everyone well and then stayed to talk with each of the train travelers. Bushell reminded them of various German customs and gave out the available information about timetables and fares. Keen Type had provided details on all trains from the Sagan station and, from various sources, Valenta had been able to build up a complete schedule of times and prices. With this the train travelers could plan their itinerary even before leaving the camp.

*

By this time, most of the material arrangements had been made. Nearly three thousand maps had been run off and sorted into groups, and

Johnny Travis had made up metal water bottles from old food cans and solder. In Hut 112, Canton's chefs were busy mixing hundreds of four-ounce cans of escape mixture. There were two kinds, both made to the recipe of dietary expert David Lubbock: a mixture of sugar and cereal; and a precooked solid made of cocoa, chocolate, fat, sugar, and Klim. Each can of the precooked mixture was enough to provide the necessary nutrition for two days. The hardarsers were given six cans each, and the train travelers were offered four, although many decided against carrying the cans, which would instantly identify them as escaped POWs if they were searched.

As the escape drew nearer, many of the lads wrote home, some hoping it would be their last letter from captivity. 'I've got an important part to play in one of our kriegie plays,' wrote George Wiley to a friend in Canada, 'and am a bit nervous about doing my part well . . . may see you sooner than expected.'

By the morning of March 23 there was still a good six inches of snow on the ground, but the winter seemed to have broken at last. There was a new mildness in the air, and a very slight thaw had set in. Spring was clearly on its way. There was still a snap in the air, but it was more electricity than cold, for everyone knew that the break was due in the next couple of days. The opinion of the optimists was further borne out when the leaders of X Organization were seen making their way slowly and circuitously toward Hut 104 for another meeting. One of the men who walked up the steps to 104 was not a regular at those meetings and, to those who knew him, his presence was significant.

The new face was Flying Officer Len Hall, of the RAF Meteorological Branch, who had the dubious distinction of being one of the few officers in Sagan who had been sunk instead of shot down. The vessel taking him to England from Nigeria had been torpedoed in the Caribbean, and Len spent four weeks as a prisoner on a U-boat before getting back to dry land. The Germans evidently didn't know what to do with him because they moved him between Dulag Luft and a naval transit camp for almost two months before finally deciding to stick him in Luft III. The organization was glad of that decision, for they were in great need of a trained weather forecaster.

Since the kingpins of the organization all knew the score, the first questions went to Len.

'How do things look for the next couple of days, Len?' asked Roger quietly.

'Quite good, actually,' began Len. 'As you know, it's dark of the moon now, and there should be pretty good cloud for the next couple of nights to make it even darker. I'm afraid the temperature won't be too helpful, but you'll likely have a bit of wind to cover up the noises. That's the best I can do with what I have to go on.'

'Can you give me anything longer-term?' queried Roger.

Len shook his head. 'Sorry, Roger. This German weather can get damned nasty, and it's still too early to say that the winter's over for good.'

Roger grunted and looked around at his lieutenants. It was clear that he wanted to get moving. 'Well, we'll have to wait until tomorrow morning to decide for sure, but I think we should give it a go if the weather doesn't change. Any objections?'

Everyone in the room knew Roger well enough to recognize when he had made up his mind, and this was one of those occasions. They all shook their heads. Tim Walenn said that he needed as much notice as possible to stamp and sign all of the forged documents, and Ker-Ramsay wanted at least half a day to make the final preparations in the tunnel. Aside from that, there was nothing further.

After the meeting broke up, Johnny Marshall hung back to have a word with Roger.

'What about the hardarsers, Roger?' he asked. 'There's still three feet of snow in the forests – they won't stand a chance in those conditions.'

Bushell was firm. 'It's a chance they'll have to take. We can't risk keeping Harry until the next no-moon period. You've seen the trap – it's warping more every day. We're on borrowed time as it is. If we don't move soon, the odds are that we'll lose everything.'

'How about putting out some train travelers now, and closing Harry up until the weather improves? The walkers would have a much better chance in a month's time.'

'Come on, Johnny,' said Roger. 'You know the tunnel would never make it through a big search if we used it once. Besides, it's got to be all or nothing. The entire plan depends on getting large numbers of escapers out in one go – a few train travelers just wouldn't do.'

It was useless to discuss it further, especially since Marshall knew that all of Bushell's points were valid. Still, the conversation forced

Big X to reconsider the problem of the walkers, and after mulling it over for the afternoon, he sought the advice of Wings Day. He told Wings that he hated to make a decision that would jeopardize the hardarsers' chances but that he saw no other alternatives.

Wings was quick with his reply. 'We both know, Roger, that the odds are stacked against the hardarser at the best of times. We've both done our fair share of walking in the past – you know as well as I do that the odds are a thousand to one against, even in the best conditions. Besides, no one's going to freeze to death – if things get bad they can just turn themselves in. It's usually warm enough in the cooler!'

Roger smiled when he saw Wings's big grin. 'That's bloody true enough!' he said grimly.

'In any case, there's a bigger question here. You've said it yourself a dozen times that the greatest value in an escape is the number of chaps who get out in the first place, not the number who get home. Even if none of the hardarsers lasts two days, they'll have had an impact just by getting outside the wire.'

Bushell was silent for a moment and then looked up and said simply, 'Thanks, you're right,' before wandering off to his hut.

Wings watched him stride across the compound and reflected on what the South African had been able to achieve. He had taken a camp full of very different characters and given them a uniting purpose. Soon he would turn loose up to two hundred escapers and, for the seventh time, Wings Day would be one of them.

There was a heavy snowstorm that night and the issue was again in doubt when the committee members met on the morning of the twenty-fourth to come to a decision. At 11:30 A.M., they gathered in a room in Hut 101. Just ten minutes later, they all emerged again. It was on.

Tim Walenn went straight off to start date-stamping and signing the papers. This job had to be left until the very last minute so the escapers could get the greatest possible use out of their limited-time travel documents. Also, most of the documents had to be signed, including Roger Bushell's genuine visa, which he had procured in the course of one of his escapes. Cassie painted on the visa stamp in purplish pink watercolor and then signed it with the name of a chief of police whose real signature they had. Alex practiced the signature for two days so that he could get it just right.

Meanwhile, Crump went down Harry to do the final tunnel work. He started by hanging two blankets in the exit chamber to block the light and sound. As an added precaution, strips of cloth were nailed to the first and last fifty feet of trolley rail. Blankets were also spread on the floor of both the entry and exit shafts to deaden any sounds and were laid down in both halfway houses so that the haulers wouldn't get their clothes filthy. Next, extra lights were installed every twenty-five feet to give a bit more illumination to comfort those who were inclined toward claustrophobia. Finally, the trolleys had to be modified to handle the large number of men who would be using them. Extra planks were added on top to provide a better platform for the escapers to lie on, and four hundred feet of one-inch-thick manila rope intended for the camp's boxing ring was taken down and attached to the trolleys. Finally, four twisted shoring boards were replaced and a specially constructed wooden shovel was taken to the exit shaft for use in breaking the tunnel.

Meanwhile, the Little X's were making their way around the various departments of the organization to pick up all of the gear for the escapers in their hut. They had already grilled each escaper and carefully examined his clothing, luggage, and papers and now had to hand over the bundle of gear and a few last bits of advice. The Little X's also gave each man explicit instructions on when and how to go to Hut 104. For days before the escape, watchers had kept a tally on the number of men going in and out of the block on a normal day. To avoid an increase in traffic on the day of the escape, these figures were used to arrive at a series of routes and timetables. There was a thirty-second interval between movements, and each escaper had a specific time and direction to go. When he got to 104, he would be directed to a bunk to wait for his number to come up. The regular occupant of that bunk would then make his way to the other fellow's hut and remain there until the following morning.

Around the camp, tension was mounting. There were a few more forced grins, and many of the kriegies tried to calm their nerves with meaningless conversation. Len Hall's afternoon meteorology class was noticeably smaller than on previous days, and there were fewer people hanging around the theater. The night before had seen a dress rehearsal of the new production of *Pygmalion*, with Roger Bushell as Professor Henry Higgins. An understudy waited in the wings, lest the star be unavailable.

Back in his room, Hank Birkland hunched over one last letter to his family. 'I got a letter last month to which I will not be able to reply,' he wrote in his typical straightforward style. 'I am not in a position to carry on a letter-for-letter correspondence for long.'

Just after six, a few men gathered in Johnny Travis's room for a last supper of bully beef fritters and barley glop, a mixture of barley, Klim, sugar, and raisins. Roger Bushell, Bob van der Stok, Digger McIntosh, and Shorty Armstrong were all there, but there was little conversation. No one seemed to have much of an appetite, despite Travis's guarantee that the feast would keep you filled for days.

In Hut 112, George Wiley was setting a few things straight before leaving for 104. Of all the escapers, George was the youngest-looking. Though he had turned twenty-two in January, his fair hair and gentle features made him look about sixteen, and George was used to jibes about the authorities having to let kids into the air force to do a man's job. This day, though, George's boyish face showed as much trepidation as excitement. He spoke no German and realized that his chances of making a clean escape were almost nil, especially as his leg was again giving him trouble in the cold. He expected to be picked up in the Sagan area and thought he would probably spend a week or two in the cooler before being put back in the compound.

As George was cleaning up his bunk, he chatted with Alan Righetti, who would be staying behind in 112. The Australian could tell that his roommate was uneasy and tried to buck him up with a few words of encouragement. Alan had been involved in a couple of breaks in Italy and knew what it was like for a first-time escaper in the hours before a break. George was comforted by Alan's words but as he got up to make his way to 104, the Canadian turned to his roommate and held out his watch and a few other things that he had collected over his year in captivity.

'Alan, if I don't make it,' he began, 'will you see that these things get back to my mother in Windsor?'

'Okay, George,' said Alan quietly. 'You sure you don't want to hang on to them? You may see her before I do!' he added cheerfully. Wiley smiled and clapped his pal on the back with a word of farewell. As he turned to leave the room, Righetti couldn't help but think that George Wiley looked so young and innocent to be heading out into the snowy unknown of a cold March night.

*

As dusk fell, the exodus continued. Pulling on his greatcoat, Mike Casey bade farewell to his roommates in Hut 122. 'I'm off, lads,' he said with a wave. 'It's about time for my run in the woods!' Mike reported to 122's controller, who consulted his time sheet, got the nod from his stooge, and pushed the Irishman out the door with a hearty clap on the back. Casey walked east, around the south end of Hut 121 and then entered 109 by the south door. He went directly to Room 17, where Wings Norman sat with another time sheet.

'Ah, Mike,' said Norman cheerily, 'spot on time as usual. Off you go, then, and don't get yourself into any trouble!' With a firm handshake, Mike was sent on his way. He continued up the corridor to the northern end of 109, where another stooge stood holding the door shut. He peeked through the crack and then quickly opened the door and gave Mike the thumbs-up as he passed. The Irishman crossed the path running beside the firepool and paused on the southern steps of Hut 104.

The door swung open and Casey reported to Dave Torrens, who gave him a room and bunk assignment. Mike had escaped before, but in his nearly five years as a prisoner, he had never seen anything quite like this. Inside the crowded hut was the oddest collection of characters, some in rough working clothes and others in smart business suits. Some were just standing and smoking, others were chatting softly, and two pairs were huddled over a game of bridge. Many just sat and said nothing, glancing up briefly with a smile as Mike passed.

Twice every minute, the door opened for another kriegie, who came in quietly and was checked off by Torrens. Everything had gone exactly according to plan so far. Then, at about a quarter to eight, the door opened again. Instantly, a hush fell over the corridor and Casey poked his head out of the room to see what was up. There, at the end of the hall, stood a Luftwaffe corporal.

Chapter 15

BEYOND THE WIRE

DAVE TORRENS LOOKED UP from his list at the same moment and threw down the papers as he bounded from his chair. He started down the corridor with the intention of doing anything necessary to subdue this goon until the escape was over. Then he stopped and recognized a familiar face under the Luftwaffe cap. It was Paweł Tobolski, Wings Day's running mate. Dave had been warned that Tob would be coming in goonskin but had forgotten in the excitement. Peace and calm restored, the movements continued.

A few minutes later, Jimmy Wernham came in and went to change bunks with a fellow Canadian. Jimmy was in high spirits, his eyes shining with excitement at the prospect of his first escape, and he joked about the hospitality they would receive from friendly Czechs once they crossed the border. 'The Dodger and I probably won't make it all the way, but I'm sure we'll have a pretty good outing!'

Down the hall, Des Plunkett and Freddie Dvorak were going over some last details. 'With any luck, we'll be at the station within thirty minutes,' said Des, looking at his watch. 'It's now . . . it's now . . . ten minutes to two? Hmmm. My watch seems to have stopped,' he said resignedly as he shook it and pressed it to his ear.

'Stopped? What bloody good is it to us now?' asked Freddie, his nerves starting to show through. 'What sort of cheap watch is it, anyway?'

'Sir, that watch was presented to my father,' replied Des, trying his best to sound affronted, 'on the occasion of his retirement in 1926. I will ask you to have some respect.'

'Sorry, Desmond,' smiled Dvorak. 'Getting a bit edgy. We'll make do, I'm sure.'

Belgian Henri Marchal had heard the conversation and walked over to the pair. His spot was back in the second hundred.

'Look, I will trade you watches,' said Henri, waving away the protests of Des and Freddie. 'No, take it. You have a train schedule to keep to. I'm only walking – it really does not matter if I get to my next night's barn a little late! Take it – we'll swap back in London in a couple of weeks.' Des took the watch with thanks and gave Henri his own. With a firm handshake, the little Belgian ambled back to his bunk.

While all this was going on, the ferret Rudi sat with Billy Griffith in Hut 112, blissfully enjoying a cup of real coffee and some Red Cross chocolate.

At about 8:30 P.M., Crump Ker-Ramsay finally emerged from Harry and announced that everything was ready. Taking up a position at the base of the entry shaft, where he would act as overall controller, Crump had a few words with the fellow working the air pump. At the top of the shaft sat Jimmy Davison, who would direct the escapers down into the tunnel, and off in the corridor stood Dave Torrens, in charge of ensuring that everyone got to the trap at the allotted time.

At eight-forty, the first seventeen escapers began entering the tunnel. First went Johnny Marshall, looking dapper in a dark civilian suit, and then Johnny Bull, who would open the tunnel. They were followed by Sydney Dowse, taking care of the hauling duties at the exit shaft for the first twenty men, and then Roger Bushell, Bernard Scheidhauer, and Wally Valenta.

Another forty minutes passed before everyone was at their places in the tunnel and Johnny Bull could begin clearing the last six inches of soil. However, twenty minutes later, Bull was still wrestling with the boards that formed the ceiling of the exit shaft. As time ticked away, the escapers packed in the tunnel began to get edgy.

After half an hour, Johnny came back down the exit shaft, his dirt-stained face streaked with sweat. 'Someone else'll have to have a go – I'm done in,' he said with a gasp. 'Those boards have swelled up with the snow and I'm damned if I can loosen them.' He slumped against the wall of the chamber, his head hanging between his knees.

Without a word, Johnny Marshall stripped off his neat civilian suit and clambered up the shaft in his underwear. He worked at the boards for fifteen minutes before he was able to get a finger under one and wrench it free. The other ones came away easily, and Johnny returned down the shaft to redress while Bull went up to finish the final few inches.

It was now ten-fifteen, more than an hour after the scheduled opening time, and Bull worked quickly to avoid losing more time. He pulled down the clods of earth and dropped them to the floor of the tunnel, where they were stashed in a small dispersal chamber. Once he reached the surface, he would act as the first exterior controller, lying on his stomach beside the exit to monitor the movement of escapers. As each man reached the top of the ladder, Bull would put his hand on the fellow's head and, peering through the tree trunks, make sure that the coast was clear. Then he would give the fellow a quick tap on the head and the escaper would scoot away, following a rope into the woods for seventy yards to the marshaling point.

Carrying a blanket to lie on and a coil of rope, Johnny Bull at last poked his head out of the tunnel. But he saw not the sheltering trunks of the black fir trees. Instead he saw flat ground, snow-covered and frighteningly open. He looked to one side and saw the trees, a good ten feet off. The other way, Bull was horrified to see that the goon box was a scant forty-five feet away. He could see the guard quite clearly, silhouetted against the lighted compound, his breath making clouds around his helmet. Despite all of the careful surveying work, Harry had come up short.

Johnny dropped quickly back down the shaft and pushed aside the blankets leading to the exit chamber. The smiles of the waiting escapers vanished when they saw Bull's solemn expression.

'We've got a problem, Roger,' he whispered urgently. 'We're about twenty-five feet short of where we wanted to be.' In the silence that followed, Johnny Marshall hared up the shaft to look for himself. He returned cursing softly.

'And what's worse,' continued Bull, 'is that we're only fifteen yards or so from the goon box.'

*

Bushell, Marshall, and the others recovered quickly from the shock and began to discuss the problem rationally. 'It's not the goon box that worries me,' began Roger; 'it's the patrolling guards. The goon in the tower will be watching the compound, but the perimeter guards are going to be walking straight past the hole. And we'll be bloody easy to see against the snow.'

'So we close up and dig the rest of the way to the woods,' suggested someone, 'and go out during the next no-moon period.'

'Or,' cut in another, 'we go now and do as best we can – it could be ages before we're spotted.'

Johnny Bull spoke next. 'We could dig the last few feet in a couple of ⟨...⟩ but you all saw Harry's trap – it's so warped I doubt if it would last another week, let alone until the next no-moon period. And besides, we'd have to get everybody out of 104, collect all the gear, and get it hidden. That's going to be a big job.'

'I can think of a bigger problem,' whispered Roger slowly. 'The papers – they're all stamped with today's date. If we don't go now, we'll have to scrap the lot. No, we've got to go tonight – all we have to do is find a way to minimize the risk.'

The group was silent for a moment and then Johnny Bull spoke. 'I've got an idea: You remember those ferret fences that the goons used to spy on us? There's one of them in the trees near the hole. If we put a controller behind it, he could watch the guards and direct traffic from there. It would be the same as lying beside the hole, only a bit more comfortable!'

'How's he going to get word to the man in the tunnel? He sure as hell won't be able to whistle,' said someone.

'We'll just add another signal rope,' answered Johnny. 'I'll do the first shift, and take the rope out to the ferret fence. When you're waiting at the top of the ladder, you hang on to the rope. When you feel two tugs, out you come and follow the rope to the fence. Everything else can go exactly as planned.'

'It's the best we can do,' said Roger. 'There's no reason why it shouldn't work, provided everyone's patient enough to wait for the signal.' Pulling a pencil stub from his pocket, Bushell wrote the instructions on the wall of the exit chamber: 'Wait at top of shaft. Hold signal rope tied to rung. On receiving two tugs, crawl out. Follow rope to shelter.'

'Right, then,' said Bull cheerily, 'I'm off – see you all in the woods.' Carrying an extra coil of rope, he took off up the shaft, closely followed by Johnny Marshall, who paused at the top of the ladder and waited for the signal. Feeling two tugs, he heaved himself up and followed the rope to the ferret fence.

'Looks a damn sight better from the outside than it does from the inside,' Marshall remarked to Bull as they watched the lighted compound. 'Take care, old chum – see you at the RAF Club a week from Tuesday.'

'It's a date,' said Bull with a smile. With that, Johnny Marshall bent double and ran to the rendezvous point, paying out the seventy yards of rope as he ran. Less than fifteen minutes had passed since Bull broke the tunnel. It was now ten-thirty and the escape itself could begin, ninety minutes late.

*

Back in 104, the tension mounted as the minutes ticked away. The escapers tried to keep still, but it was difficult. Pumped up with adrenaline, the body had to do something to release energy, even if it was just pacing the corridor. Dave Torrens tried his best to maintain calm by keeping everyone informed with constant progress reports. Every few minutes, muffled whispers raced through the hut: 'Johnny Bull has started,' or 'They're having trouble with the exit.' Finally, Davison felt a breath of cool air waft up the shaft. 'We're through,' he said quietly, and a wave of relief spread through the hut.

It was dashed only minutes later by another circulated whisper. 'Harry's too short,' said a dozen strained voices, and the hut buzzed with conversation as the escapers tried to figure out what had gone wrong. Then a few minutes later came the signal that they had all been waiting for. Still quietly and calmly, Davison said to Torrens, 'They've started – let's have the next few fellows ready.'

As the escapers moved down the corridor to the last room in 104, they had time for a few hurried words to the marshals along the way. Tony Hayter was in the next group to go underground, and he looked very dapper in a dark civilian suit as he strode down the hall. He stopped to chat with Paddy Byrne, directing traffic in a doorway, and was excited at the approaching adventure. Tony's German was excellent after two years of study in captivity, and he had money and papers to get him to his destination, the city of Mulhouse on the French border. He had no qualms about traveling alone and confidently accepted Paddy's best wishes and handshake before taking his place in the tunnel room.

Later, Gordon Brettell and Henri Picard left their assigned bunks and moved down the corridor. Before leaving Hut 120, Gordon had exchanged a few words with his fellow forger, Alex Cassie. Brettell, too, was confident about his chances and was sure that he and Picard could pull off their disguise as French workers. Just before turning down the corridor, Brettell turned to Cassie and said, 'If by any chance I don't make it through, please write to my parents for me.' It was a routine request, and Alex quickly assented, adding that Gordon could tell them just as well himself when he got home. With a happy chuckle, Gordon was gone.

For Alex Cassie, it had been a difficult night, having watched all of his roommates leave for the tunnel. Realistically he knew that some, if not all, of them might not return to the camp. He hoped some would reach home, but there was an equal chance that they would be purged to Colditz or another punishment camp upon recapture. So, when he said good-bye to each of them as they left for the tunnel, he knew that the happy pattern of their shared lives together had come to an end. He would have only his memories of the Amiable Lunatics and their antics.

*

Outside the wire, the movement continued as the rest of the early escapers clambered out of Harry and snaked past Bull to join Marshall at the rendezvous point. Wally Valenta, Marshall's partner, came next, followed by Bushell and Scheidhauer, John Stevens and Johannes Gouws, Halldor Espelid and Nils Fuglesang, and Des Plunkett and Freddie Dvorak. When they all had arrived, a hurried conversation was held. According to the original plan, the various pairs were to take different trains away from Sagan to reduce the risk of discovery. However, the long delay meant that many had already missed their connections, leaving the group with the undesirable prospect of taking the same train. With no other alternative, the pairs set off at five-minute intervals to make their way through the forest to the railroad station. It was there that many would run into problems. Since the last briefing, a shed had been built over the subway entrance, and it was not easy to recognize as such. This new shed was to be a major obstacle for the escapers.

Of the first ten, only Bushell and Scheidhauer and Plunkett and Dvorak were able to make it through the woods without difficulty. Roger and Bernard got to the station first, went straight to the subway to save time, and bought two third-class tickets for the Berlin–Breslau express. When the train arrived, the pair boarded without incident.

Des and Freddie reached the station a few minutes later but found the eastern entrance blocked by a gang of Soviet prisoners on a work detail. Undaunted, they continued along the road toward the footbridge at the western end. They were still trying to find it when they heard the pulse of bomber engines in the distance. The sound grew louder, and then the scream of air-raid sirens broke the night air.

Dvorak grabbed Plunkett's arm and tersely uttered 'Come,' pulling him toward the subway. Inside, they were stopped by a railroad employee, who refused to sell them tickets. Instead she summoned a soldier, who began to manhandle the pair toward an air-raid shelter built into the subway. At that moment the Berlin–Breslau express arrived and, with the guard's attention diverted, Des and Freddie slipped away and sprinted through the ticket barrier toward the platform. They reached it just as the train was slowing down, and ran along the pavement toward the last car.

When the train stopped, the door nearest them was thrown open and a frazzled-looking conductor stuck his head out. *'Ist ein Alarm hier?'* (Is there an alarm here?) he asked hurriedly. *'Jawohl'* (Yes, sir), answered Des, and the conductor disappeared back into the train, hotly followed by the two escapers. As they pulled the door closed behind them, the train started to move. Only two minutes had passed since they first entered the subway.

The only problem was that they had no tickets, but only two-pfennig platform passes clearly marked Sagan station. With all the compartments full, Freddie and Des stood in the darkened corridor and discussed the problem.

'We must throw away our platform passes,' whispered Freddie urgently. 'They show that we came from Sagan.'

'So what? We can always say that we mistook these for tickets and pay the difference at the other end,' replied Des.

'No, it's too dangerous. If a warning goes out and we've got passes saying we boarded at Sagan, we're sure to be suspected. We should throw them out the window. When we get to Breslau, I'll do the talking,' went on Freddie. 'I'll say that we got on at Leignitz. That way we won't have to pay so much.'

Des still did not think it was wise to discard the platform passes and thought any ticket was better than none. However, he deferred to Freddie's experience in Continental travel, and the incriminating passes were pushed out the window. The two fell silent, watching the countryside speed by in the faint light reflected off the virgin snow.

Then a well-dressed man ambled up and grasped Plunkett's hand. Looking up, Des was surprised to see Roger Bushell, who was scanning the train to see how many escapers were onboard. He passed Des to shake Freddie's hand and then disappeared down the corridor. Buoyed by Big X's brief visit, Des and Freddie felt renewed hope as they stared out the grimy windows.

After about forty minutes, the train slowed. 'This must be Leignitz,' said Freddie. The two got off with the masses of people and spent a few minutes stretching their legs on the platform. Around them milled German soldiers and civilians, blissfully ignorant of their identity. It seemed as if half the population was in uniform.

When the train left Leignitz there were quite a few empty compartments, and Des and Freddie were able to secure one for themselves. In the next compartment a very agitated woman from Berlin was describing how her entire family had been killed in a recent air raid. She was leaving the capital because she had had enough of bombing. She then went on to describe, in some detail, exactly what she would do to a British airman if she could get her hands on one. Des and Freddie listened in silence and tried to sink a little deeper into their seats.

At about midnight the train slowed again and pulled into Breslau station. As the crowds piled off and made for the ticket kiosks, the escapers held back in the hopes that something would present itself. Soon they spotted a civilian arguing with the ticket collector at the middle kiosk. Seizing the opportunity, the two pushed through the crowds and squeezed behind the man. In an instant they were past the checkpoint and stood perusing a timetable innocently. The railroad police and Gestapo at the ticket kiosks never even looked at them.

While Bushell, Scheidhauer, Plunkett, and Dvorak were on their way to Breslau, other escapers arrived at Sagan station to find it blacked out. They walked up and down the road outside the station, trying in vain to locate the now hidden subway entrance, watching helplessly as trains came and went. There were strained queries in English and muffled curses as escapers watched their trains leave without them. More vital minutes ticked away.

Bob van der Stok, eighteenth out of the tunnel, arrived at the station a bit unnerved after running into an armed soldier who had demanded to know what Bob was doing roaming the woods during an air raid.

'I am a foreign worker,' replied Bob in a thick Dutch accent, 'and I am trying to find my way to the railroad station. But I heard the air-raid sirens and now I must find a shelter.'

'It's all right,' reassured the soldier. 'Just follow this path and it will take you directly to the station – there is a shelter there.' With a wave, he sent Bob on his way, and the Dutchman found the station without further inconvenience.

Finally, after what seemed like ages of pacing along the road, Johnny Marshall and Wally Valenta gamely walked into what they thought was a toolshed and discovered the long-lost subway. Once inside they were immediately stopped by a ticket inspector.

'Haven't you heard the siren?' he asked angrily. 'No one may enter the station during an alarm – you must go to the shelter!'

'But we must catch a train,' pleaded Wally. The inspector cut him short and waved them toward the shelter. Temporarily stumped, Wally and Johnny retreated to the woods to rethink their plans. As they left the station, they saw other escapers faced with similar dilemmas standing in the road and trying to work things out. The air raid had thrown a monkey wrench in the works.

*

Back in Hut 104, the escape had also suffered some setbacks. In the original plan, two to three minutes had been allowed for each escaper to travel the length of the tunnel. However, no one reckoned on the problems that the cases carried by the train travelers would create.

Because of nerves and the excitement of the moment, few escapers remembered the instructions given by Marshall and Ker-Ramsay. Some got their cases wedged behind frames and had to reverse back along the tunnel to free them, while others dropped their cases in front of them, forcing the hauler to crawl up and retrieve them. Many held the cases too far forward, throwing them off balance and tipping the trolley. Rather than wait for the escaper to disentangle himself and crawl up the tunnel, the hauler usually decided to crawl up himself and help the man back on. This was a tricky operation, made more difficult by nerves. The escaper had to take his weight on his fingers and toes so the hauler could get under him and reposition the trolley; then the hauler had to crawl backward down the tunnel and start pulling, hoping the same thing didn't happen again. With these delays, it was taking five or six minutes for each man to make his way through the tunnel. Sometimes it slowed down to one man every twelve minutes. By eleven-thirty, only six escapers had been summoned to follow the first group of seventeen.

Then came the air raid. The sirens wailed and, minutes later, the power in the camp was cut, leaving the tunnel in darkness. Many of the escapers had never been underground before, and the feeling of claustrophobia was bad enough when Harry was fully lit. In total blackness, some of the escapers panicked. Wings Day, waiting at the base of the shaft to be hauled up, realized that the panic could easily bring disaster and set out to get the fat lamps lit. Slowly he worked his way up the tunnel, lighting all the wicks and reassuring people as he went. It took thirty-five minutes to finish the job, but he was able to restore comparative calm.

However, there was still some confusion. Arriving at the exit chamber, Wings was surprised to see Sydney Dowse still working the hauling ropes.

'What the hell are you still doing here?' Day whispered. 'You're supposed to be out by now!'

'I know,' replied Sydney. 'Danny's gone already, although I had a bit of a tough time getting him through – he's got pretty bad claustrophobia. Hank Birkland's supposed to be taking over from me – God knows where he's gotten to!'

'Birkland's hauling in Leicester Square – I just passed him,' said Day quickly. 'He must have picked up the wrong instructions. You'd better get going. I'll take over here – Tobolski's coming through after me, so I can stick around for a bit.' With a quick nod, Sydney was off, up the shaft.

Farther down the tunnel, Gordon Brettell was having some difficulties, too. He was pulling an empty trolley from Leicester to Piccadilly when the rope broke somewhere in the middle. Unsure of what to do, he pulled the rest of the rope through to avoid getting himself tangled and set out to crawl up the tunnel. Ivo Tonder, arriving in Piccadilly seconds later, asked the hauler there what had happened, but the hauler had been fixing a break of his own. So Ivo had to crawl up to the trolley, attach a rope, and then return to Piccadilly to be hauled up.

In the tunnel room, Ker-Ramsay had taken over as above-ground controller, assisted by Henry Lamond. With the delays in mind he inspected everyone who entered the tunnel and removed anything that might impede their passage. Johnny Dodge, bundled up a bit too well against the cold, was asked to divest himself of some of his clothing before proceeding underground, and Pop Green was relieved of two large loaves of German bread that he had stuffed in his pockets. However, Crump didn't have the heart to deprive Tim Walenn of his huge suitcase, which the forger insisted would see him through any eventuality.

Then the inevitable happened. Tom Kirby-Green, being pulled from Piccadilly to Leicester Square, shifted a bit on the trolley and overbalanced it. In his attempts to get the wheels back on the rails, he nudged one of the box frames and brought three feet of tunnel down on top of him. When Hank Birkland in Leicester Square felt the rope tighten, he knew something was wrong. As he peered down the tunnel and realized he could no longer see the fat lamps in Piccadilly, he prepared himself for the worst.

He reached Kirby-Green to find the squadron leader well buried. Carefully, he heaved him out from under the sand and lay flat while Tom crawled over him and up the tunnel. Then Hank went to work.

Luckily, none of the boards had broken, so it was merely a matter of replacing them and putting the sand back. In the cramped quarters of a dark tunnel, though, this was no mean feat. Working entirely by feel, he located all of the sideboards and wedged them back into place, packing sand behind them as he went. Then he turned his attention to the ceiling, where a three-foot-high dome had opened in the fall. One by one he fitted the ceiling boards back in and stowed the sand as best he could. The whole job took him an hour, and he finished just as the lights came back on.

In the now-bright tunnel, Hank was relieved to see that the electric cable had not been damaged in the fall. However, he also discovered that there was a good bit of sand left that had not fit behind the shoring, so the only thing he could do was spread it over the floor between the rails. This done, he went back to Leicester Square and started hauling again.

The lights were now on, but the problems continued. Shortly after Kirby-Green's fall, Cookie Long was buried about twenty feet before Piccadilly. He was able to free himself and crawl away, but Bob Nelson, hauling in Piccadilly, had to worm back and fix the fall. That took thirty minutes. Then two others got stuck. One of them was Neville McGarr, who had packed himself with food and clothing that he laughingly insisted would ensure his survival for months on end. Both were able to free themselves, but soon after, Les Brodrick was stranded temporarily in the middle section when the rope on his trolley broke. Then, between Piccadilly and Leicester Square, Sandy Gunn was caught in a fall. Cookie Long, who had escaped his own burial to relieve the hauler in Leicester Square, made his way back to free Sandy and shore up the collapse. That took another twenty minutes.

The problem in many of these falls was the blanket rolls carried by the hardarsers. Some had been made too long, so that the ends caught on the box frames. Others hung too loosely around the escaper's neck, so that they dragged on the rails and caught under the front wheels, derailing the trolley and nearly strangling the man. Sometimes it was taking up to fourteen minutes for a man with a blanket roll to get through. Faced with this, Ker-Ramsay made a tough decision: No more blanket rolls would be allowed. It would create even greater hardship for the hardarsers, but it was the only way to avoid more dangerous accidents. The other controllers, Dave Torrens in the corridor and Muckle Muir at the base of the entrance shaft, agreed completely. Without the blanket rolls, things started to go more smoothly.

For Les Brodrick, however, the difficulties continued when he reached the base of the exit shaft. In the pitch darkness, he was unable to get oriented and then discovered that he could not lift his leg up to the rungs without becoming wedged in the shaft. Consequently he had to pull himself up with his arms, pausing for a rest whenever he could get a foot on the ladder. When he finally emerged, Les was just about done in with exhaustion. The shock of finding himself out in the open galvanized him, though, and he crawled down the well-worn path to the woods where the marshaler, Hank Birkland, was waiting patiently. Sheltered behind a tree, Les glanced back toward the camp and was astonished to see a column of steam rising from the tunnel mouth; he could not imagine how the guards had failed to spot it.

Soon there appeared Denys Street, a twenty-one-year-old Lancaster bomber pilot who was the son of Sir Arthur Street, the British permanent undersecretary of state for air and secretary of the Air Council. Denys was followed by Hunk Humphreys, Paul Royle, and the rest of the group of ten. Birkland got them organized and moved off into the woods. Before long they stumbled on a small building, but it was unguarded and apparently abandoned. Breathing a collective sigh of relief, the party continued westward.

*

At the railroad station, the delays caused by the air raid were compounding. Granted, the rate of exit had speeded up as the guards started watching the compound for signs of trouble rather than the wire and woods, but the escapers merely began to clog up at the station. Men who should have caught trains hours before were still waiting in the ticket hall. The only advantage they had over those who had arrived earlier was that, by watching other travelers, they realized that most people ignored the air-raid provisions and marched right past the officious railroad employees and into the booking hall. There Paweł Tobolski strolled around in his Luftwaffe uniform while others stood in the shadows in their tailored suits, trying to look inconspicuous. Dennis Cochran's dark violet-dyed uniform looked a bit garish as he stood in the center of the station but his pale, freckled face held an expression of supreme confidence. There were a few guards from the camp lounging around and a group of girls sat on a windowsill, singing softly among themselves.

Gordon Kidder and Tom Kirby-Green, the latter still a bit shaken by his near-burial, were approached by a member of the camp censor staff, who smiled pleasantly and asked who they were. Playing the part of a Spanish laborer, Tom replied carefully in a mixture of Spanish and broken German but the woman was not satisfied. She summoned a policeman, and Tom went through his story again. The policeman nodded with no small measure of disinterest and waved the two off. Later the woman picked on Bob van der Stok, but he escaped his second close call of the night. She seemed to have an inclination to talk, and Bob was relieved when his train pulled in.

Wings Day, finally getting to the station at about 12:45 A.M., was surprised to see so many escapers still there and wandered up to Gouws and Stevens, who were standing in the shadow of a newspaper stall.

'What's everyone still doing here?' Day asked softly in German.

John Stevens turned toward Day with a feigned look of disgust, as any businessman would do if approached by a vagrant. 'All the trains have been delayed by the air raid – who knows when we'll get out of here!' he answered.

Not wishing to test his marginal German further, Wings smiled meekly and wandered off to rejoin Tobolski.

Then the loudspeakers crackled to life: '*Breslau, Bahnsteig fünf, Breslau, Bahnsteig fünf*' (Breslau, track five). With that, the booking hall began to empty as escapers and civilians moved through the ticket barrier into the subway leading to the platforms above. Bob van der Stok went through, followed by Gouws and Stevens, Kidder and Kirby-Green, and Tony Hayter. Dennis Cochran was one of the last to go through, looking completely bored with the whole experience. At 1:00 A.M., the train slowly began to move off. The second group of travelers was on its way.

Just over an hour later, another express arrived, the 2:04 A.M. to Frankfurt-an-der-Oder. Looking dapper and buoyed by the ease with which they had moved through the tunnel and reached the station, Jens Müller and Per Bergsland confidently boarded a car. After them came Rene Marcinkus and the three forgers Tim Walenn, Gordon Brettell, and Henri Picard. That train, too, chugged away, leaving a much smaller group waiting in the ticket hall. At 3:15 A.M., the express to Berlin pulled in and Day, Tobolski, and Sailor Neely climbed aboard. Just as it was drawing away from the platform, Jimmy Catanach, Arnold Christensen, Halldor Espelid, and Nils Fuglesang trotted up and swung themselves onto one of the last cars.

That left one escaper in the booking hall, a French former radio technician named Raymond van Wymeersch, who had been downed over Dieppe in August 1942. Earlier he had discovered to his dismay that the ticket clerk had given him a ticket, not to Breslau, but to Lissa, well north of Breslau. Rather than risk a scene by trying to get a replacement or chance discovery by boarding without a ticket, he waited until the Lissa train arrived and boarded that. Upon arrival, he bought a ticket for Breslau and got there just a little behind schedule.

*

The 1:00 A.M. Berlin–Breslau express reached the Breslau station at two-thirty, and there many of the escapers met up again. Des Plunkett and Freddie Dvorak, having missed their first connection to Glatz, were still waiting for the next train, at six o'clock. Desperate to sleep, they looked in vain for somewhere to lie down for a few hours. As a last resort, they sat on their cases at the side of the booking hall and tried to catch a few winks. Conversation was impossible because of the many people leaning over the balcony above them. All they could do was sit.

They hadn't been there long when Roger Bushell strolled through the hall. A short while later, Roger passed again, paused, and said politely to Freddie, '*Avez-vous un peu de feu, monsieur?*' (Have you a light, sir?). Producing a match, Freddie replied, '*Certainement, monsieur,*' and Roger lit his cigarette. In a low voice, Dvorak went on to ask what had happened to Bernard Scheidhauer.

'Oh, he met a Frenchwoman in the restaurant,' replied Bushell. 'He's gone off to her flat – she may be able to help us.' With that, Roger blew out a cloud of smoke, smiled to Des and Freddie, and disappeared into the crowd in the booking hall. Looking around, Des and Freddie spotted a few others from the camp. John Stevens and Johannes Gouws stood off on the other side of the hall, while in the waiting room, Bob van der Stok sipped a glass of stale beer. Within a couple of hours everyone was gone but Plunkett and Dvorak. They remained sitting on their cases, patiently waiting for the train to Glatz.

*

At the camp the early dawn hours had heightened the tension and brought further delays. At about four o'clock, Roy Langlois emerged from the tunnel to relieve George McGill at the ferret fence. Langlois signaled out the next two escapers, Dutchy Swain and Bob Stewart and then noticed that small groups of guards had started to gather near the wire. They stood around in twos and threes, showing no inclination to leave. Then Langlois realized that it was changing time. For the next twenty minutes, off-duty guards wandered around before slowly moving off to the guardhouse. During that period Roy could get only another two men out.

A few minutes later, Langlois got another shock. He heard a shout from the goon box and instinctively crouched a little lower behind the fence, half expecting a shot to ring out. Then an answering call came from one of the patrolling guards, who ambled over and climbed the ladder to the box. The tower guard came down and started walking directly for the tunnel mouth. As he got closer, Roy tried to sink lower, conscious only of his pounding heart. A scant five feet from the hole, the guard turned, unhitched his pants, and squatted down. For five minutes the guard squatted there, nonchalantly going about his business, while Roy tried to slow down his heart. Then he remembered the unfortunate escaper standing on the ladder, just a few feet from the goon. He's the one with the worst of the situation, thought Roy. Finally the goon finished and carefully fastened his pants before returning to the tower. Uttering a silent word of thanks, Roy gave two tugs on the rope and the next man darted past him.

*

At about ten minutes to five, the controllers in Hut 104 decided that the last man out would be number 87, at about five o'clock. With dawn spreading, this was the very latest they could go. The final escapers were put down the tunnel, and the haulers, Tim Newman at Piccadilly, Red Noble at Leicester Square, and Shag Rees at the exit shaft, were told to get out once they had pulled their last man through.

For Roy Langlois behind the ferret fence, it was far too light already. He felt as if he had aged ten years in the past hour, and things did not look like they were going to get any easier. Once more the guard reached the end of his beat and, once more, Langlois tugged on the signal rope. The seventy-sixth man, Lawrence Reavell-Carter, emerged from the hole and began making his way along the second rope to the rendezvous point. There he met up with Tony Bethell, who was just assembling his group before moving off toward the railroad line. Next out of the hole was Keith Ogilvie, who also snaked past Roy to join Reavell-Carter in the woods. From their vantage point in the trees, they watched as number 78, New Zealander Mick Shand, popped out of Harry and crawled toward them. He had just passed the ferret fence when Len Trent, number 79, emerged.

Then both Langlois and Reavell-Carter noticed a deviation in the guard's path. Instead of staying close to the wire, he was widening his beat as he walked and was on a direct course for the tunnel. Immediately Roy tugged both ropes desperately, and Trent and Shand froze on the ground. The guard kept coming, and Langlois expected a repeat of the last episode. But this time the guard didn't stop. Step by step he neared the tunnel mouth; on one step his foot missed the mouth by inches, while on the next, it nearly landed on Len Trent. There the guard paused.

Chapter 16

BATTLING THE ELEMENTS

THE GUARD MUST HAVE spotted Mick Shand lying on the slushy path beyond the ferret fence, for he unslung his rifle and pointed it at Mick. With his head buried in the snow, Shand was blissfully unaware of this development, as were Trent and Langlois, also hugging the ground for cover. But Reavell-Carter, watching from the comparative safety of the trees, saw the guard draw a bead on Shand. Without hesitation, he jumped into the open, waving his arms and yelling, *'Nicht schiessen!'* (Don't shoot!). All hell broke loose.

The guard, startled by Reavell-Carter's shout, fired wildly and, at the shot, Mick Shand bounded to his feet and ran for the woods. Keith Ogilvie did the same. Slowly Reavell-Carter walked forward with his hands raised; then Trent stood up right beside the goon. The poor guard jumped a foot when he saw Len standing beside him. With no other choice, Langlois, too, stood up behind the ferret fence and raised his hands. Fumbling for a flashlight, the guard shone the beam into the tunnel, where it rested upon the wan but smiling face of Bob McBride, number 80. 'Wings' Maw, waiting behind Bob at the base of the shaft, had already taken off up the tunnel. Recovering his wits, the guard pulled out his whistle and blew it for all he was worth. It was all over.

*

As soon as they heard the shot, the controllers in 104 sprang into action. Davison gathered up all the exit order lists and stuffed them into the stove, while Ker-Ramsay went down the tunnel to get everyone out. However, communication in a tunnel is very difficult and, try as he might, Crump could not make Tim Newman in Piccadilly understand that the escape was over. Finally he grabbed the rope and tried to pull Tim back, but that only led to a tug of war, which ended when the rope came apart. Eventually the message got through when the last escapers began to come back up the tunnel. The first to emerge was Newman, then Muckle Muir and Michael Ormond. They were followed by Red Noble and Wings Maw, each insisting that there was a goon hard on his heels. The next man, Shag Rees, emerged sweaty and breathless and confirmed to Crump that he was the last.

The trap was closed, the stove was returned to its normal position, and the lockers that had been concealing the entrance were moved back against the wall. All of the blankets that had been spread around the trap were returned to the bunks, and the would-be escapers set about destroying the evidence. Their first concern was to burn everything incriminating, including papers, money, and maps, and reconvert their clothing to service issue. Some even tried to consume all of their escape rations, although no one was able to get halfway through them.

A few tried to make it out of the windows and back to their own huts. In 109, one kriegie heard a frantic banging on the shutters and threw open the windows to let in a breathless escaper, who tore off his civilian clothes and jumped into a bunk, waiting for the whole hut to be turned out. He was one of the few to make the attempt before a burst from the nearest goon box put a stop to the practice.

At 5:30 A.M., the *Hundführer*, a harmless little fellow who had helped the escape organization in the past, came into 104 with his dog. He was completely overwhelmed by the situation and told everyone to stay in their rooms. Then, despairing of anything better to do, he collected all the greatcoats from the corridor, put them in a pile, and sat his dog on top of them. The Alsatian promptly went to sleep.

In the tunnel room, Crump Ker-Ramsay heard a faint scratching coming from under the stove. After confirming with Torrens that all of the escapers had been brought out, Crump concluded that it was a goon and decided to let him find his own way out.

Back outside the camp, Len Trent, Bob McBride, Roy Langlois, and Lawrence Reavell-Carter were being marched to the guardhouse. When they got there, their escort was dismayed to discover that most of the guards were still asleep, and he had quite a job rousing them. So, with only two guards to keep an eye on them, the four frustrated escapers took turns sidling up to the small stove and stuffing in their papers, maps, and money.

Eventually von Lindeiner threw open the door and stormed in, his eyes wild and bulging. With a great effort at restraint, he began to question the four about the break. How many had escaped? Who were the instigators? Where did the tunnel start? The four merely stood there, looking dumb and smiling pleasantly. This was not at all what the commandant had in mind, and he flew into an uncontrollable rage. He became virtually incoherent in his speech and spewed forth threats, accusations, and invective. 'You have no idea what you have done,' he screamed. 'The Gestapo will have a hand in this, you mark my words!' His face was the most startling shade of red, and his limbs shook with anger.

Pieber was a bit more controlled. He just looked at the four and shook his head sadly. 'You will never be allowed to return to the camp,' he said dolefully. For two hours they waited in the guardroom before being stripped, searched, and marched to the cooler. There they were kept without food, heat, or washing kit for two days. According to the sentry, it was von Lindeiner's order.

At about 6:00 A.M., a fully armed riot squad trooped into the compound and formed a ring around 104. Machine guns were set up at each door, and a small knot of ferrets and camp officers stood off at a distance, regarding the scene with some embarrassment. One by one the escapers were pulled out of the hut, each half expecting to be shot, and stripped down to their underwear. Anything that had been even slightly altered to civilian apparel was seized and thrown in a pile, to which was added any escape gear that hadn't been destroyed. Most of the escapers had been able to drop their compasses in the snow on the way out of 104, but one or two fellows realized after they had been stripped that their escape maps were still tucked in their shorts. With the help of the kriegies around them, the maps were slowly chewed up and swallowed.

Meanwhile, Simoleit, one of the commandant's adjutants, was obviously getting edgy and eventually located Bill Jennens in his bunk. He said imploringly that Charlie Pfelz, a likable and totally harmless ferret, was down in the tunnel and would soon suffocate if he was not let out. Knowing full well that plenty of air came in through the mouth, Jennens dawdled and hemmed and hawed, demanding to know what Pfelz was doing in their tunnel at this hour of the morning. Slowly he pulled on his pants and ambled out of the room, trailing an anxious Simoleit behind him.

Taking full advantage of the situation, Jennens paused and chatted with a few of the half-naked escapers standing in the compound and then finally located Red Noble and went to open the trap. Charlie emerged, blinking in the light, and grinned as he told Rubberneck and von Lindeiner, who had just arrived, about the tunnel. Few of the ferrets cared for Rubberneck, and the whole situation was obviously making him very uncomfortable.

Hearing about the tunnel whipped up von Lindeiner's rage again and he drew his pistol, waving it viciously with a half-crazed look in his eyes. The security officer, Broili, was doing his best to hold his weapon steady but couldn't quite manage it. The only one who appeared to be in control was Rubberneck, whose face was mottled red but who exuded a sort of psychotic calm. He was evidently looking for someone to vent his anger on.

Then he spotted Shag Rees and Red Noble. He had always regarded the two as his mortal foes, and when he saw them standing outside 104, he rushed over and grabbed them by their collars. Shag and Red, still pumped up from their trip back along the tunnel, pulled away and moved back a step, looking defiant and ready for a fight. Seeing this as his challenge, Rubberneck slowly leveled his pistol on Red, while another goon drew a bead on Shag. It could have gone either way, but in the end the tension subsided and Shag and Red allowed themselves to be stripped and marched off to the cooler.

One young wag couldn't resist putting in his own two cents' worth by making strange clucking noises in his throat. Von Lindeiner turned toward him without expression. 'Cooler,' he said stonily. A friend of the clucker evidently thought this a great sport and let out a chuckle as his pal was marched away. The commandant turned to him next: 'Cooler.'

In time another goon appeared with the photo identification cards to verify the names of everyone who had come out of 104. Then, for nearly two hours, the staff went through each hut to determine who was missing. Armed guards had been posted at the doors of each block, so it was impossible to leave. Slowly the staff compiled a list of those who had escaped.

Pieber appeared in the door of Sandy Gunn's room in 122 and asked wearily, 'Where is Flight Lieutenant Gunn?' The others replied that he must be in another hut. Pieber made a note and stalked out. Later he poked his head into a room in Hut 106 and stood at the door, pointing at the various bunks. 'Hmm, Flying Officer Cochran and . . . ah, Mr. Lyon has gone to England as well!' Unfortunately for the latter, Jack Lyon was standing in the compound at that moment, shivering with everyone else.

Finally, with the count complete, the group from 104 was formed up and marched toward the cooler. At the gate, they stopped. Pieber gave them a short speech and a few mild reproaches and then stood by, contemplating his boots. The group waited. Half an hour later, a ferret appeared with a message for Pieber. The Austrian sighed audibly and then invited the prisoners to dismiss. It turned out that there was not enough room in the cooler for them. In fact, few of them would ever serve their full twenty-eight-day sentences.

*

While the count was going on, von Lindeiner had retired to his office to institute the search procedure. Though he did not yet have any idea of the number missing, he felt sure that a full alert would be necessary. First he telephoned his immediate superior in the OKW POW office, who dispatched an official to the camp, and then he informed his superior in the Luftwaffe chain of command. Most important, he telephoned Max Wielen, head of the Breslau Kripo office, which would be responsible for coordinating the search. Wielen immediately ordered a *Kriegsfahndung*, a general alert, and then quickly upgraded it to a *Grossfahndung*, the highest level of national security alert. He instructed von Lindeiner to continue setting up the search apparatus while he notified the Kripo chain of command.

Von Lindeiner made thirty-nine more telephone calls during those early-morning hours. He alerted local railroad stations and, unaware that the train travelers were long gone, ordered that every train leaving Sagan be searched. Nearby airfields were put on warning, and the Kriegsmarine in the Baltic ports notified. Home Guard and local defense detachments in the area were also called out. They were to stop every vehicle on the roads, patrol every lane and street, and search every farm, house, and hotel within fifty miles of the camp. Everyone in authority, and many who were not, was instructed to take to the countryside to round up the escapers. Blissfully unaware of what was going on around them, the lowly hardarsers trudged through the snow, trying to get clear of the camp.

*

Just before 1:30 A.M., after the last of the train travelers had left the tunnel, the first of the foot sloggers emerged in the person of Willy

Williams. The big Aussie was to lead a group of twelve escapers disguised as a bunch of workers on leave from a local woodmill. They were to head for Tschiebsdorf, a small station southeast of the camp, where Jerzy Mondschein would use a forged pass to buy tickets for Boberröhrsdorf, near Hirschberg on the Czech border. Once there the group would split up and go their separate ways.

After Williams and Mondschein came the redoubtable Johnny Dodge, struggling to get his big frame out of the tunnel, and Pop Green, the oldest man in the escape at fifty-seven. Rusty Kierath and Jim Wernham followed Pop up the ladder; then came the Poles Tony Kiewnarski and Kaz Pawluk. The ninth member of the group was Doug Poynter, and bringing up the rear were Jimmy James, resplendent in an altered flying tunic and a pair of desert-issue trousers he had lain inside the door of his hut to give them a suitably grubby appearance, and Nick Skantzikas, decked out in a cut-down, dyed overcoat and a cloth cap. Once they were assembled, the party picked up its twelfth member, Johnny Bull, who had just been relieved at the signal rope.

It was dreadfully cold and windy, and nerves already frayed became even more raw. Every few hundred yards one of the escapers whispered that he had heard voices, but Willy Williams's calm drawl would cut in to silence the crew, reminding them that the only people stupid enough to be out on a night like that were other kriegies. After about an hour's walking through the forest, they still had not found the railroad line. Pausing for a hurried conference, they decided to bear due east so as not to miss it. Eventually they came to the rails, headed south, and entered the station at Tschiebsdorf.

Mondschein went to the booking window, thrust the pass forward, and asked the clerk for twelve tickets to Boberröhrsdorf.

'Zwölf?' the clerk asked in disbelief before turning his back on Jerzy to give some serious thought to the situation. It was only a moment before he was back at the window.

'Zwölf Fahrkarten?' he repeated.

Mondschein was losing patience. 'Ja, zwölf!' he answered menacingly, and the clerk again turned to his ticket trays. Finally he reappeared with the twelve tickets, which Mondschein accepted without a word.

The rest of the kriegies were draped around the waiting room while this episode was going on, trying to look nonchalant as their stomachs tied in knots. When Jerzy returned with the tickets, they breathed a collective sigh of relief. It was nearly 6:00 A.M. before the train arrived, and the escapers climbed on and crammed themselves into three full compartments. The train steamed south, stopping at every little hamlet on the way, and gradually filled up with workers and children. Everyone seemed to ignore the escapers, except for a large conductress who used her considerable lungpower to berate one of them for smoking in a nonsmoker. When they reached Boberröhrsdorf just after nine o'clock there wasn't even a ticket check as they left the station. With brief good-byes and handshakes, they separated.

*

Nick Skantzikas and Jimmy James walked out of the village and then turned off the road into the foothills of the Riesengebirge. As they got higher into the hills, the snow became deeper, and by midafternoon it was up to their waists. Occasionally they happened upon a rough trail, but for the most part it was heavy slogging through virgin snow. Crossing the valley of the Bober, they clawed their way up the opposite side, using tree roots and saplings as handholds, and eventually reached a small plateau, barren of trees, on the other side of the valley. They sheltered for a while in a deer stall, one lying in the straw-lined trough while the other huddled around a tiny fire, but it was soon obvious that they had to keep moving and find better shelter before nightfall. Jimmy and Nick dragged themselves up and pushed off southward, up gently sloping ground to the top of another broad valley. Across the valley lay a range of rugged, snow-covered mountains and, off to the east, the city of Hirschberg. By their calculation, they still had another forty miles to go before reaching the Czech border.

Jimmy James had spent some time in Canada before the war and was used to cold winters, but he was beginning to doubt whether they could make it across the mountains with their poor rations and clothing. Nick was in worse shape. Accustomed to warm, Adriatic weather, he was shivering and blue with cold. The only option was to hit the roads. On the valley road to Hirschberg, the two escapers began to gain confidence. No one seemed to pay any attention to them, and the few who did merely called out cheerful remarks about the weather. They were on the road for Polaun when they decided to risk going into Hirschberg West station and buying tickets for somewhere closer to Czechoslovakia.

They didn't even get to the ticket kiosk. A policeman and a civilian official headed them off in the booking hall and demanded their papers, which the policeman quickly tucked in his pocket. After a perfunctory search of their packs, Nick and Jimmy were taken by the arm and marched out of the station to police headquarters. By late evening, most of the rest of the original party had joined them.

*

Tony Kiewnarski and Kaz Pawluk had reached Hirschberg without incident but were arrested in the afternoon while walking through the town. Pop Green, despite the fact that his age made him a less conspicuous traveler, had not even gotten away from Boberröhrsdorf. Wearing an old khaki tunic with civilian buttons, khaki battle dress trousers, and a blue balaclava cap, Pop carried a roll of felt stuffed with food and extra clothing and had papers identifying him as a Czech worker going home on leave. Exiting the station, he followed Johnny Bull and Jerzy Mondschein for about three hundred yards and, when he lost them, continued in his plan to skirt around the main part of Boberröhrsdorf. After watching the town from a sheltered copse for a couple of hours, he came to the conclusion that there was no easy way around and decided to make a bold bid at walking straight through the town. Though his age and appearance were valuable assets, Pop didn't get far before he was stopped.

The German who stopped him seemed suspicious and, after studying Green's papers, asked why he had not traveled straight to Czechoslovakia instead of getting off at Boberröhrsdorf. Putting on his best sheepish expression, Pop said sadly that he had lost all of his money gambling and could only borrow enough for a ticket to Bober. The soldier was unconvinced and insisted on taking Pop to the local post office, where a call was placed to the Hirschberg police station. The official on the other end instructed that Pop be taken into custody, and his escape bid was over.

*

Johnny Dodge and Jim Wernham, traveling with papers identifying them as French volunteer workers, made an odd-looking pair. The

Dodger's big frame was clad in an altered RAF enlisted man's greatcoat and pants, while the lean Scots-Canadian was lucky enough to have a suit of real civilian clothes. After leaving the group, they walked south along the riverbank to a small station on the outskirts of Hirschberg, where Jim Wernham tried to buy tickets to a station on the Czech frontier. Because of restrictions on travel to border zones, he was refused, so they continued their trek southwest, this time along the main road. After very slow going through deep snow, they finally reached the Hirschberg main station, where Wernham again tried unsuccessfully to purchase tickets. Eventually the Dodger was able to buy two third-class tickets to a small station farther down the line, but the pair were questioned and arrested shortly after boarding the train at 4:00 P.M. Taken to the railroad police office, Johnny and Jim had no choice but to admit their identities. They were questioned briefly and taken to the Kripo office, arriving shortly after dusk.

*

Doug Poynter was the last to rejoin the party at Hirschberg. Wearing a naval greatcoat with civilian buttons and one of Tommy Guest's cloth caps, Doug found a hiding place in the woods south of Boberröhrsdorf after leaving the rest of the group. He remained there until midafternoon; then, driven by intense cold and heavy snowfalls, he started walking southwest. After about eight miles, Doug reached the main Hirschberg–Polaun railroad line, went to the nearest small station, and bought a third-class ticket to Polaun. To avoid scrutiny, he waited until the very last minute to board the train and then bustled past the ticket inspector and forced his way into the crowded car. The train chugged slowly south for about three hours but, just before 9:00 P.M., it was boarded by two civilian policemen and a member of the Hitler Youth. The police were satisfied with Doug's papers but, just as they were about to leave the compartment, the Hitler Youth member spotted a tiny defect. Poynter stuck to his story of being a French worker but was taken off at the next stop and driven to the police station at Hammersdorf. When another car arrived to take him to the Hirschberg Kripo office, Doug realized that the game was up and admitted his identity to the chief of police.

The rest of the party had no better luck. Pop Green had seen Johnny Bull and Jerzy Mondschein trekking away from the railroad station at Boberröhrsdorf, and eventually they linked up with Willy Williams and Rusty Kierath for the journey southward. The four made it into the Riesengebirge but were arrested by a mountain patrol and taken to the Reichenberg prison, inside Czechoslovakia.

*

Closer to Sagan, the deep snow and biting cold were causing problems for the rest of the hardarsers, too. Numbers 54 and 55 out of the tunnel, Hunk Humphreys and Paul Royle, respectively, got clear of the camp at about 2:30 A.M. and joined Hank Birkland's party for the trek away from the vicinity. Aside from their brush with the abandoned building, they had no further difficulty and reached the north–south railroad line after about an hour's walking.

Hunk and Paul left the group there and, once they had arranged their kit and decided on a direction, turned toward the southeast. They were lucky enough to find a series of firebreaks that had been cut in the forest where the going was fairly easy, though the knee-deep snow occasionally gave them problems. They heard the occasional bark of a deer but nothing else. By dawn they still had not reached the autobahn and decided to lie up for the day. After trying unsuccessfully to boil some water on a little fat lamp heater they had brought, Hunk and Paul bundled up to sleep. What with nerves and the cold, though, each managed barely an hour's sleep.

The pair started off again at dusk but were soon forced, against their better judgment, to take to the roads to escape the slushy and sticky snow. They reached the autobahn without incident (the only other person they saw was a suspicious individual who appeared from the woods, darted across the road, and vanished into the trees on the other side – likely another kriegie, they decided) and crossed it without difficulty. They tried the fields again but were soon driven back to the road. Four times they were forced to take cover to avoid civilians, but each time they escaped detection. On the fifth occasion, just after passing through the village of Tiefenfurt, their luck ran out.

A party of three elderly Germans appeared on the road in front of them and, since it was impossible to duck into the woods to avoid them, Humphreys and Royle tried to bluff it out. The three Germans were having none of it. With weapons drawn, they waved away the escapers' story and called for reinforcements. Soon a policeman and a soldier arrived to join the party.

The policeman and the Home Guard types were grim-faced and uncommunicative but as they walked back to the village, the soldier chatted with Hunk and Paul in their broken German. Sympathetically he congratulated them on their effort and told them to ignore the sullenness of the others. 'They're not real soldiers like us,' he said. 'They don't count,' he added, casting a look of disgust toward the elderly men.

At about 3:00 A.M. on March 26, the party reached the local jail, and Hunk and Paul were shoved into a tiny cell no more than seven feet square. They were about to lie down for a rest when the door opened. The first to enter was Shorty Armstrong, who had done a stint on the signal rope before walking away from the camp with Jack Grisman's group. He had also found the snow in the fields too deep to handle and had been forced onto the road. It may have been he whom Hunk and Paul spotted crossing the autobahn so furtively. On the second night of his trek, Shorty was spotted by two Local Defense men and taken into custody.

The next two to enter were more of a surprise to Hunk and Paul. Johnny Marshall and Wally Valenta had been the first pair out of the tunnel and were traveling as Czech workers (Johnny carried papers identifying him as Petr Kovalkov, a glassworker, and wore a dark civilian suit with a ski cap). They had nearly two hundred Reichsmarks to buy their train tickets to Mittelwalde on the Czech frontier, where they planned to cross the border on foot. Once in Czechoslovakia they would link up with some of Valenta's contacts or, failing that, head toward Yugoslavia to try to reach Tito's partisans. Everyone expected them to be miles away from Sagan by now.

However, due to the confusion at the train station, Johnny and Wally had retreated to the forest to rethink their plans. There was another train at 1:00 A.M., but that would mean waiting at the station for about two hours, a very risky proposition. It would also prevent them from catching their 3:00 A.M. train to Mittelwalde. Reluctantly, the pair decided to walk the eighty-odd miles to the Czech frontier. From there, their experiences were much the same as the others'. Forced onto the roads by the deep, slushy snow, Wally and Johnny crossed the autobahn easily, only to be stopped in a small village on the other side. Wally took command of the situation, chattering away to the men in his perfect German, but they soon became interested in Marshall's silence. They started firing questions at him, and Johnny, whose German was not good, elected to answer in French. Unfortunately, one of the Germans was fluent in French, and the game was up.

They were taken to the burgermeister's house and then to the local jail to await transport to Tiefenfurt. Johnny was able to save some of his German money by taping it to the sole of his shoe, but he stuffed their forged papers into a fire.

*

Humphreys, Royle, Armstrong, Marshall, and Valenta remained in the tiny cell for the rest of the night and at dawn were herded into a car by six policemen. Pleased to be returning to Luft III, their satisfaction quickly evaporated as the car passed the camp and pulled up outside the police station in Sagan. They were searched and questioned briefly and then locked in a smelly and bug-infested cell furnished only with wire mesh bunk beds.

Shortly after their arrival, a group was brought in from Halbau. Keith Ogilvie had managed to escape from the fray at the tunnel mouth but was forced to leave his traveling companion, Lawrence Reavell-Carter, and much of his escape gear behind. The Canadian turned south, made his way into the middle of the woods, and settled down to pass the day. Unable to sleep, he munched on some chocolate and just waited. At dusk he set off again but, like so many others, was forced to the roads by the snow and slush. After passing through a couple of villages, he was stopped by an elderly man on a bicycle who produced a pistol and arrested him. Keith was taken to an inn in Halbau, where he gratefully relaxed before a fire. Just as he was dozing off, the door to the inn was thrown open and three more kriegies walked in, surrounded by a brace of ancient reservists.

Ogilvie recognized Chaz Hall and Brian Evans, who looked completely exhausted after their trek, and also the little Canadian Tommy Thompson. The three had had a very interesting, if short, escape. Thompson had been sixty-eighth out of the tunnel, following his running mate, fellow Canadian Bill Cameron, and the pair covered only about two hundred yards before hearing the shots at the tunnel mouth. They pressed on for two or three miles and then hid under a pile of brush for the day. That evening they set off again and were trudging silently through the forest when two figures suddenly appeared from behind a stand of trees. Thinking they might be armed, Tommy fought the urge to bolt and, as he peered at the pair, realized that they looked oddly familiar. He took a step forward and recognized them: Brian Evans and Chaz Hall.

The four were delighted to meet up and quickly exchanged stories, which turned out to be almost identical. Talking further, they decided that there was nothing to be lost by traveling together, so they all set out again. At about four in the morning they found a barn at the edge of a field and made themselves comfortable in the hayloft for the day. By this time, though, Bill Cameron was starting to feel the effects of cold and exposure. He began to shake uncontrollably and before long was hallucinating and talking to himself. The options open to them were limited.

It was obvious that Bill was unfit to travel, but there were no other buildings visible where they might get help for him. They even considered giving themselves up, but a brief reconnaissance failed to turn up anyone to surrender to. Finally they decided that Bill was safest where he was. They bundled him up well, left some of their escape rations, and headed off on their own, leaving the barn door unlatched in the belief that the owner would realize there was someone inside. The plan worked: A few hours later, Bill was awakened by a farmer armed with a pitchfork, a shotgun, and a vicious-looking Alsatian. He was escorted to a nearby house and from there to the local military post. Bill was then taken by car to the Sagan police station at 7:00 A.M. on March 26, arriving shortly after Humphreys, Royle, Armstrong, Marshall, and Valenta.

Chaz, Brian, and Tommy continued their trek in the hopes of jumping a freight train somewhere, but they got no more than a couple of miles before being picked up by the Home Guard on the outskirts of a small village. Now, unwilling to give in, Tommy Thompson was arguing in French with one of his escorts, maintaining angrily that he was a French worker on his way home and demanding to know why he had been arrested with these criminals. Keith Ogilvie had to stifle a laugh as Tommy tried to cope with the questions of the guard, who obviously spoke much better French than he did. Eventually, after many embarrassing pauses as Tommy slowly translated the question and worked up an answer in his mind, the Canadian gave up. He did, however, buy enough time to stuff his papers behind a cushion on the couch. Then Keith, Brian, Chaz, and Tommy were driven to Sagan, arriving shortly after the group from Tiefenfurt on the morning of the twenty-sixth.

*

At about noon on March 27, yet another party of escapers was brought to the Sagan jail. Les Brodrick and Denys Street had planned to travel together as French workmen, and Hank Birkland, who had the same idea but no running mate, elected to join them. The first part of their trek took them across open ground in deep snow, and it was nearly dawn before they passed the first obstacle, the main road they had been warned about.

After another hour of backtracking to avoid farm buildings, the three decided it was time to lie up and settled down in a hollow in a fairly open pine plantation. They were able to brew some hot drinks and, though their blankets were soaking wet, bundled themselves up and dozed for the day. Once in a while they awoke with a start at the sound of voices, but no one disturbed them.

The pattern continued on the second night. They plodded through the often hip-deep snow, resting occasionally and circling to avoid farmhouses. Les spotted one or two people off in the distance, but none was near enough to pose any threat. Now cold, tired, and hungry, there was little conversation among the three and at dawn they hid again, this time in a thicket, and passed a miserable day. Late in the afternoon, numb with cold and tortured by inactivity, Les, Denys, and Hank elected to continue their trek even though it was still light. People occasionally appeared far ahead of them, and once Denys saw a pair who looked suspiciously like escaped POWs. Still, they were not challenged. By the time darkness fell, they had entered yet another pine forest, and the going became even more difficult. The trees seemed to go on forever, and the snow was so deep that each man could trudge only a few hundred yards at best before collapsing in exhaustion. One of the others would soon come up from behind and urge him on, only to collapse himself before long.

The cold and damp were starting to affect Hank, who began to talk ceaselessly to himself as he walked, and Denys and Les decided that they would have to find somewhere to lie up and dry off. The first farm they approached had no suitable outbuildings, so they opted to try a lighted house that was visible in the distance. Denys, who was fluent in German, approached the cottage and knocked. When the farmer appeared, Street said that they were French workers who had become lost while on the way to a new job. The farmer was silent for a minute and then peered out of the house at where Les and Hank were sheltered.

He told them to wait. Almost immediately, there was a commotion in the farmhouse and four soldiers rushed out and surrounded Denys, Les, and Hank. Their escape bid was over.

They were marched to the police station in the small village of Kalkbruch but were able to dump their compasses along the way. The police station turned out to be the house in which the policeman lived, and the three were put into a makeshift cell that obviously had not been used for some time. Their escort, an army sergeant, was quite friendly and, mindful of their plight, started a small fire in the broken old stove in the room. They were locked in and immediately set about making Hank comfortable on the rough bed. Then they quickly stuffed their maps and forged papers in the fire and set about reconverting their clothing to service dress, which simply meant pulling the cloth button covers from their battle dress and enlisted men's greatcoats. They had just begun the more legitimate task of spreading out their blankets before the fire when the policeman returned and demanded their papers. Les happily and truthfully told him that they had none. The man left satisfied and returned a few hours later to take them to the Sagan police station.

*

Later on the twenty-seventh, another pair arrived at Sagan from Halbau. After leaving Jack Grisman's party, Bob Nelson and Dick Churchill headed south, trudging through the thick pine forests until dawn. Then, in the middle of a pine thicket, they stopped for the day and broke off some pine boughs to make a bed. The limbs made a hefty crack when they were snapped off and, as the pair settled down to lie up for the day, they heard similar noises coming from another part of the woods. They discovered later that it was Shorty Armstrong, doing exactly the same thing. Huddled in the pine boughs, Bob and Dick opened their bundles to munch on some escape food, but Nelson was surprised to see that his pack contained someone else's clothing and socks. Then it struck him. While hauling in Piccadilly he had stowed his bundle behind him, planning to pick it up on the way out. Another escaper must have grabbed his pack by mistake, leaving his own. Bob wondered if he would ever find out whose gear he was using.

At dusk they started off again and continued until they reached the main road. In the darkness, the paved highway looked like a canal, so

Bob crawled up and tried to dip his hand in to test the temperature of the water. He felt a little sheepish when his fingers touched the cold tarmac. Crossing the road, Nelson and Churchill continued through the deep snow and slush until, near dawn on March 26, they came upon a barn at the edge of a village. Exhausted and wet through from walking in the snowy and sodden countryside, they decided to lie up for as long as it took to dry out and get their strength back. The following night they ventured into the village for a wash and drink at the water pump, which made a terrific racket. No one was alerted, though, and they crept back to the barn unobserved.

The day passed without incident but on the afternoon of the twenty-seventh, a pack of civilians threw open the barn door and started a vigorous search with pitchforks. Luckily, Bob and Dick were discovered before they were perforated. The leader of the search party, a red-faced, corpulent fellow who was the owner of the barn, took great pleasure in driving the pair into the village at the point of his pitchfork. Soon the self-important burgermeister of Halbau arrived, waving a tiny pistol, and escorted the bedraggled escapers to the local inn, where they were held to await pickup. Before the van arrived to take them to the Sagan police station, Bob and Dick were able to shove their forged papers behind the piano in the inn.

At Sagan they were searched and interrogated by two officers and were then put into a large cell with the others. John F. Williams arrived shortly afterward, followed a few hours later by George McGill and Neville McGarr.

The last to be brought in was Flight Lieutenant Alistair Thompson McDonald, a craggy little Scot from 1 PRU. He had been picked up in much the same circumstances by a couple of Home Guardsmen who made a halfhearted attempt to rough him up before changing their tactics and ignoring him. When he finally arrived at the police station, he had been able to destroy his papers and reattach the RAF buttons to his tunic.

Williams, McGarr, McGill, and McDonald had all gone through the same conditions: knee-deep, slushy snow that forced them onto the roads; hunger and intense cold; and exhaustion and disorientation. All arrived worn out and soaked to the skin.

*

Now there were nineteen escapers languishing in the civilian jail in Sagan. They were not mistreated but were given nothing to eat save a piece of dry bread and a mug of ersatz tea. Then, at 2:00 A.M. on March 28, a party of uniformed police turned up and piled the lot of them into a large van. The escapers assumed that they were being taken back to the camp, so it was with some trepidation that they noticed the driver had passed Luft III and was leaving Sagan. They drove for about forty minutes, came to a largish town, and eventually pulled through a gate into a small courtyard. A sign informed them that this was the Görlitz civilian prison.

To say that the cells were spartan was an understatement. They were dreadfully cold and measured roughly ten feet by six feet, with a tiny, barred window high on the outside wall. For sleeping, a solid board folded down from each wall and met in the middle of the cell. A couple of well-worn blankets were tossed in a corner. Four men were put in each cell and when the bed was folded down, it was a case of 'one turns, all turn.' Each morning they received a thin slice of bread with ersatz jam and coffee, and at noon, half a slice of bread and a small cup of watery cabbage-beet soup. Dinner was the same as lunch, except there was no soup. The dolorous guard who brought the food always promised sausage that night, but there was never any variety in the menu. For lavatory facilities there was a bucket in each cell and another one at the end of the corridor. Since their shoes had been confiscated, it was a trip that was not looked forward to.

In spite of all this, morale was fairly high as the men chatted about prewar things and concocted imaginary menus. Bob Nelson was even able to discover the exchanger of his pack. Denys Street had accidentally picked it up instead of his own on the way out the tunnel.

Through March 28, more and more escapers were brought to the Görlitz prison, alone or in pairs: Mike Casey, pleased at having had his run in the woods but a little exhausted from the experience; Cyril Swain; Tom Leigh; Jack Grisman; Ian Cross; Sandy Gunn; Pat Langford; Harold Milford; George Wiley; and Bob Stewart. The cells continued to fill up and stories were exchanged, though cautiously in case the cells were bugged.

On the evening of the twenty-ninth, another bunch arrived from the Sagan police station. The first pair of this group, Tony Bethell and Cookie Long, had left the tunnel quite late, and Tony was actually the marshaler of the last group of ten to get away from the camp. He assembled his party and set off into the woods and was still trying to navigate to the railroad line when the shots rang out. The group immediately scattered and quickly lost their bearings in the maze of pine trees. Before they knew it, they had come up against the wire of the Soviet compound, one of the places they had been told to avoid. After Bethell rounded them up, they set off into the woods again and finally reached the railroad line, where they split up. Tony and Cookie set off toward the northwest, walking for about two miles before hiding for the day.

The next night they made excellent progress, walking along the main rail line to Frankfurt-an-der-Oder for about thirteen miles. Unfortunately, all of the trains were going much too fast to hop, and they were forced to give up their plan of riding the rails to Stettin via Berlin.

On the morning of March 26 they came to the village of Benau, where they were able to hole up in a barn. Their plan was to wait until nightfall and then try to circle around the village under cover of darkness. On their first attempt, Tony and Cookie became badly bogged down in a plowed field and decided to return to their barn and try again the next night. They met with the same result, so they tried to find a slow freight train at the local rail yard. When this, too, proved futile, they returned in disgust to the barn.

On the following morning, the twenty-eighth, they realized that the village would be impossible to bypass in darkness so Tony and Cookie waited until noon, when they believed most of the workers would be at lunch, and set off along the slightly raised shoulder of the plowed field. They were cheered by their progress and had nearly made it around the village when a uniformed Home Guardsman stopped them. He seemed quite thick and had no idea who they might be, but decided to arrest them anyway. The pair spent a few hours in the local lockup and were then escorted to the Kripo office in Sorau, where their identities were verified. Once they admitted to being escaped POWs, Tony and Cookie were taken directly to the Sagan prison.

They spent the rest of the night there, and later in the morning Adam Kolanowski was brought in, having fallen afoul of the Home Guard nearby. In the afternoon, Johnny Pohe and Al Hake appeared. They had had a particularly rough journey and were suffering from frostbite, Al being the worse affected.

There was a sixth member of this group. On the night of March 27, Flight Lieutenant Max Ellis had escaped from Belaria by hiding in the tarpaulin of a truck that came into the camp with a load of stones. Ellis got clean away and began walking north toward Stettin but was recaptured at Christianstadt and taken to the Sagan police station. When the five from North Compound were shipped to Görlitz on the evening of the twenty-ninth, he was included in the purge.

*

At the Görlitz prison, Al Hake's frostbite was causing some concern, and Pat Langford and Johnny Pohe were crouched over Al in their cell trying to find some way to soothe the pain. Suddenly the door banged open and in walked Mick Shand, the last man to get away from the camp on the night of the escape.

After running from the scene, Mick walked due south for about an hour and then hid for the day, starting again at dusk. For three more days he repeated the ritual, walking by night and resting by day, until the morning of March 29, when he had traveled as far as Kohlfurt. There he was waiting by a siding to jump a freight train when he was questioned and detained by a pair of railroad workers. He was immediately turned over to the police but in the shuffle was able to discard his papers identifying him as a Romanian worker.

Mick Shand was the last to reach Görlitz, by which time there were thirty-five escapers packed into the tiny cells. They were a pretty ragged-looking lot, but most had been able to reconvert their roughly altered service dress by pulling off the cloth button covers or reattaching service buttons and insignia that had been carried for that very purpose. Now they looked more or less like normal prisoners of war. Both Ogilvie and Shand wore army battle dress and greatcoats, while Les Brodrick and George Wiley wore RAF battle dress with enlisted men's greatcoats, shortened to look less military. Tony Bethell finished off a similar wardrobe with US Army boots. Denys Street looked the most presentable of all, despite the heavy trek in the snow. He wore an RAF officer's tunic, complete with buttons and rank stripes, service trousers, and an army greatcoat.

*

On the morning of the escape, the regular conference at Hitler's headquarters had gotten off to a bad start. The Führer was in a testy mood because of the night's raid on Berlin, and Gestapo chief Heinrich Himmler was sullen and grim-faced. OKW chief Wilhelm Keitel said little as well and was hoping to get through the meeting without news of the escape reaching Hitler's ears. Keitel believed that most of the escapers could be recaptured during the day, thereby avoiding much embarrassment for all concerned, particularly himself. So Keitel squirmed in his seat a bit when Himmler started to speak toward the end of the conference.

'One more small point, *mein Führer*,' he began. 'There has been another escape from the prisoner-of-war camp at Sagan. It appears that upward of seventy air force officers may be at large at this moment. The search procedures have been instituted but I imagine we will have to mobilize perhaps seventy thousand auxiliaries to deal with the matter.'

Keitel was furious with Himmler for spilling the truth, but his anger was overshadowed by Hitler's rage. 'That is the tenth time that dozens of officer prisoners have escaped!' he screamed at his OKW chief. 'These officers are an enormous danger. You don't realize that in view of the six million foreign people who are prisoners and workers in Germany, they are the leaders who could organize an uprising!' Stopping for a moment to regain his breath, Hitler said more quietly, 'The escaped air force officers are to be turned over to Himmler immediately.'

Himmler listened to Keitel's halfhearted protests, which only seemed to whip Hitler into a greater rage. 'They are all to be shot!' he screamed. 'All of them – they will not trouble us again!'

At this, Himmler finally spoke up, waving down Keitel's objections. 'I am sure the Führer doesn't mean all of them,' he said soothingly. 'That would do great harm to our relations with the neutral countries. Executions must certainly take place, but not all of them.'

'More than half, then!' barked Hitler. 'More than half of these escapers are to be shot!'

'Perhaps fifty would be a suitable number,' suggested Himmler. 'Very well, I shall contact my deputy Kaltenbrunner and have him draft an order. Leave the matter in my hands, *mein Führer*.'

And so it was decided.

Chapter 17

THE TRAIN TRAVELERS

IN THE CELLS AT Görlitz, an informal postmortem of the escape was under way. The prisoners had been able to make a rough count of their own number and realized that they accounted for a good percentage of the walkers, which was not unexpected. But everyone was curious to know how the train travelers were faring. Surely some of them must be well on their way by now, they said. Had the men in Görlitz known the truth, their spirits would not have been buoyed, for the train travelers were not doing as well as many had hoped. They had covered great distances but in many cases had lost their liberty even before some of the hardarsers.

*

Ironically, Roger Bushell and Bernard Scheidhauer were the first of the train travelers to be recaptured. After talking to Plunkett and Dvorak at Breslau, they made good progress in their journey westward but on the morning of March 26 were stopped at the Saarbrücken station and arrested when a recent change in form in their papers was noticed. Roger's efforts to sway the official with his faultless German were waved away, and the two were immediately taken into custody. After many months of careful preparation, Big X's escape came as a terrible anticlimax.

*

Leaving Breslau, John Stevens and Johannes Gouws split up for the middle portion of their journey, planning to rendezvous again near Konstanz to cross the Swiss border together. Stevens, with a better command of German, traveled by express train, while Gouws took local trains. They both got south of Munich but were recaptured following paper checks at different stations on the morning of the twenty-ninth. They met up again at the Munich police station, where Johannes and John were stuffed into a tiny cell measuring no more than two feet by five feet. The police interrogated them at length and examined the scant possessions they carried in two cardboard boxes, later stripping them and going over their clothes with a fine-tooth comb. The officials tried to squeeze full confessions out of the two, but the South Africans refused to cooperate.

*

The train from Sagan to Berlin had reached the German capital at about seven-thirty on the morning of the twenty-fifth. There had been no paper checks, and Arnold Christensen, Jimmy Catanach, Halldor Espelid, and Nils Fuglesang took this as a good omen. They continued north toward Denmark, but their luck ran out at Flensburg, near the border, on March 28. A suspicious policeman asked to see inside their briefcases, which contained cans of escape food and then examined their altered greatcoats, which were lined with a material not found in civilian clothes. Tipped off by this, the policeman took the four in and passed them on to the Kripo. The Kripo were evidently quite pleased with their catch and photographed each of them, looking a bit drawn but still resolute.

*

The express to Frankfurt-an-der-Oder pulled into its destination at 6:00 A.M. on the twenty-fifth, but Tim Walenn, Rene Marcinkus, Gordon Brettell, and Henri Picard stayed on the train, which was continuing to Küstrin. The four spent the night of March 26–27 in Willenberg but the next day were pulled off a train at Schneidemühl and put in Stalag XXB Marienburg. They were supplied with army battle dress in exchange for their tailored civilian clothes, and then taken by truck to the Danzig police prison. A cheerful Kripo deputy director told them that they would be given the best cells and good treatment because they were officers.

*

While waiting for the train to leave the Küstrin station, Rene Marcinkus had looked across the platform to see another of the escapers, the Norwegian Jens Müller. Looking very dapper in a converted airman's tunic, cuff pants from Tommy Guest, and a cloth cap made from blue dyed blanket material, Müller stared at Marcinkus for a few seconds and then turned to rejoin his partner Per Bergsland, who wore a civilian suit made from a Royal Marines uniform, an RAF greatcoat with flattened, leather-covered buttons, ordinary shoes, and a black tie.

Müller suggested that they go to the station waiting room for a glass of beer. There an official asked to see their papers but gave them no more than a cursory glance. Per and Jens caught the 10:00 A.M. train to Stettin, arriving just after 1:00 P.M., and divided the afternoon between a movie theater and a beer hall. Then they decided to try the address on Klein Oder Strasse that had been given out by Roger. They couldn't remember what the place was but decided it was worth a look. Watching the building, which bore a shabby sign that read 'Zur Ostsee,' they saw sailors coming and going and, thinking that it must be some sort of seamen's club, walked in to see what they could find out.

They entered a long room with chairs and couches on one side and a well-stocked bar on the other. Assuming it to be some sort of public house, Jens and Per sat down and waited for someone to appear. Finally, a scantily clad woman with heavy makeup came in and approached Per. 'What have you brought for me today?' she said with a smile, her bad breath cascading down on Bergsland. Immediately, the penny dropped: The establishment was a brothel. Quickly recovering himself, Per demurred.

'I'm afraid I have no money,' he said, hoping they would be turned out.

Unfazed, the woman looked down at his briefcase. 'That will do,' she said, turning toward the door. 'Let's go upstairs.'

'But I need that,' Per stammered. 'My friend and I will go and borrow some money from an acquaintance – we shall be back.' With slight bows, the two hurried out.

Coming down the steps, they were stopped by a young Pole who asked in German if they had any black-market goods to sell. They replied in the negative and said they were looking for a Swedish sailor to help find an old friend sailing out of Göteborg. The Pole hailed a passing man, introduced him to Per and Jens, and sidled off. Quickly revealing their identities, the Norwegians asked about the prospects for stowing away. It turned out that the Swede's ship was due to leave that night, and he told them to meet him at the same spot at 8:00 P.M. and that they would be smuggled aboard. Hardly able to contain their excitement, the two passed a few nervous hours before returning for the rendezvous. The sailor led them by a roundabout route to the docks and eventually smuggled them through the gate and told them to wait behind a pile of cargo for his signal. The sailor vanished up the gangplank, and Per and Jens waited. After an hour, no signal had come and then the two were dismayed to see the ship prepare to sail. As they hunched behind the crates, their ticket to freedom steamed up and pulled away from the pier.

Their disappointment turned to alarm when the Norwegians realized that they were now stranded on the dock. Should they be discovered there, the punishment would be dire. With no other option, Bergsland and Müller marched straight toward the gate, resolved to take the bull by the horns. As they passed the rows of ships, Per took note of one of the names and memorized it, in case it might come in handy. They reached the gate, and the guard immediately asked who they were. 'We are electricians,' replied Per, 'doing some work on one of the ships.'

'Which one?' demanded the guard, and Per gave him the name he had memorized. The guard checked a list and then waved the two past without asking to see their papers. They hurried away into the shadows, hardly believing their luck. Hoping to meet up with some other sailors, they returned to the brothel, but it was now 2:00 A.M. and the building was closed. Badly in need of rest, Per and Jens found a small hotel and asked for a room. Their papers satisfied the hotelkeeper, and the two slept until the middle of the following afternoon. They checked out and strolled around the countryside, only returning to the city when darkness fell.

At about six, Per and Jens returned to the brothel, where they met a couple of Swedes coming out. The two were delighted to take the escapers to their ship, which was lying at Parnitz, and they left for the dock immediately. Arriving at the gate, the Swedes showed their papers first, and then the guard asked Müller and Bergsland if they were from the same ship. Quickly nodding, the two Norwegians were waved through the gate. It had all been too easy.

Jens and Per were hidden in the anchor chain compartment and told to wait quietly. It would be about thirty-six hours before the ship sailed, and there were sure to be searches. A couple of times over the next day and a half, Per and Jens heard the comforting footsteps of one of their helpers coming into the hold to lower a bag of food and coffee over the high bulkhead of the compartment. The Norwegians munched their sandwiches and talked occasionally but mostly just sat and thought.

Very early in the morning on March 28 they heard different footsteps, the clear and ringing sound of German jackboots. They descended into the hold, and Per and Jens listened tensely as a couple of guards searched the compartment with flashlights. Whistling softly to themselves, the Germans worked slowly and methodically and had just about finished when Per noticed a flash of light on the steel above his head. His heart in his mouth, Per saw the beam pause on the roof above him as one of the guards came over to look.

First Per spotted a couple of fingers over the top of the bulkhead, but they quickly disappeared. Then came the sound of a crate being dragged toward them. Trying in vain to press himself farther down into the chain, Per watched in horror as a gray-clad arm appeared over the wall and began feeling around. Unable to move for fear of making a sound, he just lay there as the hand came closer. The German felt all around his head and then the worst possible thing happened: The soldier's finger landed squarely in Per's eye. Blinking in pain, Per could hardly believe his luck when the hand continued on its way and was pulled out of the compartment. '*Nichts*' (Nothing), huffed the guard, and the pair moved off, their footsteps slowly receding. For the first time in minutes, Per and Jens let out deep breaths.

A few hours later, at about seven, the ship sailed. At 11:00 P.M. on March 29, it steamed into Göteborg, Sweden. The Great Escape of Jens Müller and Per Bergsland was over, and it had gone almost without a hitch. They were through the tunnel in less than three minutes, in Stettin by lunchtime on the day after the escape, and safely in Sweden just three days later. Theirs was the perfect escape.

On the advice of the crew, Per and Jens remained on the ship until it reached Stockholm the following day. Not wishing to take any chances, they scaled the fence at the dock and went straight to the British consulate. The consul regarded them rather coldly and straight off asked if they had reported to the Swedish police. When Per and Jens shook their heads, he sharply rebuked them. 'Don't you know there's a war on?' he asked in complete seriousness.

*

At the Gestapo building in Breslau, a secret teletype had been received from Berlin, the same teletype that had been sent to every district Gestapo office in Germany. It originated from Kaltenbrunner's office at the RSHA and expressed disappointment at the lax security that had resulted in the escape from Sagan. As a deterrent, it ordered that more than half of the recaptured escapers be shot during their return to the camp. It was to be reported that they had resisted arrest or attempted to escape again. Finally, the names of all the recaptured escapers were to be transmitted to Kripo headquarters in Berlin, where a decision would be made as to who would die. Then the final execution orders would be transmitted to the relevant offices.

*

Ninety miles to the west, the thirty-five at Görlitz were trying hard to stave off boredom. They were shifted around fairly frequently, so everyone had heard everyone else's story. Now it was a matter of waiting until each was called for interrogation.

Les Brodrick and his three cellmates begged a piece of paper from one of the guards and tore it up to make tiny playing cards. Each morning they played hands of rummy to decide who would get the first choice of bread at lunch. One morning they were in the middle of a hand when a car pulled up outside. Jumping up to the window, Les saw three civilians in leather greatcoats and black fedoras get out of a small black car. He caught only a glimpse of them before the guard threw open the cell door and hustled him away from the window, but he did not like the look of them.

Down the hall, Keith Ogilvie shared a cell with Paul Royle, Neville McGarr, and Chaz Hall. For lack of anything better to do one morning, Chaz dug a pencil stub out of his pocket and wrote on the wall, '*Morituri te salutamus*' (We who are about to die salute you). The four of them had a good laugh over that.

At regular intervals the prisoners were summoned for questioning and marched through the town to a dirty gray building identified only by a small sign: *Geheimestaatspolizei*. Les Brodrick found his interrogation quite civil, in contrast to their treatment at the prison. In the Gestapo building he paused with some trepidation in front of a large and ornate door, took a deep breath, and entered. Instead of the burly thugs with whips whom he expected, Les was relieved to see that the room was occupied only by a middle-aged, clerkish man and a female secretary. They motioned him to a chair and proceeded to ask him about the escape organization.

'I'm afraid I won't be too much help to you,' Les said disarmingly. 'I only moved the sand to where I was told.' With this, he lowered his head in a slightly embarrassed way. To his complete and utter surprise, the clerk apparently believed the story and merely asked Les to sign a statement that the secretary had been typing. This he readily did, after checking to see that it contained nothing incriminating, and Les was led back to the jail with renewed confidence.

Tony Bethell found two civilians and a stenographer awaiting him in the interrogation room. At first the proceedings were fairly polite, with Tony providing his name, rank, and number. Then the scene turned ugly. The two men began to shout questions at him, pushing him around and generally being very rude. Finally Tony shouted that they shouldn't raise their voices because there was a lady present, and to his surprise, the two men stopped, blinked a few times, and became quite civil again. Tony then became very helpful, though instead of answering their questions, he launched into monologues about the importance of an officer's duty. Soon the interrogators tired of this tack and resignedly closed the file on the desk, waving Tony away.

However, the interrogations did not always go so smoothly. The first thing George Wiley heard from the civilians was that he probably would never see his parents again. Mike Casey and Sandy Gunn were told they would lose their heads, while Denys Street was threatened with shooting. The interrogators warned Ian Cross that the escapers were being sent to a special camp because the Luftwaffe evidently could not hold them. Jack Grisman and Harold Milford were told that their wives would never see them again.

When Bob Nelson was taken into the interrogation room, he felt as if he had entered a Hollywood movie. A bright light shone on him, while his interrogators were in semidarkness, and there was a strong smell of Gaulois cigarettes. The session began with fairly routine questions about Bob's family background, questions that he decided were safe to answer. However, on correctly giving his mother's name as Rebecca, one of the interrogators accused Bob of being a Jew, saying he would be shipped off to a concentration camp. When they began asking questions about the escape, Bob became decidedly evasive. He admitted that he had been making for England but decided not to argue the matter when his interrogators pointed out that he had been captured on the way to Czechoslovakia. As Nelson became more reticent, his interrogators became more agitated, throwing around angry threats of dire punishment, physical beatings, and worse. Finally, he was given a pretyped statement to sign. Bob promptly refused and was taken back to the jail.

Tom Leigh was shown a similar statement, which he also refused to sign. He, too, was told he would be shot. Adam Kolanowski wouldn't say what he had been told but returned to his cell looking very depressed. Wally Valenta came back from the Gestapo building and, with a grim smile, said that he expected the East European officers to have a rough time. He said that the interrogators had been very angry with him and constantly insisted that he would never escape again.

On the other hand, Paul Royle didn't have much of a chance to say anything. His interrogation began with a five-minute speech about how he could be made to disappear and that the police were under no obligation to inform the camp or even prove that he was a spy or a saboteur. 'I'm afraid I've told you all I can,' was Paul's only reply. The German started another monologue. 'It's not up to us to prove anything against you,' he rambled. 'If some act of sabotage has occurred in this area, it will naturally be assumed that you were responsible. You will then be made to disappear.' He droned on, talking vaguely about political events, the Soviets' treatment of German prisoners, and the bomber offensive. There was no hostility, only a dull monotone. Then an interpreter with an American accent told him to stand up and answer the questions put to him. They were fairly standard, and Paul was deliberately hazy about his recollections of the escape preparations and the break itself. He merely said that he was sick of captivity, so he decided to escape. 'I'm sure you would feel the same,' he said earnestly to the interrogators. He was then returned to the cells to await further developments.

Later, Max Ellis from Belaria was questioned. He wasn't even inside the room yet when the interrogator bellowed, 'Who organized the escape from North Compound?' Ellis answered quietly that he had not escaped from North Compound but from Belaria, whereupon the German seized his telephone, yelled something into the receiver and then slammed it down. 'This interrogation is now concluded,' he said ferociously, trying his best not to look sheepish.

*

In Berlin, the names of the recaptured escapers were slowly filtering into the Kripo main office. Artur Nebe, head of the Kripo, instructed a clerk to draw up a list of the names and collect the photo identification cards from the central filing system. Once these arrived on his desk, Nebe and the clerk sat down to make the final decisions. For Artur Nebe, the experience was strange. As a commander of one of the notorious *Einsatzgruppen* execution squads in the Soviet Union, he had condemned thousands to summary execution, but this task was different. Faced with the photographs and personal details of the men he was to condemn, Nebe became agitated, as if he was finally aware of the monstrous deeds he was about to do. Finally he grabbed a handful of cards and pushed another pile toward the clerk. 'See whether they have wives and children,' he said tersely.

As the clerk shuffled through the cards, he was occasionally interrupted by Nebe muttering to himself. 'Ah, he is so young,' he said, 'but HE is for it.' After studying the cards for quite some time, Nebe had two piles on the desk in front of him and stared at them for a number of minutes. Suddenly he took a card from one pile and transferred it to the other, pushing the stack toward the clerk.

'Here, make a list of these,' he said. 'Quickly!' The clerk rushed out to dictate the list to Nebe's secretary, who transmitted the execution orders to the various Kripo offices. The wheels were beginning to roll.

*

At the Hirschberg police station, the members of Willy Williams's party were also undergoing lengthy interrogation. In turn, each was taken in for questioning, which consisted of alternating doses of kindness and abuse, and then either put in a converted lavatory that served as a holding cell or stuck in the corridor outside the interrogation room. In time the escapers were taken out of the police station and marched to the town jail, each manacled to a police officer. The cell into which they were put was small and dank, but they were asleep in no time.

The next morning, things began to look a little brighter. An attractive Polish girl brought a tray of black bread and ersatz jam and, with a bit of food in their stomachs, the eight cheered up. They talked about their escapes and, for lack of anything better to do, the Dodger led the group in some songs. By coincidence, Johnny was taken away early the next morning.

Unaware of what lay in store, the remaining seven went on as before. Jimmy Wernham talked ambitiously of his plans to make money in Canada after the war, while Kiewnarski and Pawluk took turns chatting out the window to Russian and Polish women working in the courtyard below. The warden angrily warned them away from the window and later came into the cell and dragged Doug Poynter into the corridor. He pointed his revolver at Doug and shouted incoherently, but Poynter waved him aside and demanded to see the prison commandant.

Surprisingly, the commandant stormed into the cell later that day, listened to their requests for exercise, razors, and more food, and stomped off in a rage at their presumption. Still, on Tuesday the twenty-eighth, they were taken out to the courtyard and allowed to walk around for half an hour. The following morning the warden came into the cell and summoned Jimmy Wernham and Nick Skantzikas. They were given only a few minutes to gather their possessions and say good-bye and then were gone. Later that day the warden reappeared, this time calling for Doug Poynter and Pop Green. Two days later, on the afternoon of the thirty-first, Kaz Pawluk and Tony Kiewnarski were taken away. That left only Jimmy James cooling his heels at Hirschberg, not knowing where the others had gone and unsure of what the future held.

*

As the interrogations were proceeding, a few of the escapers were still trying to make their way out of Germany. Sailor Neely, who had been twenty-eighth out of the tunnel, wore a naval uniform with civilian buttons, a greatcoat, and a beret. He had a French identification card, papers allowing him to travel to Stettin via Berlin, 500 francs, and 150 Reichsmarks. After reaching Berlin, Sailor wandered around the city for the day before catching the 4:20 P.M. train to Stettin. Arriving at about seven-thirty, he found a small hotel and had a good sleep, checking out at ten the next morning, the twenty-sixth. Neely decided to try the address he had been given and made his way to Klein Oder Strasse. It was only after he went to a house and spoke to two women that he realized he was at the wrong address.

Sailor fortified himself with a restaurant lunch before going back to Klein Oder Strasse, where a woman at the brothel told him there were no Swedes in at the moment but that he was welcome to wait. He stayed until five-thirty and then gave up and left. By a stroke of luck, he happened to meet a Frenchman who was delighted to help and took Neely to meet a friend working in a hospital kitchen.

For the next two nights, Sailor sheltered in the hospital, staying hidden during the day but venturing out with one of the helpers at night to look for Swedish sailors. Finally they met a sailor who worked on a harbor tug. From him came the discouraging news that there were no Swedish ships in at the moment but that he would let them know when one arrived.

Disheartened, Sailor went back to the hospital to wait it out, but on March 28 the building was searched by the police, Sailor barely managing to escape out the back. He returned to the brothel but found no Swedes in the area and then went to the city's main bridge, where he had arranged to meet Wings Day and Paweł Tobolski to compare notes. When they failed to show up, Sailor assumed that they had been recaptured. That, combined with the incident at the hospital, convinced Neely that the city was becoming too dangerous. He went directly to the railroad station and caught the 8:00 P.M. train to Berlin.

Neely was surprised that there were no paper checks on the train, and he reached the capital without incident. Intending to travel all the way to France, he boarded a Munich-bound express at 11:00 A.M. on March 29. Running short of food and money, Sailor wanted to get as far south as possible and decided to risk traveling on an express train, knowing full well that it was more likely to be patrolled. Sure enough, at Nuremberg a plainclothes policeman checked his papers and became suspicious because Sailor's identity card looked new, when it was supposed to have been issued months ago. He was arrested as a runaway French worker and taken to Munich.

In the midafternoon of March 30 Neely was interrogated and immediately owned up to being from Sagan. It was much safer being an escaped prisoner than a deserting laborer. A very affable policeman told him that two others from the camp were also being held. Though he gave no names, it later turned out that they were Gouws and Stevens.

The interrogation continued in a very pleasant vein until the air-raid sirens moaned a few hours later. While everyone else in the building hurried toward the shelters, Sailor was returned to his cell. To his protests, the guard only replied, 'Your countrymen are doing the damage – you must stay here and endure it!'

Ironically, Sailor Neely had probably missed Wings Day and Paweł Tobolski by minutes, for they were indeed at the bridge in Stettin at the appointed time. After reaching Berlin, Wings and Tob went directly to their contact address, where they were well received and treated to a hearty lunch, complete with Schnapps and Moselle wine. They had a short nap; then, inventing an engagement as an excuse to get out of the apartment, they spent the afternoon in a small workers' café. There Tobolski got all the information he needed about a leave and transit center where soldiers could get a free meal and a bed.

They returned to the contact's house and were surprised with a beautiful dinner. The Danish lodger, however, proved to be a disappointment. He was foppish and effeminate and took no interest in the war, despite the fact that his homeland was occupied. Worse still, he spent most of the evening extolling the virtues of his German girlfriend, who was an ardent Nazi. Wings and Tob spent the night there but had already decided to leave the next morning.

Early on March 26 Tobolski and Day, the latter wearing their host's hat, which he had stolen, left the house and decided on their next move. They had a steaming plate of vegetable soup in a café occupied mainly by German officers and then split up to carry on separate investigations. Tob would visit the leave center to see if it was possible to get on a military train going west, while Wings was to go to the main railroad station to see about the connections to Stettin. They were to meet up again at the Winterfeldplatz the following morning.

Day accomplished his task quickly. It was easy to get to Stettin, so he memorized the connections and times and then set off in search of something else to do. With no particular place to go, he went into the station bar and ordered a beer. The next thing he knew, Day was being shaken awake by a waiter. He had fallen asleep while sitting at the table. However, no one seemed to pay any attention to him, so he ordered another beer, quaffed it, and took his leave. Wings tried to find a movie theater to kill some time but had no luck, so he resigned himself to passing the night in the cellar of a bombed house. Finding it too cold to stay there, he retreated to another bar but left again in equal haste when the air-raid sirens sounded. Day was leery about spending the night in a shelter packed with civilians, but the paucity of gutted houses that were not boarded up left him with no other choice. He followed a string of people into the nearest shelter and spread his coat on the floor between two families. The police arrived for a paper check just as the all-clear sounded, but Wings was able to slip out before they got to him.

The next stop was the subway station, where Day had a wash and brush-up before going to meet Tobolski. However, the Pole failed to arrive for the first rendezvous so Wings went to a nearby café, had some acorn coffee and a bit of escape food, and read a newspaper.

At the 2:00 P.M. rendezvous Day was relieved to see Tobolski waiting patiently. He had passed a very restful night in the leave center but had found that it was too risky to get the paperwork necessary for a military train to the west. He did, however, get some authentic stamps on his forged paybook. After a short discussion, they resolved to try Stettin, where there were three options: the address given by Roger; French POWs known to be working in the city; and Tob's sister, with whom he had corresponded while in Luft III.

At the railroad station, they split up to go through separate civilian and military gates. There was a paper check, but both got through without difficulty. Arriving at the destination, Paweł got another genuine stamp on his paybook and then left Day in a café while he went to visit his sister. When she saw Paweł, the poor woman was terrified. Because she was married to a German, she begged him to try somewhere else. As a last resort, she allowed that they might hide in her toolshed.

Disappointed, Tob returned to the station and told Wings the bad news. They tried the brothel next but found no Swedes. With no other options, they returned to Tob's sister to spend the night in her shed. There they found she had left milk, eggs, and bread for them. The next morning the two left the shed separately and met up at the main bridge, where they were to meet Sailor Neely. When he failed to turn up, they decided that Tobolski, the more presentable of the two, should remain in the city to pick up any leads while Day reconnoitered the dock area. They were to meet again at noon or 6:00 P.M.

Wings found the dock area surrounded by fields and a twelve-foot-high fence, so he picked up a tree limb and scouted around the area, poking his branch into culverts and trying to look busy when anyone walked by. Then he spotted a rank of unescorted French POWs coming up the road. When they passed, he dropped his probe and fell in with them. As they walked toward the city, Wings decided to go for broke.

'I am an English officer prisoner of war,' he said in French. 'Can you help me to escape?'

The Frenchmen to whom he spoke reacted enthusiastically. Certainly they would help him, but it was not easy. Stowing away was difficult and you needed somewhere to hide until the right opportunity came along. However, if the Englishman and his friend would be so kind as to meet them at the bridge at nine o'clock that evening, they would see what could be done.

Tobolski had been unable to find any Swedes while wandering the cafés so the pair decided to throw in their lot with the Frenchmen. They waited at the bridge but when the poor workers saw Tobolski's Luftwaffe uniform, they bolted. It was with some difficulty that Wings was able to catch up with them and convince them that Tob was his friend. The pair were taken to the French barracks, which apparently were never disturbed by the Germans, and received warmly in spite of Tob's goonskin. Wings and Paweł passed around their escape food and Red Cross chocolate and made friends with their new roommates. They went to sleep with new confidence about their chances.

That confidence was rudely shattered early the next morning, the twenty-ninth. The tramp of boots and guttural voices awoke them, and in minutes they were being hauled out of the barracks by six uniformed policemen and two plainclothesmen. Tob and Wings were taken to the local police headquarters, where Day gave a long and fully false statement and chatted amiably with a policeman who had served in Shanghai at the same time as Wings. This official also revealed that the pair had been betrayed by one of the Frenchmen.

'Do not worry,' said the policeman soothingly, waving aside Wings's pleas to be allowed to strangle the man. 'These types soon outlive their usefulness. When this one does, we shall inform his comrades, as we have done in the past. We usually find the bodies floating in the harbor.'

The official dismissed them and they were shown into another office, where a red-faced civilian examined their false papers. When he came to Tobolski's and noticed the genuine stamps, he blew up, screaming nearly incoherent questions at the Pole. Tob merely looked vacant and said nothing. The German was about to turn his anger on Day when the wing commander stopped him.

'Stop shouting!' he barked. 'I am an officer and a colonel who has served his king for more than twenty-five years. You will be civil when you address me!'

Taken aback, the German simply stared at him. He probably had never been spoken to like that by a prisoner. He sat down, pressed a buzzer on his desk, and said nothing as the two were ushered from the room.

They spent the next four days in a tiny cell, unable to lie down because the beds were left chained to the wall all day. Then, on the fifth day, they were taken by train to Berlin, escorted by four police officials. Outside the railroad station in Berlin, the escapers saw two cars waiting. Day was shown toward one and Tobolski toward the other. Wings immediately protested. He knew that the Pole was in even greater danger having been recaptured in a German uniform.

'This man is an officer of the Royal Air Force,' said Day. 'I am his senior officer – he must remain with me.'

'I am sorry, Herr Colonel,' said one of the officials, 'but you are required for further interrogation. Your companion is going back to the camp. There will be no further questions,' he added quickly as Wings began to speak again. Realizing he was powerless, Day turned to Tobolski, who saluted sharply. They shook hands and exchanged a few words and then Wings watched as Tob was driven away. He saw that the Pole still had the same charming, poker-faced expression. Day was pushed into another car and driven to Albrechtstrasse, the notorious Gestapo headquarters.

There he came face to face with Artur Nebe, the man responsible for the recapture of the Sagan escapers. He was tall and gaunt with dark eyes and a bony nose; his face was completely expressionless. He began speaking in a dull monotone, telling Day what a nuisance he had been in escaping, despite the kindness and hospitality shown by his captors. 'Evidently the Luftwaffe is incapable of holding you,' he said grimly, 'so you will now be taken to a place from where there is no escape. That is all.'

Wings protested that, as a British officer, it was his duty to escape, but Nebe was not interested. 'This matter is now concluded,' he said without expression. 'Take him away.'

Day was led outside by two leather-coated thugs and put into a brown car. As they left the city and drove north through open fields dotted occasionally with tufts of pine trees, Wings Day wondered if this would be his last ride.

*

Interrogations at Görlitz continued in an atmosphere that was apparently carefully calculated to cause fear. Shorty Armstrong, upon refusing to answer any questions, was curtly informed that his head would be cut off and no one would be any the wiser. Cyril Swain was also told that he could be disposed of without a trace. His interrogator pointed out that they had always been moved at night so no one knew where they were. If anything unfortunate happened, the police would just claim that he had not been recaptured.

Tommy Thompson refused to say who had organized the break, drawing a stern rebuke from his interrogator. 'I must warn you,' he said through an interpreter, 'that you are not in the hands of military authorities but what you in England call the Secret Service. Anything might happen to you without that protection – you might never go back to the camp.'

'I don't care who you are,' retorted Tommy, 'I'm still protected by the Geneva Convention.' The German's only response was a laugh.

'Well, I don't think Göring would be very happy if anything happened to me,' the Canadian went on. 'We met once, you know, back in 1939.'

The official was unimpressed. 'Be that as it may, you are in civilian clothes – you are probably a spy. You show me your camp identity disk, but how do I know that your superiors did not issue it to you in London?'

'Just call von Lindeiner at the camp – he can tell you who I am,' said Thompson.

'I have no time for such things. No, we will examine your clothing.' He pressed a buzzer and a young woman entered. She fiddled around with Tommy's clothes, checking the seams and feeling the material. After a few minutes, the interpreter spoke again.

'It has been determined that you are dressed in military clothing. You are lucky – you will not be punished.' With that, Tommy was taken back to the cells.

Keith Ogilvie had a similar experience. At the end of his interrogation, the official conferred with a typist and said, 'You are fortunate – you have escaped in a soldier's uniform; therefore you will be tried before a military court. The others will not be so lucky.' John F. Williams was also told that he would go back to the camp because he had rank stripes on his RAF tunic. He was told that three others would be returning with him. In fact, only two of the thirty-five were wearing anything that resembled civilian clothes. Consequently, Johnny Marshall and Wally Valenta had particularly difficult interrogations.

As the escapers talked about their interrogations, they discovered that many of them had been asked about Czechoslovakia: why they were all going to Prague, who they were to meet there, and other ominous questions. Though many of the Görlitz group had carried maps of the Czech border area, they didn't know that Willy Williams's group had been rounded up near the frontier. They also didn't know that other escapers had recently made their way through Czechoslovakia.

*

Twenty-first and twenty-second out of the tunnel were Johnny Stower and Ivo Tonder, respectively, who were hoping to retrace Johnny's route to Switzerland via Czechoslovakia. Their papers identified them as engineers at a Focke-Wulf aircraft factory, and both were ostensibly on their way to a vacation camp at Mladá Boleslav. Once inside the country Johnny and Ivo would head for the same inn where Stower had been helped before.

They left the tunnel just before midnight and were to walk directly to the Sagan station to begin their journey, but because of the delays, the pair elected to avoid the backlog at the station and set out on foot. They spent their first day at large holed up near Halbau and their second sheltering in a woods just south of Kohlfurt, but on the morning of March 27 they had the misfortune to be spotted by a young girl near Stolzenberg. She lost no time in warning the local authorities, but Johnny and Ivo easily evaded the three civilians sent to look for them. They waited near Rothwasser for the search to peter out and then returned to Kohlfurt and boarded a train for Görlitz.

Arriving there, Ivo went into the booking hall to buy tickets for Reichenberg, inside Czechoslovakia, but after leaving the window noticed to his dismay that the clerk had given him tickets for another destination. To make matters worse, a young SS officer had stood behind Ivo in the line and was now regarding the pair with some suspicion.

Rather than avoid contact, Tonder decided to take the initiative and strode up to the officer, thrusting forward his papers and speaking in deliberately bad German. He explained his predicament, suggesting that the clerk must have misunderstood him, and meekly asked for the officer's assistance. For emphasis, he clapped Johnny on the back and shoved him forward, muttering something about 'my Spanish friend's first visit to Czechoslovakia.' Luckily, Johnny looked the part, and the young SS man bowed solemnly to him before taking their tickets and elbowing his way to the front of the line. The unfortunate woman behind the window found herself on the receiving end of a tirade about mindless bureaucrats harassing valued foreign workers and, after stamping his foot and banging his fist a few times for effect, the officer returned to Johnny and Ivo and gave them the correct tickets. With another solemn bow, he wished them a pleasant journey and headed for the platforms.

Hardly believing their luck, Tonder and Stower quickly left the hall and boarded their train. When a group of Kripo officials entered their compartment just after Zittau for a routine paper check, they gladly handed over their identification. The documents were returned with scarcely a flicker of interest, but as the policemen were leaving, one of them turned back and looked carefully at Johnny's trousers, which were Australian Air Force blue. Having seen the same color trousers once already, on Willy Williams, the policemen became suspicious and began a thorough search of the two escapers. This time even Ivo Tonder could not explain the absence of lining in their clothes or the English chocolate and cigarettes in their briefcases. The game was up, after only three days on the run.

Ivo and Johnny were taken to the civilian jail in Reichenberg, where they ran into Johnny Bull, Jerzy Mondschein, Willy Williams, and Rusty Kierath, who had been arrested the previous day. The two groups were kept in different cells but were able to chat briefly, and the four mentioned that they had been through a pretty rough interrogation. At least one of them, Willy Williams, was told that he would be shot. They had little time for conversation, though, for at 4:00 A.M. on March 29, the four were removed from Reichenberg for return to Sagan.

Left alone in the jail, Stower and Tonder had ample time to go over their escape between rounds of questioning, most of which centered on any help they had received from Germans in the camp. Then, at 8:00 A.M. on March 31, Johnny Stower was taken away. Ivo Tonder shouted his protests, thinking that he was being left behind because he was a Czech while Stower was returning to the camp, but they were waved away by the warden.

*

Another pair also came to grief in Czechoslovakia. After narrowly escaping being nabbed by the camp censor at the Sagan station, Tom Kirby-Green and Gordon Kidder made it safely to Breslau, where they caught a train for Czechoslovakia. In time they hoped to reach

Yugoslavia. They crossed the border without difficulty but on March 28 were recaptured at Hodonín in southern Moravia, close to the Austrian frontier. Taken to the Zlín prison, they were the only prisoners to be mistreated during their interrogation. There is evidence that their handcuffs were torn off without being opened, and it seems likely that other deeds were perpetrated against them as well.

Chapter 18

GÖTTERDÄMMERUNG

BACK IN GÖRLITZ, THE interrogations had started to wind down, and most of the escapers were expecting to be moved out any day. Keith Ogilvie had spotted a list of about twenty names on his interrogator's desk and theorized that they would make up the first group to be returned to the camp. Unfortunately he couldn't get close enough to the desk to read all of the names.

Then, early on the morning of March 30, it began. Tony Bethell was jolted awake by the slamming of car doors and clambered up to the window to see three large staff cars and eight or ten plainclothes Gestapo thugs. Down the corridor, Johnny Marshall, Keith Ogilvie, Paul Royle, and Alistair McDonald heard the sound of tramping feet and harsh voices, and Keith immediately banged on the door and demanded to be taken to the lavatory bucket at the end of the hall. As he waited, he heard six names being called and then the sound of cell doors opening.

Finally, the guard came and took Keith to the toilet area. Immediately he spotted the six being led away in handcuffs by heavily armed guards. At the front of the rank were Mike Casey, Ian Cross, Tom Leigh, and George Wiley, while Al Hake and Johnny Pohe straggled a few paces back, slowed down by their frostbitten feet. Quickly catching up with them, Keith whispered a few words to Al and asked where they were going.

'No idea,' was the reply. 'I imagine we've got another round of questioning ahead of us.'

A guard's shout broke up the conversation and the party was quickly hustled out of the jail. Other prisoners, watching from the windows, saw the six appear in the courtyard and get into a covered truck. Tony Bethell asked one of the guards where they were going, but the guard didn't know. Someone thought that Pohe and Hake were being taken away to receive treatment for their feet. There was a lot of guessing, but no one could say for sure.

Twenty-four hours later, the episode was repeated. Cars were heard to draw up and then the sound of guttural voices filled the corridor.

This time Keith Ogilvie squeezed up to the tiny window in the door and peered out, just in time to watch another group being led away. He saw Hunk Humphreys, Dutchy Swain, Chaz Hall, Brian Evans, and Wally Valenta; following them were George McGill, handcuffed to a tall, pugilistic-looking civilian, Pat Langford, Adam Kolanowski, Bob Stewart, and Hank Birkland.

Again, the remaining prisoners rushed to the windows and saw the group being herded into a covered truck. 'You lucky bastards,' someone yelled, 'it's back to Sagan for you!' But the cheery call sounded forced and nervous. Soon the excitement died down and the apprehension of the remaining escapers grew.

*

On the other side of Germany, yet another of the train travelers had recently lost his liberty. Dennis Cochran was aiming for Freiburg and planned to enter Switzerland by the Rhine at Basel. He reached Breslau with no difficulty and on March 26 was spotted by another escaper with a group of French workers in Frankfurt-am-Main. Just a day after the escape, he had covered more than two-thirds of his 550-mile journey. Sadly, the last part was always the most difficult, and Dennis was picked up just south of Lorrach, within five miles of the Swiss frontier, on March 30. He was taken to the Kripo prison at Ettlingen near Karlsruhe and subjected to an all-night interrogation. The following morning three plainclothesmen in a green Mercedes came for Dennis. They said he was being driven to a transit camp before returning to Sagan.

The fellow who had spotted Dennis Cochran was Frenchman Raymond van Wymeersch, who had taken the wrong train from the Sagan station. However, that bad start did not delay him and, getting back to Breslau, Raymond boldly bought a direct ticket for Paris. He traveled through Dresden, Leipzig, and Frankfurt, where he saw Cochran but didn't speak to him, and then passed through the district control check at Mainz, arriving at Metz on March 26. Ironically, once inside France, Raymond's troubles began. Bushell and Scheidhauer had just been recaptured at Saarbrücken, and police in the entire border area were on the alert. In fact, van Wymeersch was apprehended on the same technicality that had cost the other pair their freedom: All three sets of papers were missing the same series of stamps.

Taken to prison in Metz, Raymond underwent some pretty rough treatment. He was left handcuffed in a tiny cell for four days without food and water, though occasionally a Gestapo thug came in to break up the monotony by kicking him in the ribs or threatening to shoot him. The second day, an oily police official appeared and ordered him to sign a prepared statement. When Raymond refused, he was told that his mother would be arrested and that his father, who was already in a concentration camp, would be killed. Finally, on March 30, he was driven to the Alexanderplatz prison in Berlin. On the way there, the Gestapo inspector accompanying him bragged that he had arrested Bushell and Scheidhauer in Saarbrücken. Raymond merely looked blank and said that he didn't know who the Gestapo man was talking about.

*

On April 1, the exodus from Görlitz continued. That night, Keith Ogilvie, Tommy Thompson, Alistair McDonald, and Paul Royle were herded together into one cell. When they asked why, one of the guards told them they were going back to the camp. 'You are lucky,' he said, 'because you are recognized as military. The rest are wanted for civil investigation.' The four were encouraged but still leery after the events of the previous few days. Later that night, Alistair McDonald heard the tramp of boots and peered out the cell door window. He saw a party of four Luftwaffe guards come into the corridor and take up residence in the cell directly opposite them. That alone was encouraging enough, but better yet, McDonald actually recognized two of the men as guards from the camp.

With this news, the four began to think their luck was changing. Early the next morning, Keith, Tommy, Paul, and Alistair were taken from the prison under escort. The party of Luftwaffe guards who accompanied them had spent the night in the cell. They were marched to the train station and from there were taken by rail out of Görlitz.

*

It was now more than a week since the escape but, for some of the airmen, the drama was far from over. Tony Hayter was traveling as a Danish businessman and, like Dennis Cochran, was on his way to the Swiss frontier. After leaving Breslau he headed west and eventually arrived at Mulhouse, just inside the French border and close to Basel.

He spent a couple of days there planning his assault on the border and on April 4 started to head south.

The *Grossfahndung* was still in force, though, and when Hayter was stopped by three Home Guardsmen on the road between Mulhouse and Altkirch, he was told that all foreigners were being taken to the frontier police post at Zillesheim. There the inspector noted that, on Tony's papers, the issuing office of Leipzig had been misspelled as Leipsich in one place. Further investigation revealed that there was too much color variation in the official stamps. Tony had no alternative but to admit his identity. He was taken to the police station in Mulhouse, and was then transferred to the district Kripo office in Strasbourg. From there, two policemen bundled him into a car and started driving east, toward Sagan.

*

The day after Tony Hayter's recapture, yet another group was taken away from Görlitz. Early on the morning of April 6, Tony Bethell heard a truck draw up and peered through the viewhole in his cell door to see what looked like a Luftwaffe sergeant and two guards. The sergeant pulled a piece of paper from his pocket and called out six names: Denys Street, Neville McGarr, Jack Grisman, Sandy Gunn, Harold Milford, and John F. Williams. Mick Shand, who had been listening from the cell he shared with Denys Street and a couple of others, had a brainwave.

'That Luftwaffe bloke,' he whispered to his cellmates, 'must mean they're going back to the camp. If I can get in with that group, I might be able to have a bash at hopping out of the truck on the way there. Nothing to lose, anyway. How about it, Denys? Mind waiting around for another shipment so I can have a go?'

'Sorry, Mick,' said Denys with a smile. 'I'd just as soon get back to the camp and put my feet up.'

'That's all right, mate – no harm in asking,' said Shand as Denys was summoned from the cell. 'See you back in the camp!' With a wave, Denys Street was gone, to join the rest of the group in the corridor.

*

With the departure of the fourth group, the mood in Görlitz became even more uneasy. They had been there for more than a week, and some were starting to get a bit anxious about their fate. A couple thought they might have been singled out for special treatment. All of them just wanted to get back to normal camp life and a good meal. The night before, when the guard entered their cell to distribute dinner, Johnny Marshall had noticed that the letter S was chalked on the door.

'Good show!' said one of the inmates. 'S for Sagan – that means we're going back to the camp!'

'Perhaps it's S for *schiessen* [shoot],' offered another, less optimistic, soul.

Then at 9:00 A.M., just a couple of hours after the last group had left, three Luftwaffe guards stalked into the corridor. They, too, had spent the previous night in the prison and were anxious to get on their way. With little ceremony, they sorted out Mick Shand, Shorty Armstrong, Johnny Marshall, Dick Churchill, Tony Bethell, Bob Nelson, Bill Cameron, and Les Brodrick and marched them down to the courtyard. They were piled into the back of a truck and driven away from the prison.

That left just two escapers, Cookie Long and Max Ellis, in the Görlitz prison. Throughout the past week they had been moved to cells farther and farther down the hall until, on April 6 they were placed in a cell at the end of the corridor. The two stayed there for another five days, but on April 11 Ellis was moved to a separate cell while Cookie was using the lavatory.

Later that afternoon, Ellis saw Long in the corridor and asked if he could borrow his comb. The next day it reached Max's cell wrapped in a piece of paper. He used it and then asked the guard to return it to Cookie with the request that he borrow it again the following day. On the thirteenth, when the comb didn't arrive, Max assumed that the guard had forgotten to mention it to Cookie. In the afternoon, though, Ellis's cell door was opened and a civilian asked politely if he was Long. 'Sorry,' said Max with a smile, and the civilian went to the next cell. Ellis heard no more until late in the afternoon, when a truck pulled into the courtyard. He heard no voices, and in a few minutes the truck departed.

Max was puzzled by the incident, but none of the guards could enlighten him, so he tried to ignore it and think of other things. The next morning he again asked the guard to borrow Cookie's comb. 'He left yesterday,' was all the guard said. Max Ellis returned to his cell, suddenly feeling very much alone.

*

On April 6, a police 'wanted' poster appeared in railroad stations and public buildings around occupied Europe. It was the third such poster issued in the wake of the escape but, after the recaptures of the previous week, this poster included details and photos of only seven fugitives. The first photo showed the smiling face of Sydney Dowse.

From the beginning, the escape had not been kind to Sydney Dowse. Originally intending to travel to Berlin and stay in a safe house arranged by his contact, Hesse, before continuing to Stettin, Dowse's departure was delayed by the extra stint of hauling he did in the tunnel. When he finally did get out, the air raid had started and things were hopelessly tied up at the station. With his old friend Danny Król, Sydney decided on a change of plans.

The pair, Sydney as a Dane and Danny as a Slav, would walk east to Poland and link up with some friends of Danny's. From there they would get in touch with Król's family, who were leaders in the Cracow underground and could arrange their journey for them. Their chances were good. Danny was a very capable cross-country traveler, thanks to excellent orienteering skills. In addition, Sydney had a three-week supply of real ration cards, also from Hesse, which would allow them to get enough food to keep their strength up. For twelve days and nights the pair followed the railroad line east. They made a strange-looking couple, Sydney in a real civilian suit (yet another gift from Hesse) and an enlisted man's greatcoat dyed plum red and Danny wearing undyed officer's trousers, several pullovers, and a greatcoat borrowed from Henry Lamond.

The going was tough, but they made steady progress. As dusk approached on April 6, Sydney and Danny were about to leave their hiding place and strike out again. They had spent the night in a barn about four miles west of Kempen, near Breslau, and were getting close to the Polish border. Just as they were about to leave, though, the owner of the barn arrived and threatened them with a pitchfork. They were able to convince him that they were Polish workers resting on their way home for a vacation, and the farmer allowed them to stay until dark. He even brought them some bread and a flask of coffee. Pleased with this success, Dowse and Król were enjoying their snack when a member of the Hitler Youth threw open the barn door, summoned the Home Guard, and took the pair into custody. They were a scant two miles away from the Polish border and comparative safety.

Sydney and Danny were clapped into the civilian jail at Oels and visited by officials from the Breslau Gestapo. The interrogation was long and arduous and at the end of it all, Sydney was told that he would have to go to Berlin for further questioning. Danny, he was assured, would be returned to Sagan. As he was being led out of the prison, Sydney Dowse broke away from his escort and ran to Król's cell. 'It's okay, Danny,' he whispered, 'you're going back to the camp – I've got to go to Berlin for more questioning.'

A look of terror swept across the Pole's face. 'No,' he pleaded. 'If you leave me, I'm finished – you must stay, or it will be the end of me!'

Concerned by his friend's obvious distress, Sydney tried to reassure him but was manhandled away from the cell by his escort. 'Everything will be okay, Danny,' he called as he was hustled down the corridor. 'I'll see you back at the camp in a few weeks.' With a final look back, Sydney was pushed from the corridor.

*

With the recapture of Sydney and Danny, only five were left at large: Per Bergsland and Jens Müller, now safely in Sweden; Bob van der Stok; and Des Plunkett and Freddie Dvorak.

After their long wait at the Breslau station on the morning of the escape, Des and Freddie were relieved when their departure time finally rolled around. Just after 5:00 A.M. on the twenty-fifth, they heard the station loudspeakers calling for Sturmbahnführer So-and-so and Untersturmführer Something-or-other, and they decided to make their move to the platform immediately. It was already crowded when they got there, but their hunch had been correct. Looking back toward the ticket hall, they watched as the police set up a checkpoint at the entrance to the platform and began examining the papers of all travelers.

Finally, the train pulled in and Des and Freddie were able to get two seats in a crowded car. It was a local train that stopped at every tiny station, and the journey was unnerving. A talkative lad in a Hitler Youth uniform tried to engage Des in conversation, but Plunkett found it easy to act exhausted and indifferent. Eventually the German gave up and pestered someone else. After a four-hour trip the train pulled into Glatz. The snow had stopped but it was still very cold, and the two didn't relish the thought of slogging through deep snow for the thirty miles to the Czech frontier. So they bought third-class tickets for Bad

Reinerz, fifteen miles closer to the border, with the intention of walking from there. Their train reached Bad Reinerz at about noon, and the two were glad to see a throng of skiers in the station. Welcoming the anonymity offered by the crowd, they dodged into the men's room to relieve themselves before pressing on.

Standing at the urinals, Des did his job and then said in a cheery voice to Freddie, 'Ah, that's better!' In an instant he realized his mistake. A German soldier at the next urinal turned and stared at Des with a puzzled expression, but Plunkett and Dvorak quickly ducked out of the lavatory and into the street. Luckily, a heavy snowfall had just started, and within minutes their footprints were obliterated by newly fallen snow. By the time the soldier recovered his wits, Des and Freddie were long gone. From then on, Plunkett was very conscious about speaking only Czech, in which he was passably competent. If a slip was made again, they might not be so lucky.

Now faced with the daunting prospect of a cross-country walk in a heavy snowstorm, the pair headed west, toward the frontier. They hoped to reach the village of Nový Hrádek, just inside Czechoslovakia, and find shelter there. Again Fate smiled, and before they were a mile out of Bad Reinerz, the snow stopped. Buoyed by the change in the weather, they continued their trek. Though the border was only fifteen miles away as the crow flies, they had to walk at least twenty miles around the hills and valleys. At the top of the first hill they had a short rest and munched on some of the food that Freddie had brought. Then, pulling out his detailed map of the area, Des plotted their course. Ahead, just beyond the woods that sheltered them, was a valley with a tarmac road running through it. Carefully picking their time, they descended toward the road, darted across it, and made their way up the other side, along a footpath leading to the top of the next hill.

Reaching the top, Des and Freddie were soon out of sight of the road and continued along the ridge westward. The farther they went, the more difficult the terrain became. The hip-deep snow was very soft and sticky but if they stopped to rest, the escapers faced the very real possibility of freezing to death. Freddie, the slighter of the two, was having more difficulty negotiating the drifts, so Des carried their suitcase for a while. They plodded on in the gathering darkness.

A short time later they came upon a uniformed man on skis. 'Good afternoon,' he said cheerfully. 'You two should have brought your skis also – you would find it much easier.'

'You're right,' answered Freddie, 'but we had no idea the weather would be so bad. We haven't far to go in any case.'

'And where are you going?' inquired the man, starting to look a little wary.

'To Grunshubel,' offered Dvorak, giving the name of the nearest village. 'I don't think it's far.'

'About two miles, in the valley ahead. You'd best hurry up, though – you don't want to be out here after dark.' With that, the man turned on his skis and disappeared into the forest.

Thinking he was probably a frontier guard, Des and Freddie picked up their pace and by sunset had reached the top of the hill overlooking Grunshubel. It was a tiny village, with perhaps a dozen cottages, but there seemed to be lots of people around. Boldly, Freddie stopped an old rustic in the street and asked if there was an inn anywhere, saying that they had some machinery to fix in the morning. To his surprise, the man answered in perfect Czech and Freddie continued in his native tongue. He introduced himself as Bohumil Dostal and Des as his simple-minded friend, Sergei Bulanov, and said they were Siemens technicians working in the area. The old man looked rather oddly at Des's dyed and recut RAF uniform with leather-covered belt buckle and buttons but made no remarks.

He chuckled and said there was no inn in Grunshubel and then began to ask passersby where the most convenient hotel might be. To the escapers' dismay, it soon became almost a town meeting on the main street as the villagers tried to help the visitors. Just in the nick of time, a wizened little man who seemed like he might be able to help strolled up. It turned out that he worked three days a week as a barber in Germany to escape being called into the army. He lived in Nový Hrádek and made the ten-mile walk to work three times a week. He offered to help Des and Freddie, and the two accepted with alacrity. They left the villagers still chatting, glad to be out of Grunshubel.

Setting off toward Nový Hrádek, Des and Freddie immediately had trouble keeping up with the little barber. His twenty-mile walk to and from work each day had allowed him to build up quite a pace and, after their exertions in the hills, the escapers were on the point of giving up when they spotted the border post ahead in the distance. Leaving the road to avoid the barrier, Des and Freddie climbed into the fields and jumped across the stream that the barber had told them marked the Czechoslovakian border. They kept to the fields for a few hundred yards and then returned to the road, where they met up with the barber again. They were now safely inside Czechoslovakia. It was just after 8:00 P.M. on March 25.

Des and Freddie paused on a hill overlooking the village of Nový Hrádek to take stock of the situation. The little barber pointed out the inn where they would be able to stay and then wished them good luck. The escapers gave the fellow some money for his troubles and bade him farewell. Now almost completely exhausted and with huge clods of snow hanging from their clothing, Des and Freddie headed into the town to locate the inn. Because there was a blackout in effect, they quickly became lost and had to ask the way from a number of passersby. After what seemed like ages, they finally came to the inn. It was warm and dim inside, and Freddie went to the receptionist to ask for the manager while Des waited by the door.

When the manager appeared, Freddie identified himself and asked for help. After having a quiet word with the receptionist, who happened to be his daughter, the manager directed the two to the lounge and told them to sit beside a large cast-iron stove that was glowing hot. Within thirty minutes Des and Freddie were warm and dry, though there were large pools of meltwater on the floor all around them. However, no one seemed to notice. The lounge was filled with skiers who were drinking and having a fine old time and not paying the least attention to the two bedraggled specimens huddled beside the stove.

In time the lounge emptied, and after the last patron had gone to bed, the manager appeared again and talked to Freddie until nearly midnight. Only able to understand snatches of the conversation, Des dozed peacefully as they chatted. Then the two were shown upstairs to a room with a large feather bed. There was another guest in the dressing room attached to the escapers' room but he was fast asleep. And Des and Freddie, not having slept since the night before the escape, were quick to follow him.

In the morning, the manager anxiously told them they would have to leave as soon as possible. He had spent the night worrying about the consequences of sheltering two escaped POWs in his hotel and decided that it was too risky. Plunkett and Dvorak, however, told him that it was far too dangerous to leave in daylight and that they would have to wait until dark to make their move. Realizing that they were right, the manager relaxed a little and spent the next hour discussing the possibilities with the two. Obviously the first priority was to get to Prague, but such a trip was too hazardous because the roads were still patrolled under the provisions of the *Grossfahndung*. Finally, after much discussion, Freddie was able to convince the manager to let them stay in the hotel until it was safe to travel. They arranged an emergency escape plan in case the police pounced.

The manager had enlisted the help of various friends in trying to find a way for the escapers to get to Prague, and one of these fellows had foolishly mentioned the matter to his wife. The man returned to the hotel in a very agitated state, babbling that his wife had threatened to inform the police about the escapers' whereabouts. Now completely terrified, the manager again said that they must leave the inn. Knowing that the man and his daughter could face a death sentence for sheltering escaped POWs, Des and Freddie agreed and left the inn that night, walking back through the village to the house of one of the other helpers. Unfortunately, the man's wife answered the door, and when Freddie said who they were, the poor woman let out a blood-curdling scream that was loud enough to wake the dead. Thinking that she was about to have a heart attack, Plunkett and Dvorak hurried back to the inn and told the manager what had happened. At great risk, he agreed to put them up again.

Again they talked about the options. The escapers still badly wanted to get to Gbel in Prague, where Johnny Stower had been helped before, but it seemed as if the escape was common knowledge and that everyone was out looking for the fugitives. Des and Freddie suggested that they hide in a truck or even hire a private car to take them to Prague but the manager said that the roads were still patrolled regularly and all vehicles were being searched. Many civilians had already been rounded up, and it was clearly unsafe to move around.

However, the manager had found a farmer who was willing to let them stay in his barn. It was a far cry from the feather beds at the inn, but it was much safer. So, early on the evening of the twenty-seventh, Plunkett and Dvorak began the seven-mile walk to the barn. The night was clear and cold and, despite the curfew, there were many people walking the streets. No one gave them anything more than a pleasant 'Good evening,' and they came to the barn after a three-hour walk. There was plenty of straw available but, spoiled by the warmth of the inn, Des and Freddie spent a very uncomfortable night, shivering most of the time and sleeping only in snatches.

The following afternoon the owner of the barn turned up and had a talk with Freddie. He said that rumors were flying around the village of escaped POWs hiding nearby and told them they would have to leave immediately. Freddie replied that even if there were patrols out looking for them, it was much safer to remain hidden in the barn than to try to make their way away from the farm. As long as no one saw them, they would be quite safe. The farmer reluctantly agreed.

On Tuesday morning, the twenty-eighth, a laborer came into the barn and started to shift the straw around with a pitchfork. Des and Freddie buried themselves a little deeper, but the man came closer and closer. Finally, just as he was about to stick Freddie, the two escapers leaped out. The surprise of seeing them combined with the shock of finding out who they were sent the old man into a fit and he angrily threatened to call the police. Realizing that he was not about to listen to reason, Freddie replied in the same tone that they would kill him if he informed on them. This seemed to calm the fellow down a bit and, after a good hour's arguing, Freddie was able to convince him to keep his mouth shut. However, when the farmer heard the story, he, too, became very excited. The man was known about the town to have a loose tongue and likely would not keep his discovery to himself for long.

Anxious to get moving, both to spare the farmer more worry and to get on with their journey, Des and Freddie reconsidered their plans. It had started to warm up and the snow had stopped, but there were still regular patrols on the roads. And, since their travel permits had already expired, they had only their forged identity cards to travel on. It was still far too dangerous to move.

It was March 31 before they decided it was safe enough to travel and, late that afternoon, Des and Freddie finally resumed their journey south. The farmer and a friend led them away from the barn, with Des and Freddie following fifty yards behind. When they reached the top of the hill, the locals turned around, walked back past the escapers, and gave them directions and a quick farewell as they passed. Shortly, Plunkett and Dvorak came to the tiny village of Spik, which consisted of no more than twenty cottages, each with a dog that barked whenever anyone approached. Taking the bull by the horns, Freddie proceeded to knock at every single cottage, starting a row of barking each time, to ask for help. They were about to give up when the farmer in the last house agreed, after much persuasion, to allow them to sleep in his hayloft. He said, however, that they would have to leave before dawn.

When the farmer came to wake them, Freddie refused to budge, saying that it was far too risky for all concerned to leave in the morning. Again, the farmer agreed and became quite friendly, providing baskets of food and bringing them up to date on the progress of the war. He also passed on the encouraging news that the road patrols were due to end that night, April 1. With that news, Plunkett and Dvorak resolved to leave at the first opportunity.

When it was good and dark, Des and Freddie thanked the farmer and set out. They had to cover the fifteen miles to the main line station at Náchod within eight hours. They stopped at an inn along the way and had a beer, but Freddie didn't trust the manager, and they left quickly. Back on the road, the trek soon turned into the hardest part of the escape. It was a clear and crisp night, and the two battled fatigue and cold all the way. They said nothing and must have walked half of the distance in their sleep. The only thing that kept them going was the prospect of getting to Prague. By dawn they were within half a mile of Náchod and could see the town stretched out in front of them.

'Your papers, please.' The voice of the policeman came as a shock to the two, for he had appeared out of nowhere. Had they been more alert they might have noticed him before and avoided him, but now they were at his mercy.

'You,' said the policeman, pointing at Plunkett with his identity card, 'have shaved off your mustache – the picture on your card does not resemble you so much anymore.' Des merely shrugged disarmingly.

'Let me see inside your cases,' barked the policeman, 'and why don't you tell me who you are while I'm looking?'

'We are Siemens technicians from the factory at Breslau,' began Freddie, 'and we were in Nový Hrádek doing some work on a piece of machinery. But the work took longer than expected and our travel passes have expired. Rather than renew them, we decided to finish up the job quickly and get straight back to Breslau.' As he spoke, Freddie realized for the first time just how flimsy their story sounded.

The policeman listened carefully. 'There are many escaped prisoners of war about,' he said after asking a few general questions, 'so we've been told to keep our eyes open. And frankly, your story stinks. But,' he said with a hard look at the two, 'I'm going to let you go anyway.' With that, he handed back their papers and walked away.

For at least a minute, Des and Freddie stood stock still in the middle of the road, speechless. Perhaps the policeman couldn't be bothered doing all of the paperwork involved in arresting fugitives. It was very early in the morning; perhaps he just wanted to get home. Or maybe he was a Czech with Allied leanings. Des and Freddie would never know; all that mattered was that, twenty minutes later, they were on the platform at Náchod holding tickets for Pardubitz.

The train left at 8:00 A.M. and stopped at every little station along the way. Though the third-class benches were hard and uncomfortable, Des and Freddie could not have been happier to be on their way again. At Königgrätz the train stopped for about an hour and the platform filled with men in Luftwaffe uniforms. Looking out the window, Des and Freddie spotted dozens of aircraft circling the town and surmised that there must be a big airfield nearby. They also took advantage of the delay to go into the lavatory and spruce themselves up a bit.

At Pardubitz Freddie had one call to make. Before the war, he had rented an apartment there from a local woman. Now he went to ask if she could help. Dvorak was with the woman barely five minutes. Her apartment was across the street from Gestapo headquarters and the woman had been arrested and interrogated for months after Freddie escaped from Czechoslovakia in 1939. She was terrified of going through the same ordeal again, so Freddie left her in peace. He returned to the station, where Des was waiting, and the pair boarded the train for Prague.

They got to the capital and reached the suburb of Gbel before dusk but found the inn closed and went around the back to see if there was another way in. The rear staircase was guarded by a pack of Alsatians, but they seemed quite friendly. Leaving them behind, Des and Freddie climbed the darkened stairs to what they thought was the inn. However, once inside they found the corridor filled with men in Luftwaffe uniforms. Staring at a notice board for a few minutes while trying to size up the situation, Plunkett and Dvorak spotted two orderlies carrying trays of medical supplies and realized that they had accidentally entered an emergency medical clinic, likely for the local airfield. Turning on their heels, they were out of the building in an instant.

Plunkett and Dvorak went to an inn in the suburb of Libeň and learned from the manager that the owner of the Gbel hotel was away until Thursday, April 6. To kill time, the escapers took a train to Kolin and spent the day there. Leaving the platform, Freddie was horrified to see a plainclothes policeman stop Des and ask for his papers. Plunkett handed over his identity card, which the official removed from its cellophane packet and studied carefully, turning it over and over in his hands. Finally he gave the card back to Des and, with a smile, wished him a good trip. Returning nonchalantly to his partner, Des found Dvorak in a complete flap, calling him all sorts of terrible names in Czech. Plunkett did his best to calm his excited friend and the two went to the station restaurant, where, having no food coupons, they drank ersatz coffee all day.

Returning to Prague that afternoon, the pair went to see a barber who had helped Johnny Stower on his earlier escape. Waiting until all of the other customers had been served, Freddie identified themselves and asked the barber for help. The man was delighted to meet them and greeted them effusively. He gave them some money and, more important, some ration cards and food to tide them over. He also said that they could stay at any third-class hotel, but only for one night. After one night the registration cards were given to the police, who might track them down. Des and Freddie spent nearly two hours with the barber and left with the best shave and haircut they had ever had.

To kill some more time, the pair took a train back to Pardubitz and tested the barber's suggestion. The clerk in the hotel seemed completely uninterested in them and, after glancing at their identity cards, directed them upstairs to a palatial room with a huge feather bed and a private bath. They had a luxurious clean-up and an excellent meal, and spent a few hours discussing their itinerary. Eventually they decided to make for Switzerland, which was only a day's travel from the Czech border. They would follow Johnny Stower's route and hopefully avoid the mistake that he had made.

At noon on April 6, Plunkett and Dvorak returned to Prague, feeling a hundred percent better about their chances. For the first time in days, they were clean, well rested, and well fed. They returned to visit the barber and then went to the Gbel hotel to see the manager, who had just returned from vacation. Despite the fact that the hotel bar was full of Luftwaffe personnel, the manager was quite happy to help them and told them to relax over a beer. When the pub closed, they were instructed to follow the crowd toward the exit and then duck through a door that the manager would leave ajar.

Everything went like clockwork. Des and Freddie hung back behind the main pack of patrons and slipped through the door. They passed through another lounge into a conservatory and picked out two sofas to sleep on. They were just about to lie down when the manager reappeared, carrying two large plates of food. The escapers accepted gratefully, and Freddie had a long talk with the fellow, interpreting to Des as they went.

The manager confirmed that the best option was to follow Johnny Stower's route southwest to Switzerland. From Taus on the German border, he told Plunkett and Dvorak, it would take two days' traveling at most to reach Switzerland. With this in mind, Des and Freddie resolved to set out first thing the following morning, April 7. Very early on Friday, the two escapers left the Gbel hotel, with ration cards and money provided by the manager. In the predawn darkness they made the short walk to the railroad station and arrived to find it packed with people. Only then did it dawn on them: It was Good Friday, and the trains would be full of travelers. Des and Freddie took this as a good omen. With more people on the trains, they were less likely to be singled out for questioning.

A local train took them to the main railroad station at Prague, where the pair boarded the train for Taus. At about lunchtime there was a stop in Tabor for an hour, so the escapers used the time to walk into the town and have a plate of vegetable stew at one of the local pubs. At Pisek there was another delay, and it was almost 6:00 P.M. before they pulled into Taus. Unsure of where to spend the night, they finally decided to walk into the town and take a room at one of the small inns lining the main street. Freddie paid in advance for their accommodation, dinner, and breakfast, and he and Des felt most uncomfortable as the manager spent an inordinate amount of time examining their identity cards. Finally, after what seemed like an age, he showed them upstairs to a spacious and pleasant room.

The escapers had a very good dinner in the inn's restaurant, though their complete enjoyment of the meal was prevented by the fact that the manager's son was now scrutinizing their identity cards, which they had left at the front desk according to standard practice. To cap it all off, as Des was returning from the men's room after dinner, he accidentally bowled over a German officer in the darkened corridor. It was difficult to tell who was more embarrassed by the collision, and after profuse apologies on both sides, Des and the officer parted the best of friends. Freddie, however, was distraught when he heard of the incident and begged Des to be more careful in the future.

After dinner, Plunkett and Dvorak discussed their next move and, for the first time in their fourteen-day trek, they had a serious disagreement on strategy. The two agreed that the hotel manager would probably report them to the police first thing in the morning, and Des believed that they could safely get away from the town and cross the border to Fürth, in Germany, on foot. Freddie, however, insisted that they go back up the line to Klattau, to throw the police off their trail by making it appear as if they were going into Czechoslovakia for Easter. Then they could double back to the border and cross on foot after the fuss had died down. For most of the evening they argued the point, Des maintaining that Johnny Stower had had no difficulty crossing the border the previous year and Freddie insisting that they had to make some kind of diversion. In the end, Dvorak's judgment won out. Remembering their agreement that Freddie would have the final say on everything while they were in Czechoslovakia, Des reluctantly agreed to go back to Klattau.

At ten the next morning, Des and Freddie left Taus. The journey went without incident at first, but the train stopped about two hundred yards outside the Klattau station and all of the passengers disembarked to walk to the ticket collectors' boxes. There was a large crowd and no policemen were visible, so Des and Freddie were not unduly worried. Dvorak went first and passed through the barrier unhindered, but Des was stopped by a Czech railroad policeman, who asked for his travel permit, which Plunkett did not have. Watching from the safety of the booking hall, Freddie unwisely decided to go back and help Des out of the jam. He argued volubly with the policeman, but his explanations were ignored. The man insisted that they go to the local police station, where a call would be placed to Breslau, the issuing office listed on their *Ausweise*, to verify their identities.

Realizing that the game was up after two weeks, Des nearly collapsed on the platform as the stress of the past two weeks finally caught up with him. He managed to collect himself, though, and he and Freddie were led to the police station and placed in the cells. After an hour, the policeman returned and informed them that their identities had been proved false. They would have to accompany him to the Gestapo office, he said. The two were put into a cell together while the Gestapo tried to establish their identities. When they became convinced that the escapers were actually paratroopers who had been dropped from England, Des and Freddie decided that it was time to own up. However, their interrogation at Klattau got off to a bad start. When asked for their birth dates, Des and Freddie refused to cooperate and were told that they would be shot if they persisted in being unhelpful. With apparently genuine curiosity, Des replied, 'How do you expect to get our birth dates if we're dead?'

This was not at all what the Gestapo wanted to hear. The agent interrogating the two flew into a rage and screamed at them to cease their impudent behavior. After a long tirade, he finally calmed down enough to continue the interrogation, which progressed in Czech, with Freddie interpreting for Des. They had already agreed on a story to shield their helpers, and Freddie stuck doggedly to the concocted tale, stressing again and again that it was an officer's duty to escape. Finally, an escort was summoned and the escapers were taken back to their cell. Realizing that further interrogation likely awaited them, Des and Freddie went over their story again and again, to make sure there were no loopholes. After repeating the tale upward of a hundred times, both could almost recite it in their sleep.

The following day the two were put into separate cells and left to ponder their fate. Freddie was visited by a German policeman, who assured him that they would both be shot. Des was a little more optimistic, believing they were facing an indefinite stay with the Gestapo. So with that amount of time to while away, Plunkett invented all sorts of mental problems to keep his mind occupied. One of his pastimes was to devise a new numeric system based not on ten but on twelve, with extra numbers after four and nine. That little problem kept his thoughts occupied for a good many days. Later he decided to pull his little table up to the cell window and see what was happening in the courtyard. The sight that greeted him was appalling. In the middle of the courtyard stood a man with barely enough flesh to cover his bones. Occasionally he took a few shuffling steps, but the mere effort of moving seemed to exhaust him. He seemed to have barely enough energy to fall into his grave. Angered by the sight, Des challenged his guard about the walking skeleton. He was told that looking out of the window was strictly forbidden and he would be shot if it happened again.

Finally, on May 4, a large black touring car pulled up to the prison. Plunkett and Dvorak's meager possessions were returned to them and they were pushed into the backseat of the car. It was a beautiful, sunny day, but as the car drove through the green and treed countryside, Des and Freddie could only wonder if the threats they had received at Klattau would be carried out.

*

That left one still unaccounted for. From Breslau, Bob van der Stok had boldly bought a direct ticket to Alkmaar in Holland. It meant three changes – at Dresden, Hannover, and Oldenzaal – but Bob decided it was worth the risk to get as far away from the camp as quickly as possible. He caught the train for Dresden and found a seat in a stuffy, packed compartment. The smell of stale food and body odor was almost suffocating, but the feeling of freedom made Bob enjoy every moment of the trip.

It was about 10:00 A.M. when the train pulled into the huge Dresden station, and van der Stok had most of the day to kill before his next departure. He sought the dark anonymity of a movie theater and spent the afternoon watching cartoons, short comedies, and German war newsreels. At dinnertime it was back to the station, where he ordered a glass of beer and a portion of bread and sausage. The beer was stale and the sausage tasteless, but everyone else on the platform was partaking, so Bob joined in. Just before 8:00 P.M., the loudspeaker crackled: '*Hannover, Oldenzaal, Bahnsteig fünf.*' The voice was muffled and guttural but still strangely comforting to the escaper; just hearing the name of a Dutch town made Bob's goal seem that much nearer. There was an hour's wait at Hannover, and then the train continued to Oldenzaal. This was the border checkpoint into Holland and would be the most dangerous part of the journey so far.

Bob would have preferred to get off at a small station and cross the border on foot, but because Oldenzaal was inside Holland, he was forced to go through the police checkpoint. As a precaution, he took a package of coffee, carried for bartering, out of his briefcase and hid it in the lavatory. With his pulse quickening, Bob got off the train with the rest of the passengers and lined up before the desk on the platform. After a few minutes, he was at the front of the line.

'*Papieren*,' asked the Gestapo man curtly. Bob produced his train ticket and the Gordon Brettell–forged travel pass. The man turned over the pass and looked at the fake stamp on the back.

'*Wohin?*' (Where to?) he inquired.

'Alkmaar,' replied Bob, exaggerating his Dutch accent.

Again the agent looked at the ticket and travel pass. Finally he initialed the back of the pass and handed both back to Bob. '*Weiter*,' he called, waving van der Stok through. Bob went back to the train, retrieved his coffee, and sat down again in the compartment. It had all been too easy. The time was 6:00 A.M., twenty-four hours after the discovery of the tunnel.

Now in Holland, Bob could breathe a little easier, but his mind was still racing. He admitted to himself that by now the Germans would have discovered the tunnel and would likely have the names of those prisoners who had escaped. And if the Gestapo knew that a Dutchman had escaped and that someone had bought a ticket from Breslau to Alkmaar, they might well put two and two together and be waiting for him at the station. When the train pulled into Utrecht, the stop before Alkmaar, Bob got off.

It was a strange feeling to be a fugitive in a city where he had once lived as a student. He passed many familiar haunts but didn't dare go in any of them. The occupation had changed Holland, and it was difficult to know who could be trusted. Finally, Bob decided to call on two of his university professors about whom he had no doubts. When he rang the bell of the first house, a young girl answered and asked him in. The professor and his family greeted him warmly, gave him a meal, and let him have a bath. They were not overly shocked by his arrival. On the contrary, they seemed to regard the visit of a wanted man as something of an everyday occurrence. The other professor was invited over, and the three talked for hours about Bob's experiences in the RAF and in camp, and about the ever-deteriorating situation in Holland. For Bob, it felt just like a family reunion.

A safe house was arranged for him in Amersfoort, and van der Stok was welcomed by another family that was risking so much to help him. He spent three weeks there, but the local underground could do little to assist him. Perhaps they had been hurt by recent arrests, or perhaps they were just not convinced of Bob's identity. In any case, the Dutchman decided to strike out on his own and follow the route he had tried to use in 1940, during his first escape from Holland. The underground gave him directions to a safe house near Maastricht, where other resisters would help Bob cross the Maas River into Belgium. He was spirited across the river at night, given refreshments at a farm on the Belgian side, and put on a tram for Hasselt. There he was on his own again. It was April 20, almost a month after van der Stok had left the tunnel at Sagan.

With no Belgian money and little prospect of getting any, Bob's options were limited. Resorting to boldness again, he marched into a bank, said that he had lost his wallet, and asked to telephone his uncle in Antwerp, who would advance him some funds. Within thirty minutes, he was back on the street again, with plenty of Belgian money and a safe address, provided by his uncle. Van der Stok went directly to that address and spent the next three weeks in the Brussels suburb of Uccle with the director of an insurance company and his family.

His new hosts were quite well off and Bob lived comfortably, eating with the family and even playing tennis with friends and visitors. To everyone he was just an uncle from Holland. But again there was trouble in the Resistance. Three top people in the local cell had been arrested the month before, and the rest of the members were nervous. They were suspicious of everyone, and Bob was no exception. When it became clear that they were unwilling to assist him, Bob again decided to go on his own.

His host was able to provide a worker's pass for Bob to cross the frontier to Valenciennes and also gave him a contact in Paris, a man he was supposed to meet on the steps of the Opéra subway station. With his next step arranged, Bob started the eight-hour train journey to Paris. It was a full twenty-four hours before he arrived in the French capital. The train had spent several hours shunting back and forth in a badly bombed railroad station and later was evacuated because an air raid seemed imminent. When he finally reached Paris, Bob was famished and thirsty and had also missed the all-important meeting with his only contact. He was on his own again.

After spending the night in the station waiting room, Bob decided to head south, to Toulouse. He went to the Gare St. Lazare, crossed out 'Paris' on his travel permit and wrote in 'Toulouse,' and bought a ticket, for which he had to surrender the vital permit. He walked to the platform, armed with only his ticket.

'*Ihre Passe, bitte,*' grunted the German soldier who was checking tickets.

'The man at the ticket stall kept it,' replied Bob in German. 'How else would I have bought this ticket?' he challenged, hoping this was the right tack.

'*Natürlich,*' said the soldier and waved him by. Another hurdle overcome, but it had been the closest shave so far.

After changing at Lyons and Rodez, Bob arrived in Toulouse and took a local train to the small town of St. Gaudens, where one of the Belgian resistance workers had given him a contact address. Unfortunately Bob had forgotten the name of the café, remembering only that it would be easy for a Dutchman to recognize. Wandering the streets, he noticed that every second building seemed to house a café. Then he saw it – l'Orangerie. How could he possibly have forgotten something so close to the name of the Dutch royal house, he asked himself.

Van der Stok introduced himself as an English airman and was invited into the back by the patroness. Her first request was that he change his appearance a little, so as not to look so obviously foreign. His beret was moved to the right side of his head, and the light-colored overcoat he had worn for weeks was discarded in exchange for a heavy sweater. Finally, a pair of sturdy boots was provided to replace his RAF escape shoes. Then, a couple of nights later, he was taken some miles out of town to a farmhouse that was full of fugitives, including a Canadian, an American, two other Dutchmen, and thirteen German Jews. He was now in the hands of the Maquis, the French underground army.

The group was briefed by a couple of heavily armed guerrillas about their journey across the Pyrenees to Spain. They would walk in single file behind the guide, and there would be no talking or smoking. Anyone who stepped out of line or tried to run would be shot. Finally, to finance the operations of the group, all French money would be surrendered to the guide. That night, the trek began. The going was rough in the dark, and many times they stumbled over fences and stones along the way. Finally, exhausted and hungry, they reached a desolate farmhouse in the foothills of the Pyrenees, where they would rest and strengthen themselves. Ahead of them was an arduous four-day climb through the mountains.

Bob and the American volunteered to accompany one of the Maquisards to a local café to pick up provisions for the group. Crouched behind a rocky outcrop, the two escapers watched as the Frenchman descended and entered the back door of the café. Then all hell broke loose. A patrol car full of German soldiers careened toward the café, drawing a hail of rifle fire. Two of the soldiers were hit as the car pulled over to return fire, but reinforcements were already on their way. Another car and a truck sped toward the café with all guns blazing and then screeched to a halt and stopped firing. Suddenly it was quiet as the dust gradually settled around the café. The two escapers raced back to the farmhouse to find that their guides had already learned of the disaster. A sheep was requisitioned from the reluctant farmer, and the group ate while the Maquisards tried to locate another guide. The group was then taken to the ruins of an old castle, evidently a regular stronghold of the Maquis.

In time another guide arrived and the party set off again. They walked all night and in the morning reached a farmhouse where milk was supplied. They rested there for the day, and in the late afternoon were on their way again. As they went higher in the mountains, the going became more difficult. Often the path vanished completely as the group straggled over boulders and streambeds. Once they sheltered in an icy cave that would have been beautiful had it not been too cold to enjoy. By this time the trek was beginning to take its toll. The Canadian was suffering badly from fever and found it difficult to walk, while one of the Jewish women was dizzy and close to fainting. They kept going only by carrying each other.

The group reached the top of the mountain and inched along the barren rocks in the bright sunshine. Even the sun, though, could do nothing to lessen the penetrating cold. With the icy winds gusting constantly, it was impossible to rest for longer than ten minutes. Finally they began heading down again. The going was a little easier but still required great care. A broken or twisted ankle at this point could have dire consequences. After a few hours of the downward trek, the guide stopped and pointed toward a grassy mountain pass in the distance.

'On the other side of that pass is Spain,' he said calmly. 'You must make your own way from here. Good luck to you and good-bye.' With that, he was gone.

The group elected to separate, with the German Jews going in one bunch and the military types in another. That way, if either group ran into trouble the other should make it through. With the objective in sight, their spirits rose. The walking was also easier. It was still mostly ups and downs, but at least they were now walking through mountain meadows, keeping under cover of the trees to avoid taking any chances at this stage. Finally Bob's group reached the highest point of the grassy pass and looked down into the valley on the other side.

'Well, fellows,' said Bob, 'this is it – we're in Spain!'

*

In Stalag Luft III, the weeks following the escape were surprisingly calm. The tunnel was thoroughly inspected (during the inspection a young airman boldly peered through a window of 104 – he found himself face to face with von Lindeiner and was instantly hustled off to the cooler) and then filled in. The entry shaft was filled with sand and the final 2½ feet sealed with concrete. Raw sewage was pumped into the other end to close up Harry completely.

The expected reprisals never materialized, though there was a constant Gestapo presence in the camp. Special searches were instituted and an extra *Appell* was added each day. There was also some temporary interruption of Red Cross parcels, and the camp theater was closed until further notice. Unused to the ways of the prisoners, the Gestapo found nothing in the course of their searches. They did, however, leave behind a hat, two pairs of gloves, two scarves, a flashlight, and a packet of papers that they were too embarrassed to mention.

On April 26, a call came through from the Sagan police station to say that a number of escapers were being held there. The policeman asked if they should be brought back to the camp according to standard procedure. Still very distraught at the events of the weekend, von Lindeiner exploded. He angrily refused to accept the prisoners back into the camp, saying that they had wanted out so they would have to stay out.

'But they will have a hard time of it if you do not receive them back,' said the policeman carefully.

'Let them have a hard time of it, then! It is no longer any concern of mine,' yelled the commandant, slamming down the receiver. Later that afternoon, von Lindeiner suffered a minor heart attack and retired to his bed. The next morning came the expected communiqué: Von Lindeiner was relieved of his command.

*

On March 29 Doug Poynter and Pop Green were brought in from Hirschberg, the first of the escapers to return to the camp. However, a Luftwaffe interpreter told them that their return was a mistake and that the new commandant had ordered them to be handed back to the police. An escort was summoned and the two were taken to the Sagan police station. No one there seemed to know what to do with them, and they were left sitting in the interrogation room. Later an SS officer arrived and asked Doug and Pop a few questions. He assured them that they were indeed to go back to the camp, and he left to make the arrangements. An hour later he came back and took them to Luft III himself, placing them directly in the cells. In time they were joined by two groups from Görlitz, first Keith Ogilvie, Tommy Thompson, Paul Royle, and Alistair McDonald, and then Mick Shand, Shorty Armstrong, Tony Bethell, Johnny Marshall, Dick Churchill, Bob Nelson, Bill Cameron, and Les Brodrick. Sailor Neely was also brought in, from Berlin. They were supposed to be in solitary, but the cooler was so full that they were packed three or four to a cell.

Gradually their stories got out. They were allowed daily exercise in a yard that happened to be right next to the parcels store, so the returned escapers took turns giving running narratives of their experiences while circling the small yard. Prisoners working in the parcels office made notes from the monologues and reported them to the senior officers. When word got around that only fifteen of the seventy-six who got clear of the tunnel had returned to the camp, a wave of concern spread. Given the poor weather in the week after the escape, it was assumed that many more hardarsers would have come back. Perhaps, suggested some, they had all been purged to Colditz, as had happened in the past.

All the while, rumors ran rife in the compound. Someone said they heard that the camp security officer, Broili, had been dishonorably discharged, and another kriegie said that two of the camp staff had been shot by the Gestapo after a search of the North Compound and the *Kommandantur*. One prisoner learned from his contact goon that Roger Bushell had been recaptured on the Dutch frontier dressed as a nun.

There were a few disquieting incidents, too. Shortly after the escape, one of the camp officers visited John Casson and casually remarked that he was glad that John hadn't escaped because something terrible was going to happen to those who had. He would not elaborate, but Casson noticed that he did look more nervous than normal.

*

The sixth of April began as most days had since the escape. The now familiar contingent of police officials watched glumly as *Appell* was held, and eventually the prisoners were dismissed to return to their diversions. There was a bit of excitement after roll call when the last group of escapers returned from Görlitz, and those who were involved in X Organization looked forward to hearing more news of the break. Just before lunch, a solemn Pieber came into the compound and requested Massey's presence at a meeting with Colonel Braune, the new commandant. 'What is it this time?' demanded the feisty group captain. 'More reprisals?'

'I cannot say,' replied Pieber, who looked a bit paler than usual, 'but the matter is the most terrible thing that I have had anything to do with since I was in prisoner-of-war camps.'

Massey summoned his interpreter, Wank Murray, and, feeling a little troubled by Pieber's manner, followed the Austrian to the *Kommandantur*. They were shown directly into Braune's office and found the tall, weary-looking commandant standing solemnly behind his desk. Pieber and the adjutant Simoleit took up positions beside Braune and stared at the floor. With a stiff bow, Braune motioned for Massey and Murray to sit down.

The commandant remained standing and began to speak in a slow, measured voice. 'I have been ordered by a higher authority to pass on certain information to you,' he said. Then he cleared his throat nervously and read from a prepared statement. 'With reference to the recent escape from the North Compound of Stalag Luft III, Sagan, I am instructed by the German High Command to state that forty-one of the escapers were shot while resisting arrest or in their endeavors to escape again after having been rearrested.' Without looking up, Braune carefully folded the piece of paper and laid it on his desk.

Unable to speak German, Massey sat in ignorance of what was going on, but Wank Murray listened to the statement in stunned disbelief. Hoping that his German had confused him, he asked, 'How many were shot?'

'Forty-one,' replied the commandant, and Wank knew that he had heard correctly the first time. Slowly and carefully, Murray translated the statement to Massey. The group captain's reaction was exactly the same.

'How many were shot?' he asked, dumbfounded.

'Forty-one,' answered Wank.

The silence that followed was dreadful. Braune, still standing, looked more tired than ever, and Simoleit fixed his gaze on the baseboard. The only sound was a slight creak as Pieber shifted his feet. Finally, after what seemed an age, Massey turned to Murray and spoke.

'Ask him how many were wounded,' he said, staring straight at Braune as Wank translated.

The commandant shifted in an effort to escape Massey's gaze. He glanced briefly at the paper again and then turned to look out the window. 'I am only permitted to read the statement,' he said uneasily, 'and not to give any further information or answer questions.'

'Ask him again,' barked Massey when Braune's reply was translated.

Braune looked at Pieber and Simoleit, who never took their eyes off the floor, and then gazed out the window. Still avoiding Massey's stare, he said quietly, 'I think that none were wounded.'

'None wounded!' exclaimed Massey. 'Are you asking me to believe that forty-one men were shot in those circumstances and not a single one was wounded? Every man was killed?'

'I can only read from the communiqué,' said Braune solemnly. 'I have no further information.'

'You will provide me with a list of the names,' returned Massey sharply.

'I do not have that information,' repeated the commandant. 'I have only the information contained in the communiqué.'

'I expect to be given the names as soon as possible,' said Massey.

'Of course.' There was a slight pause and then Braune spoke more quickly. 'You should know that I am only acting under orders. The higher authority has directed me what to divulge; I am unable to say more.'

'Who is this higher authority?' demanded the SBO.

Braune shrugged. 'Just a higher authority.'

It was clear to Massey that there was no point in continuing the interview. After getting Braune's assurance that the protecting power would be notified, he stalked out of the office, followed by Murray and Pieber.

Before they parted, Pieber turned to the group captain. 'Please be assured that the Luftwaffe had nothing to do with this terrible occurrence. We were not involved in it in any way.' He shook his head slowly. 'It is a terrible thing . . . terrible.' Ashen white and visibly shaken, Pieber bowed to the two officers and returned to the *Appell*.

The news was kept quiet while Massey summoned the senior officer from each room to meet in the camp theater. When they were all seated, Massey came onto the stage, told them the news, and briefly described the course of the interview. When the SBO dismissed them, they remained seated in stunned silence for a few minutes before slowly rising and filing out. Within minutes the entire compound knew. An eerie silence fell over the camp as the prisoners talked quietly about the news or just sat and tried to take it in. Those who had worked in X Organization remembered the events of two weeks ago, and the series of triumphs and disappointments that had marked the night of the escape. But most of all, the prisoners wondered whose names would be on the list.

*

Pieber's opinion about the deaths was not unique in the camp, for most of the staff were visibly ashamed and took great pains to point out to the prisoners that the matter was entirely a police affair and had nothing to do with the Luftwaffe. In fact, from the very first day of the manhunt, a rift had been growing between the military and the police over Hitler's execution order. The officials responsible for the OKW POW office, Generals Walther von Grävenitz and Adolf Westhoff, had argued bitterly when Keitel told them of Hitler's orders and demanded that the entire episode be documented so that Keitel would realize the gravity of the step. However, there was nothing further von Grävenitz and Westhoff could do; the Gestapo moved too quickly and cut them out of the matter. Though they should have been kept informed of the progress of the search, neither the OKW nor the Luftwaffe POW organization received a single report from search headquarters at the Breslau Gestapo office, nor from the Gestapo command post at the camp. They were completely in the dark.

In the days following the escape, Westhoff kept up the pressure. He went directly to Kaltenbrunner at the RSHA in Berlin and told him bluntly that the whole thing was madness. He insisted that the affair must be stopped immediately, even if it meant approaching the Führer about it. Kaltenbrunner said nothing. He merely thanked Westhoff for expressing his concerns and ushered him from the office.

*

On April 15 some of the escapers were released back into North Compound, where they learned the shocking news of the shootings. Many thought at first that it was a cruel joke, but they were quickly convinced by other prisoners. They cast their minds back to their interrogations and realized in horror that the threats that had been made were quite serious. The fact that they had survived while most of the others with them had not seemed too terrible to contemplate at that moment.

Just before dusk that day, a lone goon entered the compound and stuck a piece of paper on the bulletin board. That was nothing unusual, and it flapped in the wind for some time before anyone bothered to read it. When one chap finally decided to have a look, he let out a shout.

'It's a list of the names!' he bellowed, and within seconds a knot of kriegies had gathered at the board. They milled around, trying to get close enough to read the list before a fellow at the front called for silence and read out the names. When he finished, someone piped up from the back, 'That's not forty-one – it's forty-seven!' and there were mutters of disbelief as the list was tallied again and again. There were indeed forty-seven names. Slowly the prisoners melted away to pass on the news to friends and roommates. Within the hour, everyone in the camp knew the list.

To those who had been in Görlitz, the shock was perhaps the greatest, for twenty-two names were of men who had been held there. So Keith Ogilvie had actually spotted the death list on his interrogator's desk that morning. The first two groups taken from the prison had been driven to their deaths, as had the fourth group. Many who had been in Görlitz recalled the sinister appearance of the guards who led the groups away. Over the next few days, the prisoners of Luft III lived with their own private memories of the dead. As a mark of respect and mourning, each kriegie sewed a small black diamond on his sleeve. It would be years before the full story of the deaths would be uncovered, but for now, it was important to come to terms with the tragedy.

*

Roger Bushell and Bernard Scheidhauer had been gunned down in a field near Saarbrücken. Roger's death was not unexpected. Sydney Dowse and others had tried to warn him before the escape, but he was determined to go regardless. Many said that he had been living on borrowed time since his recapture in Prague.

Mike Casey's 'run in the woods' ended in a spray of bullets outside Görlitz. With him died Ian Cross, Tom Leigh, George Wiley – the young-looking Canadian who had never been sure of his chances in the first place – Johnny Pohe, and Al Hake. The last two, with their severe frostbite, certainly had not made any further escape attempts.

As they remembered Mike Casey, many prisoners recalled what he had said about his Roman Catholicism: 'One of the things that keeps me going is that, if anything happens to me, I know that my faith will not be in doubt.' Mike had been among the most devout of all the prisoners. At Dulag Luft he had been responsible for securing facilities for Mass, and at Luft III, he had received Holy Communion each day. Casey, like Al Hake, had never lost faith that God would take care of him in whatever circumstances.

Dennis Cochran was murdered on the way to Natzweiler concentration camp, making jokes during the ride that would be his last. When asked by one of his guards about the US Army Air Force's equivalent of flying officer, Dennis replied with a chuckle, 'Never mind the title – the fact is that he gets paid four times as much as I do!'

One fellow who did a lot of soul-searching during those days was Alex Cassie. Scanning the list, he felt instantly sick upon seeing the names of four of his roommates among the dead: Tim Walenn, Henri Picard, and Gordon Brettell, all three murdered with Rene Marcinkus near Danzig; and Tony Hayter, shot by the side of the road near Natzweiler. Of Alex's other roommate, Des Plunkett, there was no word. Cassie sat on his bunk, going over the lunatic antics that he and his friends had engaged in, and felt devastatingly lonely.

Wally Valenta and Adam Kolanowski both had their fears borne out: They lost their lives with Hunk Humphreys, George McGill, Cyril Swain, Pat Langford, Brian Evans, Bob Stewart, and Hank Birkland in a clearing just outside Görlitz. With them died Chaz Hall, who had jokingly written 'We who are about to die salute you' on the cell wall.

John Stevens and Johannes Gouws met their end near Munich, and the thugs who killed them also took the time to fire some slugs into a telegraph pole to make it look like they had been shot while running away. Tom Kirby-Green and Gordon Kidder, after having been brutalized at Zlín, were taken out and shot near Mährisch Ostrau.

When Mick Shand read the list, he uttered an oath at seeing the name of Denys Street, who had been murdered with Neville McGarr, Jack Grisman, Sandy Gunn, Harold Milford, and John F. Williams. Were it not for Denys's desire to get back to Sagan, Shand would have taken Street's place on that last ride.

Nor had Jimmy Wernham had a chance to enjoy any Czech hospitality. He had been taken from Hirschberg and shot with the two Poles Tony Kiewnarski and Kaz Pawluk, and the cheery Greek Nick Skantzikas. Not far from them had died Willy Williams, Johnny Bull, Rusty Kierath, and Jerzy Mondschein. Poor Jerzy turned out to be right: He never would see his wife and child again. Johnny Stower died in the same area, too, the precise time and place unknown. Though he did not know it at the time, Ivo Tonder had been the lucky one, remaining in the Reichenberg prison.

The four who had been making for Denmark – Jimmy Catanach, Arnold Christensen, Halldor Espelid, and Nils Fuglesang – rounded out the list. They were taken from the Kiel prison in two cars, Jimmy Catanach in the first and the other three in the next. On the way through Kiel, Johannes Post, the Gestapo officer riding with Jimmy, chatted pleasantly and pointed out the sights. Then he said blandly, 'We must get going – I have to shoot you.'

Unsure of what he had heard, Jimmy merely said, 'Pardon?'

'I said I must shoot you,' replied Post without emotion.

'Enough of the bad jokes,' smiled Catanach. 'I've got to get to the cooler at Sagan. I've done nothing wrong except escape from a prison camp – you can't shoot me.'

'Those are my orders,' returned Post, watching for some sort of reaction. Catanach merely sat in silence. When the car drew up to a meadow and Jimmy was invited out, there was no longer any doubt in his mind. Post said again that he was to be shot.

Jimmy Catanach's eyes were clear and his voice steady. 'Why?' was all he said.

The second car pulled up a few minutes later, and Halldor, Nils, and Arnold were taken out into the meadow. There they saw Jimmy's body lying face down on the wet grass. One of them let out a yell and made a dash but only got two steps before the pistols opened up. All three were dead after the first volley. Arnold Christensen died without ever seeing his father's Danish homeland.

It would be more than a month later, on May 18, before a second list appeared on the bulletin board, this list containing just three names: Danny Król, Cookie Long, and Paweł Tobolski. The fears of Danny and Tob had been well founded, and when the news of Cookie's death reached Belaria, Max Ellis remembered hearing the truck pull into the courtyard that day in mid-April and the disappointment he felt on learning that Cookie was no longer there to share their discomforts.

Chapter 19

'THE AIR MINISTRY REGRETS . . .'

W ORD OF THE SHOOTINGS spread like wildfire to the rest of Luft III. In East Compound, morning *Appell* had usually started with the duty officer coming onto the parade ground and calling, 'Good morning, gentlemen!' to which the assembled POWs would roar good-naturedly, 'Good morning, sir!' The day after news of the killings got out, the duty officer appeared on the *Appell* ground and bawled in his typical, jolly manner, 'Good morning, gentlemen!' From the thousand or so kriegies standing stiffly at attention, there was nothing but stony silence.

The next day it was decided that everyone in East Compound should be rephotographed, to make identification easier in the event of an escape. Halfway through the process, some of the lads started a brawl near the photo area and, in the ensuing melee, the camera was stolen. Before they would return it, they forced the terrified photographer to give them a couple of rolls of film for their own camera.

Later the camp held an auction of the possessions of the fifty, the proceeds going to the families. Bids were in sterling, with checks written on blank paper given to those who ran the camp's finances. Knowing where the profits were going, the men bid briskly and were urged on by Glemnitz, who was temporarily reassigned to North Compound. He stood at the back of the room, periodically calling, *'Bieten, mein Herren, Bieten!'* (Bid, gentlemen, bid!) to encourage the bidders. Pat Langford's personal clothing fetched 104 pounds, while Jack Lyon paid 25 pounds for Tom Kirby-Green's wooden suitcase. It did yeoman service for Jack over the next few months, but he had to abandon it on the march in 1945.

Weeks after the escape, an official communication arrived for Cookie Long. 'We are pleased to inform you,' it read, 'that you have successfully completed the requirements for the degree of Bachelor of Arts in Economics.'

Later, perhaps as a reminder that the Gestapo meant business, the bunks of the murdered airmen were filled with POWs who had spent time in concentration camps. Pat Leeson's roommates were joined by an American bombardier who had come from Auschwitz. He said little about what he had seen there, but the message conveyed by his presence was crystal clear.

In spite of the assurances of Colonel Braune, the protecting power had not been notified about the deaths of the escapers and did not learn of them until a routine inspection of the camp on April 17. At the same time, further information about the incident was given to the Swiss by Group Captain Massey, who was being repatriated to England on account of his injured leg. With the few details they had, the Swiss pressed the German Foreign Ministry for an inquiry into the matter, but the Foreign Ministry demurred, saying that the RSHA operated under a veil of secrecy. Temporarily stonewalled, the Swiss decided to forward what little information they had to London. After a short delay while the next of kin were notified, Anthony Eden made an announcement about the killings before the House of Commons. His statement was necessarily brief, but the news stunned the Allied countries and made headlines around the world. The greatest effects, though, were felt in the homes of the fifty.

*

Late one evening in May, Brian Evans's mother awoke with a terrible fright in her house in Cardiff. In a freakish nightmare, she had seen Brian, with blood pouring from his head, tapping on the window of her bedroom. She turned on the light, but of course there was nothing outside but the blackness of night. That morning, a telegram arrived: 'The Air Ministry regrets to inform you . . .'

In the Octagon Chapel in Taunton, the local youngsters were gathered for Sunday school. A few minutes late, Cecil Long entered the hall, looking much more solemn that usual. He asked for silence and then, in a quivering voice, he announced that his son Leslie had been among the airmen murdered after the escape from Sagan. Many of the congregation knew Les well, and they sat in stunned silence at the news. Then, with tears streaming down his face, Cecil led a prayer for the fifty, beginning with the words that the youngsters from the Octagon Chapel knew so well: 'Heads bowed, eyes closed, no talking please . . .'

The months following the announcement of the murders were hard on the families of the fifty. Neither Morley Wiley nor William Catanach lived long after the deaths of their sons, and there were double tragedies for the Casey and Scheidhauer families as well. Not only did Margery Casey lose her husband, but her sister also lost her husband in March 1944, in Burma. At least Jeanne Scheidhauer didn't have long to endure the loss of her son Bernard. In September she was killed when the family's apartment in Brest was destroyed by an Allied bomb.

Those relatives in Britain, however, found solace together at a memorial service in London at St. Martin in the Fields on June 20, 1944. Dignitaries, families, friends, and repatriated POWs began arriving midmorning, entering between two lines of Dominion air crew boys, and by the time the service began at noon, the church was packed. On the southern side of the church sat the relatives of the fifty, mothers and fathers, brothers and sisters, wives and children, friends and loved ones. From Cardiff came Captain and Mrs. Evans and Brian's brother Noel, in the uniform of the Durham Light Infantry. The Hayter family was there from Burghclere Grange, and beside them sat Anthony's unofficial fiancée, Cynthia Henstock. The Brettells from Chertsey, the Walenns from Golders Green, the Grismans from Hereford, and Dr. and Mrs. Gunn from Auchterarder – all were seated in the first pews of the church. With them sat Sir Arthur and Lady Street, who gave up their seats with the dignitaries to be with the other families of the murdered airmen.

Behind the relatives sat repatriated prisoners and squadronmates, all attired in full military dress. In the first seat was Group Captain Massey, his lame leg stuck out into the aisle, and beside him was Paddy Byrne, who had feigned insanity to gain repatriation. Between the two of them, they knew more about what had gone on in Sagan over the past year than anyone else in the British Isles.

Across the aisle, in the northern part of the church, were seated the highest officials of the Royal Air Force: Chief of the Air Staff Sir Charles Portal; Chief of Bomber Command Sir Arthur Harris; Chief of Transport Command Sir Frederick Bowhill; Secretary of State for Air Sir Archibald Sinclair; and the commanders of the RCAF, RAAF, and RNZAF. Also present were Lord Dowding and Lord Trenchard, now well into his eighties but still retaining a deep personal interest in the service that he had helped to found, and representatives of the Admiralty and the Army Council.

Behind the military were the political representatives, including the ambassadors of Belgium, Czechoslovakia, Greece, Norway, and

Poland, and the high commissioners of the Union of South Africa, Canada, Australia, Southern Rhodesia, and New Zealand. A member of the French National Committee and the secretaries of state for the Dominions and India were also in attendance. Significantly, the commissioner of police for the metropolis, the judge-advocate general for the forces, and the Central Criminal Court were also represented.

Promptly at noon, the swell of Elgar's 'Nimrod Theme and Variations' filled the church as the service got underway. Then, accompanied by strings and organ played by airmen, the congregation sang the first hymn, 'For All the Saints Who from Their Labors Rest.' From the flower-decked pulpit, the Reverend Eric Loveday read Psalm 23, 'The Lord is my shepherd, therefore can I lack nothing,' before Sir Charles Portal came to the front to read the lesson, taken from the Wisdom of Solomon and the Book of Revelation. 'In the sight of the unwise they seemed to die,' he read, 'and their departure is taken for misery, and their going from us to be utter destruction, but they are in peace. For though they be punished in the sight of men, yet is their hope full of immortality.'

Following the hymn 'Let Saints on Earth in Concert Sing,' RAF chaplain-in-chief, the Reverend J.A. Jagoe, gave the address. 'Their sacrifice was touched by the finger of God,' he read in a loud, clear voice. 'Their indomitable courage, unquenchable hope, and supreme sacrifice had about it, even in these days of many patterns of heroism, something that was unique. Their freedom in a measure lost, they still fought on, doing their duty twice over.' It was a moving and evocative epitaph that was made even more powerful by the final hymn, 'I Vow to Thee, My Country, All Earthly Things Above.' The blessing, delivered by the Bishop of Fulham, was followed by the clear and crisp trumpet tones of the 'Last Post' and 'Reveille,' which rose through the church and enveloped the congregation. To the tones of Purcell's 'Trumpet Voluntary,' the mourners slowly filed out of the church.

In the months after the escape, Sir Arthur Street maintained the link between the families, using his official position to keep them informed about the case. He kept in touch with as many of the families as he could and carefully passed on any news about the affair that he was able to turn up.

*

As the storm of outrage grew and began to spread to the neutral countries, the German government decided that it could no longer ignore the matter. Keitel instructed a liaison officer at the Foreign Ministry to prepare a response giving the German side of the story, but the official knew nothing of the case and could get no information from either Keitel or the OKW POW office. As a last resort, the official went to the RSHA and was given the falsified reports on the deaths that had been prepared by the individual Gestapo offices. These reports were passed on to Foreign Minister Joachim von Ribbentrop, with the instructions that they be used as the basis for the German reply. Neither von Ribbentrop nor his subordinates seriously believed the RSHA version of the killings, but with no other information to work from, had to use them to draft their statement.

That statement, when it finally appeared in June, clung to the story that the prisoners had been shot while resisting arrest or attempting further escape. Furthermore, it claimed that the escape had been planned and coordinated from London as an attempt to destabilize Germany and paralyze her administration. The Foreign Ministry's statement was, of course, dismissed out of hand by the British government, with Anthony Eden promising that the murderers would be brought to exemplary justice. Again, a wave of public opinion swept through the Allied and neutral countries. With the tide of opinion now solidly against them in Portugal, Switzerland, and Sweden, the Nazis were pushed to make a further explanation.

At Berchtesgaden, representatives of the Foreign Ministry and the RSHA met with the Führer to discuss the next volley in the war of words. After due consideration, von Ribbentrop presented a draft note to Hitler, who rejected it and demanded that it be rewritten. That version, too, was found wanting by the Führer, who, after a peevish silence, decreed that there would be no further discussion of the matter. The case was to be considered closed.

As a parting shot, a final accusatory telegram was sent to London in late July. It reaffirmed the original German position and stated proudly that the 'systematic action' planned in London had been frustrated by the security forces. Finally, the note said that no further correspondence on the affair would be accepted.

All things considered, the Foreign Ministry was probably glad to be done with the matter. Concerned with public opinion in the neutral countries, von Ribbentrop likely chafed at having to defend the deeds of the Gestapo to the world, while the security service hid behind its cloak of secrecy. Between the Foreign Ministry and the RSHA, the aftermath of the Great Escape left nothing but bad feelings.

*

While the war of words raged, there were still nagging fears in the minds of all concerned, both in Luft III and in the Allied countries. Fifty escapers had been confirmed dead and another fifteen had returned to the camp, leaving eleven unaccounted for. News would soon come out that Jens Müller, Per Bergsland, and Bob van der Stok were on their way to England, but the fate of the other eight would not be known until the war was over. Their stories were, in many ways, the strangest of all.

The black car that picked up Des Plunkett and Freddie Dvorak in Klattau drove them all the way to Prague, to the infamous Pankrac prison. Before leaving Klattau, Des was taken to Gestapo headquarters for a final interrogation. Having rehearsed his story so many times, he could now tell it freely and without hesitation. He gave a false description of the man who had provided the ration cards and, when asked who produced their forged papers, maintained that he had received all of his escape equipment in one package and had no idea who had produced any of it. Throughout the entire interrogation, Des continually broke the line of questioning by interrupting the interpreter and correcting him on points of English grammar and pronunciation. By midafternoon, the interrogators gave up and instructed that Plunkett be returned to the prison.

For the next two months, nothing happened. Des and Freddie sat in their cells, waiting for punishment to be meted out. Then, one day in early July, their wing of the prison was emptied into the courtyard while soldiers searched the cells for contraband. Sitting on the grass enjoying the sun, Des suddenly heard a faint voice calling, 'Plunk! Plunk!' and looked up to see a familiar face in one of the upper windows. It was Ivo Tonder.

Des was delighted to see his old friend and escape partner and, for the next hour, they swapped stories about their travels. Tonder had languished in the Reichenberg prison until April 17, when a guard came into his cell and announced that he was being taken back to Sagan. However, he was instead driven to Prague, where he was put in the position of having to direct his captors, who had never been to the city before, to Pankrac.

After a week there, he was taken across town to Gestapo head-quarters for interrogation, an ordeal that went surprisingly well. Ivo was shown into a beautiful office, complete with a lovely secretary, and was motioned to sit on a small stool in front of his interrogator's desk. Realizing that this would put him at a distinct disadvantage, he walked toward the desk and, with a single motion, hooked a nearby straight-backed chair with his foot and sat down, smiling. The official gave him an almost imperceptible wink, and the interview proceeded on friendly terms from there. The man seemed most interested in Ivo's escape to England in 1939 and only mentioned the break from Sagan in passing. There were no death threats or dire warnings. It was all quite civilized. Later Ivo was given a demonstration of the other side of the Gestapo's methods when the prison barber slipped him a note saying that his mother, his brother, his brother's new wife, and both of her parents, neither of whom Ivo had ever met, had been arrested and put in Pankrac as well. The parents were detained for six weeks and the sister-in-law for two months. Ivo's mother and brother remained in Pankrac until the end of the war.

On November 21 Ivo and Freddie Dvorak were transferred to the military prison in Prague and at the end of the month were taken to Barth. They were released into the main compound, but two weeks later were rearrested and sent to Leipzig to be tried for treason. Hardly surprisingly, both were condemned to death (despite the services of an excellent lawyer, Ivo said at the time) and sent to Colditz to await the execution of their sentences. Time was on their side, for on April 16, 1945, Ivo's birthday, the camp was liberated and he and Freddie were freed.

*

Des Plunkett remained in Pankrac after Ivo and Freddie had left and had a very rough time. On a number of occasions spies were put into his cell to try to get information, but Des doggedly stuck to the story that he and Freddie had agreed upon. Thanks to his resolve, all of the resisters who had helped them survived the war. On December 1 Plunkett was transferred to the Hradcin military prison, and from there to Barth on January 25, 1945.

Not until he arrived at Barth did Des learn of the shootings. He was horrorstruck. For days he was unable to take in the information and then he began to believe that he must have said something under interrogation to incriminate his fellow escapers. Countless times he went over his months in Pankrac, running through the events in his mind and trying to remember if he had let anything slip to one of the spies. To make matters worse, no one in Barth knew Des, and one officer accused him of being a German plant. Convinced that he had done something to cause the deaths of the fifty, Des prepared to end his life.

Taking some razor blades from his last parcel, he went to the lavatory and was about to slit his wrists when something inside him said, 'Why are you being such a coward? Why don't you face the music?' The voice jolted him, and Des dropped the razor blades and ran back to his room, shaking uncontrollably with the realization that he had come so close to killing himself. The next day Plunkett was removed to the camp hospital. Two Canadians spent hours talking to him and were finally able to convince Des that he had had nothing to do with the deaths, especially since forty-eight of the fifty had been murdered before he and Freddie were even recaptured. When he at last admitted that fact to himself, Des Plunkett had conquered the biggest obstacle to his recovery.

*

Jimmy James was kept waiting in the Hirschberg prison until four-thirty on the morning of April 6, when his cell door banged open and he was summoned out by two civilians. They marched him through the predawn to the railroad station, where they boarded a train for Berlin. Once in the German capital, Jimmy was driven to Albrechtstrasse Gestapo headquarters and left in an outer office. He attracted the interest of a good-looking secretary, who seemed quite amused by him. Anxious to avoid her wide-eyed stare, he picked up a police magazine, only to have it snatched from his hands by a passing clerk, who barked that it was for internal consumption only. After a long wait, James was taken outside again and driven away by a very chatty policeman, who pointed out the sights, or what was left of them, as they wound their way out of Berlin. An hour's drive brought them to thick pine woods, which suddenly broke to reveal a high, camouflaged wall topped with electrified wire and sentry towers. At the front gate stood an SS guard, who was grinning widely through a row of straight, chrome teeth.

James was taken past the guardroom to a small compound, about seventy yards by thirty, containing two huts and surrounded by more electrified wire. One of the first people he saw was Wings Day.

'Glad to see you, Jimmy!' said Day with a smile, shaking James's hand vigorously. 'Welcome to your new home!'

'Is this Colditz?' inquired James.

'No, I'm afraid not. This is Sachsenhausen concentration camp. We're in Sonderlager A. The small compound beside us seems to contain some very important prisoners, or at least some people that the goons don't want us to see. The rest of the camp is for political prisoners, resisters, and other 'undesirables.' We don't see a lot of them either, although you can occasionally hear their screams.' The wing commander looked grim.

'Who else is in this compound, then?' asked Jimmy.

'Well, there are a few renegade Irishmen who played the part of collaborators for a while – we're still not really sure which of them can be trusted. Then we have some Russians – mostly from Vlasov's White Russian Army, fellows who joined up to fight with the Germans in the East and then thought better of it. By and large they're a fairly decent lot. A couple of Italian orderlies, two Poles in the RAF who were on a supply drop . . . oh, and this fellow here.'

Jimmy turned to see the smiling face of Johnny Dodge. 'Hello again, Jimmy,' said the Dodger with a grin.

A week later there was another new addition. Sydney Dowse, fresh from further interrogation at Albrechtstrasse, was brought into the compound. He appeared none the worse for wear and was anxious to start on another escape plan.

Sydney immediately realized that a tunnel was the only way out. The ground was quite firm, so shoring was unnecessary, and the prisoners were left entirely on their own during the day. However, security was going to be a major problem because no one knew if the others in the compound were completely trustworthy. To keep things secure, only the Brits and their two Italian orderlies knew of the tunnel's existence.

A trap was cut with a serrated table knife in the corner of the room shared by Sydney and Jimmy, and the tunnel was pushed out from there at a depth of about 5 feet. To reach safety, an uncompleted and empty compound, they had about 120 feet to dig. Then they would scale the outer wall using a 15-foot ladder that was left in the compound and hare away. All of the digging was handled by Sydney and Jimmy. Day and Dodge wanted to help but were too conspicuous; their absence from the compound might bring questions and lead to a general search. It was no problem for the two experienced diggers, though. They scraped away the firm soil from the face and stashed it under the passageway of the hut. It was necessarily a very basic tunnel. There was no shoring, no electric lighting, no air pump, and no trolley system. Still, it headed toward the outside world, and that was all that mattered.

One day in July, Wings Day happened to spot an article in the newspaper *Völkischer Beobachter*. It was a ringing condemnation of Anthony Eden's recent speech to the House of Commons protesting the murder of fifty airmen who had escaped from Sagan. Wings reread the paragraph and then read it again, carefully translating each word to be sure he had the meaning right. There was no mistaking it. Grimly he called Dowse, James, and Dodge into his room and told them the news. What they did not know was that each of them had lost his running mate in the massacre. They talked briefly about the greater danger of escaping and the merits of continuing, but their decision was never really in doubt. Sydney and Jimmy would keep digging.

Shortly afterward there was another addition to the compound in the person of commando colonel 'Mad Jack' Churchill. He joined the digging team, and the extra pair of hands was very welcome, though the tunnel was only large enough for one man to work in it at a time. As the tunnel neared the wire, they sank it a bit deeper, to about eight feet. There were rumors that electrified probes had been buried around the perimeter.

By September the tunnel was complete, and on the twenty-third, the five escapers made their way through the hole. It was very small, barely two feet square, because of the limited space available for dispersal, and in fact came up under the roadway, forcing the escapers to dig a new exit shaft before they could get away. Finally clearing the mouth of the tunnel, they crossed the empty compound and, sure enough, the builder's ladder lay just where it had for weeks. In minutes all five were over the ladder, landing easily on the soft ground on the other side of the wall.

*

Sydney Dowse and Wings Day had the name of a local labor contractor who had been friendly with one of the Irishmen. He offered to give the fellow a ride to France anytime in one of his trucks. For Dowse and Day, it seemed too good to be true. They would take a suburban train from the Oranienburg station to Mahlsdorf, south of Berlin, and walk to the man's house. From there, everything would be easy. Unfortunately, when they arrived at the Oranienburg station they had missed the last train and had to wait until the first connection, at 6:00 A.M. The journey went without incident, although the pair had to change compartments upon realizing that they were leaving a trail of pebbles and tunnel soil around them. They reached Mahlsdorf by 9:00 A.M., but their hopes were dashed. The house of their contact was nothing more than a gutted ruin. Uncertain of what to do next, they sheltered in the cellar of a bombed house to work on another plan. In the meantime, a woman living in the next basement made the decision for them. She summoned the police, and Sydney and Wings were picked up.

They were first taken to a military prison near the Lehrter station by two very friendly guards, but a day later the Gestapo came and took them to Albrechtstrasse. Then they were driven in separate cars back to Sachsenhausen and chained to the floor in the *Zellenbau*, or cell block. In Sachsenhausen, the *Zellenbau* was the last stop before execution.

*

Johnny Dodge's plan was simple and direct: Walk west and hope to be liberated. Leaving the camp, he was able to locate the main railroad line running to Rostock and followed it for about twenty miles before meeting up with some French workers. They hid him in a hayloft above a pigsty and brought him the necessary provisions each day. In this rather fragrant perch the Dodger spent four weeks before he was recaptured.

*

Jimmy James and Jack Churchill had planned to ride freight trains to one of the Baltic ports and pick up a Swedish ship, and they made good progress at first. On their fourth night, they came to the little station of Dannenwalde and, munching on some foraged fruit and vegetables, watched the yard to see if any freights stopped. When none did, the pair looked at the various trains in the yard and found three wagons bound for Stettin. They boarded one, and after being carried back and forth for some time while the trains shunted, finally started moving north. The train went past Neustrelitz and when it started shunting again, James and Churchill decided to get off and try again later. Unfortunately, Jack sprained his ankle jumping from the wagon, so the pair elected to lie up for a few days and let it heal. On the eighth night Jack's ankle was better, so after switching the destination plates on some wagons, they started walking again. Just south of Waren they shared a very enjoyable meal with some Soviet woodcutters, but the next night they ran into a bit of bother while trying to steal some lamp oil from a signal post on an embankment. On the morning of October 5, Jimmy and Jack were stopped by a foreman supervising a group of Polish women workers but managed to escape in the fog. Their luck was clearly starting to run short, though, and that afternoon they were recaptured by the Home Guard and taken via Güstrow back to Sachsenhausen, where they joined the others in the *Zellenbau*.

In time they learned who else was in the *Zellenbau*, or the bunker, as the prisoners called it. Sigismund Payne-Best, one of the British officers kidnapped by Germans agents in Holland in November 1939 (the notorious Venlo Incident), was the longest-serving resident of the bunker. There were four saboteurs who had been caught trying to blow up the Corinth Canal in 1941, and a number of other British and Continental agents. Dr. Fritz Heberlein, the German ambassador to Spain, his wife, and the Duke of Mecklenberg, all considered unreliable by the Nazis, were also held in the bunker. Another eminent prisoner was Pastor Martin Niemöller, a captive of the Nazis since 1937.

In early 1945 there was another new arrival: General Artur Nebe, the man who had selected the fifty to die and who had dispatched the others to Sachsenhausen in the first place. Some say he had been deeply affected by his role in the selection process, while others say he simply saw the winds of change beginning to blow and wanted to take advantage of them. For whatever reasons, he involved himself in the July plot on Hitler's life and was sent to the concentration camp to be executed. He died, suspended on a noose of piano wire, while the escapers he had sent to Sachsenhausen lived on.

*

In February, strange things began happening. Sydney Dowse was approached by the Germans with a proposition that he be allowed to escape and carry a message of peace to England. He curtly refused the offer. The following week the same proposal was given to the Dodger but he was given no option. One morning he simply disappeared, and the others were told that he had been taken to Berlin to meet with the Foreign Ministry. Then, on February 15, the unthinkable happened. The escapers were informed that they would be returning to Sonderlager A. Back in their old home, they were heartily welcomed by the inmates, who had given them up for dead. Among the group they spotted another familiar face, that of the little Frenchman Raymond van Wymeersch. In many ways he, too, had come back from the dead.

Raymond had been given a pretty rough time in Berlin's Alexanderplatz prison. Put in a room with 150 others of all nationalities, he was held as a criminal despite protests that he be accorded the proper treatment. He remained in the huge cell for weeks, but on the morning of May 24 the prison was hit by a stray American bomb. With three French housebreakers, Raymond picked through the rubble and made off into the streets, taking shelter at the house of one of the criminals. The next day, though, they were back in captivity, this time in the notorious Plötzensee prison. For another five months van Wymeersch languished, apparently forgotten by his captors, until November 7, when he was taken to Sachsenhausen. He had exchanged the proverbial frying pan for the fire.

*

In the meantime, the population of the camp was being systematically reduced. On April 3 came the beginning of the end. Very early in the morning, the inmates were awakened and told to be ready for a move. The first stop was the Flossenburg concentration camp, where the group remained for just under two weeks. On April 15 they moved again, this time by truck, to the Dachau concentration camp. There they joined a mass of eminent prisoners from across Europe, all waiting to see what the Nazis had planned for them.

The group, when assembled, read like a Who's Who of European society. There were noblemen, such as Prince Philip of Hesse, Prince Frederick Leopold of Prussia, and Prince Xavier de Bourbon, and clerics, such as the noted Niemöller; Gabriel Piguet, the bishop of Clermont-Ferrand; and Johann Neuhausler, the canon of Munich. There were other resisters, such as the ex-mayor of Vienna Richard

Schmitz, who had spoken out against the *Anschluss*. The Heberleins from the *Zellenbau* were there, and so was Colonel John McGrath, who had led a pro-Nazi Irish brigade until the Germans realized that he was really organizing escapes and sabotage. Also, there was Fabian von Schlabrendorff, one of the few to survive Hitler's wrath after the failed July plot.

On the evening of April 17, they were off again, this time in coaches through Munich to an SS camp near Innsbruck. There they were joined by another convoy of *Prominenten,* as they came to be known. The new arrivals included some senior officials in Hitler's regime: Dr. Hjalmar Schacht, former president of the Reichsbank and minister of economics; the industrialist Fritz Thyssen and his wife and daughter; General Alexander von Falkenhausen, once governor-general of occupied Belgium and northern France, who had been implicated in the July plot; General Franz Halder, formerly the chief of the General Staff, and his wife; and Colonel Bogislaw von Bonin, who was made the scapegoat for the loss of Warsaw. Others were relatives of resisters such as Carl Goerdeler and Claus von Stauffenberg, and the rest were individuals who had been branded 'undesirable' by the Nazis: Dr. Kurt von Schuschnigg, one-time chancellor of Austria; former Hungarian prime minister Miklos Kallay and members of his cabinet; Wassili Molotov, a nephew of the Soviet foreign minister; Greek Field Marshal Alexander Papagos; Léon Blum, ex–prime minister of France; Richard Stevens, captured at Venlo with Payne-Best; and the son of Admiral Miklos Horthy, Hungary's former pro-German regent. There were dozens of others, from all nations, connected by the fact that the Nazis hoped that they might prove useful some day.

On April 27, the odyssey resumed. In motorcoaches, the group continued south with a contingent of heavily armed SS guards. The buses wound their way toward Italy through the Brenner Pass and then turned down the Pustertal, a beautiful Tyrolean valley. The scenery was breathtaking as the sun glinted off the white-capped mountains. Below, tiny Alpine cottages nestled in folds of green. It might have been an enjoyable ride had not the escort been with them, carrying the threat of imminent execution. Finally, the convoy ground to a halt when two of the buses ran out of gas and the third had a flat tire. Nervously, the prisoners waited while their guards held a conference some distance off. It seemed the perfect opportunity to liquidate the lot, as the captives well knew.

Meanwhile, Wings Day had slipped away from the group to track down the local partisan leader, who, it turned out, was anxious to launch a quick and savage attack on the SS party guarding the group. Initially excited by the plan, Wings quickly returned to his senses and counseled against an immediate attack. He said there would be too many casualties and convinced the partisans to put their plan on ice for a while.

Some of the wealthier members of the party considered offering the SS leaders a bribe to take them to the Swiss frontier, but it proved impossible to act on the idea. Most of the guards were now well into their cups and were becoming more insensible, and perhaps more dangerous, by the hour. Someone managed to lift the wallet of one of the SS leaders. In it was an order, signed by Himmler, for the execution of the entire party should there be any danger of their falling into Allied hands.

Eventually the whole group moved to accommodations arranged by Tony Ducia, a local who appeared to be working for the Germans as billeting officer but who was in reality a Resistance chief in the area. Again, the local partisans were anxious to attack but were pacified by the knowledge that von Bonin had placed a call to an old friend who was commanding a German Army unit in the area. He explained their predicament and von Bonin's friend assured him that a Wehrmacht party would be sent to rescue the captives from the clutches of the SS.

On the morning of April 29, the Wehrmacht unit finally arrived and there was a tense standoff with the SS. The latter were convinced by two heavy machine guns to drop their weapons. Half of them commandeered a car and drove north toward Austria, not making it far outside the village before partisans caught up with them and strung them from telegraph poles. The other half threw in their lot with the hostages.

The next day the group moved again, to the Pragser Wildsee Hotel, a beautiful Alpine resort with a well-stocked wine cellar. While the rest of the party awaited developments, Wings Day and Tony Ducia headed off in Ducia's road-weary Volkswagen toward Allied lines. After discarding the broken-down car, and a number of other vehicles that carried them anywhere from a couple of hundred yards to two miles, the two finally contacted an American Army unit near Trento.

On May 4, a flying column of the 339th Infantry Regiment pulled up to the Pragser Wildsee Hotel to relieve the *Prominenten*. For Sydney

Dowse, Jimmy James, Wings Day, and Raymond van Wymeersch, it was a strange end to a strange year that had begun when they crawled out of the tunnel at Luft III more than thirteen months earlier.

*

Johnny Dodge's final weeks in captivity were, if anything, even more bizarre than those of his comrades. Taken from Sachsenhausen in early February, Dodge was driven to Berlin by a pleasant young officer, who bought him an entire suit of new civilian clothes and installed him in a beautiful apartment occupied by an SS major and his family. The situation was so odd that Johnny had no idea what to think.

After receiving assurances that he would not be compromised by accepting the civilian clothes, Dodge was introduced to Dr. Hans Thost of the Foreign Ministry. Thost showed Johnny to a car and drove him to Berlin's finest hotel, the Adlon. Still asking what was going on, Johnny was ushered into a private room in the sumptuous but bomb-damaged hotel, where he came face to face with a large, fleshy man with a loud voice and a wide smile. Thost introduced him as Dr. Schmidt, Hitler's interpreter. Still in a bit of a daze, Dodge dubiously accepted a glass of Scotch whisky and pondered his lot. He was brought back to attentiveness by the booming voice of Schmidt.

'You are going home, Major Dodge,' he bellowed, 'and I imagine you will be seeing your kinsman Mr. Churchill when you return.' Dodge's ears pricked up and Schmidt leaned closer to him. 'I want you to remember three things when you get back to England. First, no unconditional surrender. Secondly, ethnographical boundaries. Third, the balance of power in Europe must be maintained, for all our safety. I am sure you know what I mean,' he added with a slight smile.

At last, Dodger understood. He was to be a peace emissary in the last days of the war. The Germans must really be desperate, he thought with grim satisfaction.

A few days later, Thost and Dodge drove to Dresden, where they narrowly escaped incineration during the big fire raid. Their hotel in ruins, the pair continued to Weimar and were bombed again. Johnny considered making an attempt at escaping but was unsure what it would achieve. He decided to stay with Thost and see what turned up.

At Regensburg, someone overheard Thost and Dodge speaking English in a small café and summoned the police, who arrived within minutes and arrested them as spies. For Johnny this was nothing new, but Thost was outraged, screaming at the policemen and threatening all sorts of dire punishments. Finally, by the greatest of ironies, they were released by the local Gestapo, who had received an urgent message to that effect from Berlin.

After a couple of days in Munich, Dodge and Thost reached the Swiss border near Bregenz. It was April 25, 1945. That night the pair separated and Johnny walked across the border into St. Margrethen. Two days later he was lunching with intelligence officers in Bern and within a week was back in England. Two days before VE Day, Johnny Dodge finally dined with Churchill and recounted his adventures. The prime minister listened to the whole story with undisguised delight.

*

In the aftermath of the escape and the killings, X Organization was reconstituted in Luft III under Wing Commander John Ellis as Big X. Conk Canton and Crump Ker-Ramsay took over as chiefs of the tunneling section, while Alex Cassie was asked to rebuild Dean and Dawson. Though there were no major escape plans in the works, it was deemed advisable to have a corps of capable forgers ready if needed.

Conk and Crump, meanwhile, had started another tunnel from the theater block. Code-named George, this hole had its trap under one of the seats, so dispersal was a simple matter. The sand was merely taken out of the tunnel and spread around under the theater floor, where there was still plenty of space on top of Harry's spoil. Again, though there were no concrete plans for an escape, it was thought wise to finish the tunnel and see what transpired in the meantime.

Gradually, as the military fortunes of Germany declined after the Normandy invasion, some of the camp staff began giving subtle hints that the prisoners were in grave danger should Germany fall. With this in mind, the new SBO, Group Captain Wilson, formed the Klim Klub, a sort of last-ditch defense force for the camp. Everyone in North Compound was assigned to a unit of the Klub, and each unit was given a specific task, such as gaining control of the cooler or one of the guard towers. No one really thought that unarmed kriegies could do much if the SS arrived to liquidate everyone, but it was always better to go down fighting.

In the summer, one of the stenographers in the *Kommandantur* sent word that it was now official policy that all escaped POWs be shot upon recapture. Undaunted, a bony Scot named McCulloch wanted to give it a try anyway and asked Big X for permission, which was grudgingly given after much consideration. McCulloch did get out of the camp under a pile of cans in the garbage wagon, only to be picked up by some German soldiers a few hours later. They returned him to the camp but things certainly would have gone a lot worse for the Scot had he fallen into the hands of the SS or the Gestapo.

Early in September, there was another, more direct, warning when a small red and black poster was affixed on the bulletin board in the camp. 'The escape from prison camps is no longer a sport!' it read and went on to say that certain forbidden zones, called death zones, had been created in Germany. Anyone who strayed into these unmarked zones would be shot on sight. 'Stay in the camp, where you will be safe!' the poster concluded. 'Breaking out of it is now a damned dangerous act. The chances of preserving your life are almost nil!'

By this time it was possible for Allied aircraft to venture almost at will over Germany, and many formations of bombers were spotted passing over the camp. On one occasion a small force of American aircraft bombed a target a few miles from the camp and, even with the guards' warnings to remain inside the barracks, the kriegies were able to voice their delight at the raid. Shortly afterward, though, the mood was sobered when bits of charred papers thrown up in the bombing began to drift into the compound. They were pages from a Bible.

*

In November the snow began to fall again and the escape organization decided to suspend work on George. He now reached beyond the wire, and it had already been decided to use him only if things turned nasty in the compound. Ironically, the completion of George coincided with another event that brought back memories of the big escape the previous spring.

On December 4, 1944, a funeral service was held for the fifty just outside camp, at a memorial cairn that had been designed and built by the prisoners using materials donated by Colonel von Lindeiner. The Anglican Reverend E.B. Jones and the Roman Catholic Father P. Goudreau officiated, and attendance was limited to thirty officers: Group Captain Wilson and fifteen others, representing the nations of the dead, from North Compound; and seven officers each from East Compound and Belaria. No Americans were allowed to attend. Messieurs Naville and Feldscher of the Swiss legation attended on behalf of the protecting power, and Colonel Braune's adjutant represented the camp staff. The service was short, lasting only fifteen minutes, but was dignified and moving. After addresses by both chaplains, a prisoner from each compound laid a wreath on the cairn, followed by Feldscher for the protecting power. A trumpeter from North Compound's orchestra sounded the 'Last Post'; then an honor party of camp guards fired a volley in salute as the prisoners filed back to the compounds.

*

The New Year brought word of another major Soviet offensive in the East, and the prisoners in Luft III listened carefully to the BBC news on their radio, hoping that they would be overrun in the advance. It was not to be.

After much confusion, the evacuation of the entire Sagan complex began on the morning of January 27, 1945. In six columns, the prisoners marched west to Spremberg in nightmarish conditions. The weather was appalling, and the Germans provided few supplies. Many kriegies collapsed by the roadside from exhaustion, to be picked up by rescue parties that trailed the columns. Hundreds fell ill and some died.

At Spremberg, cattle cars were on hand to take the kriegies to various destinations. The Americans went south, to Moosburg, near Munich, while the inmates of Belaria and East Compound went north, to Stalag IIIA at Luckenwalde, south of Berlin. The occupants of North Compound were taken to Marlag und Milag Nord, a naval camp near Bremen, where they were installed in the former ratings' compound. The camp was in a terrible state, but despite everything, morale was good, now that the end was definitely in sight.

Then, on April 9, came the order to march again, back toward the east. On this march the weather was much better and the kriegies had enough Red Cross goods to barter for food and supplies along the way. Though the column was strafed by Allied fighters and a few kriegies were killed, the march was not nearly as bad as the previous one.

The prisoners traveled to within about ten miles of Lübeck and then stopped and sent advance parties to inspect the accommodations that the Germans had arranged for them. Finding the buildings rife with vermin and unfit for human habitation, the prisoners refused to march any farther and settled themselves on two large estate farms, Wulmenau and Trenthorst. As a precaution, some of the prisoners hung out banners that read 'RAF POWs Ahead' and 'Good pull-in for tanks – 100 yards.' On May 2, after the sound of gunfire had been heard toward the west, two tanks rumbled up to the farm and rotated their turrets menacingly. Unsure of whether they were German or Allied, the prisoners waited breathlessly. Then one of the hatches popped open and a Tommy in a black beret climbed out. Before the prisoners had time to react en masse, one of their number stepped forward and said in a shaky voice, 'I've been waiting for this moment for five years.'

'Hey, Nobby!' called the Tommy down the hatch. 'This bugger's been 'ere for five fuckin' years!' At that moment the kriegies knew they were back in civilized hands.

EPILOGUE

AFTER THE WAR, THE British government acted upon Anthony Eden's promise that exemplary justice would be done for the Stalag Luft III killings. A small detachment of the RAF Special Investigation Branch was given the task of reconstructing the crimes and tracking down the perpetrators. In this they were eminently successful, identifying seventy-two murderers and accounting for sixty-nine.

On July 1, 1947, the first trial in the Stalag Luft III case began at the Curio Haus in Hamburg. It lasted fifty days and produced many sensations, not the least of which was the testimony of Colonel von Lindeiner.

Relieved of his command and court-martialed after the escape, von Lindeiner had been sentenced to a term of imprisonment by the Nazis for his failure to prevent the break. Now he was called as a witness for the defense, who were interested to know what warnings he had given to the prisoners about the dangers of escaping. The colonel replied that he had had no direct information to pass on but that he had warned the SBO nonetheless because he felt uneasy about the change in climate regarding escapes. Then, after reminding him that he had taken an oath of unquestioning obedience to the Führer, the defense counsel asked von Lindeiner what he would have done had he been given the order to shoot the officers himself.

Von Lindeiner, who had lost none of his military bearing, glared down at the defense counsel as if he were a pariah. 'I would have put a bullet through my head,' he said calmly.

When it was all over, fourteen of the first eighteen defendants were sentenced to hang. One of the verdicts was reduced to life imprisonment upon review, but on February 27, 1948, the other thirteen were hanged in the Hameln jail. Among them were the devout Alfred Schimmel of the Strasbourg Gestapo, who had ordered Tony Hayter killed on Maundy Thursday to avoid the stain of committing a crime on Good Friday, and three members of the Karlsruhe Gestapo, condemned for the murder of Dennis Cochran. For killing Tom

Kirby-Green and Gordon Kidder, Erich Zacharias of the Zlín Gestapo also was hanged. His partner in the crime cheated the noose by cutting his own throat. The murderers of John Stevens and Johannes Gouws were hanged too, as was Emil Schulz, who pulled the trigger on Roger Bushell and Bernard Scheidhauer. Finally, Johannes Post and three of his henchmen were executed for the murders of Jimmy Catanach, Arnold Christensen, Halldor Espelid, and Nils Fuglesang. Post was the only defendant who remained totally unrepentant to the end, claiming that he wished he had been able to wipe out more *Terrorfliegers* and subhumans, as he called them. When asked why he wished to offer no affidavits in mitigation of his sentence, Post replied sharply that he could not have been a National Socialist for so many years and suddenly put in affidavits from Communists, Jews, or 'freethinkers.'

Over the next twenty years, efforts to trace the rest of the killers and bring them to trial continued. In May 1968, the last trial in the Stalag Luft III case concluded, with Fritz Schmidt of the Kiel Gestapo receiving a two-year prison sentence for his part in the deaths of Catanach, Christensen, Espelid, and Fuglesang.

Unfortunately, the SIB had comparatively little success in tracing members of the Breslau Gestapo, who were responsible for the deaths of the officers from Görlitz prison. Wilhelm Scharpwinkel, head of the Gestapo office, was held by the Soviets, who refused to hand him over. They later claimed that he died in prison, but many involved in the investigation believe that he merely put on a new uniform and took a job with the Soviet police. Max Wielen received a life sentence at the Hamburg trial and two others were tried a year later, though neither went to prison. Of the rest of the murder squad, there was little trace. Many had likely been killed in the bitter defense of Breslau in 1945, while others had simply disappeared.

*

Late in 1945, New Zealander Geoff Fallows was able to get leave and fulfill a promise to see Johnny Pohe's family. He found them still mourning their son. In a low and measured voice, Johnny's father asked if *utu* (revenge) had been done for the crime. Geoff said he did not know but would contact the authorities to find out. Months later he received a reply from the Ministry of Defence saying that an official investigation was under way but that no results could be expected for some time. Geoff returned to the Pohe farm and met again with Johnny's father. His son's death had aged the man, and he had lost much of his vigor. With this in mind, Geoff said solemnly that *utu* had indeed been done. The old farmer immediately straightened up a bit and gave Geoff a firm handshake. As Pohe walked back to his plowing, Geoff noticed that he exuded a new strength.

It was late 1946 before Alan Righetti could fulfill his promise to George Wiley. He was returning to Australia after studying at Leeds University in England and, while passing through the United States, made a stop in Windsor, Ontario. Darkness was falling and there were big, heavy snowflakes floating down as Alan pulled up to the Wileys' modest house.

George's mother and sister put up a brave front, but it was obvious that they were still devastated by the loss of their son and brother. Alan handed over the watch and the few other personal possessions that George had entrusted to him the night of the escape and told them what he remembered about his time in captivity. They were hungry for information and pumped Alan for every word that George had said in Sagan. They talked of their relief when word came through that George was a prisoner and of their belief that, once out of battle, he was sure to come home safely. But mostly they spoke of the shock when notification of the murders had reached them, and of the grief that had devastated their family and led to the premature death of Morley Wiley. It was a difficult evening, full of tears and anger.

Alan went to bed exhausted by the ordeal and got up early to find his car buried in thick, wet snow. As he dug it out after a hurried breakfast, he wondered if it had been worth the opening of old wounds to return the few belongings to the Wiley family. He looked back at the house before pulling away and saw the pained faces of George's mother and sister through the half-steamed window. Alan Righetti never contacted the Wileys again.

*

And what of the prisoners themselves? Those who were liberated at Trenthorst were flown back to England and, with a few squirts of DDT powder and a meal of tea and biscuits, were given leave to visit their families. Some remained in the service, and some took their release at the first possible moment. For the most part, the years of peace were kind to the survivors of the Great Escape.

After returning to England from Sweden, Per Bergsland was posted to Canada as a flying instructor. Then, seven months later, he transferred to Transport Command and finished the war flying out of Montreal. In late 1945 he went back to Norway and became the first pilot for Fred Olsen Aviation, eventually becoming company president in 1968. The following year, Olsen Aviation bought up a bankrupt carrier and Per formed his own company, Widerøes Flyveselskap, which eventually grew to serve thirty-seven airports in Norway. Per enjoyed a short retirement from the pursuit that had been his life for more than forty years and died in 1992.

Like Per Bergsland, Bob Nelson and Jens Müller both took up flying jobs with airlines after the war, Bob with KLM and Jens with SAS. They met from time to time in various European airports but lost touch when they moved up to bigger aircraft and intercontinental routes. Jens retired in Oslo, while Bob, after spending some time in Portugal, returned to England to live. Both men died in 1999.

Tommy Thompson returned to his home in Penetanguishene, Ontario, and went on to study law. He practiced in his hometown, served a term as mayor there, and was eventually appointed the assistant district attorney for Simcoe County in 1967. Tommy retired in 1980 and stayed in Penetanguishene until his death in 1985.

Jimmy James remained in the RAF until 1958 and served in various capacities, including attaché to the Foreign Office in Berlin. Upon retirement he returned to Canada for a short time and then took a job with a timber exporting firm in Ghana. In 1960 Jimmy became general secretary of the Great Britain/USSR Association in London, a Foreign Office–sponsored organization created to foster cultural contacts between the two nations. Four years later James transferred to the Foreign Office proper and, after serving in West Berlin, Prague, Bern, Paris, Lagos, and Durban, retired in 1975. He died in 2008.

Johnny Dodge returned to England after the war and was awarded a Military Cross for his activities in captivity. He ran as the Conservative candidate for Gillingham in Kent but was defeated in the big Labour landslide of July 1945. That ended the Dodger's political career. He returned to the business world, working with a London stock brokerage firm, but kept in touch with some of the people he had met in Germany, particularly Theo Rumpel, the commandant of Dulag Luft, and Hans Thost, who had accompanied Johnny on his journey to freedom in 1945. Dodge died of a heart attack in November 1960.

After crossing into neutral territory, Bob van der Stok and his companions entered the village of Canejan, where they narrowly escaped internment as undesirables. Bob, however, convinced their unfriendly hosts to transport them to the British embassy in Madrid. It was there that he learned of the murder of the fifty, from none other than Sir Arthur Street.

Returned to England via Gibraltar, Bob was initially passed unfit for active service due to an ear injury sustained in his crash in 1942, but Prince Bernhard of the Netherlands pulled a few strings and in no time Bob was on his way to 67 OTU at Hullavington, flying occasional operational sweeps with his old unit, 91 Squadron. Eventually promoted to squadron leader, van der Stok was given command of 322 (Dutch) Squadron, which flew Spitfires over Holland.

When his native land was liberated, Bob was at last able to see his parents again. When Bob escaped from Sagan, his father was arrested and tortured, an ordeal that left him partially blinded. Then, when Bob's two brothers were identified as Resistance members, the elder van der Stok was taken into custody again and subjected to further torture. Though he was eventually released, both of Bob's brothers were murdered in Nazi prisons. So when Bob saw his father that day in 1945, he was a broken man, devastated by the loss of two sons. He seemed to be living only for the return of his third son, for the day after Bob's visit the elder van der Stok died.

After serving on the Dutch General Staff in The Hague for a time, Bob van der Stok turned down an offer to become chief of flying services for KLM and went back to his medical studies. He graduated from the University of Utrecht in 1951 and then immigrated to the United States and set up a private practice in New Mexico. He worked on the Skylab project for NASA before moving with his wife to Hawaii, where he continued his practice. Van der Stok died in Virginia in 1993.

Freddie Dvorak returned to Czechoslovakia after the war but found life difficult under the new Communist regime. He remained in touch with a number of his fellow prisoners but eventually fell into ill health. He died in the early 1960s, a victim of Bright's disease.

Des Plunkett remained in the RAF after the war, serving with 10 Squadron in Karachi, Pakistan. He was demobilized in Bombay in 1947 after turning down an offer to become Lord Mountbatten's pilot in India. Instead, he took a job as a salesman with Hindustani Aircraft Company, selling flying boats until he realized that there was little future in the job. Then Des returned to instructing at the Bengal Flying Club in Barrackpore, and in January 1949 he started a career in survey flying. He immigrated to Rhodesia, now Zimbabwe, and did not give up flying until 1972. He died in 2002.

Ivo Tonder returned to the air force in Czechoslovakia after the war but demobilized when it became clear that the Communists would take over the country. He and his wife bought a farm near Marienbad and settled down to a peaceful life. That peace lasted only a few short years. After the Communist election victory in 1948, Ivo and his wife decided to escape from Czechoslovakia with their two small children and convinced a friend to drive them to a spot near the Austrian border. However, with no maps or compass, the family became lost at night and were picked up by border guards. Tonder's wife and children were soon released, but Ivo was put in prison. After a number of other abortive attempts, Tonder eventually escaped to Vienna in December 1949; his wife followed in October 1950, but their children were not spirited out of Czechoslovakia until June 1951. The Tonders eventually settled in England, where Ivo ran a textile business. He died in 1995.

Les Brodrick spent another year in the RAF after liberation and then took up teaching. In 1955 he immigrated to South Africa, where he taught in elementary and secondary schools in Johannesburg and Natal. He died in 2013, followed by Australian Paul Royle in 2015. With that, Dick Churchill became the last survivor of the Great Escape.

Len Trent requested an assignment to Transport Command after the war and it was during that assignment that he learned he had been awarded the Victoria Cross for the Amsterdam raid. The investiture took place at Buckingham Palace on April 12, 1946. Trent rose through the ranks of the air force, occupying various staff and instructional positions before being posted to command 214 Squadron, flying Valiant jets from Marham. It was in a Valiant that Len flew his last operational mission, a bombing raid during the Suez crisis of October 1956. In April 1958 Trent became wing commander for training at 3 Group headquarters at Mildenhall. His commanding officer at the time was

Kenneth Cross, the elder brother of Ian. In June 1962 Len Trent became the Bomber Command representative with the British embassy in Washington. After three years there he left the service, spending much of his retirement in Matheson's Bay, New Zealand. Trent kept active during his retirement, playing golf and traveling to various Victoria Cross and Bomber Command functions around the world. To the great shock of his family and many friends, he died suddenly in May 1986.

In 1949 Len had gone on a skiing trip to St. Moritz. A reasonably competent skier, he was about to start down the Chantarella with his guide when he spotted a sign, the only one in English, that said 'Bushell Run.' Understandably curious, he asked his guide about it.

'That run is named after a man,' began the guide proudly, 'who made the fastest time on this dangerous run. He was a very brave man and a very good skier, but he was killed by the Germans during the war. I had the honor of calling him a friend,' he added quietly.

'Odd coincidence,' said Len. 'I was in prison camp with Roger Bushell, and I, too, had the honor to call him a friend.'

'Then we shall pause here,' said the guide, digging in his ski poles, 'and you shall tell me everything you remember about our friend Roger from the camp.' Len gladly obliged, recounting the story of X Organization and the escape to the guide, who listened with obvious fascination. When Len had finished, the guide shook his hand warmly.

'I am most grateful to you for telling me that story,' he said. 'Many times I have thought about my old friend, and I have often wondered what his life was like in the camp. Now we shall think of him as we ski down the Chantarella. And maybe someday,' he added, giving Len a broad smile, 'you shall be proficient enough to try the Bushell Run yourself!'

SUGGESTED READING

Allen Andrews, *Exemplary Justice* (London: Harrap, 1976)

Ted Barris, *The Great Escape: A Canadian Story* (Toronto: Thomas Allen, 2013)

Patrick Barthropp, *Paddy: The Life and Times of Wing-Commander Patrick Barthropp, DFC, AFC* (London: Howard Baker, 1987)

Paul Brickhill, *The Great Escape* (London: Faber and Faber, 1951)

Paul Brickhill and Conrad Norton, *Escape to Danger* (London: Faber and Faber, 1948)

Kingsley Brown, *Bonds of Wire: A Memoir* (Toronto: Collins, 1989)

T.D. Calnan, *Free as a Running Fox* (London: Macdonald and Co., 1970)

Tim Carroll, *The Dodger: The Extraordinary Story of Churchill's Cousin and the Great Escape* (London: Mainstream Publishing, 2012)

Albert P. Clark, *33 Months as a POW in Stalag Luft III* (Golden, CO: Fulcrum, 2004)

Aidan Crawley, *Escape from Germany: The Methods of Escape Used by RAF Airmen during the Second World War* (London: HMSO, 1985)

Eugene L. Daniel, *In the Presence of Mine Enemies: An American Chaplain in World War II German Prison Camps* (privately published, 1985)

Arthur A. Durand, *Stalag Luft III: The Secret Story* (London: Patrick Stephens, 1988)

Don Edy, *Goon in the Block* (privately published, 1961)

Larry Forrester, *Fly for Your Life: The Story of Wing-Commander R.R. Stanford-Tuck, DSO, DFC and two bars* (London: Frederick Muller, 1956)

Anton Gill, *The Great Escape: The Full Dramatic Story with Contributions from Survivors and their Families* (London: Review, 2002)

Laurence Green, *Great War to Great Escape: The Two Wars of Flight Lieutenant Bernard 'Pop' Green, MC* (Hitchin: Fighting High, 2011)

John R. Harris, *Serving and Surviving: An Airman's Memoirs* (privately published, 2004)

George Harsh, *Lonesome Road* (New York: W.W. Norton, 1971)

Barbara Hehner, *The Tunnel King: The True Story of Wally Floody and the Great Escape* (Toronto: Harper Trophy, 2004)

B.A. James, *Moonless Night: One Man's Struggle for Freedom, 1940–45* (London: William Kimber, 1983)

Robert Kee, *A Crowd is Not Company* (London: Eyre and Spottiswood, 1947)

Murdo Ewen Macdonald, *Padre Mac: The Man from Harris* (privately published, 1992)

Donald MacDonell, *From Dogfight to Diplomacy: A Spitfire Pilot's Log, 1932–1958* (Barnsley: Pen and Sword, 2005)

Gwyn Martin, *Up and Under* (privately published, 1989)

Walter Morison, *Flak and Ferrets: One Way to Colditz* (London: Sentinel Publishing, 1995)

Keith C. Ogilvie, *The Spitfire Luck of Skeets Ogilvie: From the Battle of Britain to the Great Escape* (Toronto: Heritage House, 2017)

Simon Pearson, *The Great Escaper: The Life and Death of Roger Bushell. Love, Betrayal, Big X and the Great Escape* (London: Hodder and Stoughton, 2013)

Oliver Philpot, *Stolen Journey* (London: Hodder and Stoughton, 1950)

Roland Plett, *Ginger's Great Escape* (privately published, 2011)

Jack Rae, *Kiwi Spitfire Ace: A Gripping World War II Story of Action, Captivity and Freedom* (London: Grub Street, 2001)

Simon Read, *Human Game: The True Story of the 'Great Escape' Murders and the Hunt for the Gestapo Gunmen* (New York: Berkley Caliber, 2012)

Ken Rees, *Lie in the Dark and Listen: The Remarkable Exploits of a WWII Bomber Pilot and Great Escaper* (London: Grub Street, 2004)

Jerry Sage, *Sage: The Man They Called 'Dagger' of the OSS* (Wayne, PA: Tobey Publishing, 1985)

James Sanders, *Venturer Courageous: Group Captain Leonard Trent, VC, DFC* (Auckland: Hutchinson, 1983)

Sydney Smith, *Wings Day: The Man Who Led the RAF's Epic Battle in German Captivity* (London: Collins, 1968)

Delmar T. Spivey, *POW Odyssey: Recollections of Center Compound, Stalag Luft III, and the Secret German Peace Mission in World War II* (privately published, 1984)

Marc H. Stevens, *Escape, Evasion and Revenge: The True Story of a German-Jewish RAF Pilot who Bombed Berlin and Became a POW* (Barnsley: Pen and Sword, 2009)

George Sweanor, *It's All Pensionable Time: 25 Years in the Royal Canadian Air Force* (privately published, 1981)

Nick Thomas, *Kenneth 'Hawkeye' Lee: Battle of Britain and Desert Air Force Fighter Ace* (Barnsley: Pen and Sword, 2011)

Tyler Trafford, *Almost a Great Escape: A Found Story* (Fredericton, NB: Goose Lane, 2013)

Bob Vanderstok, *War Pilot of Orange* (Missoula, MT: Pictorial Histories, 1987)

Marilyn Jeffers Walton and Michael C. Eberhardt (eds), *From Commandant to Captive: The Memoirs of Stalag Luft III Commandant Col. Friedrich Wilhelm von Lindeiner gennant von Wildau* (privately published, 2015)

Geoffrey Willatt, *Bombs and Barbed Wire: My War in the RAF and Stalag Luft III* (Tunbridge Wells: Parapress, 1995)

Louise Williams, *A True Story of the Great Escape: A Young Australian in the Most Audacious Breakout of WWII* (Sydney: Allen and Unwin, 2015)

'Quickly, I climbed up to the surface and immediately found the rope … I felt no signal, so it was not safe yet. Then I felt three distinct tugs and slowly popped my head up … The nearest "Goonbox" was at least two hundred feet away; but, indeed, I was twenty feet from the edge of the woods.'

On the night of 24 March 1944, Bram (Bob) Vanderstok was number eighteen of seventy-six men who crawled beyond the barbed-wire fence of Stalag Luft III. This story details the real Great Escape as depicted in the 1963 cult movie classic *The Great Escape*.

This memoir sets down the incredible adventures Vanderstok experienced, starting even before he was incarcerated in Stalag Luft III. As a pilot in the Dutch Air Force he witnessed the occupation of the Netherlands and, after several false starts, managed to escape to Britain, where he joined the RAF and became a Spitfire pilot.

Shot down over France in April 1942, he was captured and sent to Stalag Luft III. In extraordinary detail he describes various escape attempts, culminating in the famous March breakout.

THE GREAT ESCAPE
FROM
Stalag Luft III
THE MEMOIR OF
JENS MÜLLER

Foreword by JON MÜLLER
Introduction by ASGEIR UELAND

'It took me three minutes to get through the tunnel. Above ground I crawled along holding the rope for several feet: it was tied to a tree. Bergsland was wearing a civilian suit he had made for himself from a Royal Marine uniform, with an RAF overcoat slightly altered with brown leather sewn over the buttons. A black RAF tie, no hat. He carried a small suitcase which had been sent from Norway. In it were Norwegian toothpaste and soap, sandwiches, and 163 Reichsmarks given to him by the Escape Committee.'

Jens Müller was one of only three men who successfully escaped from Stalag Luft III in March 1944 – the break that later became the basis for the famous film *The Great Escape*.

In a vivid, informative memoir he details what life in the camp was like, how the escapes were planned and executed and tells the story of his personal breakout and success reaching RAF Leuchars base in Scotland.

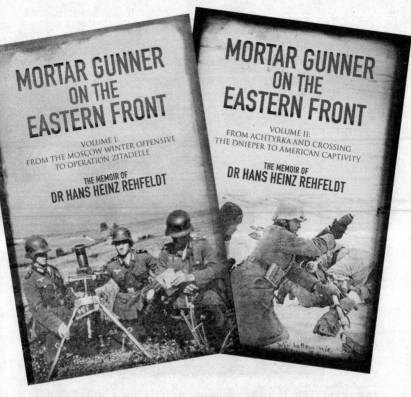

MORTAR GUNNER ON THE EASTERN FRONT

VOLUME I:
FROM THE MOSCOW WINTER OFFENSIVE
TO OPERATION ZITADELLE

THE MEMOIR OF
DR HANS HEINZ REHFELDT

MORTAR GUNNER ON THE EASTERN FRONT

VOLUME II:
FROM ACHTYRKA AND CROSSING
THE DNIEPER TO AMERICAN CAPTIVITY

THE MEMOIR OF
DR HANS HEINZ REHFELDT

'The accursed Russian MG was still firing into our flank ... I was studying a barn about 500m from the village when by chance I saw a Russian steel helmet and the muzzle fire. I pointed out my discovery to the artillery spotter. At once he gave new orders ... the next round blew up the barn, boards and beams whirled in the air. Direct hit!'

Rehfeldt was trained on the heavy mortar and heavy machine gun with *Grossdeutschland* Division. Still only 18, he was on the Eastern Front in 1941, fighting for the city of Tula, south of Moscow. The descriptions in these diaries of the privations are vivid and terrifying as they battling in freezing conditions, at its lowest -52°, with no winter uniform, cold and uncamouflaged in the snow.

Illustrated with over 240 photographs and maps hand-drawn by the author, this fascinating account of a man who kept bouncing back from near death is a testament to the author's sheer strength of spirit.

IMAGES OF WAR
STALAG LUFT III
THE GERMAN POW CAMP THAT INSPIRED *THE GREAT ESCAPE*
RARE PHOTOGRAPHS FROM WARTIME ARCHIVES

CHARLES MESSENGER

In early 1942 the Third Reich opened a maximum security Prisoner Of War camp in Lower Silesia for captured Allied airmen. Called Stalag Luft III, the camp soon came to contain some of the most inventive escapers ever known.

Squadron Leader Roger Bushell, code-named 'Big X', masterminded an attempt to smuggle hundreds of POWs down a tunnel build right under the notes of their guards. This remarkable escape would be immortalised in the famous Hollywood film *The Great Escape*, in which the bravery of the men was rightly celebrated.

Charles Messenger served for twenty years in the Royal Tank Regiment before retiring to become a military historian and defence analyst. He is the author of some forty books, mainly on twentieth century warfare.

OTTO KRETSCHMER
THE LIFE OF THE THIRD REICH'S HIGHEST SCORING U-BOAT COMMANDER

LAWRENCE PATERSON

Otto Kretschmer was only in combat from September 1939 until March 1941 but was Germany's highest-scoring U-boat commander sinking 47 ships totalling 274,333 tons.

His nickname 'Silent Otto' referred to his ability to remain undetected and his reluctance to provide the regular radio reports required by Dönitz: he had guessed that the Allies had broken German codes.

In the Bowmanville POW camp he was instrumental in the 'Battle of Bowmanville' that lasted for three days in October 1942. His antics behind the wire became the inspiration for the 1970 film *The McKenzie Break*. Postwar he answered the call for volunteers upon the establishment of the Bundesmarine.

This definitive work details his personal story and the political backdrop from his earliest days.

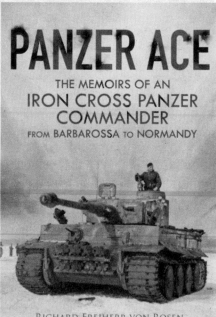

PANZER ACE

THE MEMOIRS OF AN
IRON CROSS PANZER
COMMANDER
FROM BARBAROSSA TO NORMANDY

RICHARD FREIHERR VON ROSEN
FOREWORD BY ROBERT FORCZYK

Richard Freiherr von Rosen was a highly-decorated Wehrmacht soldier
and outstanding panzer commander. His memoirs are richly illustrated
with contemporary photographs, including key confrontations of
World War II.

After serving as a gunlayer on a Pz.Mk.III during Barbarossa, he led
a Company of Tigers at Kursk. Later he led a company of King Tiger
panzers at Normandy and in late 1944 commanded a battle group (12
King Tigers and a flak Company) against the Russians in Hungary in
the rank of junior, later senior lieutenant (from November 1944, his
final rank.)

The author has a fine memory and eye for detail. His account is easy to
read and not technical, and adds substantially to the knowledge of how
the German Panzer Arm operated in the Second World War.

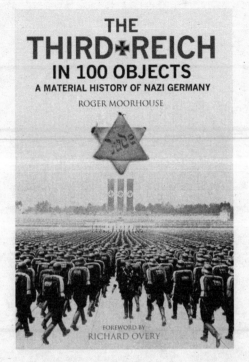

THE
THIRD✣REICH
IN 100 OBJECTS
A MATERIAL HISTORY OF NAZI GERMANY

ROGER MOORHOUSE

FOREWORD BY
RICHARD OVERY

Hitler's Third Reich is still the focus of numerous articles, books and films: no regime of the twentieth century has prompted such interest or such a body of literature. This is an accessible, compelling, sometimes shocking and often revelatory guide to the Third Reich that has been collated and presented by one of the world's leading historians of Nazi Germany.

The photographs range from documents and postcards to weapons and personal effects, including Pervitin, Hitler's Mercedes, Hitler's grooming kit, the Messerschmitt 262, the Luger pistol, the Tiger Tank, Eva Braun's lipstick case, the underpants of Rudolf Hess, and, of course, the Swastika and *Mein Kampf*.

Roger Moorhouse is a historian of the Third Reich. He is the author of the acclaimed *Berlin At War*, *Killing Hitler* and *The Devils' Alliance* and has been published in over twenty languages.